FROMMER'S

COMPREHENSIVE TRAVEL GUIDE

THE VIRGIN ISLANDS
'94 -'95

by Darwin Porter
Assisted by Danforth Prince

PRENTICE HALL TRAVEL

NEW YORK • LONDON • TORONTO • SYDNEY • TOKYO • SINGAPORE

FROMMER BOOKS

Published by Prentice Hall General Reference
A division of Simon & Schuster Inc.
15 Columbus Circle
New York, NY 10023

ISBN: 0-671-84911-5
ISSN: 1055-5447

Design by Robert Bull Design
Maps by Geografix Inc.

Frommer's Editorial Staff
Editorial Director: Marilyn Wood
Editorial Manager/Senior Editor: Alice Fellows
Senior Editor: Lisa Renaud
Editors: Charlotte Allstrom, Thomas F. Hirsch, Peter Katucki, Sara Hinsey Raveret, Theodore Stavrou
Assistant Editors: Margaret Bowen, Christopher Hollander, Ian Wilker
Editorial Assistants: Gretchen Henderson, Bethany Jewett
Managing Editor: Leanne Coupe

Special Sales
Bulk purchases of Frommer's Travel Guides are available at special discounts. The publishers are happy to custom-make publications for corporate clients who wish to use them as premiums or sales promotions. We can excerpt the contents, provide covers with corporate imprints, or create books to meet specific needs. For more information write to Special Sales Prentice Hall Travel, Paramount Communications Building, 15 Columbus Circle, New York, NY 10023.

Manufactured in the United States of America

CONTENTS

LIST OF MAPS

AN INVITATION TO OUR READERS

In researching this book, I have come across many intriguing establishments, the best of which I have included here. I am sure that many of you will also come across recommendable hotels, inns, restaurants, guesthouses, shops, and attractions. Please don't keep them to yourself. Share your experiences, especially if you want to comment on places that have been included in this edition that have changed for the worse. You can address your letters to:

Darwin Porter
Frommer's The Virgin Islands '94-'95
c/o Prentice Hall Travel
15 Columbus Circle
New York, NY 10023

A DISCLAIMER

Readers are advised that prices fluctuate in the course of time, and travel information changes under the impact of the varied and volatile factors that affect the travel industry. Neither the author nor the publisher can be held responsible for the experiences of readers while traveling. Readers are invited to write to the publisher with ideas, comments, and suggestions for future editions.

SAFETY ADVISORY

Whenever you're traveling in an unfamiliar city or country, stay alert. Be aware of your immediate surroundings. Wear a moneybelt and keep a close eye on your possessions. Be particularly careful with cameras, purses, and wallets, all favorite targets of thieves and pickpockets.

CHAPTER 1

INTRODUCING THE VIRGIN ISLANDS

Former stamping ground for some of history's most famous sea marauders, the Virgin Islands are now invaded by tourists who arrive by the thousands daily either by plane or cruise ship. Due east of what they call their "giant neighbor" (Puerto Rico), less than 30 minutes away by air, the islands lie about 1,100 miles southeast of Miami.

These green, hilly islands rise from a clear blue sea, about 100 in all, counting the rocks that jut out from the sea. Owned by the United States or Great Britain, most of the islands are so tiny that they are uninhabited except by a few birds or an adventurous boating party stopping off for a little skinny-dipping.

Coral reefs often shield the best beaches from the wicked surf of the Atlantic Ocean, which fronts their northern shorelines. The southern island rims open onto the usually calmer waters of the Caribbean. St. Croix, south of St. Thomas and St. John, is entirely in the Caribbean Sea.

The major islands—and the most famous ones—are owned by the United States: St. Thomas (which attracts the most visitors, many from cruise ships) and St. Croix. St. John is the smaller of the three, an enchanting little island made famous by one of its early promoters, Laurance Rockefeller. Of the dozens of British Virgin Islands, Tortola is the best known. Virgin Gorda tends to attract more discriminating (and well-heeled) visitors to its swank "hostels by the sea."

The main towns are Charlotte Amalie, capital of St. Thomas; Christiansted, capital of St. Croix; and Road Town, capital of Tortola.

The name "Virgins" came from that great labeler of Caribbean Islands, Columbus, who sailed by them. In 1493, impressed by their number, he named them *Las Once Mil Virgenes* in honor of St. Ursula's 11,000 martyred maidens of Christian belief.

Part of the archipelago known as the Lesser Antilles, the Virgins are for the most part rich in vegetation, even lush, and they are of volcanic origin. The Lesser Antilles more or less mark the spot where the Atlantic Ocean ends and the calmer and more tranquil Caribbean Sea begins.

The Virgin Islands, both British and American, possess the most ideal temperatures in the West Indies, thanks to the ever-present trade winds which keep the air from getting too hot. The Virgins report lower humidity than many of the other Caribbean islands, which makes them an ideal vacation paradise, both in summer or winter. The greatest numbers of tourists visit between December and April. Summer is slower and a bit hotter, but, to compensate, all hoteliers lower their prices then. The islands report an average annual temperature of 78°F. The welcome showers do come, but they pass quickly, except during hurricane season (more about that later). On nearly any day of the year, you can count on sunshine, at least for part of the day. The lowest known temperature ever recorded in the Virgin Islands is 61°F.

Most of the local Virgin Islanders are descended from African slaves who worked on plantations for European owners until their emancipation in the mid-1800s after a period of often great violence.

In recent years, the local population has swelled with an influx of "down islanders," people from other islands in the Caribbean chain, which stretches to South America. Many Puerto Ricans have also moved into the U.S. islands nearby, as well as many Americans from the mainland in the north.

The old ways of the islands are all but gone in bustling St. Thomas and St. Croix, but may still be found in some pockets in the British Virgins, especially on Virgin Gorda.

Each island has a unique personality. The shopping mecca of St. Thomas, the favorite cruise-ship arrival port in the Caribbean, is remarkably different from the more laid-back St. Croix. And sleepy St. John, when compared to its two bigger islands, is just a short boat ride from St. Thomas but miles and miles away in charm and personality. As for the British Virgin Islands (often called "BVI" for short), they loudly proclaim their differences under their Union Jack flag, and invite you over for a look.

1. GEOGRAPHY, HISTORY & POLITICS

GEOGRAPHY

The Atlantic Ocean is to the north of the U.S. Virgin Islands, and on the south they open onto the Caribbean Sea. St. Croix, entirely in the Caribbean Sea, is the largest island, followed by St. Thomas and tiny St. John. All the U.S. islands combined, including such small ones as Water Island, form a landmass of 132 square miles. The British Virgin Islands make up the eastern part of the Virgin Islands archipelago, a landmass of 59 square miles.

Over some 25 million years, volcanoes formed these islands. The soil tends to be stony and thin, and water is sometimes hard to come by (the islanders are forced to collect rainwater in cisterns). The islands are hilly, especially St. Thomas, which is split by a ridge of high hills that runs across the island from east to west.

Most of the U.S. Virgins are uninhabited. All of them are considered part of the

IMPRESSIONS

There could never be lands any more favorable in fertility, in mildness and pleasantness of climate, in abundance of good and pure water. A very peaceful and hopeful place that should give all adventurers great satisfaction.
—CAPTAIN NATHANIEL BUTLER, HM FRIGATE *NICODEMUS*, 1637

Leeward Islands and the Lesser Antilles. The population of all the U.S. islands is more than 100,000.

HISTORY

EARLY HISTORY

Christopher Columbus is credited with discovering the Virgin Islands in 1493, but in fact, they had been inhabited for 3,000 years. It is believed that the original settlers were Ciboney (or Siboney) Indians who came up from the mainland of South America.

These Indians were nomads living off the fish and the vegetation. The first real homesteaders of the islands were the peaceful Arawak Indians, who arrived from Venezuela, presumably in dugout canoes with sails. Stone tools and shell jewelry have been found from these early settlers.

For about 500 years the Arawaks occupied the Virgin Islands until the arrival of the cannibalistic Carib Indians in the 15th century.

THE AGE OF COLONIZATION

On his second voyage to the New World, Columbus spotted the Virgin Islands in November of 1493. His men were thirsty, and he was short of water, so he decided to put in at what is now Salt River on St. Croix's north shore. Instead of water, his men were greeted by a rainfall of arrows. Embittered, Columbus named the area *Cabo de Flechas* or cape of the arrows. He sailed on his way, heading for Puerto Rico.

Spain laid claim to the Virgin Islands, but didn't consider them worth colonizing, having greater goals in the Greater Antilles to pursue.

It did, however, in the years to come, occasionally raid the islands in search of slave labor for the Dominican gold mines, which eventually led to the extermination of the native population. With reports of gold, pirates circulated throughout the islands for decades. After a raid, they could always find a safe cove to hide in in one of the dozens of Virgin Islands.

The year 1625 was the turning point in the history of the islands. Both the English and the Dutch established opposing frontier outposts on St. Croix which Columbus had called Santa Cruz. Struggles between these two powers for control of the island continued for about 20 years, until the English won out.

The islands soon became a virtual battleground, as one European power vied with another for control. In 1650 alone, Spanish forces sailing from Puerto Rico overran the British garrison on St. Croix. Soon after they were raided by the Dutch, and in 1653 the island fell into the hands of the Knights of Malta, who gave it its current name. The aristocratic French cavaliers weren't well suited to being

DATELINE

- **1493** Columbus sails by the Virgin Islands, and is attacked by Carib Indians on St. Croix.
- **1625** Dutch and English establish frontier outposts on St. Croix.
- **1650** Spanish forces from Puerto Rico overrun English garrison on St. Croix.
- **1671** Danes take over St. Thomas.
- **1672** England adds British Virgin Islands to its empire.
- **1674** The king of France adds St. Croix to his empire.
- **1717** Danish planters from St. Thomas cultivate plantations on St. John.
- **1724** St. Thomas is declared a free port.
- **1733** Danish West India Company purchases St. Croix from France; slaves revolt on St. John.
- **1792** Denmark announces plans to abandon the slave trade.
- **1801** England occupies the Danish Virgin Islands for 10 months.

(continues)

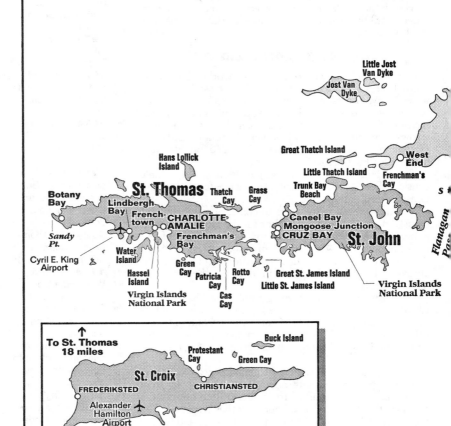

N

0 — 8.55 km
0 — 5 mi

☐ **British Virgin Islands**
▨ **U.S. Virgin Islands**

ATLANTIC

Little Jost
Van Dyke

Jost Van
Dyke

Great Thatch Island

West
End

Little Thatch Island

Frenchman's
Cay

Hans Lollick
Island

Trunk Bay
Beach

Botany
Bay

St. Thomas Thatch Grass
Cay Cay

Lindbergh
Bay French-
town

Caneel Bay
Mongoose Junction

Flanagan Pass

CHARLOTTE
AMALIE

CRUZ BAY **St. John**

Sandy
Pt.

Frenchman's
Bay

Cyril E. King
Airport

Water
Island

Green
Cay

Virgin Islands
National Park

Hassel
Island

Patricia
Cay

Rotto
Cay

Great St. James Island

Little St. James Island

Virgin Islands
National Park

Cas
Cay

To St. Thomas
18 miles

Protestant
Cay

Buck Island

Green Cay

St. Croix

FREDERIKSTED

CHRISTIANSTED

Alexander
Hamilton
Airport

CARIBBEAN SEA

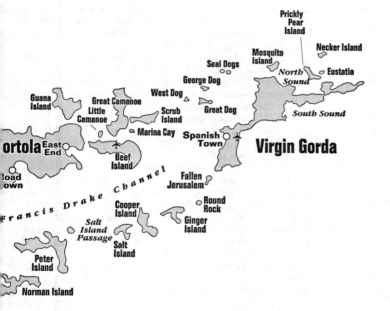

Anegada

The Settlement

OCEAN

Prickly
Pear
Island

Necker Island

Mosquito
Island

Seal Dogs

*North
Sound*

Eustatia

George Dog

West Dog

Guana
Island

Great Camanoe

Scrub
Island

Great Dog

South Sound

Little
Camanoe

Marina Cay

Spanish
Town

Virgin Gorda

ortola East
End

Beef
Island

Francis Drake Channel

Fallen
Jerusalem

load
own

Cooper
Island

Round
Rock

*Salt
Island
Passage*

Ginger
Island

Salt
Island

Peter
Island

Norman Island

CARIBBEAN SEA

DATELINE

● **1807–15** England occupies Danish Virgin Islands again.

● **1834** England frees 5,133 slaves living in BVI.

● **1848** Under pressure, the governor of St. Croix grants slaves emancipation.

● **1870** U.S. Senate rejects treaty with Denmark for sale of the Virgin Islands.

● **1902** Danish Parliament rejects U.S. offer of $5 million for sale of its islands.

● **1916** Denmark signs treaty with the U.S. and sells islands for $25 million.

● **1917** U.S. Virgin Islands fall under the control of the U.S. Navy for 14 years.

● **1927** U.S. grants citizenship to island residents.

● **1936** Under FDR, the first Organic Act is passed, granting voting rights.

● **1940** Population of U.S. Virgins increases for the first time since 1860.

● **1946** First black governor of the islands is appointed.

● **1954** Revised Organic Act passed; islands under jurisdiction of

(continues)

West Indies plantation overseers, however, and their debts mounted. By 1674 the French king decided to occupy St. Croix and make it part of his kingdom.

The English continued to war against Dutch settlers in Tortola, which was viewed as the most important of the British Virgin Islands. It wasn't until 1672 that England added the BVI to its ever-growing empire.

A year before, in March 1671, the Danish West India Company made an attempt to settle St. Thomas. They sent two ships, but only one arrived, the *Pharaoh*. About 90 of the original 239 crew, which included some Norwegians, were still alive. Eventually more boats arrived to reinforce the colony. By 1679, at least 156 whites were reported living on St. Thomas, along with their slaves who worked the fields to send indigo, cotton, tobacco, and dyewood back to Denmark. In 1724, St. Thomas was declared a free port, a position it holds today.

Captain Kidd, Sir Francis Drake, Blackbeard, and the other legendary pirates of the West Indies continued to use St. Thomas as their base for raids in the area. The harbor at St. Thomas—now a cruise-ship venue—also became notorious for its slave market.

In 1717 Danish planters sailed over to St. John to begin cultivation of plantations there. Opposite St. John, St. Thomas was formally declared a free port in 1724, a position it holds today.

The St. John planters were successful and by 1733 an estimated one hundred sugar, tobacco, and cotton plantations were operating on the island. That same year the slaves rose up and rebelled against their colonial masters, taking control of the island for about 6 months and slaughtering many Europeans. It took hundreds of French troops to quell the rebellion. Those who did not get killed or commit suicide were slaughtered.

In the same year, France sold St. Croix to the Danish West India Company, who divided the island into plantations and continued its flourishing slave trade. Some historians report that as many as a quarter of a million slaves were sold on the auction blocks at Charlotte Amalie before being sent elsewhere, often to the Deep South of the United States. By 1792 the country changed its mind, and announced that it officially planned to end the slave trade. It was not until 1848, however, that they did so. The British had freed their 5,133 slaves in 1834.

Denmark was thus in complete control of what is now the U.S. Virgin Islands. In 1801 Britain occupied the islands again, but left 10 months later. They returned to the Danish-held islands 6 years later, but left for good in 1815.

The great economic boom that resulted from the plantations of the Virgin Islands was wilting by the 1820s. The introduction of sugar beet virtually bankrupted plantation owners, as demand for cane sugar dropped drastically.

The latter half of the 19th century was marked by one

setback after another. Cholera swept through the islands. Drought and hurricanes were suffered and labor riots occurred. Plantations were set afire in 1878, and a rebellion broke out on St. Thomas in 1892 over the rapidly deteriorating economy.

Cuba eventually took over the sugar market in the Caribbean. By 1872 the British had so little interest in the British Virgins that they placed them in the loosely conceived and administered Federation of the Leeward Islands.

ENTER THE U.S.

In 1867, the U.S. attempted to purchase the islands from Denmark, but the treaty was rejected by the U.S. Senate in 1870. The asking price was $7.5 million.

Following its takeover of Puerto Rico in 1902, the U.S. expressed renewed interest in acquiring the Danish islands. This time the U.S. offered to pay $5 million, but the Danish parliament spurned the offer.

Upon the eve of its entry into World War I, the U.S. Navy began to fear a possible German takeover of the islands. The U.S. feared that using the islands as a base, the Kaiser's navy might prey on shipping through the Panama Canal, so they made another attempt. This time Denmark was ready to sell, and it did so for $25 million, a staggering sum to pay for island real estate back then.

In 1917, the United States was in full control of the islands, and Denmark retreated from the Caribbean after a legacy of nearly two-and-a-half centuries. The U.S. Navy looked after the islands for 14 years, and in 1954 they came under the Department of the Interior.

A little money came to the islands during the prohibition era, as some islanders made rum and shipped it illegally to the United States, often through Freeport, Bahamas. In 1927, the United States granted citizenship to the island residents. President Hoover inspected the islands in 1931, calling them "effective poorhouses."

In 1936, under FDR, the first Organic Act was passed, giving the islanders voting rights. This act later was revised in 1954, granting the islanders more self-government.

It took the jobs generated by World War II to wake the islands from their long economic slumber. In 1940, one year before the attack on Pearl Harbor, the U.S. Virgin Islands had their first population increase since 1860.

After World War II a major change in the economy of the islands occurred as tourists started to appear on the island. In the postwar economic boom that swept across America, the Virgin Islands at long last found a replacement for King Sugar.

The British Virgin Islands, which few people had heard of in years, was finally freed from the Leeward Islands Federation. In 1966 Queen Elizabeth II visited this remote colonial outpost, and in 1967 the British Virgin Islands got a new constitution.

Tourism was slower in coming to the BVI, but it is now the mainstay of the economy.

POLITICS

U.S. Virgin Islanders are not allowed to vote in national elections, a source of contention among some of the local residents. Many Virgin Islanders want to become the 51st state; others want to keep the status quo.

Since the 1936 Organic Act of the Virgin Islands, passed under the Roosevelt administration, residents 21 or over were granted suffrage and could elect two municipal councils and a Legislative Assembly for the islands.

In 1946, the first black governor of the islands, William Hastie, was appointed. In 1970 U.S. Virgin Islanders were granted the right to elect their own governor and lieutenant governor instead of having these officials appointed. Dr. Melvin Evans was elected the first governor.

Today, the U.S. Virgin Islands remain an unincorporated territory administered by the U.S. Department of the Interior. It sends a nonvoting delegate to the House of Representatives.

Governors serve 4 years in office, and Virgin Islanders also elect 15 senators to their own legislature.

The British Virgin Islands remain a dependent territory of Britain. Their governor is appointed in London, and he presides over an Executive Council consisting of a chief minister, an attorney general, and a trio of other ministers. The islands, in spite of their British overseer, are largely self-governing, and they have a 12-member Legislative Council.

2. FAMOUS VIRGIN ISLANDERS

Christopher Fleming (1851–1935) Born in the East End of Tortola, Fleming spent most of his life at sea, and may even have been a smuggler. In 1890, a BVI Customs officer seized a native boat, and in protest, Fleming led a group of armed men to the commissioner's house. Danish soldiers from St. Thomas put down the rebellion, and Fleming got 6 months in jail. Today, islanders look upon Fleming as a hero who protested against poverty and unfair economic conditions.

John Coakley Lettsom (1744–1815) Born into a Quaker family on Jost Van Dyke, he was educated in England and completed his medical education in Edinburgh. Rising rapidly and brilliantly, he founded the Royal Humane Society of England, the Royal Seabathing Hospital at Margate, and the London Medical Society. Regrettably, he is mainly remembered today for this famous but libelous doggerel: "I John Lettsom . . . Blisters, bleeds, and sweats 'em. If, after that, they please to die . . . I, John Lettsom."

Fredrick Augustus Pickering (1835–1926) Born in Tortola, he became a civil service worker who by 1884 had risen to become the first black president of the British Virgin Islands. He held the post until 1887, and was the last man to be known as president, since the job description after him was changed to commissioner.

John Pickering (1704–68) Born into a fervent Quaker family in Anguilla, Pickering moved in the 1720s to Fat Hogs Bay in Tortola. In 1736, he became the leader of a congregation of Quakers, and by 1741 he was named first lieutenant governor of the island. Fearing the Virgin Islands would be drawn into a war between Spain and Britain, he resigned his post because of his Quaker beliefs. Apparently, he was an "enlightened" plantation owner, as hundreds of slaves islandwide mourned his death. Or perhaps they feared their new master.

3. ARCHITECTURE & LITERATURE

ARCHITECTURE

Some of the architectural legacy left by the colonizing Danes still remains in the islands, especially in Christiansted and Frederiksted on St. Croix and in Charlotte Amalie on St. Thomas.

Many of the commercial buildings constructed in downtown Charlotte Amalie are restrained in ornamentation. Pilasters and classical cornices were commonplace on many buildings. Most door arches and windows were framed in brick. To "dress up" a building, ornamentation such as cornices was added in the final stages. The walls were covered with plaster, but in recent decades this plaster and stucco have been stripped from the walls. Underneath the rubble, well-designed shapes and patterns of old brick and blue bitch were discovered, which is a stone made of volcanic tuff. The old masons may have known what they were doing—once stripped, the walls don't stand up well in the Caribbean sun and salt air.

Cast-iron grillwork on some of the second-floor overhanging balconies displays a certain architectural flair. Many of the buildings in St. Thomas originally had courtyards, or still do. These added to the living space on the second floor. In the courtyard were the kitchens and, almost more vital, cisterns to capture the precious rainwater.

Many of the building techniques used on St. Thomas were also used on structures that went up on St. Croix. Although tremendously damaged by Hurricane Hugo in 1989, Christiansted remains one of the most historically authentic towns in the West Indies, true to its original Danish colonial flavor.

The basic style was a revival of the European classic look of the 18th century, but with variations to accommodate the tropical climate. As early as 1747, the Danes adopted a strict building code, which spared Christiansted from some of the violent fires that virtually wiped out Charlotte Amalie. Frederiksted, the other major town of St. Croix, has a well-designed waterfront, with blocks of arcaded sidewalks. The quarter is protected by the government as part of Frederiksted's National Historic District.

Great architecture was never the forte of the British Virgin Islands. During a time when major buildings might have been created, the BVI was too economically depressed to find the funds for major structures of lasting significance. Therefore, for much of its history, its people have lived in typical West Indies shanties, with an occasional public building constructed that vaguely imitated 18th-century Europe in style.

Curiously enough, although the BVI didn't leave the world any lasting architectural heritage, it did produce a native son, William Thornton, whose designs were used for the U.S. Capitol building in Washington. Many major buildings in America adopted his general classic style, including the Octagon, headquarters of the American Institute of Architects Foundation.

LITERATURE

The only piece of "great literature" to have come out of the Virgin Islands thus far is American writer's Herman Wouk's *Don't Stop the Carnival*, allegedly inspired by the old hotel on Water Island, off the coast of St. Thomas.

But that doesn't mean that the island is without its stories and legends. One person who wants to keep alive the stories of the old days in the Virgin Islands is Arona Petersen, author of *The Food & Folklore of the Virgin Islands* (Romik, Inc., 1990). This St. Thomas food writer and folklorist is also the author of *Herbs and Proverbs* and *Kreole Ketch 'N' Keep*. Many people consider her the authority on the history and culture of the Virgin Islands. *Kreole Ketch 'N' Keep*, published in 1975, is a collection of West Indian stories. Ms. Petersen has a keen ear and recaptures the flavor of old island days, interspering stories with recipes.

In her stories she remembers the sound and the idiom of the old days and the island's colorful language. In her story, "What does 'Tomorrow' Mean? In Any Language, Wait," appears this passage: "Wat I trying to say is dat waitin is wat life is about. Everybody waitin fo someting or udder, mannin or nite. Tain get wan purson wat, livin ain waitin—fo a bus, fo a taxi, fo a airplane, fo a steamer, fo a letter to come back. Some doan even know wat dey waiting for but dey still waitin."

4. RELIGION, MYTH & FOLKLORE

The native Virgin Islanders have strong spiritual beliefs. The early Christian missionaries were zealous. The slaves took quickly to the Christian religion, but the way they practiced it was unique. Many times they incorporated a belief in magic powers and a host of superstitions that they had brought over from Africa. As the islands' multitude of churches, most of which are Protestant, attest, religious fervor is still strong.

The two most famous mythological figures of the Virgin Islands are the Obeah and the jumbie. Originally, belief in the Obeah was not strong among native Virgin Islanders, but it did enjoy cult status "down island," a reference to the islands that sweep downward toward South America. With the influx of so many down islanders into the Virgin Islands looking for work and better economic opportunities, the Obeah arrived.

Basically, the Obeah is a "superstitious force" that natives believe can be responsible for both good and evil. It is considered prudent not to get on the bad side of this force, which might reward you or make trouble for you.

If you encounter an old-time islander and ask, "How are you?" the answer is likely to be, "Not too bad." The person who may actually feel great says this so as not to tempt the force, which might be listening.

"Don't let the jumbies get ya!" is often heard in the Virgin Islands, particularly when people are leaving their hosts and heading home in the dark. Like the Obeah, jumbies are also said to be capable of good and bad. These are supernatural beings that are believed by some to live around households. It is said that new settlers from the mainland of the United States never see these jumbies, and therefore need not fear them. But many islanders believe in their existence, and if queried, they may enthrall you with tales of sightings.

No one seems to agree on exactly what a jumbie is. It's been suggested that it is the spirit of a dead person that didn't go where it belonged. Some islanders disagree with this assessment. "They're the souls of live people," one islander told me, "but they live in the body of the dead." The most prominent jumbies are "Mocko Jumbies," actually carnival stilt-walkers seen at all parades.

The folkloric tradition in the Virgin Islands came not from Christian missionaries, but from the memories and oral traditions from Africa that were passed down from generation to generation.

Weed women have a firm place in the folklore of the Virgin Islands. These women used old recipes handed down from generations. Apparently, some of their potions were amazingly effective, and some are still in use. They produced herbal teas and had "secret remedies" for any sickness or ailment, ranging from infertility to cancer.

5. CULTURAL & SOCIAL LIFE

Long before the arrival of Columbus in 1493, the culture of the Virgin Islands was already under way, the result of the settlement by Arawak Indians and later the cannibalistic Caribs, who destroyed these kind people, either by working them to death as slaves or by eating them. With the advent of the European colonial powers these cultures and people were completely wiped out.

Nothing was to shape the destiny and culture of the Caribbean more than the arrival of slaves from various parts of Africa, who brought their superstitions, gods, and beliefs with them. Although converted to Christianity, they kept their traditions alive through fairs and festivals.

Except for that rare festival or fair, the cultural and social life of the communities revolved almost completely around the church, and the church was instrumental in bringing the community together.

The art of story-telling was also practiced. It was through storytellers that the past was kept alive for each new generation, since little of it was written down. Today some of the old stories are being collected and published in an attempt to preserve a cultural memory before it disappears completely.

Many British traditions are still maintained in the BVI, especially in the judicial system, and other matters. But once the Americans took over their own islands, the big neighbor in the north dominated the Virgins more than any colonial foreign force ever did. The American way of life prevails today in the U.S. Virgins, and it has swept across to the BVI.

The herbal teas and secret remedies from the weed woman, and the self-reliant arts of fishing, boatbuilding, farming, and even hunting are all but gone. Today when islanders need something, they have it shipped down from Miami. In clothes, in cars, in food, in entertainment, in currency, America, not Britannia, rules the seas around both groups of islands.

But the annual festivals, the fungi bands, and even the belief in jumbies help to keep yesterday alive.

6. SPORTS & RECREATION

Sports and recreation are why many visitors go to the Virgin Islands. Coral reefs and beautiful beaches provide a panoramic background for an array of water sports. Horseback riders, golfers, tennis players, and others will find many tempting opportunities as well. St. Thomas and St. Croix have many boating possibilities, and Tortola is virtually the yachting capital of the Caribbean. Of course, many visitors come to both the USVI and the BVI to indulge their passion for lying on the beach, and I'll have more comments on the best beaches in the individual island chapters.

In this section, I'll present a general overview to aid those who make vacation plans with sports in mind. Under the "Sports and Recreation" sections of the individual islands, more details are provided.

CAMPING   The best campsites are those on the island of St. John. The campgrounds at **Maho Bay** and **Cinnamon Bay** are considered the finest in the entire Caribbean.

In the BVI, the best campsite is **Brewers Bay Campground,** which rents tents and basic equipment, and is open year-round.

GOLF   The major golf course in the Virgin Islands is the 18-hole **Carambola Golf Course,** designed by Robert Trent Jones. It took a beating with the 1989 Hurricane Hugo that devastated St. Croix, but it has been restored. Originally called Fountain Valley, this golf course is open to the general public. Call 778-0747 for details.

On St. Thomas, the 18-hole **Mahogany Run** (tel. 775-5000), lies on the north shore, and is known for its scenery. This 6,350-yard, par-70 course was designed by Tom and George Fazio, and its special hazard is the "Devil's Triangle," with the 13th, 14th, and 15th holes bordering a cliffside.

SAILING & YACHTING   The Virgin Islands are a yachting paradise, offering smooth sailing through turquoise waters. There are seemingly endless coves and inlets, along with protected harbors, for anchoring for the day.

If you're qualified, it's possible to sail your own craft. If you're well heeled, or you join with a number of others to form a party, you can charter a vessel with a full crew. Most visitors are content to go on day sails, and in the individual island chapters I give plenty of information on the possibilities, which exist in profusion in St. Thomas. In St. Croix, the most popular day sail is to the natural paradise of Buck Island.

If you don't know how to sail but would like to learn, that too is possible. Sailing schools exist on St. Croix. Service is provided by **Annapolis Sailing School,** 1215 King Cross St., Christiansted, St. Croix, USVI 00820 (tel. 809/773-4709, or toll free 800/638-9192). Using three 24-foot day sailers, they charge $185 for a 2-day lesson, per person, and $270 for a 3-day lesson. No class or sailing excursion has more than four students.

A nonprofit organization, **Virgin Island Charter Yacht League,** Homeport, St. Thomas, USVI 00802 (tel. 809/774-3944, or toll free 800/524-2061), provides prospective yachters with information on how to go about it.

Yachting possibilities abound on Tortola in the BVI. The major center for this activity is **The Moorings,** Road Harbour, Wickhams Cay (tel. 809/494-2332) in Tortola. This 100-slip marina has complete facilities and yachting services and also arranges rentals.

The BVI is also the headquarters of the **Offshore Sailing School,** Treasure Isle Jetty, Road Town (tel. 809/494-2501), offering sailing instruction year-round. For information before you go, write Offshore Sailing School, 16731 McGregor Blvd., Ft. Myers, FL 33908 (tel. 813/454-1700, or toll free 800/221-4326 in the U.S.).

The Yachtsman's Guide to the Virgin Islands, for 25 years the classic cruising guide to this area, is annually updated. The detailed 240-page text is supplemented by 22 sketch charts, more than a hundred photographs and illustrations, and numerous landfall sketches showing harbors, channels, landmarks, and such. Subjects covered include piloting, anchoring, communication, weather, fishing, and more. Copies of the guide are available at major marine outlets, bookstores, and direct from Tropic Isle Publishers, Inc., P.O. Box 610938, North Miami, FL 33261-0938 (tel. 305/893-4277), for $15.95 postpaid.

SNORKELING & SCUBA DIVING   These sports abound on St. Croix where the warm waters are perfect. The most popular site is the underwater trails off Buck Island, to which numerous day sails go from Christiansted at the harbor. St. Croix is also known for its "dropoffs," including the famous Puerto Rico Trench, which at 12,000 feet is the fifth-deepest body of water on earth. Scuba instruction, both day and night dives, and rental of the necessary equipment are provided at many places on St. Croix, and snorkeling possibilities abound and are very easily and informally arranged.

On St. Thomas all major hotels rent fins and masks for snorkelers, and all the multitude of day-sail charters feature this type of equipment on board. Many firms on St. Thomas, such as the St. Thomas Diving Club, feature scuba programs.

The best snorkeling on Virgin Gorda is around its major attraction, The Baths. Lying off Anegada Island, Anegada Reef has been the "burial ground" for ships for centuries, an estimated 300 wrecks, including many pirate ships. The wreckage of the RMS *Rhone,* in the vicinity of the westerly tip of Salt Island, is the most celebrated dive spot in the BVI. This vessel went under in 1867 in one of the most disastrous hurricanes ever to hit the Virgin Islands.

SPORTFISHING   In the last 25 years or so, about 20 world records have been set in the waters off the U.S. Virgin Islands. Many of these records were for the capture of the blue marlin. Other abundant fish include bonito, tuna, sailfish, and skipjack. But you needn't go to sea to fish. On both St. Thomas and St. John, the U.S. government posts lists where shoreline fishing is possible. Local tourist offices will advise.

In St. Croix, grouper, wahoo, snapper, mahimahi, and the blue dolphin (not the mammal) are major prizes from the sea. Cruzans claim the world billfishing record. Numerous places arrange fishing trips.

TENNIS This is a major sport in the Virgin Islands, and most courts are all-weather or Laykold. Because the heat at midday is intense, many courts are lit for night games. Pro instruction and pro shops are found on all the major islands, especially St. Croix and St. Thomas.

St. Thomas offers six free courts, on a first-come, first-served basis. If the courts at the various major hotels aren't occupied by resident guests, most hotels will allow you to play for a fee. Bolongo Bay and Marriott's Frenchman's Reef Beach Resort have four courts each.

On St. Croix, the Buccaneer Hotel has the best courts, eight in all, each maintained in perfect condition. Its pro shop is state of the art. The island also has seven public courts.

On Tortola, most of the tennis action centers along Prospect Reef with six courts, available at times for a fee to the general public. If you're a serious tennis buff and are contemplating staying on Virgin Gorda, make your hotel selection Little Dix Bay, which has seven courts—the best on the island—reserved for guests only.

7. FOOD & DRINK

Fungi, Gundy, Callaloo.
Plantains, Seagrapes, boiled Foo-Foo.
Paw Paw, Soursop, thick Goat Stew.
Johnny Cakes and Jug Jug too!

FOOD

Just as food critics were about to publish their eulogies to old island cooking in the Virgin Islands, there occurred a last-minute resurgence. Many of the old island dishes have come back into vogue, and every island now has its little taverns—often shanties—offering regional specialties. Therefore, for·a good price you can escape from the hamburgers and the hot dogs and taste some real island flavors. Under individual island chapters, I'll recommend specific restaurants offering the best in West Indian or Virgin Island cuisine.

MEALS & DINING CUSTOMS

Of course, a visit to the Virgin Islands hardly means a diet of local cuisine. These islands often have some of the best chefs in the Caribbean, hailing from the United States and Europe, and they prepare a sumptuous cuisine of elegant French, continental, and American dishes.

When dining in the Virgins, try some fish, which is often delectable, especially dolphin (not the mammal), wahoo, yellowtail, grouper, and red snapper. These types of fish when broiled with a hot lime sauce as an accompaniment may represent your most memorable island meals. Sweet-tasting Caribbean lobster (different from the Maine variety) is likely to be the most expensive item on the menu.

Elaborate buffets are often a feature in the major resort hotels on all the islands. Usually these buffets feature a variety of West Indian dishes along with other more standard fare, and they are almost always reasonable in price. Entertainment is most often from a West Indian fungi band. Even if you are not staying at a particular hotel, you can call hotels featuring buffets on any given night and make a reservation to attend.

Before checking into a hotel, it's a good idea to have a clear understanding of just what is included in the various plans offered.

To save money many visitors prefer to request a MAP rate when checking into a hotel. This means "Modified American Plan," and it offers a room, breakfast, and one main meal of the day, nearly always dinner. That leaves the visitor free to take lunch somewhere else on the island or else near one of the beachfront places. Often if the hotel has a beach, many guests will order a light à la carte lunch at their hotel which is added to the bill for MAP guests.

If you want to go out for your main meals, request CP, which means "Continental Plan," with only breakfast included. EP is "European Plan," with no meals included. AP is "American Plan," with a room and three meals a day included. Even with meals included, you'll still have to pay extra for your drinks and wine consumption.

Frankly, it's difficult for first-time visitors in rented cars to take to the unsatisfactory roads of the USVI or BVI at night looking for that special little restaurant where the food is so good. The food may be good, but getting there can be a little dangerous, because roads are narrow and not well lit. To complicate matters, *both* island groups, even the American islands, require motorists to drive on the left.

If you go out for dinner, consider taking a taxi. All taxi drivers know these badly marked roads well. Once at the restaurant, you can arrange for the taxi to pick you up at an agreed upon time or else have the restaurant call the taxi when you are ready to go.

THE CUISINE

APPETIZERS The most famous soup of the islands is *Kallaloo,* or callaloo, made in an infinite number of ways from a leafy green vegetable similar to spinach. This soup is flavored with salt beef, pig mouth, pig tail, hot peppers, ham bone, fresh fish, crabs, or perhaps corned conch, along with okra, onions, and spices.

Many soups are sweetened with sugar, and putting fruits in soups is common. The classic red bean soup, made with pork or ham, various spices and tomatoes, is sugared to taste. *Tannia* soup is made from the root of the so-called "Purple Elephant Ear." Salt-fat meat and ham, along with tomatoes, onions, and spices, are added to the tannias.

Souse is an old-time favorite made with the feet, head and tongue of the pig, and flavored with a lime-based sauce and various spices.

Salt-fish salad is traditionally served on Holy Thursday or Good Friday, as well as at other times. It's made with boneless salt fish, potatoes, onions, boiled eggs, and an oil and vinegar dressing.

Herring gundy is an old-time island favorite made with salt herring, potatoes, onions, green sweet and hot peppers, olives, diced beets, raw carrots, herbs, and boiled eggs.

SIDE DISHES Rice—seasoned, not plain—is popular with Virgin Islanders, who often serve several starches at one meal. Most often rice is flavored with ham or salt pork, tomatoes, garlic, onion, and shortening.

Fungi is a simple cornmeal dumpling that can be made more interesting with the addition of various ingredients, such as okra. Sweet fungi becomes a dessert, with sugar, milk, cinnamon, and raisins.

Okra (often spelled *ochroe* in the islands) is a mainstay vegetable, often accompanying beef, fish, or chicken. It's fried in an iron skillet after being flavored with hot pepper, tomatoes, onions, garlic, and bacon fat or butter. *Accra,* another popular dish, is made with okra, black-eyed peas, salt, and pepper. It's dropped into boiling fat and fried until golden brown.

The classic vegetable dish—some families serve it every night—is peas and rice, made with pigeon peas flavored with ham or salt meat, onion, tomatoes, herbs, and sometimes slices of pumpkin. Pigeon peas, one of the most common vegetables in the islands because they flourish in hot, dry climates, are sometimes called congo peas or *gunga*.

FISH & MEAT Locals gave colorful names to the various fish brought home for dinner, everything from "ole wife" to "doctors." "Porgies and grunts," along with yellowtail, kingfish, and bonito, show up on many tables. Fish is usually boiled in a lime-flavored brew seasoned with hot peppers and herbs, and is commonly served with a creole sauce of peppers, tomatoes, and onions, among other ingredients. Salt fish and rice is another low-cost dish, the fish flavored with onion, tomatoes, shortening, garlic, and green pepper.

Conch creole is a tasty brew, flavored with onions, garlic, spices, hot peppers, and salt pork. Most beef is shipped in from the mainland or from Puerto Rico. A local favorite main dish is chicken and rice, made with Spanish peppers. Curried goat, the longtime "classic" West Indian dinner, is made with herbs, including *cardamom pods* and onions.

The famous johnnycakes that accompany many of these fish and meat dishes are made with flour, baking powder, shortening, and salt, then fried in deep hot fat or baked. Indians may have made johnnycakes with ground corn baked on hot coals.

DESSERTS Sweet-potato pone is a classic, made with sugar, eggs, butter, milk, salt, cinnamon, raisins, and chopped raw almonds. The exotic fruits of the islands lend themselves to various homemade ice creams, including mango. Islanders in the old days invented many new dishes using local ingredients, such as orange-rose sherbet made with fragrant rose petal mortar pounded into a paste and flavored with sugar and orange juice. Guava ice cream is a delectable concoction, as are *soursop*, banana, and papaya. Sometimes dumplings are served for dessert, made with guava, peach, plum, gooseberry, or cherry, and certainly apple.

DRINKS

Water is generally safe to drink on the islands. Much of the water is stored in cisterns and filtered before it's served. Delicate stomachs, however, should stick to mineral water or club soda. All the American brands of soft drinks and beer are sold in both the USVI and the BVI. Wines have to be brought in from either Europe or the United States. Sometimes they are quite expensive.

The *vin du pays* of the islands is Cruzan rum made with sugarcane. To help stimulate the local economy U.S. customs allows you to bring home an extra bottle of Cruzan rum, over your usual 5-liter liquor allowance.

Long before the arrival of Coca-Cola and Pepsi, many islanders made their own drinks with whatever was available, many from locally grown fruits. From the guavaberry comes a liqueur rum, which is an unusual mixture, whose ingredients include sorrel, fruit, ginger, prunes, raisins, cinnamon, and rum.

8. RECOMMENDED BOOKS, FILMS & RECORDINGS

BOOKS

GENERAL

The *Food and Folklore of the Virgin Islands*, by Arona Petersen (Romik), is penned by a well-known St. Thomas food writer and "folklorist." The regional flavor of Virgin Island fare is captured in her recipes, and the idiomatic dialogues of her island people are perfectly re-created, as she spins old island tales and wisdom. *Tales of Tortola and the British Virgin Islands,* written and published by Florence Lewishohn, recounts five centuries of the legend and lore of the islands, from the coming of Columbus to the visit of Queen Elizabeth II.

Pirates of the Virgin Islands and *Mavericks in Paradise,* by Fritz Seyfarth (Spanish Main Press), are two books bound in one volume. They capture all the daring exploits of the maritime gangsters and terrorists who collected immense booties and made the Virgin Islands a pirate paradise.

Caribbean Pirates, by Warren Alleyne (Macmillan-Caribbean), attempts to separate fact from fiction. Some of this material is based on unpublished letters and documents.

Bob Shacochis's short stories, *Easy in the Islands* (Penguin), giddily re-create the flavor of the West Indies. It was the winner of the American Book Award in 1986.

Two on the Isle, written and published by Robb White, tells the story of how the writer, aided by his wife, first discovered their little nest in the BVI, which later became the Marina Cay Hotel.

Sailing enthusiasts say you shouldn't set out to explore the islets, cays, coral reefs, and islands of the BVI without John Rousmanière's well-researched and self-published *The Sailing Lifestyle.*

FICTION

Herman Wouk's *Don't Stop the Carnival* (Pocket) is "the Caribbean classic," and all readers contemplating a visit to the Virgin Islands should try to read this book before going there. It's great airport-lounge reading.

Caribbean, by James A. Michener (Fawcett), begins with the 1310 conquest of the peaceful Arawaks by the cannibalistic Caribs and ends seven centuries later with Castro.

TRAVEL

Alec Waugh's recent *Love and the Caribbean: Tales, Characters and Scenes of the West Indies* (Paragon) recaptures the "distant past and the colorful present" of the Caribbean. Kirkus Reviews called it "a delight to the armchair traveler as well as the sophisticated tourist." *The Traveller's Tree: A Journey Through the Caribbean Islands* (Quentin Crewe), by Patrick Leigh Fermor, is an account of the author's journey through the West Indies in the 1940s. It is considered the classic for depicting life in the war and postwar years.

Exploring St. Croix, by Shirley Imsand and Richard Philibosian (Travelers Information Press), is a very detailed guide of this island. The authors take you to 49 beaches, 34 snorkel and scuba sites, 125 sites of historical interest, 22 birdwatching areas, and lead you on 20 different hikes.

HISTORY

Eric Williams's *From Columbus to Castro: The History of the Caribbean,* is a well-researched saga of a land dominated by slavery, sugar, and greed by the former prime minister of Trinidad and Tobago. *The Caribbean People,* by Reginald Honychurch (T. Nelson & Sons), one of the "new historians" of the Caribbean, reveals many heretofore obscure or relatively unknown facts about the people who live in this basin. It's a well-balanced account in three volumes.

FILMS

There haven't been many. One that is available in some video stores is *Our Virgin Isle,* starring John Cassavetes and Sidney Poitier. The movie, filmed in 1958, was based on the experience of Robb White, who moved to the island with his wife. Their home eventually became the Marina Cay Hotel.

Though it takes place on the island of Martinique, *Sugar Cane Alley* (1984) can give you some insight into Caribbean history. Director Euzhan Palcy garnered lots of acclaim for her deeply felt, beautifully crafted film.

RECORDINGS

Calypso and reggae, the sounds of the Caribbean, are famous. Less well known is soca, a rock-influenced calypso, and zouk, which is a fusion of all Caribbean music, with a touch of French melody thrown in.

Some islands, notably Jamaica and Trinidad, have their own musical traditions, but Virgin Island music is influenced by the music of all of the islands, even America.

Here is a sampling of some of the best music: *The Pan in Me* (Amoco Renegades), *Caribbean Medley* (Cayman Allstars), *Brown Skin Girl* and *Bassa Roo* (Brutus Marcato/Mardi Gras Orchestra), *Gaudeamus Igitur* (Silver Stars), *Hot Hot Hot* and *Welcome the Morning Sun* (Five Star Cockspur Steel Orchestra), *Soca Man* (Success Stars), *Saturday Night* (Cordettes-Sun Islanders Steel Orchestra), and *Polonaise* (The Sunjet Serenaders Steelband).

CHAPTER 2

PLANNING A TRIP TO THE VIRGIN ISLANDS

This chapter is devoted to the where, the when, and the how of your trip to the Virgin Islands—all those issues required to get your trip together and take it on the road.

In this chapter I concentrate on what you need to do *before* you go. In addition to helping you decide when to take your vacation, I answer questions you might have about what to take, where to gather information, and what documents you need to obtain. I also cover various alternative and specialty travel options, such as educational and wilderness travel, and include tips for special travelers.

1. INFORMATION, ENTRY REQUIREMENTS & MONEY

INFORMATION

IN THE U.S. If you're going to the U.S. Virgin Islands, you can obtain much valuable information before you go at the **U.S. Virgin Islands Division of Tourism,** 1270 Ave. of the Americas, New York, NY 10020 (tel. 212/582-4520). Additional offices are found at 235 Peachtree Center, Gaslight Tower, Suite 1420, Atlanta, GA 30303 (tel. 404/688-0906); 122 S. Michigan Ave., Chicago, IL 60603 (tel. 312/461-0180); 1667 K St. NW, Washington, DC 20006 (tel. 202/293-3707); 2655 Le Jeune Rd., Coral Gables, FL 33135 (tel. 305/442-7200), and 3460 Wilshire Blvd., Los Angeles, CA 90010 (tel. 213/739-0138).

For data on the British Virgin Islands, get in touch with the **British Virgin Islands Tourist Board,** 370 Lexington Ave., Suite 416, New York, NY 10017 (tel. 212/696-0400, or toll free 800/835-8530). On the West Coast, contact the **BVI Information Office,** 1686 Union St., San Francisco, CA 94123 (tel. 415/775-0344).

Other useful sources are, of course, newspapers and magazines. To find the latest articles that have been published on the destination, go to your library and ask for the

INFORMATION, ENTRY REQUIREMENTS & MONEY • 19

Reader's Guide to Periodical Literature and look under the island/country for listings.

You may also want to contact the State Department for background bulletins. Write to Superintendent of Documents, **U.S. Government Printing Office,** Washington, DC 20402 (tel. 202/783-3238).

A good travel agent can also be a source of information. If you use one, make sure the agent is a member of the American Society of Travel Agents (ASTA). If you get poor service from an agent, you can write to **ASTA Consumer Affairs,** 1101 King St., Alexandria, VA 22314.

IN THE U.K. Tourist information for the British Virgin Islands is available at the BVI Information Office, 26 Hockerill St., Bishops Stortford, Herts., England CM23 2DW (tel. 0279/654969). For the U.S. Virgin Islands, information is available at 2 Cinnamon Row, Plantation Wharf, York Place, London, England SW11 3TW (tel. 071/978-5262).

ENTRY REQUIREMENTS
DOCUMENTS

U.S. and Canadian citizens are required to present some proof of citizenship. It's always good to have a passport when traveling abroad, even to a U.S. possession, but it is not necessary to have one to visit either the U.S. or British Virgin Islands. However, U.S. and Canadians should have either a voter registration card or a birth certificate to visit either the American or British chain of islands.

With a passport you can take an excursion to the nearby islands, which, except for Puerto Rico, are foreign destinations. Entry into one of these little island countries is always easier with a passport, even though some of them don't absolutely require it if your other documentation looks good enough.

Visitors from Europe do need a passport.

DOCUMENT PROTECTION

It is a good policy before leaving your country to make two copies of your most valuable documents, including your passport. Make a photocopy of the inside page of your passport, the one with your photograph. In case of loss abroad, you should also make copies of your driver's license, a voter registration card (if you're using that instead of a license), an airline ticket, strategic hotel vouchers, and any other sort of identity card that might be pertinent. You should also make copies of any prescriptions you take. Place one copy in your luggage and carry the original with you. Leave the other copy at your home. The information on these documents will be extremely valuable should you encounter loss or theft abroad.

CUSTOMS

American citizens clear Customs when they are leaving the U.S. Virgin Islands. The islands are duty-free ports, and U.S. citizens are allowed to bring back $1,200 worth of merchandise duty free. Americans on a direct flight from the U.S. Virgins do not have to clear Customs when they arrive in the U.S. Canadians, Australians, British, and others enter the U.S. Virgin Islands as they do the mainland.

In the British Virgin Islands, there is a Customs review upon entry. Usually items intended for personal use are allowed in. *No illegal drugs, please!*

BRINGING IT ALL HOME

U.S. Customs The government generously allows $1,200 worth of duty-free imports every 30 days, twice the amount allowed for most Caribbean Basin countries, including the British Virgin Islands, and exactly three times the $400 exemption U.S. visitors are allowed returning from most foreign countries and such French islands as Guadeloupe or Martinique. Purchases made in the U.S. Virgin Islands over the duty-free exemption are taxed at a flat rate of 5%, and 10% in the British Virgin Islands.

Joint declarations are possible for members of a family traveling together. For a husband and wife with two children, the exemption in the U.S. Virgins is $4,800!

Unsolicited gifts can be sent to friends and relatives at the rate of $100 a day, and these do not have to be declared as part of your $1,200 per person exemption. Gifts mailed from the BVI cannot exceed $50 per day.

The government allows you to bring back 5 liters of liquor duty free, and an extra liter of rum if one of the bottles is produced in the Virgin Islands, including Cruzan rum. U.S. customs exempts items made on the island, including perfume, straw hats, jewelry, and fashion. But if the value exceeds $25, you must produce a certificate of origin. Original paintings are also duty free.

Collect receipts for all purchases made abroad. If a merchant suggests giving you a false receipt, understating the value of the goods, beware: the merchant might be an informer to U.S. Customs. You must also declare all gifts received during your stay abroad.

If you purchased such an item during an earlier trip abroad, carry proof that you have already paid customs duty on the item at the time of your previous reentry. To be extra careful, compile a list of expensive carry-on items, and ask a U.S. Customs agent to stamp your list at the airport before your departure.

If you're concerned and need more specific guidance, write to the **U.S. Customs Service,** 1301 Constitution Ave., P.O. Box 7407, Washington, DC 20044, requesting the free pamphlet, *Know Before You Go.* For information on U.S. Virgin Islands requirements, call 809/774-2510 in St. Thomas.

Canadian Customs   For more information, write for the booklet *I Declare,* issued by **Revenue Canada Customs Department,** Communications Branch, Mackenzie Ave., Ottawa, ON K1A 0L5. Canada allows its citizens a $300 exemption, and they are allowed to bring back duty free 200 cigarettes, 2.2 pounds of tobacco, 40 ounces of liquor, and 50 cigars. In addition, they are allowed to mail gifts into Canada from abroad at the rate of $40 (CDN) a day, providing they are unsolicited and aren't alcohol or tobacco. On the package, mark "Unsolicited gift, under $40 value." All valuables should be declared before departure in Canada on the Y-38 form, including serial numbers, as in the case of expensive foreign cameras that you already own. Caveat: The $300 exemption can be used only once a year and only after an absence of 7 days.

British Customs   Citizens can bring in goods up to £34, and one must be 17 or older to import liquor or tobacco. Brits are allowed 100 cigarettes or 100 cigarillos, or 50 cigars, or 250 grams of tobacco. In addition, 2 liters of table wine may be brought in, as well as 1 liter of alcohol greater than 22% by volume or 2 liters of alcohol equal to or less than 22% by volume. British customs tend to be strict and complicated in its requirements. For details get in touch with **Her Majesty's Customs and Excise Office,** New King's Bean House, 22 Upper Ground, London SE1 9PJ (tel. 071/382-5468 for more information).

Australian Customs   The duty-free allowance in Australia is $400 (AUS) or, for those under 18, $200 (AUS). Personal property mailed back from U.S. or British Virgins should be marked "Australian goods returned," to avoid payment of duty, providing it is what it says on the package. Upon returning to Australia, citizens can bring in 200 cigarettes or 250 grams of tobacco and 1 liter of alcohol. If you're returning with valuable goods you already own, such as expensive foreign-made cameras, you should file form B263. A helpful brochure, available from Australian consulates or Customs offices, is called *Customs Information for All Travellers.*

New Zealand Customs   The duty-free allowance is $500 (NZ). Citizens over 16 years of age can bring in 200 cigarettes or 250 grams of tobacco or 50 cigars, 4.5 liters of wine or beer or 1.125 liters of liquor. New Zealand currency does not carry restrictions regarding import or export. A Certificate of Export listing valuables taken out of the country (that is, items you already own) allows you to take them back in without paying duty. Most questions are answered in a free pamphlet, available at New Zealand consulates and Customs offices, called *New Zealand Customs Guide for Travellers.*

Irish Customs   Irish citizens may bring in 200 cigarettes or 100 cigarillos or 50 cigars or 250 grams (approximately 9 ounces) of tobacco, plus 1 liter of liquor exceeding 22% volume (such as whisky, brandy, gin, rum or vodka), or 2 liters of distilled beverages and spirits with a wine or alcoholic base of an alcoholic strength not exceeding 22% volume, plus 2 liters of other wine and 50 grams of perfume. Other allowances include duty-free goods to a value of IR £34 per person or IR £17 per person for travelers under 15 years of age.

MONEY

CASH & CURRENCY

Both the U.S. Virgin Islands and the British Virgin Islands use the U.S. dollar as their form of currency.

A Note on Currency for British Travelers

British visitors will need to convert their pounds into U.S. dollars when visiting not only the U.S. Virgin Islands, but also the British Virgin Islands (unless a special dispensation is granted in the latter). Here's how pounds break down into U.S. dollars (subject to market changes, of course).

THE U.S. DOLLAR & THE BRITISH POUND

U.S. $	£	U.S. $	£
.08	.05	9.60	6
.16	.10	11.20	7
.40	.25	12.80	8
.80	.50	14.40	9
1.20	.75	16.00	10
1.60	1	24.00	15
3.20	2	32.00	20
4.80	3	48.00	30
6.40	4	80.00	50
8.00	5	160.00	100

TRAVELER'S CHECKS

Traveler's checks are the safest way to carry cash while traveling. Most banks will give you a better rate on traveler's checks than for cash. The list of suppliers of these checks has grown somewhat shorter in recent years because of the mergers of traveler's check facilities at several major banks. Checks denominated in U.S. dollars are accepted virtually anywhere, but in some cases (perhaps for ease of conversion into local currencies), travelers might want checks denominated in other currencies.

Each of the agencies listed below will refund your checks if they are lost or stolen, provided you produce sufficient documentation. When purchasing your checks, ask about refund hotlines: American Express probably has the greatest number of offices around the world.

American Express (tel. toll free 800/221-7282 in the U.S. and Canada) charges a 1% commission. Checks are free to members of the American Automobile Association. The company issues checks denominated in U.S. dollars, Canadian dollars, British pounds sterling, Swiss francs, French francs, German marks, Saudi riyals, and Japanese yen, although the vast majority of checks sold in North America are denominated in U.S. dollars.

Citicorp (tel. toll free 800/645-6556 in the U.S. or 813/623-1709, collect, in Canada) issues checks in U.S. dollars, British pounds, German marks, and Japanese yen.

MasterCard International/Thomas Cook International (tel. toll free 800/223-9920 in the U.S. or collect at 609/987-7300 from other parts of the world) issues checks denominated in U.S. dollars, French francs, German marks, Dutch guilders, Spanish pesetas, Australian dollars, Japanese yen, Swiss francs, and Hong Kong dollars.

Barclays Bank/Bank of America (tel. toll free 800/221-2426 in the U.S. and Canada). Through Barclay's subsidiary, Interpayment Services, Visa traveler's checks are sold which are denominated in U.S. dollars, British pounds, Swiss francs, French francs, German marks, and Japanese yen.

CREDIT CARDS

Credit cards are in wide use in both the USVI and the BVI. VISA and MasterCard are the major cards used, although American Express and, to a lesser extent, Diners Club are also popular. Credit cards can aid greatly when you travel in the Virgin Islands, sparing your valuable cash and giving financial flexibility for large purchases or last-minute travel changes. Because the U.S. Virgin Islands are such a shopping market, being able to make purchases by credit card becomes even more important.

WHAT WILL IT COST?

You can live on $50 a day or $1,000 a day in the Virgin Islands, depending on your budget and taste. This book documents a wide range of living and eating styles to suit all but the most rock-bottom of budgets. Most of the recommendations listed are moderately priced havens, which in the high-priced Virgin Islands charge painful enough tariffs. In the U.S. Virgin Islands very expensive hotels in winter can command from $216 to $440 per double room (no meals); expensive places charge from $150 to $215 double; moderately priced establishments get from $135 to $149 double, and inexpensive hotels charge $63 to $119 a night for a double. Meals are extra. Hotels that offer MAP (breakfast and dinner) add a surcharge of $25 to $55 to your tab. The good news is that mid-April to mid-December, these same hotel prices are slashed 25% to 50%.

An expensive dinner in the islands costs from $40 for one, including tip, but not wine; moderate restaurants charge from $25 to $30 for dinner; and inexpensive places ask under $25 for dinner.

There are fewer than 100 guesthouses and hotels in the **British Virgin Islands** and some of the smaller islands have only one hotel for the entire island. Price differences among these establishments are enormous. The BVI has several posh pockets that command and easily get the highest prices in the Virgin Island chain in the winter months, when guests are often asked to take half or full board when making reservations.

The highest prices for every place are charged from mid-December to mid-April. At that time, hotels judged "very expensive" charge from $290 and up per night for two persons. Hotels rated "expensive" ask for $195 to $289 per night in a double, and those ranked "moderate" charge from $140 to $190 a night for a double. In "inexpensive" hotels, charges begin at $95 per night in a double. To these rates, a 10% hotel tax and a 10% service charge are added. In the off-season (summer), reductions ranging from 20% to 50% are granted.

WHAT THINGS COST IN ST. THOMAS	U.S. $
Taxi from airport to Charlotte Amalie	4.00
Open-air taxi bus from Charlotte Amalie to Red Hook ferry	3.00
Local telephone call	.25
Double at Marriott's Frenchman's Reef (deluxe)	260.00
Double at Blackbeard's Castle (moderate)	145.00
Double at Bunker's Hill Hotel (budget)	90.00
Lunch for one at Banana Bay Club (moderate)*	16.00
Lunch for one at Eunice's (budget)*	7.50
Dinner for one at Fiddle Leaf (deluxe)*	50.00
Dinner for one at Alexander's (moderate)*	35.00
Dinner for one at East Coast (budget)*	15.00
Pint of beer in a bar	3.50
Coca-Cola in a café	1.95
Glass of wine in a restaurant	3.25
Roll of ASA 100 color film, 36 exposures	6.25
Admission to Magens Bay Beach	.50
Movie ticket	5.00

*Includes tax and tip, but not wine

2. WHEN TO GO — CLIMATE, HOLIDAYS & EVENTS

More and more, the Virgin Islands are a vacation spot for all seasons. Although they have more rain in the late spring and summer, the islands have so little variation in temperature that you can enjoy a visit there at any time. Installation of air conditioning in many accommodations, plus the whirling ceiling fans in almost every room, make for personal comfort everywhere. Sunshine is practically an everyday affair, even between the showers.

High season in the Virgin Islands, when hotels charge their highest prices, runs roughly from mid-December to mid-April. Winter is generally the dry season in the islands, but there can be heavy rainfall regardless of the season.

During the winter months, make reservations as far in advance as possible, and, if you rely on the mail, know that it sometimes takes a long time. Instead of writing to reserve your own room, it's better to book through one of the many Stateside representatives all major and many minor hotels use, or else to deal directly through a travel agent. If you don't want to do that, you should telephone the hotel of your choice in the Virgin Islands, agree on terms, and rush a deposit to hold the room. A few of the big hotels have toll-free numbers. More and more travelers, of course, are handling reservations by direct faxes to the hotel.

Air-conditioned by trade winds, the temperature variations in the Virgin Islands are surprisingly slight, averaging between 75° and 85°F in both winter and summer. Although there can be really chilly days, especially in the early morning and at night, the Virgin Island winter is usually like perpetual May.

The Virgin Islands' **off-season** is when North America warms up, and most vacationers head for Cape Cod or the Jersey shore or the beaches of California, thinking, perhaps, that the Virgin Islands are a caldron at this time. This is not the case. The fabled weather is balmy all year, with temperatures varying little more than 5° between winter and summer. The mid-80°s prevail throughout most of the region, and trade winds make for comfortable days and nights, even in cheaper places that don't have air conditioning.

Truth is, you're better off in the Virgin Islands most of the time than you are suffering through a roaring August heat wave in Chicago or New York.

Dollar for dollar, you'll save more money by renting a house or self-sufficient unit in the Virgin Islands than you will on Cape Cod, Fire Island, Laguna Beach, or the coast of Maine.

In essence, because of the trade winds and the various ocean currents, the Virgin Islands are virtually "seasonless." Even on islands where the noonday sun may raise the temperature to around 90°, cool breezes usually make the morning and late afternoon and evening more comfortable than in many parts of the U.S. mainland.

The off-season in the Virgin Islands—roughly from mid-April to mid-December—amounts to an 8-month long summer sale. In most cases, hotel rates are slashed a startling 20% to 50%. It's a bonanza for cost-conscious travelers, especially families who like to go on vacation together.

There are other reasons besides slashed prices to visit the Virgin Islands off-season. In spring, summer, and autumn a less hurried way of life prevails and you will have a better chance to appreciate the food, culture, and local customs. The atmosphere is also more cosmopolitan then with an influx of Europeans, and you'll feel less like you're at a Canadian or American outpost.

And finally, everything is less crowded off season—swimming pools, beaches, resorts, restaurants, golf courses, tennis courts, and stores.

CLIMATE

All the islands in both BVI and USVI enjoy balmy climates all year. Temperatures go up in the 80°s during the day and drop more comfortably into the 70°s at night. Don't worry about too much rain—most of the islands rarely get enough. Sometimes a tropical shower comes and goes so quickly you don't have time to get off the beach.

Average Temperatures and Rainfall in the U.S. Virgin Islands

		Jan	Feb	Mar	Apr	May	June	July	Aug	Sept	Oct	Nov	Dec
St. Croix	°F	75.9	75.8	77.5	78.7	79.3	81.9	83	83.3	82.6	82	79.8	78.3
	″	2.72	.46	1.44	4.25	7.19	2.35	1.20	4.07	2.11	3.08	7.64	2.77
St. John	°F	75.4	75.1	77.3	78.1	77.8	79.7	80.3	82.6	81.7	80.4	78.3	76.4
	″	2.08	1.03	.81	8.02	10.6	1.92	2.55	4.61	1.86	4.02	8.42	3.44
St. Thomas	°F	76.8	76.7	77.3	79	78.5	81.6	82.2	82.6	81.7	82.6	80.5	76.9
	″	1.86	.95	.97	8.32	9.25	1.62	2.25	3.6	2.04	4.43	7.77	2.46

You can obtain current weather information on many destinations, including the Virgin Islands, by calling **WeatherTrak** (tel. 900/370-8725). A taped message gives you a three-digit access code to call for the place you're interested in—in this case, the 809 area code.

THE HURRICANE SEASON

The curse of Caribbean weather, the hurricane season, officially lasts June through November. But there is no cause for panic in that. More tropical cyclones pound the U.S. mainland than hurricanes devastate the Virgin Islands. Hurricane Hugo in 1989 was exceptional, causing the most widespread damage in years, especially on St. Croix.

Islanders hardly stand around waiting for a hurricane to strike. Satellite forecasts in general give adequate warning so that precautions can be taken in time. And of course, there is always prayer: Islanders have a legal holiday in the third week of July called Supplication Day, when prayers are said that the Virgin Islands may be spared another hurricane. In late October, at the end of the season of danger, a supplemental Thanksgiving Day is celebrated.

If you're heading for the Virgin Islands during hurricane season, you can call your nearest branch of the National Weather Service. In your phone directory, look under the U.S. Department of Commerce. Radio and TV weather reports keep you posted from the **National Hurricane Center** in Coral Gables, Florida.

HOLIDAYS

In addition to the standard legal holidays observed in the United States, the U.S. Virgin Islanders also observe the following: January 6 (Three Kings' Day); March 31 (Transfer Day, commemorating the transfer of the Danish Virgin Islands to the Americans); June 20 (Organic Act Day—in lieu of a constitution, they have an Organic Act); July 3 (Emancipation Day, commemorating the freeing of the slaves by the Danes in 1848); July 25 (hurricane supplication day); October 17 (hurricane thanksgiving day); November 1 (Liberty Day); and December 26 (Christmas Second Day). The islands also celebrate two carnival days on the last Friday and Saturday in April: Children's Carnival Parade and Grand Carnival (adults') Parade.

In the British Virgin Islands, public holidays include the following: New Year's Day; March 12 (Commonwealth Day); Good Friday; Easter Monday; Whitmonday (some time in July); July 1 (Territory Day Sunday; date can vary): Festival Monday and Tuesday (some time during the first week of August); October 21 (St. Ursula's Day); November 14 (birthday of the heir to the throne); Christmas Day; and December 26 (Boxing Day).

U.S. VIRGIN ISLANDS CALENDAR OF EVENTS

APRIL

✪ **ST. THOMAS CARNIVAL** *The most spectacular carnival in all the Virgin Islands, this annual celebration has roots in Africa. Over the years, the festivities have become Christianized, but the fun and gaiety remain.*

Mocko Jumbies, people dressed as spirits, parade through the streets on stilts, nearly 20 feet high. Steel and fungi bands, "jump–ups," and parades mark the event.
Where: *Islandwide but best on the streets of Charlotte Amalie.* **When:** *After Easter, sometime in April.* **How:** *Obtain a schedule of events from the tourist office in St. Thomas.*

JULY

☐ **Carnival of St. John.** Parades, bands, and colorful costumes lead up to the selection of Ms. St. John and King of Carnival. First week of July.

AUGUST

☐ **Virgin Islands Open Atlantic Blue Marlin Tournament.** Fishermen from all over the world, some from as far as Australia, flock to this annual competition. Several marlin catches have set world records. Weekend closest to the full moon.

DECEMBER

✪ *CHRISTMAS IN ST. CROIX* *This is a major event on the calendar, as it launches the beginning of a 12-day celebration and festival that includes not only Christmas, the legal holiday December 26, New Year's Eve—called "Old Year's Day"—and New Year's Day. It ends January 6 at the observation of the Feast of the Three Kings, sometimes called Little Christmas, with a parade of flamboyantly attired merrymakers.*
Where: *Christiansted and other venues.* **When:** *December 25 to January 6.*

BRITISH VIRGIN ISLANDS CALENDAR OF EVENTS

APRIL

✪ *BVI SPRING REGATTA* *When the islands are at their best in spring, they host this regatta, the second leg of the Caribbean Ocean Racing Triangles events. Everybody from the most dedicated racers to bareboat crews out for "rum and reggae" join in the 3-day race. For the Caribbean boat crowd, it's a major event.*
Where: *Tortola.* **When:** *Mid-April.* **How:** *For more information, write BVI Spring Regatta Committee, P.O. Box 200, Road Town, Tortola, BVI (tel. 809/494-3286).*

AUGUST

✪ *BVI SUMMER FESTIVAL* *Many visitors from the other islands flock to the BVI at carnival time. Dancing to fungi and reggae bands, a Unity Day Parade, and general festivities sweep up the locals in their 3-day "big blast" for the year.*
Where: *Mainly the fairgrounds in Road Town.* **When:** *First week.* **How:** *Just join the fun at the fairgrounds, with nightly rides, games, and dancing.*

3. HEALTH & INSURANCE

HEALTH

Traveling to the U.S. or British Virgin Islands need not impair your health. Finding a good doctor in the Virgin Islands is not a problem, and all of them speak English. See "Fast Facts" in Chapter 3 and individual island chapters for specific names and addresses.

If your medical condition is chronic, always talk to your doctor before leaving home. He or she may have specific advice to give you, depending on your condition. For conditions such as epilepsy, a heart condition, or diabetes, wear Medic Alert's Identification Tag, which will immediately inform any doctor about your problem and also provide Medic Alert's 24-hour hotline, so a foreign doctor can obtain your medical records. For a lifetime membership, the cost is a well-spent $35. Contact the **Medic Alert Foundation,** P.O. Box 1009, Turlock, CA 95381-1009 (tel. toll free 800/432-5378).

Of course, carry all your vital medicine and drugs with you in your carry-on luggage, in case your checked luggage is lost.

Although tap water is generally considered safe to drink, if you have a delicate stomach it is better to avoid it and drink mineral water instead. This applies even to iced drinks. Stick to beer, hot tea, or soft drinks.

At some point in a vacation, most visitors experience some diarrhea, even those who follow the usual precautions. This is often the result of a change in diet and eating habits, not usually from bad or contaminated food and water. Mild forms of diarrhea usually pass quickly without medication. As a precaution, take along some antidiarrhea medicine, moderate your eating habits, and drink only mineral water until you recover. Always drink plenty of fluids during the course of your disturbance to prevent dehydration. Consuming more than your usual intake of salt, will help your body retain water. Eat only simply prepared foods at such times, such as plain bread (no butter) and boiled vegetables or some broth. Avoid dairy products at the time, except yogurt.

If symptoms persist, you may have dysentery, especially if you notice blood or mucus in your stool. At this point you should consult a doctor.

Sometimes travelers find that a change in diet will lead to constipation. If this occurs, eat a high-fiber diet and drink plenty of mineral water. Avoid large meals and don't drink wine.

SUNBURN

Actually, one of the most dangerous elements in the Virgin Islands and the Caribbean in general is the very thing you might have gone there to enjoy: the sun. It can be brutal, especially if you're coming from a winter climate and haven't been exposed to it in some time.

Wear sunglasses to protect yourself from the glare. When walking, wear a hat, wide brimmed if possible, and a coverup for your shoulders. In selecting a sunscreen lotion, seek one, as doctors advise you, with a high sun protection factor.

Experts also advise that you should limit your time on the beach, especially at first. If you forget and do get burned, try an aloe plant medication or a first-aid spray. Stay out of the sun until you recover. If your exposure is followed by fever, chills, a headache, or a feeling of nausea or dizziness, go to a doctor.

INSECTS & PESTS

Mosquitoes exist, but they are not the dangerous malaria-carrying kind that you might find elsewhere in the Caribbean. Nevertheless, they are still a nuisance. One of the biggest menaces is the "no-see-ums." These biting little insects appear mainly in the early evening. Even screens can't keep these critters out. You'll have to spray yourself with your favorite bug repellent.

VACCINATIONS

Vaccinations aren't needed to enter either the U.S. or British Virgin Islands if you're coming from a disease-free country such as the United States, Canada, Australia, New Zealand, or one of the countries of Western Europe such as Great Britain and Ireland.

MEDICINES

Take along an adequate supply of any prescription drugs that you need and a written prescription that uses the generic name of the drug as well—not the brand name. Consult your pharmacist about taking such over-the-counter drugs as Colace, a stool softener, or Metamucil. Other items to take include first-aid cream, insect repellent, aspirin, nose drops, Band-Aids, and hydrogen peroxide. If you're subject to motion sickness on a plane or train, remember to bring along motion-sickness medicine as well.

INSURANCE

Insurance needs for the traveler abroad fall into three categories:

1. Health and accident.
2. Trip cancellation.
3. Lost luggage.

First, review your present policies before traveling internationally—you may already have adequate coverage between them and what is offered by credit-card companies.

Many credit-card companies insure their users in case of a travel accident, providing a ticket was purchased with their card. Sometimes fraternal organizations have policies that protect members in case of sickness or accidents abroad.

Many homeowners' insurance policies cover theft of luggage during foreign travel and loss of documents—your airline ticket, for instance. Coverage is usually limited to about $500 U.S. To submit a claim on your insurance, remember that you'll need police reports or a statement from a medical authority that you did in fact suffer the loss or experience the illness for which you are seeking compensation. Such claims, by their very nature, can be filed only when you return from the Virgin Islands.

Some policies (and this is the type you should have) provide advances in cash or else transferrals of funds so that you won't have to dip into your precious travel funds to settle medical bills.

If you've booked a charter fare, you will probably have to pay a cancellation fee if you cancel a trip suddenly, even if it is due to an unforeseen crisis. It's possible to get insurance against such a possibility. Some travel agencies provide such coverage, and often flight insurance against a cancelled trip is written into tickets paid for by credit cards from such companies as VISA or American Express. Many tour operators and insurance agents provide this type of insurance.

Among the companies offering such policies are:

Travel Guard International, 1145 Clark St., Stevens Point, WI 54481 (tel. toll free 800/826-1300 outside Wisconsin), which offers a comprehensive 7-day policy that covers basically everything, including lost luggage. The cost of the package is $52, including emergency assistance, accidental death, trip cancellation and interruption, medical coverage abroad, and lost luggage. There are restrictions, however, that you should understand before you accept the coverage.

Travel Insurance Pak, Travelers Insurance Co., Travel Insurance Division, 1 Tower Sq., Hartford, CT 06183-5040 (tel. toll free 800/243-3174), offers illness and accident coverage, costing from $10 for 6 to 10 days. For lost or damaged luggage, $500 worth of coverage costs $20 for 6 to 10 days. You can also get trip-cancellation insurance for $5.50 per $100 of coverage to a limit of $5,000 per person.

Mutual of Omaha (Tele-Trip), Mutual of Omaha Plaza, P.O. Box 31762, Omaha, NE 68131 (tel. 402/345-2400, or toll free 800/228-9792), offers a "Family Deluxe" coverage, costing $3 a day for trips of a specified amount of time. Economy plans cover flight insurance, baggage and baggage delays, medical services due to accidents, sickness confinement, and a flat benefit of $50 a day, 24-hour accidental death and dismemberment policy. The plan is priced according to trip length and number of days of travel. These policies, because of their relatively small payoffs, are meant to supplement major medical or other policies a traveler might have.

In recent years, a number of companies have offered policies and help to those stranded abroad in some emergency. Each maintains a toll-free 800 number for out-of-state callers.

HealthCare Abroad (MEDEX), 107 W. Federal St., Suite 13, P.O. Box 480, Middleburg, VA 22117 (tel. 703/687-3166, or toll free 800/237-6615). One policy, good for predefined stays abroad of between 10 and 120 days, costs $3 a day, and includes accident and insurance coverage to the tune of $100,000. Medical evacuation is also included, along with a $25,000 accidental death or dismemberment compensation. Trip cancellation and lost or stolen luggage can also be written into this policy at a nominal cost.

Access America, 6600 W. Broad St., Richmond, VA 23230 (tel. 804/285-3300, or toll free 800/424-3391), offers travel insurance and 24-hour emergency travel, medical, and legal assistance for the traveler. One call to their hotline center, staffed by multilingual coordinators, connects travelers to a worldwide network of professionals able to offer specialized help in reaching the nearest physician, hospital, or legal advisor and, in obtaining emergency cash or the replacement of lost travel documents. Varying coverage levels are available.

4. WHAT TO PACK

Take mainly comfortable clothes with one dressier outfit should you decide to go to a fancy place or two. Cotton slacks or shorts are fine for going around during the day. Some women wear skirts and shifts, either with a T-shirt or a polo shirt. If you sunburn easily, wear long-sleeved shirts and trousers.

Summer travelers don't need suits, but men in winter might want to wear a jacket if they're dining in one of the more famous spots. A light sweater or jacket will come in handy in the evening and up in the hills. Some restaurants and bars are overly air conditioned, too.

In the Virgin Islands a wardrobe of lightweight cotton is best. Avoid synthetics or nylon, which become hot and sticky in these climes. Of course, anything that doesn't have to be ironed or dry-cleaned is always a good idea. Be prepared to wash your lightweights, such as underwear, in your bathroom and hang them up to dry overnight.

The general rule of packing is to bring four of everything. That means, four pairs of socks, four pairs of slacks, four shirts, and four pairs of underwear. At least two of these will always be either dirty or in the process of drying. Although garments dry quickly in the Virgin Islands, you'll occasionally have to wrap semiwet clothes in a plastic bag as you head for your next destination.

As a final rule, always take two comfortable pairs of shoes. You may get one pair soiled and that extra pair will always come in handy.

Airlines are increasingly strict about how much luggage you can bring aboard, not only carry-on items, but checked suitcases as well. Checked luggage must not measure more than a total of 62 inches (width plus length plus height). Bags mustn't weigh more than 70 pounds. Carry-on luggage must not measure more than 45 inches (width plus length plus height). Carry-on pieces must fit under your seat or in the overhead bin.

5. TIPS FOR THE DISABLED, SENIORS, SINGLES, STUDENTS & FAMILIES

FOR THE DISABLED

Disabled persons should make as many advance preparations as possible before embarking upon a trip not only to the Virgin Islands but anywhere. Hotels rarely advertise which facilities, if any, they offer the handicapped, so it's always best to contact the hotel directly. Tourist offices don't tend to keep very good data about such matters.

There are a number of agencies that can provide information to help you plan your trip. A good source is the **Travel Information Service,** Moss Rehabilitation Hospital, 1200 W. Tabor Rd., Philadelphia, PA 19141-3099 (tel. 215/456-9600). It charges a nominal fee per package of information. Each package contains names and addresses of accessible hotels, restaurants, and attractions often based on firsthand reports of travelers who have been there.

You can also obtain a copy of *Air Transportation of Handicapped Persons,* published by the U.S. Department of Transportation. The copy is sent free by writing for Free Advisory Circular No. AC12032, Distribution Unit, U.S. Department of Transportation, Publications Division, M-4332, Washington, DC 20590.

You may also want to consider joining a tour specifically for disabled visitors. Names and addresses of such tour operators can be obtained by writing to the **Society for the Advancement of Travel for the Handicapped,** 347 Fifth Ave., Suite 610, New York, NY 10016 (tel. 212/447-7284). Yearly membership dues in this society are $45 for senior citizens or $25 for students. Send a stamped self-addressed envelope.

You might also want to consider the **Federation of the Handicapped,** 211 W. 14th St., New York, NY 10011 (tel. 212/206-4200), which offers summer tours for members, who pay a yearly fee of $4 (U.S.).

For the blind, the best source is the **American Foundation for the Blind,** 15 W. 16th St., New York, NY 10011 (tel. 212/620-2000, or toll free 800/232-5463), which has much data to aid the blind person, including information on travel and various requirements for bringing in Seeing Eye dogs. An identification card for legally blind persons, issued only upon completion of a form by a doctor, costs $10 per person, and can be obtained, along with other necessary supplies and products for the blind, by calling toll free 800/829-0500.

FOR SENIORS

Many discounts are available for seniors. Be advised, however, that you have to be a member of an association in order to obtain certain discounts.

Write to *Travel Tips for Older Americans* (publication no. 8970), distributed for $1 by the Superintendent of Documents, U.S. Government Printing Office, Washington, DC 20402-9375 (tel. 202/512-2164). Another booklet—and this one is distributed free—is called *101 Tips for the Mature Traveler.* Write or phone Grand Circle Travel, 347 Congress St., Suite 3A, Boston, MA 02210 (tel. 617/350-7500, or toll free 800/221-2610). Grand Circle Travel offers extended vacations, escorted programs, and cruises, featuring unique learning experiences for seniors at competitive prices and good value.

SAGA International Holidays is well known for its all-inclusive tours for seniors. They prefer that joiners be at least 60 years old or older. Insurance is included in the net price of any of their tours. Contact SAGA International Holidays, 222 Berkeley St., Boston, MA 02116 (tel. toll free 800/343-0273).

The **AARP Travel Experience from American Express,** 400 Pinnacle Way, Suite 450, Norcross, GA 30071 (tel. toll free 800/927-0111 for land arrangements, 800/745-4567 for cruises, or 800/659-5678 for TTD). This travel planner provides travel arrangements for members of the American Association of Retired Persons, 601 E St. NW, Washington, DC 20049 (tel. 202/434-AARP). Travel Experience provides members with a wide variety of escorted, hosted, go-any-day packages and cruises to most parts of the world. AARP members are offered individual discounts on car rentals and hotels, among other discounts, through the group's Purchase Privilege Program. This is a completely separate program from the product offered by Travel Experience.

Information is also available from the **National Council of Senior Citizens,** 1331 F St. NW, Washington, DC 20004 (tel. 202/347-8800). A nonprofit organization, the council charges $12 per person or couple, for which you receive a monthly newsletter, part of which is devoted to travel tips (often on hotel and car rental discounts).

FOR SINGLES

A recent American census showed that 77 million Americans over 15 years of age are single. Unfortunately for them, the travel industry is geared toward couples. One company has made heroic efforts to match single travelers with like-minded companions, and is now the largest and best-listed such company in the United States. Jens Jurgen, the German-born founder, charges $36 to $66 for a 6-month listing in his well-publicized records. New applicants desiring a travel companion fill out a form stating their preferences and needs. They then receive a mini-listing of potential travel partners. A bimonthly newsletter gives numerous money-saving travel tips for singles. A sample issue is available for $4. For an application and more information, write to Jens Jurgen, **Travel Companion,** P.O. Box P-833, Amityville, NY 11701 (tel. 516/454-0880).

Singleworld, 401 Theodore Fremd Ave., Rye, NY 10580 (tel. 914/967-3334, or toll free 800/223-6490), is a travel agency that operates tours geared to solo travel. Two basic types of tours are available—cruises and tours for people in their 20s or 30s, or jaunts for any age. Annual dues are $25.

Another agency to check is **Grand Circle Travel,** which offers escorted tours and cruises for retired people, including singles. Once you book one of their trips, membership is included, and, in addition, you get vouchers providing discounts for future trips. Grand Circle Travel is at 347 Congress St., Boston, MA 02210 (tel. 617/350-7500, or toll free 800/221-2610).

FOR STUDENTS

The most wide ranging travel service for students is provided by **Council Travel,** 205 E. 42nd St., New York, NY 10017 (tel. 212/661-1414, ext. 1159). In addition to its

New York office, Council Travel has 37 other offices throughout the United States. This outfit provides details about budget travel, study abroad, working permits, and insurance. It also compiles a number of helpful publications, including *Student Travels,* which describes information on study and work opportunities abroad. It's distributed free, except for the $1 postage. Council Travel also issues a useful International Student Identity Card (ISIC) for $15.

FOR FAMILIES

The Virgin Islands is a contender for the number one family vacation place. The smallest toddlers can spend blissful hours on sandy beaches and in shallow seawater or pools. There's no end to the fascinating pursuits offered for older children too, ranging from boat rides to shell collecting to horseback riding, hiking, even discoing. Perhaps your children are old enough to learn to snorkel and explore the wonderland of the underwater Caribbean.

There are places to learn such skills as weaving hats of coconut-palm fronds, swimming, and windsurfing as well as a variety of other activities unique to the islands.

Most resort hotels will advise you on what there is in the way of fun for all ages, and many have play directors and supervised activities for the young of various age groups. But there are also some important pointers to keep in mind when you're planning a family vacation anywhere in the Virgin Islands.

Take protection from the sun. For tiny tots, this should include a sun umbrella, while the whole family will need sunscreen and sunglasses.

Take along anti-insect lotions and sprays. You'll probably need both to repel such unwanted island denizens as mosquitoes and sand fleas, as well as to ease the itching and possible other aftereffects of insect bites.

Arrange ahead for such necessities as a crib, bottle warmer, and car seat (if you're driving anywhere) for the very young, as well as for cots in your room for older children. Find out if the place where you're staying stocks baby food, and if not, take it with you.

Babysitters can be hired through most hotels, and nearly all of them speak English. Talk with the sitter yourself, and introduce her or him to those to be cared for before you leave the hotel room or nursery.

In addition to fundamentals that you should take along whenever you travel with children—such as children's aspirin, a thermometer, basic first-aid supplies, and medications your doctor may suggest—don't forget swimsuits, beach and pool toys, water wings for tiny mites, flip-flops for everybody, and terrycloth robes.

Family Travel Times is published 10 times a year by TWYCH (Travel With Your Children), and includes a weekly call-in service for subscribers. Subscriptions cost $55 a year and can be ordered by writing to TWYCH, 45 W. 18th St., 7th Floor, New York, NY 10011 (tel. 212/206-0688). An information packet describing TWYCH's publications that includes a recent sample issue is available by sending $3.50 to the above address.

6. ALTERNATIVE/ADVENTURE TRAVEL

Offbeat, alternative modes of travel often cost less, and can be a far more enriching way to travel. Some of the organizations arranging such travel are listed below.

EDUCATIONAL TRAVEL

The best information is available at the **Council on International Educational Exchange (CIEE),** 205 E. 42nd St., New York, NY 10017 (tel. 212/661-1414). This outfit not only arranges low-cost travel opportunities, through its travel subsidiary, Council Travel (see above), but it also offers information about working and studying abroad. Request a copy of the 500-page *Work, Study, Travel Abroad: The Whole World Handbook* ($14.45 by mail), with more than 1,000 study opportunities abroad.

One of the most dynamic organizations of postretirement studies for senior citizens is **Elderhostel,** 75 Federal St., Boston, MA 02110 (tel. 617/426-7788), established in 1975. Elderhostel maintains an array of programs throughout Europe as well as several programs in the Caribbean. Most courses last 2 or 3 weeks and are a good value, considering that hotel accommodations in student dormitories or modest inns, all meals, and tuition are included. Programs in the Caribbean do not include airfare. Courses involve no homework, are ungraded, and center mostly on the liberal arts. In no way is this to be considered a luxury vacation, but rather an academic fulfillment of a type never possible for senior citizens until several years ago. Participants must be age 60 or older. However, if two members go as a couple, only one member needs to be 60 or over. Write for their free newsletter and a list of upcoming courses and destinations.

HOMESTAYS OR VISITS

Servas, 11 John St., Suite 407, New York, NY 10038 (tel. 212/267-0252), is a nonprofit, nongovernmental, international, interfaith network of travelers and hosts whose goal is to help build world peace, goodwill, and understanding. They do this by providing opportunities for deeper, more personal contacts among people of diverse cultural and political backgrounds. Servas travelers are invited to share living space in a privately owned home with a community, normally staying for visits lasting a maximum of 2 days. Visitors pay a $55 annual fee, fill out an application, and are interviewed for suitability by one of more than 200 Servas interviewers throughout the country. They then receive a Servas directory listing the names and addresses of Servas hosts who want visitors in their homes. This program embraces 112 countries, including the Virgin Islands.

A series of international programs for persons over 50 years of age who are interested in combining travel and learning is offered by **Interhostel.** Each program lasts 2 weeks and is led by a university faculty or staff member, arranged in conjunction with a host college, university, or cultural institution. Participants can extend a stay beyond 2 weeks if they wish. Interhostel offers programs that consist of cultural affairs and intellectual activities, with field trips to museums and other centers of interest. For information, get in touch with the University of New Hampshire, Division of Continuing Education, 6 Garrison Ave., Durham, NH 03824 (tel. 603/862-1147, or toll free 800/733-9753).

World Learning Inc., Kipling Rd., P.O. Box 676, Brattleboro, VT 05302 (tel. 802/257-7751), provides a chance to sample another culture by actually living with a family. Students aged 16 to 22 are placed with families for 2 to 4 weeks, during which time they "become one of the family," taking part in daily activities. The list of 40 countries participating includes the Virgin Islands. Later, after the program ends, many students stay on and plan a tour of the Caribbean. World Learning Inc., founded in 1932 as The Experiment in International Living, is the oldest international educational services organization in the U.S. They founded the concept of the homestay, the notion that the family is the world's greatest classroom.

Friendship Force, 575 South Tower, 1 CNN Center, Atlanta, GA 30303 (tel. 404/522-9490), is a nonprofit organization existing for the sole purpose of fostering and encouraging friendship worldwide. Dozens of branch offices throughout North America arrange visits *en masse,* usually once a year. Because of group bookings, the airfare to the host country is usually less than you'd pay if you bought an individual APEX ticket. Each participant is required to spend 2 weeks in the host country, 1 week of which will be as a guest in the home of a family. Most volunteers spend the second week traveling in the host country.

HOME EXCHANGES

If you don't mind staying put and having a stranger living in your home, you can avail yourself of a "house swap," which certainly keeps costs low. Sometimes the exchange includes use of the family car.

Many directories are published detailing the possibilities for this type of service. Sometimes it's a straight house exchange for vacation purposes; at other times it's more complicated. For example, your teenage child might be housed free in exchange for free room and board when the host child visits your hometown. Sometimes the deal is for a housesitter.

Vacation Exchange Club, P.O. Box 650, Key West, FL 33040 (tel. 305/294-3720, or toll free 800/638-3841), offers the same service but has fewer listings. For $50, you get four directories a year and you're listed in one.

FOR WOMEN

A program for women of all levels of nautical expertise is offered by **Womanship, Inc.,** 410 Severn Ave., The Boathouse, Annapolis, MD 21402 (tel. 301/267-6661, or toll free 800/342-9295.) Established in 1984 as the first organization of its kind, it offers expert sailing instruction for all-women groups, up to a maximum of six students with two instructors. Participants sleep aboard the sailing vessel in cabins with six to eight berths. Tortola is the port of departure for the Caribbean destinations of this company, and most sailing instruction is taught in the many cays of the British Virgin Islands.

Most courses last a full week, but there are also weekend-long mini-courses.

Womanship attracts women from all walks of life, and includes participants aged 20 to 75. They learn sailing techniques as well as self-reliance by working as ship crew members. Upon completion of the course, participants are presented Cruising Certificates that can be used as evidence of expertise for future sailing.

The organization also charters similar cruises in Chesapeake Bay, Long Island Sound, New England, the San Juan Islands of the Pacific Northwest, and Florida.

7. GETTING THERE

BY PLANE

From North America, the fastest and most economical way to get to the Virgin Islands is by plane. In just a matter of hours you can flee the arctic winds and be lying on the beach, sipping your rum punch.

The biggest islands have air links to the North American continent, with regularly scheduled service. The smaller islands are tied into this vast network through their own carriers. For example, to reach Tortola, capital of the BVI, you might fly from Chicago to Puerto Rico, where a smaller plane will take you the rest of the way.

Ask travel agents about special stopover privileges, since "island-hopping" is becoming an increasingly popular diversion for both a summer or winter holiday.

For information on how to reach a specific island by plane, refer to the "Getting There" section in the specific chapter.

FROMMER'S SMART TRAVELER: AIRFARES

1. Shop all the airlines that fly to your destination.
2. Always ask for the lowest-priced fare—not just for a discount fare.
3. Keep calling the airlines—availability of cheap seats changes daily. Airlines would rather sell a seat than have it fly empty. As the departure date nears, additional low-cost seats become available.
4. Try to fly in summer, spring, or fall—fares are cheaper then.
5. Ask about the cost-conscious APEX (Advance Purchase Excursion) fare.
6. Sometimes it's cheaper to fly Monday to Thursday—check it out.
7. Read the section on "Other Good-Value Choices," below—bucket shops, charter flights, standby, going as a courier, and promotional fares.
8. Consider air-and-land packages, at considerably reduced rates.

REGULAR FARES

The best strategy for securing the lowest airfare is to shop around. Keep calling the airlines. Sometimes cheaper tickets are sold at the last minute if the flight is not fully booked.

For those who can't leave everything to the last minute, there are certain things to keep in mind. Most airlines charge different fares according to seasons. Peak season, which means winter in the Virgin Islands, is most expensive; basic season, during the summer months, offers the least expensive fares. Shoulder season refers to the spring and fall months.

Most airlines also offer an assortment of fares from first class to economy. The latter is the lowest-priced regular airfare carrying no special restrictions or requirements. Most airlines also offer promotional fares, which carry stringent requirements like advance purchase, minimum stay, and cancellation penalty. The most common such fare is the APEX (Advance Purchase Excursion). Land arrangements (that is, prebooking of hotel rooms) are often tied in with promotional fares offered by airlines.

OTHER GOOD-VALUE CHOICES

Bear in mind that in the airline industry what constitutes good value is always changing. What was the lowest possible fare one day can change the next day when a new promotional fare is offered.

BUCKET SHOPS A bucket shop (or consolidator) acts as a clearinghouse for blocks of tickets that airlines discount and consign during normally slow periods of air travel. In the case of the Virgin Islands, that usually means mid-April to mid-December.

Charter operators (see below) and bucket shops used to perform separate functions, but their offerings in many cases have been blurred in recent times, and many outfits now perform both functions.

Tickets are sometimes—but not always—priced at up to 35% less than full fare. Terms of payment can vary from 45 days prior to departure to the last-minute. Tickets can be purchased through regular travel agents, who usually mark up the ticket at least 8% to 10%, which obviously reduces your discount. Many users of consolidators complain that since they do not qualify for advance seat assignment, they are likely to be assigned a "poor seat" on the plane at the last minute.

In a recent survey most users estimated their savings at around $200 per ticket, and nearly one-third reported savings of up to $300. Many, however, reported no savings at all, as the airlines sometimes match the consolidator ticket by announcing a promotional fare. The situation is a bit tricky and calls for some careful investigation on your part to determine just how much you are saving.

Bucket shops abound from coast to coast, but just to get you started, here are some recommendations. Look also for their ads in your local newspaper's travel section.

In New York, try **TFI Tours International,** 34 W. 32nd St., 12th Floor, New York, NY 10001 (tel. 212/736-1140 in New York State, or toll free 800/825-3834 elsewhere in the U.S.).

In Miami, for the most popular embarkation point on the mainland for Virgin Island destinations, go to **25 West Tours,** 2490 Coral Way, Miami, FL 33145 (tel. 305/856-0810 in Miami; toll free 800/423-6954 in Florida, or 800/225-2582 elsewhere in the U.S.).

Out West, you can try **Sunline Express Holidays, Inc.,** 607 Market St., San Francisco, CA 94105 (tel. 415/541-7800, or toll free 800/786-5463).

CHARTER FLIGHTS Charter flights allow you to save money on regularly scheduled flights. Many of the major carriers offer charter flights at rates that are sometimes 30% (or more) off the regular airfare.

There are some drawbacks to charter flights that you need to consider. Advance booking of up to 45 days or more may be required. You could lose most of the money you've advanced if you cancel a flight. (It is now possible to take out cancellation insurance against such an eventuality.) You must depart and return on a scheduled date.

Charter flights are complicated, and it's best to ask a good travel agent to explain the pros and cons.

REBATORS Rebators are outfits that pass along to the passenger part of their commission, although many of them assess a fee for their services. Although they are not the same as travel agents, they sometimes offer roughly similar services. Sometimes a rebator will sell a discounted travel ticket, and also offer discounted land arrangements, including hotels and car rentals. Most rebators offer discounts averaging anywhere from 10% to 25% with a $20 handling charge.

Rebators include **Travel Avenue,** 641 W. Lake St., Suite 201, Chicago, IL 60606-3691 (tel. 312/876-1116, or toll free 800/333-3335); **The Smart Traveller,** 3111 SW 27th Ave., Miami, FL 33133 (tel. 305/448-3338, or toll free 800/226-3338.

STANDBYS A favorite of spontaneous travelers, a standby fare leaves your departure to the whims of fortune and the hope that a seat will remain open for you to claim at the last minute. Most airlines don't offer standbys.

GOING AS A COURIER This cost-cutting technique has lots of restrictions and tickets may be hard to come by. Basically, you go as both an airline passenger and a courier. Couriers are hired by overnight air-freight firms hoping to skirt the often tedious Customs hassles and delays at the other end. Don't worry—the courier service is absolutely legal: You won't be asked to haul in illegal drugs, for example. For the service, the courier gets greatly discounted airfare or sometimes even flies free.

You're allowed one piece of carry-on luggage only (your baggage allowance is used by the courier firm to transport its cargo). As a courier, you don't actually handle the merchandise you're transporting. You just carry a manifest to present to Customs.

Upon arrival, an employee of the courier service will reclaim the company's cargo. Incidentally, you fly alone, so don't plan to travel with anybody. (A friend may be able to arrange a flight as a courier on a consecutive day.) Most courier services operate from Los Angeles and New York, but some operate out of other cities, such as Chicago or Miami.

Courier services are often listed in the yellow pages and in advertisements in travel sections or newspapers.

To get you going, check with **Halbart Express,** 147-05 176th St., Jamaica, NY 11434 (tel. 718/656-8189 from 10am to 3pm daily) or **Halbart Express/Miami,** 2471 NW 72nd Ave., Miami, FL 33122 (tel. 305/593-0260).

You can also try **Now Voyager,** 74 Varick St., Suite 307, New York, NY 10013 (tel. 212/431-1616, daily from 11:30am to 6pm). At other times an automatic telephone-answering system announces last-minute specials for round-trip fares.

PROMOTIONAL FARES   To take advantage of promotional fares you'll have to have a good travel agent or do a lot of shopping or calling around yourself to learn what's currently available at the time of your intended trip.

TRAVEL CLUBS   The Caribbean is heavily featured in the discounted offerings of travel clubs. What you do is join a club that supplies an unsold inventory of tickets offering discounts in the range of 20% to 60%. Some of the deals involve cruise ships and complete tour packages.

After you pay an annual fee, you are given a hotline that you call when you're planning to go somewhere. Many of these discounts become available several days before departure, and sometimes you might have as much as a month. Some are more last minute. You're limited to what's available, so you have to be fairly flexible.

Some of the best of these clubs include the following. **Discount Travel International,** Suite 203, Ives Building, 114 Forrest Ave., Narberth, PA 19072 (tel. 215/668-7184, or toll free 800/334-9294), charges an annual membership of $45. **Last Minute Travel Club,** 132 Brookline Ave., Boston, MA 02215 (tel. 617/267-9800, or toll free 800/LAST-MIN in New England and New York, but outside Massachusetts), literally offers "last minute" bookings at slashed prices, with no membership fee. **Moment's Notice,** 425 Madison Ave., New York, NY 10017 (tel. 212/486-0500), is considered one of the best, with a members' hotline (regular phone toll charges) and a yearly fee of $45 per member. **Vacations To Go,** 2411 Fountain View, Houston, TX 77057 (tel. toll free 800/338-4962), charges an annual membership fee of $19.95, or $50 for 3 years. **Worldwide Discount Travel Club,** 1674 Meridian Ave., Miami Beach, FL 33139 (tel. 305/534-2082), presents a "travelogue" listing with about 200 discount possibilities about every 3 weeks. Single travelers pay $40 annually and families, $50.

FLIGHTS FROM THE U.K.

Though there are no direct flights to either the U.S. Virgin Islands or the British Virgin Islands, **British Airways** (tel. 081/897-4000 in London) flies directly to San Juan, Puerto Rico. Flights occur twice a week during high season (December through April), and once a week for the rest of the year. Once in San Juan, several airlines make the final connection to either St. Thomas, St. Croix, or Tortola and Virgin Gorda in the BVI.

BY SHIP
CRUISE SHIP

If you'd like to sail the Caribbean, having a home with an ocean view, a cruise ship might be for you. It's slow and easy, and it's no longer enjoyed only by the idle rich who have months to spend away from home. Most cruises today appeal to the middle-income voyager who probably has no more than 1 or 2 weeks to spend cruising the Caribbean. Some 300 passenger ships sail the Caribbean all year, and in January and February that figure may go up another hundred or so. St. Thomas is one of the major ports of call. Pick up a copy of *Frommer's Cruises* for more detailed information.

Most cruise-ship operators suggest the concept of a total vacation. Some promote constant activities, while others suggest the possibility of doing nothing but relaxing. Cruise ships are self-contained resorts, offering everything on board and sightseeing once you arrive in a port of call.

For those who don't want to spend all their time at sea, some lines offer a fly-and-cruise vacation. You spend a week cruising the Caribbean and another week staying at an interesting hotel at reduced prices. These total packages should cost less than if you'd purchased the cruise and air portions separately.

Another version of fly-and-cruise, is to fly to and from the cruise. Most plans offer a package deal from the principal airport closest to your residence to the major airport nearest to the cruise-departure point. It's possible to purchase your air ticket on your own and book your cruise ticket separately, but you'll save money by combining the fares in a package deal.

Miami is the cruise capital of the world, but vessels also leave from San Juan, New York, Port Everglades, Los Angeles, and other points of embarkation as well.

Most of the cruise ships travel at night, arriving the next morning at the day's port of call. In port, passengers can go ashore for sightseeing, shopping, and the odd meal. Cruise prices vary widely. Sometimes the same route with the same ports of call carries different fares.

Consult a good travel agent for the latest offerings.

CHARTERED BOAT

You may feel that there is no better way to have a vacation in the Virgin Islands than on the deck of your own yacht. Impossible? Not really. No one said you had to own that yacht.

Experienced sailors and navigators, with a sea-wise crew, can charter a "bareboat," that is, a rented fully equipped boat with no captain or crew. You're on your own, and you'll have to prove you can handle it before you're allowed to go on such a craft. Even if you're your own skipper, you may want to take along an experienced sailor familiar with sometimes tricky local waters.

If you can afford it, the ideal way is to charter a boat with a skilled skipper and a competent crew. Four to six people, maybe more, often charter yachts of from 50 to more than 100 feet. Sometimes a dozen people will go out; at other times, a romantic twosome.

Most yachts are rented on a weekly basis, with a fully stocked bar, plus equipment for fishing and water sports. More and more bareboat charters are learning that they can save money and select menus more suited to their tastes by doing their own provisioning, rather than relying on the yacht company that rented them the vessel.

The best for this is **The Moorings,** P.O. Box 139, Wickhams Cay, Road Town, Tortola, BVI (tel. 809/494-2331). Arrangements can be made for bareboating, with a skipper, or fully crewed with both a skipper and cook. Boats come equipped with barbecue, snorkeling gear, dinghy, Windsurfer, and linens. The Moorings has an experienced staff of mechanics, electricians, riggers, and cleaners. If you're going out on your own, you'll get a thorough briefing session about Virgin Island waters and anchorages. To make reservations in the U.S. or Canada, call toll free 800/535-7289. You can also write for information to The Moorings Ltd., 19345 U.S. 19 North, Suite 402, Clearwater, FL 34624 (tel. 813/530-5424). Bareboat rentals, without a crew or skipper, cost $1,190 to $3,185 per week in the summer (suitable from 2 to 10 passengers). In the high season (winter), weekly rentals for bareboat cruises range from $2,163 to $6,020 per week (for between 2 and 10 persons). Rentals for ships with crews, obviously, are more expensive, and vary with the number and the nature of the crew members.

PACKAGE TOURS

If you want everything done for you and want to save money as well, consider traveling to the Virgin Islands on a package tour. General tours appealing to the average voyager are commonly offered, but there are also a number of very specific tours—tennis packages, golf packages, scuba and snorkeling packages, and, for those who qualify, honeymooners' specials.

Economy and convenience are the chief advantage of a package tour, in that the cost of transportation (usually an airplane fare), a hotel room, food (sometimes), and sightseeing (sometimes) are combined in one package, neatly tied up with a single price tag. There are extras, of course, but you'll know in advance roughly what the cost of your vacation will be.

If you were to book your flight and hotel separately, you would not come out as cheaply as on a package tour—hence their immense and increasing appeal. But there are disadvantages too. You may find yourself in a hotel you dislike, virtually trapped there since you've already paid for it.

You generally have to pay the cost of the total package in advance. Transfers between your hotel and the airport are often included, which can be a financial break since some airports are situated a $40-or-more taxi ride from a resort. Many packages carry several options, including the possibility of low-cost car rentals.

The single traveler, regrettably, usually suffers, as nearly all tour packages are based on double occupancy.

Some of the leading tour operators to the Virgin Islands include the following. Consult a travel agent for a complete list of possibilities.

FOR AMERICAN TRAVELERS   Your best deal might be offered by one of the major U.S. airlines, which offer land and air packages. Call their toll-free numbers and ask for the tour desk: American at 800/433-7300, Delta at 800/221-1212, and Continental at 800/231-0856.

Other major tour operators include the following:

American Express Vacations, 3400 Robards Court, Louisville, KY 40218 (tel. toll free 800/241-1700), offering everything from honeymoon packages to all-inclusive stays at first-class resorts.

Adventure Tours, 9818 Liberty Rd., Randallstown, MD 21133 (tel. 301/922-7000 in Baltimore, or toll free 800/638-9040 elsewhere in the U.S.), featuring some interesting land-and-air packages to St. Thomas.

FOR BRITISH TRAVELERS   Package tours can be booked through **British Virgin Islands Holidays,** a division of Wingjet Travel Ltd., 26 Hockerill St., Bishop's Stortford, Herts. CM23 2DW (tel. 0279/656111). This company is the major booking agent for all the important hotels in the BVI. Stays can be arranged in more than one hotel if you'd like to visit more than one island. The company also offers staffed yacht charters and bareboat charters.

Caribbean Connection, Concorde House, Forest St., Chester CH1 1QR (tel. 0244/341131), offers all-inclusive packages (air fare and hotel) to both the U.S. Virgin Islands and the British Virgin Islands. If you'd desire a villa instead of a hotel, that too can be set up.

8. SUGGESTED ITINERARIES

IF YOU HAVE 1 WEEK

Day 1: Fly to St. Thomas and give yourself absolutely nothing to do the first day. Rest, relax, recuperate, have a rum punch, and listen to some Caribbean music. Enjoy a typical West Indian dinner, preferably at your hotel to avoid the strain of driving on the left on unfamiliar roads at night.

Day 2: After a long, leisurely morning and a late breakfast, drive or take a taxi or bus into Charlotte Amalie for a day of lunching, shopping, and taking my guided walking tour (see Chapter 4).

Day 3: Spend most of the day at Magens Bay on St. Thomas.

Day 4: Take the short boat ride from Red Hook to St. John and take a whirlwind tour of the island. Spend the remaining time at Trunk Bay, the small island's biggest attraction and a beach collector's find.

Day 5: Spend the day exploring the attractions of the capital, Charlotte Amalie.

Day 6: Spend the morning driving around the island. Take a dive on the *Atlantis* submarine.

Day 7: Take one of the many boat trips offered on St. Thomas for a day on the sea with sun, snorkeling, and an open bar.

IF YOU HAVE 2 WEEKS

Days 1–7: See above.

Day 8: Fly to St. Croix and relax at your hotel the first day, having a quiet dinner after some beach time.

Day 9: Explore the old city of Christiansted. Check out the shops of town, which have the same duty-free arrangement St. Thomas does.

Day 10: Take an all-day excursion to the white coral sands of Buck Island, now part of the National Park Service, which has an underwater snorkeling trail.

Day 11: Journey to Frederiksted to see the second city of St. Croix.

Day 12: Check out the beaches, especially Buccaneer and Cormorant.

Day 13: Devote yourself to a day of your favorite sport: snorkeling, waterskiing, golf at the Carambola Golf Course, tennis on one of the courts of the Buccaneer Hotel, fishing, windsurfing, or horseback riding at Jill's Equestrian Stables.

Day 14: After a leisurely morning in bed, and a late breakfast with tropical fruit, stroll to the beach and later have a light lunch before heading for Christiansted for a final look at the town and its shops. If they're appearing on the island, go to hear Jimmy Hamilton ("Mr. Sax"), or attend a performance of the Quadrille Dancers.

IF YOU HAVE 3 WEEKS

Days 1–14: See above.

Day 15: Fly to Beef Island and transfer by taxi to Road Town, capital of Tortola and also the capital of the British Virgin Islands. Spend the afternoon at the beach and enjoy a dinner at your hotel or attend a West Indian buffet nearby.

Day 16: Book one of the sightseeing tours offered of the island.

Day 17: Spend a day devoted to the beaches or sporting attractions, either taking one of the boat trips offering snorkeling or scuba, or else enjoying a day on the sands. Have a final dinner at Mrs. Scatliffe's Restaurant and enjoy a good-bye toast at the Moorings on the waterfront.

Day 18: Fly or take a boat to Virgin Gorda, the second-largest cluster of the British

Virgins, lying 12 miles east of Road Town. Spend the remaining time enjoying a good beach and have dinner at your hotel.

Day 19: Explore the attractions of Virgin Gorda by taking one of the escorted tours, which will take you to The Baths, a phenomenon of tranquil pools and caves formed by gigantic house-size boulders. Enjoy some beach life.

Day 20: Check out some of the sporting possibilities on the island, including Kilbride's Underwater Tours, or else do some boating or snorkeling.

Day 21: This day regrettably might be spent in transit, as you will have to get back from Virgin Gorda to Tortola, heading for St. Thomas or Puerto Rico to make your connection back to the mainland.

CHAPTER 3

GETTING TO KNOW THE VIRGIN ISLANDS

This chapter provides information on getting around the Virgin Islands, along with advice on your accommodations and dining choices. The ins and outs of the shopping scene are also detailed. And, finally, capping off the chapter are quick-reference lists of facts about both the U.S. and British Virgin Islands—here you'll find out everything you need to know to make your trip to the Virgin Islands a smooth and relaxing experience.

1. GETTING AROUND

Once you arrive, getting around the island you're on or doing some island-hopping becomes important. There are several methods outlined below.

BY PLANE

Airplanes provide the best link between St. Thomas and St. Croix and between St. Thomas and Tortola's airport at Beef Island. To reach St. John by air, passengers usually land first at St. Thomas, then travel to St. John by boat. **American Airlines** (tel. toll free 800/433-7300) provides some of the most frequent daily service from the U.S. mainland to St. Thomas, with continuing service to St. Croix.

No nonstop air service is available between the U.S. mainland and the BVI. Consequently, most visitors fly either to St. Thomas or to Puerto Rico, where airlines to either Tortola/Beef Island or Virgin Gorda (and sometimes both) are provided by **American Eagle** (tel. toll free 800/433-7300), **Virgin Air** (tel. toll free 800/522-3084), **Sunaire Express** (tel. toll free 800/524-2094), or **LIAT** (tel. toll free 800/253-5011).

BY TRAIN OR BUS

There are no **rail** connections on any of the islands.

The only island that has a really recommendable **bus** service is St. Thomas. Buses leave from Charlotte Amalie and circle the island in each direction. See "Getting Around," Chapter 4, for details. On the other islands, bus service is highly erratic and is used mainly by workers going to and from their jobs. In the BVI, Virgin Gorda offers safaris, brightly painted open-air buses, and a more economical minibus service operated by Scato's.

BY TAXI

Taxi is the main method of transportation for getting around all the islands. On St. Thomas taxi vans carry up to a dozen passengers, going to multiple destinations. Private taxis are also available. Rates are regulated and posted at the airport, where a van of taxis meets all arriving planes. On St. John both private taxis and shuttles that carry three or more passengers are available.

On St. Croix taxis are available at both the airport and in Christiansted. Even if your hotel is remotely anchored in St. Croix, your hotel desk can generally summon a cab for you in about 30 minutes, often much less. Taxis are unmetered, and you should always settle the rate before setting out.

Taxis are one of the best ways—practically the only way at times—for getting around the BVI. In the BVI, taxis service the islands of Tortola, Virgin Gorda, and Anegada, and rates are fixed by the government.

BY CAR

If you can afford it, a rented car is the best way to get around the Virgin Islands if you don't mind driving on the left. Count on paying at least $50 a day for the rental, which includes unlimited mileage. If you book a car for a week, you get a slight reduction on this rate.

All the major car-rental companies are represented in the islands, including Avis, Budget, and Hertz. (For detailed information, refer to "Getting Around" in specific island chapters.) Many local agencies also compete in these markets. Most cars are picked up at the airport on both St. Thomas and St. Croix. On St. John there are car-rental stands at the dock where the boat arrives from St. Thomas.

If you want a car for only part of your stay, you can call from your hotel, and a car will be delivered, usually with no more than a 2-hour wait. The papers are filled out on the spot. You must have a valid credit card and driver's license. In winter cars might be in short supply, so you should reserve as far in advance as possible.

In the BVI, many visitors have a successful holiday without ever bothering to rent a car. Some of the roads such as those on Tortola have been compared to roller-coaster rides. Driving on the left and many, many hairpin curves don't add to the pleasure of driving.

Rates are reasonable, about $35 a day, with mileage included. Weekly rates are slightly cheaper. You must purchase a local driver's license for $10 from police headquarters or at the car-rental desk. The minimum age limit for renting a car in the BVI is 25. Major U.S. companies, such as Budget, are represented in the islands, and there are many local companies as well.

Parking lots are found in Charlotte Amalie, in St. Thomas, and in Christiansted on St. Croix. In Frederiksted, you can generally park on the street. Most hotels except those in the congested center of Charlotte Amalie have extensive parking lots, especially the resort hotels. Parking is free on hotel grounds.

GASOLINE

This is usually in plentiful supply on St. Thomas and St. Croix, with plenty of service stations such as Mobil on the outskirts of Charlotte Amalie. Gasoline stations are also found at strategic points along the island, especially in the north and in the more congested East End.

On St. Croix, most of the gasoline stations are in Christiansted, but they are also found along major highways and at Frederiksted. On St. John, make sure your tank is filled up at Cruz Bay, the capital, before striking out on a motor tour of the island.

Gasoline stations are not as plentiful, but they are adequate in the BVI. Road Town, the capital of Tortola, has the most gas stations, at both the western and eastern approaches to town. Fill up here before embarking on extensive island touring in the hills. Virgin Gorda has a limited but adequate number of gas stations. Chances are you won't be using a car in any other island on the BVI.

DRIVING RULES

Drive on the left. This rule seems logical for the British Virgin Islands, whose parent country has long had a tradition of driving on the left. It is less understandable in the U.S. islands, and it causes endless confusion and a somewhat higher rate of accidents than on the U.S. mainland. Drive extra carefully, especially when merging into lanes of traffic.

Highway codes and signs are generally the same as those used throughout the U.S. mainland.

Canadians and Americans do not need to obtain an international driver's license.

ROAD MAPS

Adequate maps are available for free on the islands at the individual tourist offices. If you arrive by plane, go to the tourist information office at the airport and request a map. If you plan to drive in a rented car to your hotel, have the tourist staff member trace the best route for you.

BREAKDOWNS & ASSISTANCE

All the major islands, including St. Thomas, St. John, St. Croix, Tortola, and Virgin Gorda, have garages that will come to your assistance and tow your vehicle if necessary. In the likely case that the car is rented, call the rental company first. Usually someone there will bring motor assistance to you. If your car requires extensive repairs because of a mechanical failure, a new one will be sent to replace it.

BY BOAT

There is no ferry service between St. Thomas and St. Croix (it's better to fly), but ferry service forms the vital link between St. Thomas and St. John. Private water taxis also operate between St. John and St. Thomas. Launch services link Red Hook (in the east of St. Thomas) with both St. John and Charlotte Amalie, the capital of St. Thomas.

On St. Croix, the major boat link is to Buck Island, its big offshore attraction.

In the BVI getting around by ferry and private boat is the major means of travel. Many ferries link Road Town (the capital of Tortola) with the island's West End. Service to Virgin Gorda (the second major island) is also provided. Even some of the smaller islands, such as Anegada and Jost Van Dyke, also have ferry connections, often about two per day. On some of the really remote islands in the chain, boat service may be only once a week. Many of the private islands, such as Peter Island, provide launches from Tortola.

For details on these transportation connections, with sample prices, see the "Getting Around" sections of the individual island chapters.

BY BICYCLE

Much of the hilly terrain of St. Thomas and Tortola does not lend itself to extensive bicycling. A lot of St. John can, however, be covered by bicycle, and St. Croix, which is flatter, is ideal for bicycle rides. For specific information on bicycle or motor-scooter rental, see the "Getting Around" sections of the individual island chapters.

2. WHERE TO STAY

The Virgin Islands offer a bewildering choice of accommodations, ranging from cottages to condos, from West Indian guesthouses to plush resort hotels, from self-catering facilities to home exchanges. For information on home exchanges and homestays see "Alternative/Adventure Travel" in Chapter 2.

If, like most guests, you plan to stay at a hotel or resort, you'll have to determine beforehand the type of arrangement you want, including the various meal plans offered. It is generally cheaper to take the half-board rate (MAP or Modified American Plan) or the full-board plan (AP or American Plan). You'll save more money on these plans than if you stay at a hotel or resort and order all your meals à la carte. In winter some hotels may request that you book at the MAP rate. EP means European Plan, offering a room but not meals, and CP means Continental Plan, providing a room and a continental breakfast only.

HOTELS & RESORTS

It's particularly galling to learn that the couple next door who are staying in a similar room to yours, perhaps even enjoying an ocean view as opposed to your "mountain view," are paying some $200 to $300 less per week. That happens more often than you'd imagine, especially during slow months when Caribbean hoteliers want to promote business.

There are package deals galore, and though they have many disadvantages, they are always cheaper than rack rates (what an individual who literally walks in from the street pays). Therefore it's always good to go to a reliable travel agent to find out what is available in the way of a land-and-air package before booking into a particular hostelry.

There is no rigid classification of Caribbean hotels. The word deluxe is often used—or misused—when first class might be more appropriate. First class itself often isn't. For that and other reasons, I've presented fairly detailed descriptions of the properties, so that you'll get an idea of what to expect. However, even in the deluxe and first-class properties, don't expect top-rate service and efficiency. "Things," as they are called in the West Indies, don't always work as well in the tropics as they do in certain fancy resorts of California or Europe. Life in the tropics has its disadvantages. When you go to turn on the shower, sometimes you get water and sometimes you don't. You may even experience island power failures. To prepare yourself, read the Herman Wouk novel *Don't Stop the Carnival,* and go to the Virgin Islands prepared.

Facilities often determine the choice of a hotel. For example, if golf is your passion, you may want to book into a hotel resort such as Buccaneer on St. Croix. Regardless of your particular interest, there is probably a hotel catering to your need.

THE WEST INDIAN GUESTHOUSE

Most of the Antilleans stay in guesthouses when they travel to the Virgin Islands. Some of these are surprisingly comfortable, and many have private baths in each room, air conditioning, and swimming pools. The rooms are sometimes cooled by ceiling fans or trade winds blowing through open windows at night. Of course, don't expect the luxuries of a fabulous resort, but for value the guesthouse can't be topped. Staying in a guesthouse, you can journey over to a big beach resort, using its seaside facilities for only a small fee (about $3).

Although free of frills, the guesthouses I've recommended are clean, decent, and safe for families and single women. Many of the cheapest ones are not places you'd like to spend 24 hours a day in, but who wants to do that in the Virgin Islands anyway?

SELF-CATERING HOLIDAYS

Particularly if you're a family or friendly group, a housekeeping holiday can be one of the least expensive ways to vacation in the Virgin Islands. These types of accommodations are now available on nearly all the islands previewed. Some are individual cottages, others are housed in one building. Some are private homes rented when the owners are away. All have small kitchens or kitchenettes where you can do your own cooking.

A housekeeping holiday, however, doesn't always mean you'll have to work. Most of the self-catering places have chamber service included in the rental, and you're given fresh linen as well.

Cooking most of your meals yourself and dining out on occasion (such as when a neighboring big hotel has a beachside barbecue with entertainment) is the surest way of keeping holiday costs at a minimum.

RENTAL VILLAS & VACATION HOMES

Even Princess Margaret rents out her private villa on Mustique in the Grenadines. Of course, she asks $8,000 per week, but throughout the Caribbean, including the Virgin Islands, you can often secure good deals by renting privately owned villas, apartments, condos, or cottages.

Private apartments are rented with or without chamber service. This is more of a no-frills option than the villas and condos. The apartment might not be in a building with a swimming pool, and it might not have a front desk to help you. Cottages are the most freewheeling way to live in these four major categories of vacation homes. Most of them are fairly simple and many open onto a beach. Others are clustered around a communal swimming pool. Many contain no more than a simple bedroom with a small kitchen and bath. In the peak winter season, reservations should be made at least 5 or 6 months in advance.

Dozens of agents throughout the United States and Canada offer these rentals. To get you going try one of the following.

At Home Abroad, Suite 6-H, 405 E. 56th St., New York, NY 10022-2466 (tel. 212/421-9165), has a roster of private homes for rent in St. Thomas and St. John, each with maid service included. Many villas and condos are rented.

Caribbean Connection +, P.O. Box 261, Trumbull, CT 06611 (tel. 203/261-8603), offers island-hopping itineraries and accommodations of all kinds (inns, condos, villas, hotels) in the Caribbean. Golf vacations in the islands are a specialty. "Caribbean Essence" vacations customize itineraries to a client's interest by local experts.

Hideaways International, 15 Goldsmith St., P.O. Box 1270, Littleton, MA 01460 (tel. 508/486-8955, or toll free 800/843-4433), provides a booklet with illustrations of its accommodations in both the BVI and the USVI. Villas range in size from one bedroom up to 10 bedrooms. Some villas offer full staffs; others, more modest, have maid service. There's virtually something for every taste and budget. Hideaways also offers discounts at villa and condo-type resorts. Also ask about discounts on plane fares and car rentals.

Sometimes local tourist offices also advise you on vacation home rentals if you write or call them directly.

For diverse rentals in the U.S. Virgin Islands, make inquiries from **Property**

Management Caribbean, Inc., Route 6, Cowpet Bay, St. Thomas, USVI 00802 (tel. 809/775-6220, or toll free 800/524-2038). Rentals range from studio apartments to four-bedroom villas suitable for up to eight people.

Island Villas, Property Management Rentals, 14A Caravelle Arcade, Christiansted, in St. Croix (tel. 809/773-8821), offers some of the best properties on St. Croix. The outfit specializes in villa and condo rentals, really private residences with pools; many are on the beach. The range goes from one-bedroom units to six-bedroom villas, with prices ranging from $1,200 to $5,000 per week.

3. WHERE TO DINE

Dining in the Virgin Islands is generally more expensive than it is in either the United States or Canada since, except for locally caught fish, virtually everything is imported. Service (10%–15%) is automatically added to most restaurant tabs, and if service has been good, it is customary to tip something extra.

If you're booked into a hotel on MAP (half board), which some hotels require in peak season, get out and sample some of the local restaurants at lunch. That way, your stomach won't become completely hotel bound.

In some of the more sophisticated and posh havens such as Caneel Bay on St. John, it is customary for men to wear a jacket, but in summer, virtually no establishment requires it. If in doubt, always ask the restaurant or check with the policy of the hotel before going to a particular dining room or establishment.

At the better places, women's evening attire is casual chic. During the day it is proper everywhere to wear a cover up over your bathing suit if you're in a restaurant.

Whenever possible, stick to regional food, which is fresher. For a main dish, that usually means Caribbean lobster or fish caught in the deep sea. Many world-class chefs cook in the Virgin Islands, but they are only as good as their ingredients, which are not always the freshest.

Nevertheless, the food is better than ever in the islands and many fine talents, including many top-notch female chefs from California, now cook there. Many have adapted Stateside recipes with the local ingredients available, and have come up with Caribbean/California cuisine.

Check to see if reservations are required before going to a place. In summer, you can almost always get in, but in winter all the tables may be gone at some of the famous but small places.

Roads in the Virgin Islands are poorly marked, badly lit, and narrow. On top of that, driving is on the left. If you're going out in the evening, especially if you plan to drink, it is a good idea to go by taxi and arrange for the taxi to pick you up or have the restaurant call a cab for you. It generally arrives in no more than 30 minutes.

Whatever you do, try to get out and eat at some of the local places. The prices are more reasonable, and the fare is more adventurous and interesting.

4. WHAT TO BUY

The surprise is that the island's best buys are not necessarily products made within the Virgin Islands (although some of those sometimes offer good value, too). Many visitors end up buying items that are available at home, but that are cheaper because they are duty free.

U.S. residents are entitled to $1,200 worth of duty-free exports from the American islands (not Puerto Rico) every 30 days. That is three times the exemption allowed from most foreign destinations. For more information see Chapter 2.

You can protect your duty-free allowance by sending home unsolicited gifts not totaling more than $100 per day. You pay no duty and you don't have to declare such gifts on your Customs form when leaving. Many shoppers pick up such island-made, duty-free items as leather sandals, paintings, island dolls, locally made clothing, pottery, boutique canvas bags, locally recorded music, straw products, batiks, and unusual handmade jewelry.

If you're visiting only the British Virgin Islands and make purchases there, you will be taxed at the same rate as any foreign destination. Besides, selections pale in the BVI compared to the shopping malls of St. Croix and especially St. Thomas, which is the best center for shopping in all of the Caribbean.

The smart shopper will still find some good buys in Road Town (Tortola), however, because even though the capital is not a duty-free port, there is no duty on goods imported from Britain. You might find some good buys on English fabrics, china, and some other items—certainly they will be cheaper than in London. You will have to pay duty when you bring them back into the United States, if their value exceeds the limit imposed by U.S. Customs.

St. Thomas has far more shops and far more merchandise than St. Croix, and certainly more than little St. John, which has only a few shops in its capital, Cruz Bay, most at Mongoose Junction. It is estimated that prices are generally 20% to 50% lower in the U.S. Virgins than Stateside, but don't count on that. It is wise to know the Stateside price if you're in the market for a particular item. Don't rely on the merchant to tell you the price.

In general, the best buys found are liquor (because of the generous U.S. allowance—see Chapter 2), jewelry, and china. Crystal, certain clothing, porcelain, and leather goods, along with watches, and even furs, might also be bargains if you know what you're looking for.

Cigarettes are marked down, and imported beauty products such as perfume are generally excellent buys.

In clothing, the best buys are woolen items, such as sweaters. Cashmere sweaters are good value. Fashions from the East, especially China, are tremendously cheap, and European and U.S. designer labels are often generously discounted.

Ⓕ FROMMER'S SMART TRAVELER: SHOPPING

1. Get the maximum value from your $1,200 worth of duty-free exports (better than anywhere else in the world).
2. If you wish, take the full allowance on liquor, which is more generous than anywhere else outside the U.S. You also get an extra bottle of Cruzan rum included duty free.
3. Take advantage of the greatly reduced prices on jewelry, porcelain, and crystal. Best selections are in St. Thomas.
4. Island-made products are duty free—handmade jewelry, straw products, locally made clothing, leather sandals, and the like.
5. If you're making a big purchase, do some old-fashioned bargaining with the shopkeeper. Sometimes it doesn't work, but often it does.
6. Know prices in your hometown so you can identify bargains in St. Thomas, St. Croix, and St. John.

Jewelry is the most common item for sale in St. Thomas; store after store (I'll recommend some of the best) are in the jewelry business. Look over the selections of gold and gem stones (emeralds are traditionally considered the finest savings). Gold that is marked 24K in the U.S. and Canada is marked 999 (99.9% pure gold) on European items. Gold marked 18K in the U.S. and Canada has a European marking of 750 (or 75% pure), and 14K gold becomes 585 (or 58.5% pure).

In porcelain and crystal you'll find the best selections from Europe generally for about 30% less than Stateside. Most stores will arrange shipment. Name-brand watches are sold throughout Charlotte Amalie and to a lesser degree, in St. Croix.

Theoretically, bargaining is not the rule, but over the years I have found merchant after merchant willing to do so, particularly on expensive items such as jewelry and perfume. Obviously, the slow summer season is the best time to try to make deals.

FAST FACTS: THE U.S. VIRGIN ISLANDS

American Express   In St. Thomas, service is provided by Caribbean Travel Agency, Inc./Tropic Tours, Guardian Building, Havensight (tel. 774-1855). Visitors to St. John should use the services provided by the St. Thomas agency. On St. Croix, the American Express Travel Service representative is Southerland, Chandler's Wharf, Gallows Bay (tel. 773-9500).

Area Code   The area code for all the U.S. Virgin Islands is 809, which you can dial directly from the mainland of the United States.

Banks   Several major banks are represented in the U.S. Virgins. While hours vary, many are open on Mon–Thurs 9am–2:30pm and Fri 9am–2pm and 3:30–5pm.

Business Hours   Typical business hours are Mon–Fri 9am–5pm and Sat 9am–1pm.

Camera and Film   Most famous brands of film, such as Kodak, are sold in the Virgin Islands. Film isn't cheap here, nor is the cost of getting your film processed locally. It might be cheaper to send your film home for processing. Protect your camera in the Virgin Islands, not only from theft, but from saltwater and sand. It can also overheat if left in the sun or locked in the trunk of a car. For the best commercial camera stores in the U.S. Virgins, see the individual island chapters.

Climate   See "When to Go," Chapter 2.

Crime   It's here as it is everywhere. Avoid wandering around the back streets of Charlotte Amalie, Frederiksted, or Christiansted at night. See "Safety," below.

Currency   U.S. currency is used on the U.S. Virgin Islands.

Customs   See "Entry Requirements," Chapter 2.

Documents Required   See "Entry Requirements," Chapter 2.

Driving Rules   Remember to drive on the left. Obey speed limits, which are 20 m.p.h. in town, 35 m.p.h. outside.

Drugs   A branch of the federal narcotics strike force is permanently stationed in the U.S. Virgin Islands. If convicted of possession of marijuana, severe penalties are imposed, ranging from 2 to 10 years. Possession of hard drugs such as cocaine can lead to 15 years in prison.

Drugstores   Carry all prescription medicine with you, enough for the duration of your stay. If you need any other medications, such as in case of sunburn, or a prescription filled, you'll find many drugstore outlets in St. Thomas and St. Croix, with limited offerings on St. John. See specific island "Fast Facts" for drugstore recommendations.

Electricity   The electrical current in the Virgin Islands is the same as on the mainland: 110 volts AC, 60 cycles.

Embassies and Consulates   There are no embassies or consulates here.

Emergencies Police, 915; fire, 921; ambulance, 922; Coast Guard, 774-1911.

Etiquette This subject in the U.S. Virgins mainly concerns dress. Cover up in restaurants or when walking along the streets of the main towns.

Hitchhiking It isn't illegal, but it isn't widely practiced. It might be more practical on St. Croix, because of the distances involved, than on the other islands.

Holidays See "Holidays," Chapter 2.

Hospitals See "Fast Facts" for the individual islands.

Information See "Information," Chapter 2.

Laundry Often your hotel will arrange to have your clothing laundered for you, but you pay a surcharge above what it would cost in a Laundromat. See "Fast Facts" under the individual island listings for the names of Laundromats.

Liquor Laws You must be 21 years of age or older to purchase liquor in stores or buy drinks in hotels, bars, and restaurants.

Mail Postage rates are the same as on the U.S. mainland.

Maps Tourist offices provide free maps of all three islands. If you plan extensive touring, purchase a copy of the *Official Road Map of the United States Virgin Islands,* available in most bookstores. This map has detailed routes of all three islands, and city maps of Christiansted, Frederiksted, Cruz Bay, and Charlotte Amalie.

Newspapers and Magazines Daily newspapers from the mainland are flown in to St. Thomas and St. Croix every day, and local papers, such as the *Virgin Island Daily News,* available on St. Thomas and St. Croix, also carry the latest news. St. Croix has its own daily newspaper, the *St. Croix Avis.*

Passports See "Documents," Chapter 2.

Pets To bring your pet in, you must produce a health certificate from a mainland veterinarian. You will also be required to show proof of vaccination against rabies. Very few hotels allow animals, so check in advance. Both St. Croix and St. Thomas have veterinarians found under the yellow pages. If you're strolling with your dog through the national park on St. John, the dog must be on a leash. Pets are not allowed at campgrounds, picnic areas, or on public beaches.

Police Call 915. For local stations see "Police" under "Fast Facts" for the individual islands.

Radio and TV All three islands receive both cable and commercial TV stations. Radio weather reports can be heard at 7:30pm and 8:30am on 99.5 FM.

Restrooms These exist at public beaches and at airport terminals, with limited public facilities available in towns. Usually toilets are found at the main squares. Many visitors use the facilities of a bar or restaurant, but it is considered polite to order something, if only a mineral water, as in theory these facilities are restricted to patrons.

Safety There have been recent reports that the crime rate of the U.S. Virgin Islands is increasing. Exercise caution and stay alert. Be aware of your immediate surroundings. Wear a moneybelt and keep a close eye on your possessions. Be particularly careful with cameras, purses, and wallets, all favorite targets of thieves and pickpockets.

Taxes There is no departure tax for the U.S. Virgin Islands. Hotels add a 7.5% tax to rates that is not always included in the rate quoted to you. Always ask just to be sure.

Telephone, Telex, and Fax Local calls at a telephone booth cost 25¢. From all points on the mainland you can dial direct to the Virgin Islands using the area code 809. Cable service is available as well. Most hotels are equipped to send telex and fax. You can also do so at local post offices on the islands. See "Telephone, Telex, and Fax" under "Fast Facts" under individual island listings for specific addresses.

Time The U.S. Virgins are on Atlantic time, which places the islands 1 hour ahead of eastern standard time. However, during daylight saving time, the Virgin

Islands and the East Coast are on the same time. So when it's 6am in Charlotte Amalie, it's 5am in Miami; during daylight saving time it's 6am in both places.

Tipping As a general rule tip 15%. Some hotels add a 10% to 15% surcharge to cover service. When in doubt, ask.

Tourist Offices See "Information," Chapter 2. In St. Thomas, the Visitors Center is at Emancipation Square (tel. 774-8784); in St. Croix at the Old Scalehouse (tel. 773-0495) on the waterfront at Christiansted, and also in the Customs House Building, Strand Street, Frederiksted (tel. 772-0357); and in St. John at Cruz Bay (tel. 776-6450).

Visas U.S. citizens do not need a visa to enter the U.S. Virgin Islands. Visitors from other nations should have a passport and a U.S. visa. Those visitors may also be asked to produce an onward ticket.

Water There is ample water for showers and bathing in the Virgin Islands, but you are asked to conserve. Many visitors drink the local tap water with no harmful after effects. Others, more prudent or with more delicate stomachs should stick to bottled water.

Yellow Pages The telephone company of the U.S. Virgin Islands publishes an annual directory with extensive listings of services and establishments. All three islands are condensed in one book.

FAST THE BRITISH VIRGIN ISLANDS

American Express Local representatives include Travel Plan, Ltd., Waterfront Drive (tel. 42347), in Tortola, and Travel Plan, Ltd., Virgin Gorda Yacht Harbour (tel. 55586), in Virgin Gorda.

Area Code The area code is 809. When calling from outside the islands, you must then dial 49 before all BVI numbers.

Banks Banks are generally open Mon–Thurs 9am–2:30pm, Fri 9am–2:30pm and 4:30–6pm. To cash traveler's checks, try Bank of Nova Scotia, Wickhams Cay (tel. 42526) or Barclays Bank, Wickhams Cay (tel. 42171), both near Road Town.

Bookstores The best bookstore on the island is the National Educational Services Bookstore, Wickhams Cay in Road Town (tel. 43921). In spite of its name, this is a privately owned and funded bookstore.

Business Hours Most offices are open Mon–Fri 9am–5pm. Government offices are open Mon–Fri 8:30am–4:30pm. Shops are generally open Mon–Fri 9am–5pm and Sat 9am–1pm.

Camera and Film The best place for supplies and developing on Tortola is Bolo's Brothers, Wickhams Cay (tel. 42867).

Climate See "Climate," Chapter 2.

Crime See "Safety," below.

Currency The U.S. dollar is the legal currency, much to the surprise of arriving Britishers who find no one willing to accept their pounds.

Customs You can generally bring into the BVI items intended for your personal use. But if you make purchases here, U.S. Customs allows only a $400 duty-free exemption, providing you have been out of the United States for 48 hours. You can mail back home unsolicited gifts providing they don't exceed $50 per day in value to any single address. You don't pay duty on items classified as handcrafts, art, or antiques.

Dentist   In Tortola call the Department of Health (tel. 43474) for a referral.

Doctor   See "Hospitals," below.

Documents Required   See "Entry Requirements," Chapter 2.

Driving Rules   Driving in the BVI is only for those who like hairpin turns and a Coney Island Cyclone terrain. You need a valid Canadian or American driver's license and must pay $10 at police headquarters for a 3-month British Virgin Islands driving permit. Some of the larger car-rental companies keep a supply of these forms. Remember to drive on the left.

Drug Laws   Drugs, their use, possession, or sale, are strictly prohibited. Penalties are stiff.

Drugstores   The best place to go is J.R. O'Neal, Ltd., Main Street, Road Town (tel. 42292), in Tortola. It is closed on Sunday. Stock up here on any prescribed medicines or other supplies you'll need if you're planning visits to the other islands.

Electricity   The electrical current is 110 volts, AC, 60 cycles, as in the U.S.

Embassies and Consulates   There are none.

Emergencies   Thirteen doctors practice in Tortola, and there is a hospital, Peebles Hospital, Porter Road, Road Town (tel. 43497), with X-ray and laboratory facilities. One doctor practices on Virgin Gorda. Your hotel can put you in touch with the island's medical staff.

Etiquette   Unlike in some parts of the Caribbean, nudity is an offense punishable by law in the BVI.

Hairdresser   The best place for men and women is Scissors, Prospect Reef (tel. 43221), in Road Town.

Hitchhiking   Travel by thumb is illegal.

Holidays   See "When to Go," Chapter 2.

Hospitals   In Road Town, you can go to Peebles Hospital, Porter Road (tel. 43497).

Information   See "Information," Chapter 2. The headquarters of the BVI Tourist Board is in the center of Road Town, close to the ferry dock, south of Wickhams Cay (tel. 43134).

Laundry and Dry Cleaning   In Tortola, one of the best places is Freeman's Laundry & Dry Cleaning, Purcell Estate (tel. 42285).

Library   The Public Library, Main Street (tel. 43428), is in Road Town.

Liquor Laws   The legal minimum age for purchasing liquor or drinking alcohol in bars is 21.

Lost Property   Go to the police station. Sometimes they'll broadcast notice of your lost property on the local radio station.

Mail   Most hotels will mail letters for you, or you can go directly to the post office. Allow 4 days to 1 week for letters to reach the North American mainland. Postal rates in the BVI have been raised now to 30¢ for a postcard (airmail) to the U.S. or Canada, and 45¢ for a first-class airmail letter (½ ounce) to the U.S. or Canada, or 35¢ for a second-class letter (½ ounce) to the U.S. or Canada.

Maps   The best map of the British Virgin Islands is published by *Vigilate,* and is sold at most bookstores in Road Town.

Newspapers and Magazines   Papers from the mainland, such as *The Miami Herald,* are flown into Tortola and Virgin Gorda daily, and copies of the latest issues of *Time* and *Newsweek* are sold at hotel newsstands and at various outlets in Road Town. The BVI has no daily newspaper, but *The Island Sun,* published Wednesday and Friday, is a good source of information on local entertainment.

Passports   See "Entry Requirements," Chapter 2.

Pets   To bring in a pet, you'll need proof of vaccination against rabies and a health certificate from your veterinarian. You need clearance far in advance. Write to the Chief Agricultural Officer, Road Town, Tortola, BVI, or call 495-2451.

Police   The main police headquarters is on Station Street (tel. 43822) in

Tortola. There is also a police station on Virgin Gorda (tel. 55222) and another police station at Jost Van Dyke (tel. 43450).

Radio & TV Hotels subscribe to cable TV and get such broadcasts as CNN. The BVI has two local FM stations with nonstop music, including Z-HIT (94.3) and Z-WAVE (97.3).

Religious Services In Tortola, there are several small churches, including Church of Christ, Main Street (tel. 44233) in Road Town; in Virgin Gorda there is the Church of God Holiness, Manse (tel. 55248).

Restrooms Available at airports and ferry terminals, they are hard to find elsewhere, and visitors must rely on those at commercial establishments, such as restaurants and hotels.

Safety The BVI is one of the safest places in the Caribbean. But crime does exist, and you should take all the usual precautions. Don't leave items unattended on the beach. See "Safety," in "Fast Facts: U.S. Virgin Islands," above.

Shoe Repair Try Bolo's Brothers, Wickhams Cay (tel. 42867), in Road Town.

Taxes There is no sales tax. A government tax of 7% is imposed on all hotel rooms. A $5 departure tax is collected from everyone leaving by air, $3 for those departing by sea.

Telephone, Telex, and Fax You can call the British Virgins from the continental U.S. by dialing area code 809, followed by 49, and then five digits. Once here, omit both the 809 and the 49 to make local calls. Most hotels (not the small guesthouses) will send a fax or telex for you.

Time See "Fast Facts: The U.S. Virgin Islands," above.

Tipping See "Fast Facts: The U.S. Virgin Islands," above.

Tourist Offices See "Information," Chapter 2.

Visas Visitors who stay for fewer than 6 months don't need a visa if they possess a return or onward ticket.

Water See "Fast Facts: The U.S. Virgin Islands," above.

Yellow Pages All of the island phone numbers are contained in one volume, the British Virgin Islands telephone book, issued annually. In the back of the book is a helpful yellow pages section of goods and services available on the island.

CHAPTER 4

THE U.S. VIRGIN ISLANDS: ST. THOMAS

The busiest cruise-ship harbor in the West Indies, St. Thomas is about 12 miles long and 3 miles wide. It is the second largest of the U.S. Virgins and lies about 40 miles north of St. Croix, which is the largest. The U.S. Virgins' capital is Charlotte Amalie, which is also the shopping center of the Caribbean.

Vacationers discovered St. Thomas right after World War II, and they've been flocking there ever since in increasing numbers to enjoy the shopping, sights, and sun. Tourism has raised the standard of living here to one of the highest in the Caribbean. Condominium apartments and expensive villas have sprouted up over the debris of bulldozed shacks.

St. Thomas is a boon for cruise-ship shoppers, who flood Main Street, the 3- to 4-block-long shopping center in the heart of town. While this area gets very crowded, it's away from all beaches, major hotels, most restaurants, and entertainment facilities.

You can still find seclusion at a hotel in more remote sections of the island. Hotels on the north side of St. Thomas look out at the Atlantic and those on the south side front the calmer Caribbean. Because of the steep hills which divide the islands and provide sweeping views, it's possible for the sun to be shining in the south while the north experiences showers.

St. Thomas is the most cosmopolitan and sophisticated of all the Virgin Islands, either U.S. or British. It is a port not only for cruise ships but for privately owned million-dollar yachts. It is especially known for its string of beautiful beaches, including the very best, Magens Bay. St. Thomas and the Virgin Islands have been rated by *National Geographic* as among the top destinations in the world for sailing, scuba diving, and fishing.

Charlotte Amalie, with its white houses and

WHAT'S SPECIAL ABOUT ST. THOMAS

Beaches
- ☐ Magens Bay, 3 miles north of Charlotte Amalie, one of the most beautiful beaches in the world.
- ☐ Stouffer Grand Beach, one of the island's most stunning, with many water sports available.
- ☐ Sapphire Beach, with its luxury hotel complexes in the background, one of the finest on the island, and a favorite with windsurfers. The most popular Sunday-afternoon gathering place on the East End.

Ace Attractions
- ☐ Coral World, a marine complex featuring a three-story underwater observation tower 100 feet offshore.
- ☐ Jim Tillett's Art Gallery and Boutique, built around an old plantation-era sugar mill.

Great Towns/Villages
- ☐ Charlotte Amalie, the capital of St. Thomas, one of the most beautiful port cities in the Caribbean.
- ☐ Frenchtown, settled by the descendants of immigrants from the French islands, famous for its "cha-chas," or straw hats.

Historic Buildings
- ☐ The St. Thomas synagogue, second oldest in America, built by Sephardic Jews in 1833.
- ☐ Government House, at Government Hill in Charlotte Amalie, the official residence of the U.S. Virgin Islands governor.
- ☐ Fort Christian, constructed by the Danes in 1671 and named for King Christian V.

bright red roofs glistening in the sun, is considered one of the most beautiful towns in the Caribbean. Most people come here to shop, but it is also filled with historic sights. These include Fort Christian, the oldest building in St. Thomas, built by the Danes in the 17th century. The town's architecture reflects the cultural diversity of St. Thomas. In Charlotte Amalie, the doors are Dutch, the red tile roofs Danish, the iron grillwork French, and the Andalusian-style patios Spanish.

St. Thomas is known for its excellent climate and enjoys sunshine all year round, with temperatures generally in the 80°s during the day, dropping into the 70°s at night.

1. ORIENTATION

ARRIVING

BY PLANE

American Airlines (tel. toll free 800/433-7300) is the front-runner for passage to St. Thomas from most points of North America. From New York's JFK, a nonstop flight departs daily for St. Thomas early in the morning. Passengers who prefer later flights may opt for one of the airline's three daily connections through San Juan, Puerto Rico, or for one of the three daily transfers through San Juan from New Jersey's Newark airport. The San Juan hub is the only one of its kind in Latin

America, and is considered one of the largest, most efficient, and most modern within the North American network.

Passengers from the Midwest and the Middle Atlantic states transfer through American's hub in Raleigh-Durham, North Carolina. From Raleigh, a nonstop flight continues to St. Thomas every day. American also offers a daily direct flight from Chicago to St. Thomas, which touches down briefly in San Juan before continuing on to its final destination.

Passengers originating from (or transferring through) South Florida take either American's daily nonstop flight to St. Thomas from Miami or one of several different daily transfers through San Juan.

American's least expensive fare to St. Thomas from any of its hubs is a SuperSaver fare, which requires a 14-day advance payment, a stay of between 3 and 30 days, and a penalty of $25 for any alterations in itinerary. From New York, this ticket sold at presstime for a low-season promotional fare of $254 for travel Monday through Thursday, and for $282, plus tax, for travel Friday through Sunday. (At the end of this particular promotion, round-trip fares were expected to rise by around $100.) Equivalent high-season fares from New York to St. Thomas range from $403 to $443 round-trip, plus tax, depending on the day of the week. Prices are, of course, subject to change.

Delta (tel. toll free 800/221-1212) offers flights to St. Thomas, with continuing service on to St. Croix, through Atlanta, Orlando, and San Juan. (Passengers transferring through San Juan continue their journeys on another carrier.) Travelers originating anywhere within Delta's intricate network could usually make convenient transfers on to St. Thomas through any of these three points.

Continental (tel. toll free 800/231-0856) offers daily nonstop flights to St. Thomas from its hub in Newark, New Jersey. After picking up and discharging passengers in St. Thomas, flights continue on to St. Croix before turning around and heading back (nonstop) to Newark. Continental's cheapest fares require a 14-day advance payment, and a delay of between 3 and 30 days before activating the return portion of any ticket.

TWA (tel. toll free 800/221-2000) does not fly nonstop into any of the Virgin Islands, but instead offers connections on other carriers from San Juan, Puerto Rico. TWA flies to San Juan twice daily nonstop from New York's JFK, once daily nonstop from Miami, and once daily (either nonstop or with a touchdown en route) from St. Louis.

Flying time to St. Thomas from New York is 3½ hours; from Chicago, 5 hours; from Miami, 2½ hours; and from the neighboring island of Puerto Rico, 20 minutes.

A final hint: Bargain-seeking passengers should ask their airline to connect them with the tour desk. Someone there can usually arrange discounted hotel rates if a hotel reservation is arranged simultaneously with air passage. The options are so varied and complicated that only an airline staff member or a travel agent can describe them in detail.

BY BOAT

St. Thomas's capital, Charlotte Amalie, is the busiest cruise-ship port in the Caribbean. For details on cruise-ship travel, see "Getting There," Chapter 2.

St. Thomas maintains no ferry connections to St. Croix, some 40 miles to the south. The best way to get there is to fly.

If you are already in the British Virgin Islands and want to visit St. Thomas, there is a much traveled route by boat between Charlotte Amalie and Tortola, the capital of the BVI. Trip time is only an hour between these two capitals, and the one-way cost

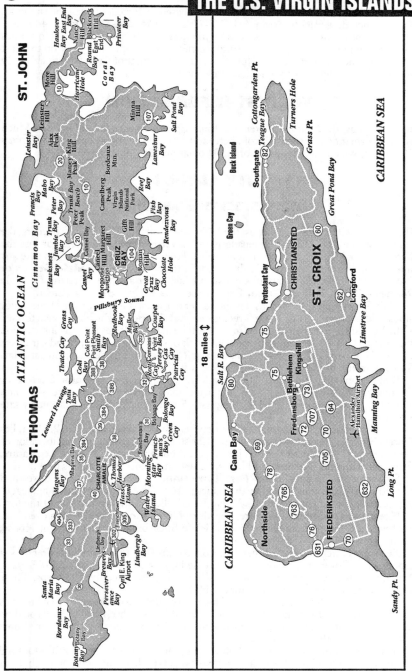

THE U.S. VIRGIN ISLANDS

N

ST. JOHN

ST. THOMAS

ATLANTIC OCEAN

Leeward Passage

Pillsbury Sound

CARIBBEAN SEA

ST. CROIX

CARIBBEAN SEA

18 miles

ranges from $28 to $35. The principal carriers based in Tortola making the run to St. Thomas include **Smith's Ferry** (tel. 775-7292) and **Native Son** (tel. 774-8685).

St. Thomas is also linked by boat to St. John, its neighbor island, some 3 to 5 miles away (depending on where you measure). Ferries depart from Red Hook on the East End of St. Thomas and reach St. John (or rather its capital of Cruz Bay) in about 20 minutes. For complete ferry schedules, telephone 776-6282.

TOURIST INFORMATION

In St. Thomas, the Visitors Center is at Emancipation Square (tel. 774-8784). Much useful information is dispensed from here, and you can pick up a copy of *St. Thomas This Week,* which includes maps of St. Thomas and St. John.

CITY LAYOUT

MAIN STREETS & ARTERIES

The capital, Charlotte Amalie, is the only town on St. Thomas. It borders the waterfront, and its seaside promenade is called **Waterfront Highway** or just the Waterfront. Its old Danish name is Kyst Vejen. From the waterfront, you can take any number of streets or alleyways leading back in to the town to the **Main Street** or Dronningens Gade. Principal links between Main Street and the Waterfront include **Raadets Gade, Tolbod Gade, Storetvaer Gade,** and **Strand Gade.**

Main Street is aptly named, as it is the center of the capital and the site of the major shops. The western part of Main Street is **Market Square,** which was once the site of the biggest slave market auctions in the Caribbean Basin. It lies near the intersection with Strand Gade. Today, it is an open-air block of stalls where farmers and gardeners on the island peddle their produce daily except Sunday and particularly on Saturday. Go early in the morning to see the market at its best.

Running parallel to Main Street and lying north of it is **Back Street** or Vimmelskaft Gade, which has many stores, including some of the less expensive ones. *Note:* It's quite dangerous to walk along Back Street at night, but it's reasonably safe for daytime shopping.

In the eastern part of town, midway between Tolbod Gade and Fort Pladsen, lies **Emancipation Park,** northwest of Fort Christian, commemorating the liberation of the slaves in 1848. Most of the major historical buildings, including the Legislature, Fort Christian, and Government House, lie within a short walk of this park.

Southeast of the park looms **Fort Christian,** crowned by a clock tower and painted a rusty red, constructed by the Danes in 1671. The Legislative Building, seat of the elected government of the U.S. Virgin Islands, lies on the harbor side of the fort.

Kongens Gade (or King's Street) leads to **Government Hill,** which overlooks the town and the harbor. Here stands a white brick building, Government House, dating from 1867.

Between Hotel 1829, a former mansion constructed that year by a French sea captain, and Government House is a staircase known as the **Street of 99 Steps.** Actually, someone, miscounted: It should be called the Street of 103 Steps. These steps lead to the summit of Government Hill.

Near here are the remains of the 17th-century **Fort Skytsborg** or Blackbeard's Tower, a reference to the notorious pirate Edward Teach, who is said to have spied on treasure galleons entering the harbor in the 1700s. Today a 22-room hotel, Blackbeard's Castle, stands here.

This should not be confused with Bluebeard's Tower, which crowns a 300-foot hill at the eastern edge of town. This is the site of what is perhaps the best known (but not the best) hotel in the Virgin Islands. It's called Bluebeard's Castle.

FINDING AN ADDRESS/MAPS

Finding an address in Charlotte Amalie is relatively easy, even though many stores don't advertise or even display their street numbers. Even numbers run up one side of the street and odd numbers up the other. No. 25 might be across the street from No. 14.

St. *Thomas This Week*, distributed free by the tourist office and handed out to cruise-ship passengers, contains a two-page map in its center, including not only a clear, easy-to-follow street plan of Charlotte Amalie, but also all the important landmark buildings. It pinpoints all the leading shops of Charlotte Amalie, giving the name of the shop on an index which corresponds with an easy-to-find number on the map. Pick up a copy of this map if you're going on a walking tour of Charlotte Amalie or a shopping spree.

NEIGHBORHOODS IN BRIEF

Charlotte Amalie is too small to be divided into neighborhoods. A highly walkable little town, it forms its own closely knit geographical unit.

It's only neighborhood of any significance is **Frenchtown** which for years was called *Cha-Cha Town,* now considered pejorative, after the straw hats worn by the original settlers of the town. Some of the older generation still speak a distinctive Norman-French dialect.

Since the heart of Charlotte Amalie is considered a dangerous place to go wandering at night, Frenchtown, with its many fine restaurants and interesting bars, has now become the center of nightlife and is a much safer place to be after dark.

To reach it, take Veterans Drive west of town along the waterfront, turning left (shortly after you pass the Windward Passage Hotel on your right) at the sign pointing to the Villa Olga.

The only other neighborhood is **Frenchman's Hill,** site of the famous Harbor View Hotel and restaurant. The Huguenots built many old stone villas here, which open onto panoramic views of the town and its harbor.

2. GETTING AROUND

If you arrive by cruise ship, you will be deposited right in the heart of Charlotte Amalie where you can begin your shopping adventures. Should you arrive by air, you will land at the Cyril E. King Airport to the west of Charlotte Amalie along Route 30. A plentiful supply of taxis always meets every arriving plane. Chances are you will be staying at a hotel east of Charlotte Amalie. Getting there can involve long delays and traffic jams on any day that a lot of cruise ships happen to visit the port.

BY BUS

St. Thomas has the best public transportation of any island in the U.S. chain. Buses (called Vitrans) leave from the center of Charlotte Amalie, fanning out east and west along all the most important highways on the island. Vitran stops are found beside the roads. You rarely have to wait during the day more than 30 minutes, and they run between 6am and 9pm daily, charging 75¢. This is an excellent and comfortable form of public transportation. You may not be delivered to your door, however.

St. Thomas also has an open-air "taxi bus" system, which runs daily from 7:15am to 5:15pm. Departures are every hour from Market Place in Charlotte Amalie, heading east to Red Hook, where the ferry departs for St. John. The one-way fare is $3. The bus will deliver you right to the door.

The **Manassah Bus** goes between Charlotte Amalie and Red Hook nearly every hour. Service starts at 6am from Charlotte Amalie and ends with the last run at 8pm from Red Hook, all for a one-way ticket cost of 75¢. Throughout the day, across St. Thomas as far west as Bordeaux, a one-way passage costs $1. For information about exact schedules, telephone 774-5678.

BY TAXI

In St. Thomas taxis are plentiful and are the chief means of transport. The cabs are unmetered, and fares are controlled and widely posted; however, it is still important to agree with the driver on a rate before you get into the car. Surcharges, ranging from $1.50 to $2, are added after midnight. If you rent a taxi and a driver (who just may serve as guide) for a day, the cost is about $30 for two passengers for 2 hours of sightseeing; each additional passenger pays $12. For 24-hour radio dispatch taxi service, call 776-0496.

Many taxis transport 8 to 12 passengers in vans to multiple destinations. Of course, it's cheaper to travel in one of these—say, if you're going from your hotel to the airport instead of renting the taxi all to yourself. For example, from the airport to the Stouffer Grand Beach Resort costs $9 individually, but only $6 per person if others are going in the same directions.

BY CAR

RENTING A CAR

St. Thomas offers reasonable base rates for car rental. However, because of the island's high accident rate (which is partly the result of dangerous roads and the unaccustomed requirement of driving on the left), insurance rates tend to be higher than you might have expected. In addition extra coverage can be arranged for between $1 and $10. Given the accident rates, it is a wise investment.

Budget (tel. toll free 800/626-4516), **Hertz** (tel. toll free 800/654-3001), and **Avis** (tel. toll free 800/331-2112) each maintain their headquarters at the island's airport, with kiosks near the baggage claim areas.

Each of the three companies offers an air-conditioned Mitsubishi Mirage, or a Nissan Sentra, in most cases with automatic transmission, as their least expensive car. The price (including unlimited mileage) ranges from $209 to $252 per week. Budget offers a booklet of coupons for free or discounted admission to the island's attractions (and free drinks or food at a selection of the island's restaurants) whose value (if you use all the coupons) exceeds $600.

Each of the three companies requires an advance booking of between 2 and 3 business days to qualify for the lowest price. Avis requires that renters be aged 25 or older, and present a valid credit card at the time of rental. All three require a valid driver's license and a valid credit card or a substantial cash deposit.

PARKING

If you can't find a place to park along the waterfront (free), go to the large, sprawling lot to the east of Fort Christian, across from the Legislature. Charges are nominal here, and you can park your car and walk northwest toward Emancipation Park or else along the waterfront until you reach the shops and attractions. Because of congested and one-way streets, don't try to drive within the town.

DRIVING RULES

Always drive on the left. The speed limit is 20 m.p.h. in town, 35 m.p.h. outside town. Be especially careful driving since roads are dangerous and poorly lit.

BY MOPED

If you're going exploring outside Charlotte Amalie, you can rent a moped if you are at least 15 years old. **Paradise Scooters,** at the Ramada Yacht Haven Hotel, Long Bay Road (tel. 775-2724), rents by the hour, day, or week, providing maps and tour information. It also has the largest selection of scooters on the island.

ON FOOT

This is the only way to explore the heart of Charlotte Amalie. All the major attractions and the principal stores are close enough to walk to. However, the other major attractions of the island, such as Coral World or the beach at Magens Bay, are long, hot hauls from the center and it's better to go by bus or taxi.

FAST FACTS ST. THOMAS

American Express In St. Thomas, service is provided by the Caribbean Travel Agency, Inc./Tropic Tours, 14AB The Guardian Building, Havensight (tel. 774-1855).

Area Code The area code is 809. You can dial direct from North America.

Airport Directly west of Charlotte Amalie, Cyril E. King Airport, Airport Road (tel. 774-3140), is a modern terminal, with 11 major gates and 10 commuter gates. A line of taxis meets all arriving flights to take you to your hotel.

Babysitters Make arrangements through your hotel.

Banks Several major banks are represented in the U.S. Virgins. While the hours vary, many are open Mon–Thurs 9am–2:30pm, Fri 9am–2pm and 3:30–5pm.

Bookstores Dockside Bookshop, Havensight Mall (tel. 774-4937), where the cruise ships dock, has a selection of books, cards, and maps.

Business Hours Typical business hours are Mon–Fri 9am–5pm, Sat 9am–1pm. Store hours are generally 9am–5pm Mon–Fri and 9am–1pm Sat. Some open Sun for cruise-ship arrivals. Usual hours for bars are daily 11am–midnight or 1am, although some hot spots stay open much later.

Car Rentals See "Getting Around," above.

Climate See "When to Go," Chapter 2.

Currency See "Information, Entry Requirements, and Money," Chapter 2.

Currency Exchange Most major hotels will cash your traveler's checks. You can also go to any of the major banks in Charlotte Amalie, including Chase Manhattan Bank, Veterans Drive (tel. 776-2222), and Citibank, Veterans Drive (tel. 774-4800).

Dentist The Virgin Island Dental Association, Four Winds Plaza (tel. 775-9110), is a member of the American Dental Association, and has the largest number of members practicing throughout the island. It is also linked with various specialists.

Doctor Doctors-on-Duty, Vitraco Park (tel. 776-7966), in Charlotte Amalie is an excellent medical facility.

Documents Required See "Information, Entry Requirements, and Money," Chapter 2.

Driving Rules In St. Thomas motorists drive on the left. Speed limits and road signs are similar to those on the U.S. mainland.

Drugstores Cathedral Pharmacy, 22 Kronprindsens Gade (tel. 776-4080), sells over-the-counter medications, but to fill prescriptions, visitors go to Apothecary, 19 Droningensgade (tel. 774-1341).

Electricity 110 to 115 V, 60 cycles, as on the U.S. mainland.

Embassies and Consulates St. Thomas has no embassies or consulates. Go to one of the various U.S. government agencies if you have a problem.

Emergencies Police, 915; ambulance, 922; fire, 921.

Etiquette U.S. Virgin Islanders tend to be a bit conservative. Save the skimpy swimwear for the beach and cover up when patronizing public places.

Eyeglasses Vision Center, 14B Norre Gade (tel. 774-2020), has the fullest optical care and services on the islands. They specialize in contact lenses and offer immediate prescription and repair services.

Hairdressers and Barbers Many hotels have a beauty shop on the premises. If not, women can go to Nora's Beauty Palace, 8 First St. Estate (tel. 776-5992), in Charlotte Amalie. Celsa's House of Beauty, Windward Passage (tel. 776-3094), has a wide range of unisex services, including facial treatments, coloring, manicures, pedicures, and permanent waves and relaxes. Call either of these places for an appointment.

Holidays See "When to Go," Chapter 2.

Hospitals The St. Thomas Hospital is at Sugar Estate (tel. 776-8311), Charlotte Amalie.

Hotlines Call the police at 915 in an emergency. Otherwise, "Hot Line" at 773-1780 provides trained counselors who offer confidential counseling and emotional support for persons in crisis. In case of boating mishaps, call the U.S. Coast Guard Rescue at 772-2943. Scuba divers should have the number of the Recompression Chamber (tel. 776-2686).

Laundry and Dry Cleaning Many of the major hotels arrange this service, but it's also more expensive, of course, than independent establishments on the island. For dry cleaning go to One-Hour Martinizing, Barbel Plaza (tel. 776-5452), in Charlotte Amalie. The island also has a few coined-operated Laundromats, including Lemon Fresh Laundry, at the Yacht Haven Marina, 4 Long Bay Rd. (tel. 774-0250), in Charlotte Amalie. A good full-service laundry is 4-Star Laundromat, 58 Kronprindsens Gade (tel. 774-8689), in Charlotte Amalie.

Libraries Go to the Enid M. Baa Library, Main Street at Gutters Gade (tel. 774-0630), in Charlotte Amalie.

Liquor Laws Persons must be at least 21 years of age to patronize bars or purchase liquor in St. Thomas.

Lost Property There is no office for recovering lost property. You can call the police at 915 to report a lost item. Leave a description of the item, your name, and mailing address should the item ever be turned in to the police.

Luggage Storage and Lockers Check with Native Son, Inc. on Veterans Drive (tel. 774-8685). They will store suitcases for 1 full day or less for passengers eventually headed to the airport. Storage is free.

Mail Postal rates are the same as on the U.S. mainland.

Maps See "Orientation," above.

Money See "Information, Entry Requirements, and Money," Chapter 2.

Newspapers and Magazines Copies of U.S. mainland newspapers, such as *The New York Times, USA Today,* and *The Miami Herald,* arrive daily in St. Thomas and are sold at hotels and newsstands around the island. The latest copies of *Time* and *Newsweek* are also for sale. *St. Thomas Daily News* covers local, national, and international events. Pick up a free copy of *Virgin Islands Playground,* with much tourist-related data, and definitely get *St. Thomas This Week,* which is packed with information and distributed free all over the island.

Photographic Needs Try Blazing Photos, Inc., Veterans Drive (tel. 774-5547), in Charlotte Amalie, with a branch office at Havensight Mall (tel. 776-5547), where cruise-ship passengers arrive. The charge for developing film in 1 hour is $20.40; 4-hour developing costs $17.40.

Police Dial 915 in an emergency.

Post Office The Main Post Office is at 46 Estate Thomas (tel. 774-1950), Charlotte Amalie, open Mon–Fri 9am–5pm and Sat 9am–1pm.

Radio St. Thomas has several radio stations, broadcasting news and music, including WIYC FM-104 and WVGN-V105 FM.

Religious Services St. Thomas has a number of churches and synagogues, including St. Peter's Episcopal Church, 22-AB Kronprindsens Gade (tel. 774-0201); Hebrew Congregation of St. Thomas, Crystal Gade (tel. 774-4312); Calvary Baptist Church, 200 Altona (tel. 774-1759), and Christchurch Methodist, Market Square (tel. 774-0797).

Restrooms See "Fast Facts: The U.S. Virgin Islands," Chapter 3.

Safety St. Thomas has an unusually high crime rate, particularly in Charlotte Amalie. It is reasonably safe during the day, but don't wander around town at night, particularly on Back Street. Guard your valuables. Store them in hotel safes if possible, and make sure you keep your doors and windows shut at night.

Shoe Repairs Go to Zora's of St. Thomas Shoe Repair, 34 Norre Gade (tel. 774-2559), Charlotte Amalie. The shop also does handbag and luggage repair. It has been in business since 1962 doing custom and ready-made sandals. It also makes high-quality canvas bags and luggage, its primary business. Hours are Mon–Fri 8am–5pm and Sat 8:30am–5:30pm.

Taxes The only local taxes are a 7.5% surcharge added to all hotel tariffs.

Taxis See "Getting Around," above.

Telephone, Telex and Fax Pay phones operate as they do in the United States. All island phone numbers have seven digits. It is not necessary to use the 809 area code when dialing within St. Thomas. Numbers for all three islands, including St. John and St. Croix, are found in the U.S. Virgin Islands phone book. Hotels will send fax and telexes for you, often for cost plus a small service charge. Long distance, international, and collect calls are made the same way they are on the U.S. mainland.

Time See "Fast Facts: The U.S. Virgin Islands," Chapter 3.

Tipping See "Fast Facts: The U.S. Virgin Islands," Chapter 3.

Television Many of the major resort hotels subscribe to cable TV, including CNN. Local TV stations include WSVI-TV Channel 8 and WTJX-TV Channel 12.

Transit Information Call 776-0496 24 hours a day to order a taxi. Call for airport information at 774-3140, and dial 776-6282 for information about ferry departures for St. John.

Water See "Fast Facts: The U.S. Virgin Islands," Chapter 3.

Weather Call the U.S. Weather Service at 791-3490.

Yellow Pages See "Fast Facts: The U.S. Virgin Islands," Chapter 3.

3. ACCOMMODATIONS

Nearly every beach has its own hostelry, and St. Thomas just might have more inns of character than any other place in the Caribbean. You're faced with a choice of staying in the capital, Charlotte Amalie, or at any of the far points of the island, including the unusual Bolongo Bay and Sapphire Beach resorts.

If you want to stay in St. Thomas on the cheap, you'll have to select one of the guesthouses or motels in the Charlotte Amalie district. All the glittering, very expensive properties lie in the East End. Hotels slash their prices in summer 20% to 60%. What follows is a breakdown of daily winter rates in double rooms with private baths. "Very expensive" means rooms ranging from $200 to $440; "expensive" is a double for $150 to $199; "moderate" is a double for $135 to $149; and "inexpensive" is a double in the $63 to $119 price range. Unless otherwise noted, the rates listed do not include the 7.5% government tax.

If you are interested in a condo rental, contact **Property Management Caribbean, Inc.,** Route 6, The Anchorage, St. Thomas, USVI 00802 (tel. 809/775-6220, or toll free 800/524-2038), which currently represents six condo complexes. Rental units range from studio apartments to four-bedroom villas suitable for up to eight people. Each has a fully equipped kitchen. Although no food is provided, a coffee starter set is. A minimum stay of 3 days is required in any season, 7 nights around Christmas.

CHARLOTTE AMALIE

VERY EXPENSIVE

BLUEBEARD'S CASTLE, Bluebeard's Hill, P.O. Box 7480, Charlotte Amalie, St. Thomas, USVI 00801. Tel. 809/744-1600, or toll free 800/524-6599. Fax 809/774-5134. 170 rms (all with bath). A/C TV TEL
$ Rates: Winter, $195–$235 single or double. Summer, $150–$185 single or double. Extra person $30. Breakfast $10 extra. MAP $50 per person. AE, DC, MC, V. **Parking:** Free.

Almost a monument in St. Thomas, this popular, all-around resort lies on one side of the bay overlooking Charlotte Amalie. In the 1930s, the U.S. government turned what had been a private home, dating from 1665 into a hotel. Over the years Bluebeard's has had many additions and extensions to accommodate the ever-increasing throng of vacationers.

Bedrooms come in a wide variety of shapes and sizes, all pleasantly decorated. You may find the best way to stay here is on a package deal (ask your travel agent for details).

Dining/Entertainment: The Terrace Restaurant commands a breathtaking view and offers many American and Caribbean specialties, open-air brunch, lunch, and late-night dining. The hotel also has another open-air restaurant, which serves an international cuisine and a piano bar.

Services: Free transportation to Magens Bay Beach.

Facilities: Freshwater swimming pool, two whirlpools, two lit tennis courts, physical fitness center, tour desk, car-rental facility, on-site free-port shopping.

EXPENSIVE

THE MARK ST. THOMAS, Blackbeard's Hill, Charlotte Amalie, St. Thomas, USVI 00801. Tel. 809/774-5511, or toll free 800/343-4085. Fax 809/774-8509. 9 rms (all with bath), 1 cottage. A/C TV TEL
$ Rates (including breakfast): Winter, $145–$215 single or double. Summer, $90–$150 single or double. Extra person $25. AE, DC, MC, V. **Parking:** Free.

Listed with the National Register of Historic Homes, this former domain of a Danish-born merchant was built in 1785 with bricks used as ballast in ships from Denmark. Today, the much-altered and expanded building stands in the midst of pleasant gardens at the top of the island's famous 99 steps. In addition to a "great room" furnished with antiques, there are comfortable bedrooms, each one suitable for one or two occupants and named after the original style or function of the room, such as Marble Room, Red Room, Library, Study. An outlying cottage, the only accommodation without a sea view, has two bedrooms and can house up to four guests. The restaurant of the small hotel is recommended under "Dining," below.

RAMADA YACHT HAVEN HOTEL & MARINA, 4 Long Bay Rd., P.O. Box 7970, St. Thomas, USVI 00801. Tel. 809/774-9700, or toll free 800/524-7877 in the U.S. Fax 809/776-3410. 151 units (all with bath), 2 suites. A/C TV TEL

$ Rates: Winter, $140–$180 single or double; $225 suite. Summer, $90–$115 single or double; $180 suite. Tax and service extra. Breakfast $8 extra. AE, DC, MC, V. **Parking:** Free.

Centrally located near the beaches and the shops on the Vitran route heading east, this hotel is adjacent to one of the largest and best-equipped private marinas in the Caribbean and to the West Indies Cruise-Ship Dock. Behind the shell-pink facade, the spacious units contain extra-large double or king-size beds, radios, and VCRs. The decor is pink and teal green.

Dining/Entertainment: The Bridge in the marina has a relaxed atmosphere for casual dining, and offers a view of the yachts and cruise ships. La Crêperie Bretonne is in the center of a court on the property, serving breakfast or lunch, and La Pizzeria provides pizza delivery to guests of the hotel and marina. Penelope's Restaurant and Lounge is located in the main hotel complex, offering panoramic views of the marina, and Splash's Pool Bar has swim-up seating in the pool.

Services: Daily shuttle service to beaches, valet laundry, guests services desk.
Facilities: Florist, beauty salon, laundromat.

MODERATE

BLACKBEARD'S CASTLE, Blackbeard's Hill, P.O. Box 6041, Charlotte Amalie, St. Thomas, USVI 00801. Tel. 809/776-1234, or toll free 800/344-5771 in the U.S. Fax 809/776-4321. 19 rms (all with bath), 3 suites. A/C TV TEL **Transportation:** Taxi.

$ Rates (including continental breakfast): Winter, $110 single; $145 double; $190 suite. Summer, $75 single; $95 double; $140 suite. AE, MC, V. **Parking:** Free.

It was the inspiration of an Illinois businessman Bob Harrington, and his Brazilian partner, Henrique Konzen, that transformed what had been a private residence into a genuinely charming inn. It enjoys one of the finest views of Charlotte Amalie and its harbor, thanks to its perch high on a hillside above town. The owners weren't alone in their appreciation of this location; in 1679 the Danish governor erected a soaring tower of chiseled stone here as a lookout for unfriendly ships. Legend has it that Blackbeard himself lived in the tower half a century later.

Each of the bedrooms has a lattice-enclosed veranda, a flat-weave Turkish kilim, terra-cotta floors, and consciously simple furniture. Guests enjoy the swimming pool and the establishment's social center, which is within the stylish bar and restaurant (see "Dining," below).

HOTEL 1829, Kongens Gade, P.O. Box 1567, Charlotte Amalie, St. Thomas, USVI 00804. Tel. 809/776-1829, or toll free 800/524-2002. Fax 809/776-4313. 12 rms (all with bath), 3 suites. A/C MINIBAR TV TEL

$ Rates (including continental breakfast): Winter, $70–$170 single; $80–$230 double; from $280 suite. Summer, $50–$100 single; $60–$110 double; from $180 suite. AE, MC, V. **Parking:** Free.

After a major restoration, this once-decaying historical site has become one of the leading small hotels of character in the Caribbean. Right in the heart of town, it stands about 3 minutes from Government House, built on a hillside with many levels and many steps (no elevator). The 1829 has been a hotel since the

19th century and has entertained such celebrated guests as King Carol of Romania, Edna St. Vincent Millay, and Mikhail Baryshnikov.

Amid a cascade of flowering bougainvillea are the upper rooms, which overlook a central courtyard with a miniature swimming pool. The units, some of which are small, are beautifully designed, comfortable, and attractive; most face the sea. During the restoration, the old was preserved whenever possible, and some rooms have antiques, such as four-poster beds.

WINDWARD PASSAGE HOTEL, Veterans Dr., P.O. Box 640, St. Thomas, USVI 00804. Tel. 809/774-5200, or toll free 800/524-7389 in the U.S. Fax 809/774-1231. 150 rms (all with bath), 11 junior suites. A/C TV TEL **Transportation:** Vitran bus.

$ Rates (including buffet breakfast): Winter, $125–$150 single; $135–$160 double; from $180 suite. Summer, $90–$125 single; $100–$135 double; from $140 suite. AE, DC, MC, V. **Parking:** Free.

Even though its charms are not immediately visible, this modern, many-balconied hotel enjoys one of the consistently highest rates of return bookings of any hotel on the island. Everything about it meets the needs of businesspeople and sports teams arriving for short-term stays.

Built in 1968 and renovated in 1990, its rooms are arranged around a massive central atrium, which contains a soaring concrete fountain, a restaurant (see "Dining," below), a bar with a devoted local clientele, a rectangular swimming pool, and a variety of facilities for children. There is no beach nearby, but there are frequent shuttle buses to and from Magens Bay, Morningstar Beach, and Sapphire Beach. Although the 54 harborfront rooms have beautiful views of some of the world's largest cruise ships, many frequent visitors request a bedroom overlooking the adjacent Emile Griffith Park, where baseball games provide the entertainment. Bedrooms are pastel colored and comfortably modern, with marble-trimmed bathrooms.

INEXPENSIVE

THE ADMIRAL'S INN, Villa Olga, P.O. Box 6162, Frenchtown, Charlotte Amalie, St. Thomas 00803. Tel. 809/774-1376. Fax 809/544-0493. 16 rms (all with bath). A/C TV TEL **Transportation:** Vitran bus line.

$ Rates (including continental breakfast): Winter, $99–$139 single or double. Summer, $75–$125 single or double. Children under 12 stay free in parents' room. AE, DC, MC, V. **Parking:** Free.

Set on a peninsula in Frenchtown, near the western entrance to Charlotte Amalie's harbor, this beachfront hotel attracts yachtspeople and divers. Modern lodging is provided in a relaxed setting with both harbor and oceanfront views. The secluded yet central location is just a short walk to town. Units lie upon a landscaped hillside, each newly refurbished in 1992. The freshwater pool was carefully terraced into the slope, and has a large sun deck and flowering borders. The recently reconstructed saltwater beach and sea pool lie a few paces from the lanai-style oceanview units. Full breakfasts and light lunches are available, and the poolside bar remains open for hotel guests throughout the afternoon and evening. Dinner is served in the on-site Chart House Restaurant (see "Dining," below). The Borns family, owner-managers, plan to add more bedrooms in the future.

BUNKERS' HILL HOTEL, 7 Commandant Gade, Charlotte Amalie, St. Thomas, USVI 00802. Tel. 809/774-8056. Fax 809/776-8056. 11 rms (all with bath), 4 suites. A/C TV TEL

$ Rates (including continental breakfast): Winter, $80 single; $90 double; $100 suite. Summer, $60 single; $70 double; $80 suite. MC, V. **Parking:** Free.

This clean and centrally situated guest lodge is suitable for anyone on an economy

ST. THOMAS ACCOMMODATIONS

N 0 ━━━━━ 1.5 mi / 2.4 km

ATLANTIC OCEAN

CARIBBEAN SEA

Grass Cay

Pillsbury Sound

Thatch Cay

Leeward Passage

Redbook Bay

Great Bay

Muller Bay **20** **19**

Coupet Bay

Point Pleasant

Coki Point

Smith Bay

Compass Point

Jersey Bay

Rotto Cay

Cas Cay

Patricia Cay

Coki Bay **23**

24 388 38

22 **21**

Redbook 322

32

Tutu Bay

Mandal Road

Magens Road

Magens Bay

Magens Bay

42

386

384

39

Turpentine Run Road

Weymouth Rhymer Hwy.

Bovoni Road

Bolongo Bay **17**

Bolongo Bay

Green Cay

394

Mahogany Run Road

35

Frenchman's Bay Road

Frenchman's **16**

Frenchman's Bay

25 38

CHARLOTTE AMALIE 316

Sugar Estate Road

313

13

14 **15**

Morningstar Bay

Virgin Islands National Park

12

9 **10** **11** **6** **5**

8 **7**

334

2

1

5 **4**

3

St. Thomas Harbor

Frenchtown

Hassel Island

Water Island

Hull Bay Road

St. Peter Mt. Road

40

Solberg Road

Harwood Hwy.

Veterans Dr.

Honeymoon Beach

404

333

37

Crown Mountain Road

Moravian Hwy.

Lindbergh Bay

305

302

Inner Brass Is.

Santa Maria Bay

West End Road

Bordeaux Bay

Botany Bay

Fortuna Road

30

Brewers Bay

Perseverance Bay

Cyril E. King Airport

Lindbergh Bay

The Admiral's Inn **3**
Blackbeard's Castle **10**
Bluebeard's Castle **12**
Bolongo Bay Beach & Tennis Club **17**
Bolongo Bay Villas **17**
Bolongo Elysian Beach Resort **19**

Bolongo Limetree Beach Hotel **16**
Bunkers' Hill Hotel **9**
Danish Chalet Inn **2**
Galleon House **6**
Grand Palazzo **20**
Heritage Manor **7**
Hotel 1829 **11**
Island View Guesthouse **1**

The Mark St. Thomas **8**
Marriott's Frenchman's Reef Beach Resort **14**
Marriott's Morning Star Beach Resort **15**
Miller Manor **5**
Pavilions and Pools **21**
Point Pleasant Resort **23**

Ramada Yacht Haven Hotel & Marina **13**
Sapphire Beach Resort & Marina **22**
Secret Harbour Beach Hotel **18**
Stouffer Grand Beach Resort **24**
Villa Blanca **25**
Windward Passage Hotel **4**

budget who doesn't want to sacrifice comfort and safety. Some of the accommodations share a small kitchenette, and 10 of them contain balconies, some with a view of the city and sea. In 1990, the hotel was upgraded, with a new lobby and improved furnishings. The kindly management prepares meals for guests with advance notice.

DANISH CHALET INN, 9E-9J Nordsidevej (Solberg Rd.), P.O. Box 4319, St. Thomas, USVI 00803. Tel. 809/774-5764, or toll free 800/635-1531. Fax 809/777-4886. 13 rms (5 with bath). TEL
$ Rates (including continental breakfast): Winter, $50 single without bath, $85–$95 single with bath; $75 double without bath, $95 double with bath. Summer, $40–$60 single without bath, $70–$80 single with bath; $60 double without bath, $80 double with bath. MC, V. **Parking:** Free.

Set high above Charlotte Amalie on the western edge of the cruise-ship harbor, a 5-minute walk to the harborfront, this is, in the eyes of many of its fans, one of the most charming bed-and-breakfast hotels on the island. Cozy, family-managed, and friendly, its trio of buildings sits on a steeply inclined acre of land dotted with tropical shrubs and bougainvillea, behind a facade of lattices and modern verandas. The heart and soul of the place is the panoramic terrace, which has a 180-degree view over the cruise ships, an honor bar where every drink costs $1, and a convivial atmosphere created by the establishment's owners, California-bred Frank and Mary Davis. Both are graduates of the Cornell School of Hotel Administration. Bedrooms are neat, clean, and colorful, all but the cheapest of which contain air conditioning and refrigerators. The others have ceiling fans.

Much of this hotel's business stems from its willingness to accept 1-night guests (many other small island hotels insist on bookings of several nights), making it popular as an island beginning or end for cruise-ship passengers.

The establishment has no swimming pool, but it does have a semisecluded Jacuzzi spa for the relaxation of its guests. No meals other than breakfast are served.

GALLEON HOUSE, Government Hill, P.O. Box 6577, Charlotte Amalie, St. Thomas, USVI 00804. Tel. 809/774-6952, or toll free 800/524-2052. Fax 809/774-6952. 14 rms (12 with bath). A/C TV TEL
$ Rates (including continental breakfast): Winter, $59 single without bath, $109 single with bath; $69 double without bath, $119 double with bath. Summer, $49 single without bath, $69 single with bath; $59 double without bath, $79 double with bath. AE, MC, V. **Parking:** Free.

The main attraction of this pleasant little guesthouse is its location, set next to the Hotel 1829 on Government Hill about 1 block from the main shopping section of St. Thomas. To get to the establishment, walk up a long flight of stairs past a neighboring restaurant's veranda to the concrete terrace that doubles as this hotel's reception area. The guest rooms are scattered in several hillside buildings, and each contains a ceiling fan and air conditioning. There's even a small pool on the grounds. Fresh baked goods are offered at breakfast, served with juice and coffee on the veranda overlooking the harbor.

HERITAGE MANOR, 1A Snegle Gade, P.O. Box 90, Charlotte Amalie, St. Thomas, USVI 00804. Tel. 809/774-3003, or toll free 800/828-0757 in the U.S. Fax 809/776-9585. 8 rms (2 with bath), 2 apts. A/C
$ Rates (including continental breakfast in winter only): Winter, $75 single or double without bath; $100 double with bath; $115–$135 apt. Summer, $55 single or double without bath; $75 double with bath; $85–$95 apt. AE, MC, V. **Parking:** Free.

This 150-year-old restored Danish merchant's town house is located in the historical district of Charlotte Amalie. Intimate and personal, it offers well-furnished, comfortable bedrooms and two apartments with kitchens. The

FROMMER'S SMART TRAVELER: HOTELS

VALUE-CONSCIOUS TRAVELERS SHOULD TAKE
ADVANTAGE OF THE FOLLOWING:

1. Off-season reductions. All hotels grant them (from 20% to 60%) from mid-April to mid-December.
2. Greatly reduced rates for children who stay in a parent's room. Sometimes children stay free.
3. Reductions in rates if you pay cash.
4. Accommodation in a West Indian guesthouse in a room with a shared bath.
5. Air-and-land packages, which in the long run usually work out cheaper for you.
6. The Modified American Plan (MAP), which usually works out much cheaper than ordering meals à la carte.
7. Any special packages offered for honeymooners, divers, tennis players, golfers, and so on.

QUESTIONS TO ASK IF YOU'RE ON A BUDGET

1. Is there a surcharge for local or long-distance calls? Usually there is. In some hotels it can be an astonishing 40%.
2. Is service included in the rates quoted, or will 10% to 15% be added to your final bill? It makes a big difference.
3. Is breakfast included? If it's not, it can easily add as much as $70 more per week to your final bill.
4. Is the 7.5% government tax included in the quoted rate? It can make a big difference in your final bill after a few days.

rooms—named Paris, Rome, London, New York, and San Francisco—contain many extras, including fans, hairdryers, and refrigerators. Most of the accommodations have a view of the harbor. The small inn has a freshwater pool installed in a former Danish bakery complete with a chimney.

ISLAND VIEW GUESTHOUSE, 11-C Contant, P.O. Box 1903, St. Thomas, USVI 00803. Tel. 809/774-4270, or toll free 800/524-2023 for reservations only. Fax 809/774-6167. 15 rms (13 with bath). TEL **Directions:** From the airport, turn right to Rte. 33. Then cut left and continue to Scott Free Rd. where you go left and look for the sign.
$ Rates (including continental breakfast): Winter, $58 single without bath, $90 single with bath; $63 double without bath, $95 double with bath. Summer, $40 single without bath, $63 single with bath; $45 double without bath, $68 double with bath. $4 surcharge for 1-night stays. AE, MC, V. **Parking:** Free.
The Island View is located within a steeply inclined neighborhood of private homes and villas about a 7-minute drive west of Charlotte Amalie. Set 545 feet up Crown Mountain, it has sweeping views over Charlotte Amalie and the harbor. Family-owned and managed, it was originally built in the 1960s as a private home. Recently enlarged, it contains main-floor rooms, two without private baths and some poolside rooms, plus six units in a recent addition (three with kitchens and all with balconies). The bedrooms are cooled by breezes and fans, and the newer ones have optional air conditioning. A self-service, open-air bar on the gallery operates on the honor system.

VILLA BLANCA, 4 Raphune Hill, Rte. 38, Charlotte Amalie, St. Thomas,

USVI 00801. Tel. 809/776-0749. Fax 809/779-2661. 12 rms (all with bath and kitchenette). TV

$ Rates (without breakfast): Winter, $115–$125 single; $125–$135 double. Summer, $70–$75 single; $75–$80 double. AE, DC, MC, V. **Parking:** Free.

Small, intimate, and charming, this small-scale hotel lies on 3 secluded acres of hilltop land that connoisseurs claim is some of the most panoramic on the island. Originally built in 1953 as the private home of Christine Cromwell, heiress to the Dodge fortune, its main building served as the private home of its present owner, Blanca Terrasa Smith, between 1973 and 1985. After the death of her husband, Mrs. Smith added a 12-room annex in her garden and opened her grounds to paying guests.

Each of the rooms contains a ceiling fan, a well-equipped kitchenette, and a private balcony or terrace with sweeping views either eastward to St. John or westward to Puerto Rico and the harbor of Charlotte Amalie. No meals of any kind are served on the premises, but nonetheless, a homelike and caring ambience prevails. On the premises are a swimming pool and a large covered patio suitable for quiet reading or socializing. The hotel is 1½ miles east of Charlotte Amalie.

FLAMBOYANT POINT

VERY EXPENSIVE

MARRIOTT'S FRENCHMAN'S REEF BEACH RESORT, Flamboyant Point, Charlotte Amalie, St. Thomas, USVI 00801. Tel. 809/776-8500, or toll free 800/524-2000 in the U.S. Fax 809/776-3054. 421 rms (all with bath), 18 suites. A/C MINIBAR TV TEL **Transportation:** Water or land taxi from Charlotte Amalie.

$ Rates: Winter, $260–$295 single or double; from $443 suite. Summer, $165–$190 single or double; from $315 suite. MAP $52 per person extra. AE, DC, MC, V. **Parking:** Free.

The Frenchmen's Reef, lying 3 miles east of Charlotte Amalie, has a winning southern position on a projection of land overlooking both the harbor at Charlotte Amalie and the sea. The hotel stands in such a conspicuous position that it's impossible to miss. Whatever your vacation needs, chances are they'll be met at The Reef. To reach the private beach, you take a glass-enclosed elevator. The bedrooms vary greatly, but most are traditionally furnished.

Dining/Entertainment: Seafood with a continental flair is served in Windows on the Harbour, which resembles the inside of a cruise ship and has a view of the harbor. You can also get meals at the Lighthouse Bar, once an actual lighthouse. In the evening, the Top of the Reef, a supper club, offers entertainment, or you can go to La Terrazza lounge. In addition, Caesar's offers an Italian cuisine at surfside.

The Oriental Terrace features Japanese exhibition cooking on the Teppanyaki Grill and traditional Chinese wok cooking from the Pacific Rim. The Raw Bar offers fresh seafood appetizers and light meals daily from 11am to 11pm.

Services: Room service, full-service beauty salon, unisex hair salon, drugstore, valet, babysitters, travel and tour desks.

Facilities: Two giant swimming pools, suntanning areas, poolside bar, four tennis courts, water sports (snorkeling, scuba diving, sailing, deep-sea fishing), private beach.

MARRIOTT'S MORNING STAR BEACH RESORT, Frenchman's Reef Beach Resort, Flamboyant Point, Charlotte Amalie, St. Thomas, USVI 00802. Tel. 809/776-8500, or toll free 800/BEACH CLUB in the U.S. Fax 809/776-8500. 96 rms (all with bath). A/C MINIBAR TV TEL **Transportation:** Water or land taxi from Charlotte Amalie.

$ Rates: Winter, $325–$425 single or double. Summer, $200–$260 single or double. MAP $55 extra. AE, DC, MC, V. **Parking:** Free.

⭐ Both the public areas and the plushly outfitted accommodations here are among the most desirable on the island. They were built on the landscaped flatlands near the beach of the well-known Frenchman's Reef Beach Resort, as the elegant twin neighbor of the older hotel. The resort has five cruciform buildings, each containing between 16 and 24 units. Guests have the amenities and attractions of a large hotel nearby, yet maintain the privacy of an exclusive enclave. Each accommodation has rattan furniture, a color scheme of lilac, plum, and red mahogany, and views of the garden or beach. Swimming can be supplemented with a wide array of water sports.

Dining/Entertainment: The popular Tavern on the Beach overlooks the ocean and serves regional American cuisine. Tavern serves breakfast from 7:30 to 11:30am and dinner from 6:30 to 10:30pm (closed for dinner on Tuesday). Caesar's Ristorante, located at the water's edge on Morning Star Beach, serves lunch, pizza, and snacks from 11am to 5pm. Dinner is served under the stars with a southern Italian menu from 6 to 10:30pm (closed for dinner on Friday). The Sand Bar is an ideal spot for sunset cocktails, and a variety of restaurants and bars are also available at the adjoining Marriott's Frenchman's Reef Beach Resort (see above).

Services: Room service, babysitting, valet, and all the services provided by Frenchman's Reef next door.

Facilities: The two giant swimming pools, four tennis courts, water-sports program, and private beach offered by Frenchman's Reef are shared by Morning Star.

EAST END

VERY EXPENSIVE

BOLONGO ELYSIAN BEACH RESORT, 8-1 Estate Nazareth, Cowpet Bay, P.O. Box 7337, St. Thomas, USVI 00801. Tel. 809/779-2844, or toll free 800/524-4746. Fax 809/775-3208. 175 rms. A/C MINIBAR TV TEL **Transportation:** Hotel-owned open-air shuttle.

$ Rates (including continental breakfast): Winter, $265–$405 single; $275–$415 double. Summer, from $200 single or double. AE, DC, MC, V. **Parking:** Free.

⭐ This elegant resort opened in 1989 on Cowpet Bay between a pair of upscale condo complexes in the East End. The resort has a European kind of glamour, and it's within a 20-minute drive of Charlotte Amalie. The thoughtfully planned bedrooms have kitchens and large balconies, and some offer sleeping lofts reached by a spiral staircase. The decor is sophisticated and tropical, with white ceramic-tile floors, rattan and bamboo furnishings, and natural-wood ceilings. Rooms are in a bevy of four-story buildings connected to lushly landscaped gardens.

Dining/Entertainment: A member of the Bolongo Bay Beach Resorts, the hotel offers elegant international dining in its Royal Palm Court Restaurant, and also has weekly barbecues on the terrace. Other dining choices include the Oasis right on the beach, serving light fare. Drinks are enjoyed either at the pool bar or in the Royal Palm Court Lounge. In season, live entertainment is offered, as well as theme nights such as West Indian Carnival night.

Services: Open-air shuttle to town, room service, masseur, babysitting.

Facilities: Fitness center, swimming pool, snorkel gear, canoes, Sunfish, tennis court.

GRAND PALAZZO, Great Bay, St. Thomas, USVI 00802. Tel. 809/775-3333, or toll free 800/283-8666. Fax 809/775-4444. 152 oceanview suites (all with bath). A/C TV TEL MINIBAR

$ Rates: Winter, $450–$495 junior suite for 2; $785–$865 1-bedroom suite for 2;

Ⓕ FROMMER'S COOL FOR KIDS: HOTELS

Sapphire Beach Resort (see p. 73). This is one of your best bets, as the resort does more for kids than most hotels on the island, and the sweeping expanses of one of the finest beaches on the island gives them plenty of room to play. Children under 12 stay and eat free when accompanied by their parents. There are even supervised activities at the Little Gems Kids Klub.

Secret Harbour (see p. 74). Children under 12 stay free at this hotel opening onto Nazareth Bay. Many units have kitchenettes where families can prepare light meals. Beach facilities are at the doorstep.

Stouffer Grand Beach Resort (see p. 74). This big resort offers a daily year-round children's program free for guests. Children aged 3 to 14 are invited to join in the fun, directed by counselor-supervised trained personnel. There's also a kiddie pool.

Bolongo Bay Villas (see p. 75). Ideal for families, these villas have programs designed to give parents some time off. Its Kid's Korner Center provides planned day activities and lunches and dinners when children are not with their parents.

$1,125–$1,235 2-bedroom suite for 4. Summer, $210 junior suite for 2; $420 1-bedroom suite for 2; $630 2-bedroom suite for 4. MAP supplement $60–$65 per person winter, $55 summer. AE, DC, MC, V. **Parking:** Free.

⭐ The recent purchase of one of the last large tracts of seafront land on the island (15 acres) was viewed as a minor triumph. Shortly after its acquisition, the developers of this luxury hotel immediately hired topnotch architects, decorators, and landscape experts to create what is today probably the most desirable hotel in St. Thomas. The hotel is near Red Hook, about 4½ miles southeast of Charlotte Amalie.

Opened in August of 1992, its accommodations lie within a half-dozen three-story villas designed with Italian Renaissance motifs and pastel versions of Mediterranean colors like yellow ocher and burnt sienna. These encircle a freshwater pond, home to a colony of Bahamian ducks. Guests register in the "reception palazzo," whose arches and accessories were inspired by a palace in Venice, before heading to bedrooms whose themes are unabashedly European. These contain all the electronic amenities you'd expect (including a digital safe), marble bathrooms, and many thoughtful touches. Public rooms carry nautical themes of navy blue and white, interspersed lavishly with verdant themes from the surrounding gardens. The largest of the two swimming pools is designed such that it appears to stretch into the sea.

Dining/Entertainment: The Palm Terrace, set beneath soaring rows of rhythmically graceful arcades, is the more formal of the hotel's two restaurants. Equally appealing is the Café Vecchio, whose lavish murals depict the botanical diversity of a latter-day garden of Babylon. On the premises are a trio of bars, one of which has a live pianist.

Services: 24-hour room service, top-notch tennis instructors, massage, concierge.

Facilities: Air-conditioned health club/gym, free use of Hobie Cats and Sunfish, a 53-foot catamaran (*The Lady Lynsey*) for cocktail sails, four tennis courts, two swimming pools.

PAVILIONS & POOLS, Rte. 6, Sapphire Beach, St. Thomas, USVI

00802. Tel. 809/775-6110, or toll free 800/524-2001. Fax 809/775-6110. 25 units (all with bath). A/C TV TEL **Transportation:** Taxi.
$ Rates (including continental breakfast in winter only): Winter, $230–$255 single or double. Summer, $175–$195 single or double. AE, DC, MC, V. **Parking:** Free.

Ideal for a honeymoon, this is the ultimate in small-scale luxury—you have your own villa with floor-to-ceiling glass doors opening directly onto your own private swimming pool. The resort, 7 miles east of Charlotte Amalie, is a string of condominium units, tastefully built and furnished. After checking in and following a wooden pathway to your attached villa, you don't have to see another soul until you check out, if that is your desire. The fence and gate are high, and your space opens into tropical greenery. Around your own swimming pool is an encircling deck. Inside, a high room divider screens a full, well-equipped kitchen. Each bedroom has its own style, with plenty of closets behind louvered doors. The bath has a garden shower where you can bathe surrounded by greenery and protected from Peeping Toms. The resort adjoins Sapphire Bay, which has an excellent beach. Honeymooners should inquire about packages.

Dining/Entertainment: A small bar and barbecue area is set against a wall on the reception terrace, where rum parties and cookouts are held. Informal, simple meals are served only on Tuesday and Friday. Occasionally a musician or singer entertains.

Services: Helpful front desk, day sails, restaurant reservations.

Facilities: Free snorkeling gear, tennis courts.

POINT PLEASANT RESORT, Estate Smith Bay No. 4, St. Thomas, USVI 00802. Tel. 809/775-7200, or toll free 800/524-2300. Fax 809/776-5694. 134 rms (all with bath). A/C MINIBAR TV TEL **Transportation:** Taxi.
$ Rates: Winter, $220–$250 single; $240–$350 double. Summer, $145–$155 single; $175–$240 double. Breakfast $10 extra. AE, MC, V. **Parking:** Free.

This is a very private, unique resort on Water Bay, on the northeastern tip of St. Thomas. From your living-room gallery, you look out on a Virgin collection—Tortola, St. John, and Jost Van Dyke. The complex is set on a 15-acre bluff with flowering shrubbery, century plants, frangipani trees, secluded nature trails, old rock formations, and lookout points. Some of the villa-style accommodations have kitchens, and the furnishings are light and airy, mostly with rattan and floral fabrics.

Dining/Entertainment: The restaurant, Agave Terrace, is one of the finest on the island, and offers three meals a day. The cuisine is a blend of nouvelle American dishes with Caribbean specialties, featuring seafood. Local entertainment is provided several nights a week.

Services: Complimentary use of a car 4 hours per day, shopping and dinner shuttle available.

Facilities: Three freshwater swimming pools, lit tennis courts, snorkeling equipment, Sunfish sailboats.

SAPPHIRE BEACH RESORT & MARINA, Rte. 38, Smith Bay Rd., P.O. Box 8088, St. Thomas, USVI 00801. Tel. 809/775-6100, or toll free 800/524-2090. Fax 809/775-4024. 171 suites and villas (all with bath). A/C TV TEL **Transportation:** Taxi.
$ Rates: Winter, $250–$345 double suite, $330–$485 double villa. Summer, $168–$198 double suite, $208–$244 double villa. Extra person $25. Children 12 and under stay free in parents' room. MAP $50 extra. AE, DC, MC, V. **Parking:** Free.

One of the finest modern luxury resorts in the Caribbean, this secluded retreat in the East End merits an extended stay. Guests can arrive by yacht and occupy a berth in the 67-slip marina or else take a superb suite or villa.

The accommodations open onto a horseshoe bay, with one of St. Thomas's most spectacular beaches, and exude casual elegance. The beaches are actually two ivory sand crescents broken by the coral-reef peninsula of Prettyklip Point. The one-bedroom suites have fully equipped kitchens with microwaves, bedroom areas, living/dining rooms with queen-size sofa beds, and large, fully tiled outdoor galleries with lounge furniture. Villas are on two levels, the main one containing the same amenities as the suites while the upper level includes a second full bath, a bedroom and sitting area with a queen-size sofa bed, and a sun deck with outdoor furniture. Suites accommodate one to four guests, whereas villas are suitable for up to six guests.

Dining/Entertainment: Meals are served at the beach bar, and at night you can dine at the Seagrape, along the seashore, one of the island's finest eating places. Sometimes a 5-piece band is brought in for dancing under the stars.

Services: Beach towels, daily chamber service, guest services desk, babysitting.

Facilities: Snorkeling equipment, Sunfish sailboats, windsurfing boards, four all-weather tennis courts, ¼-acre freshwater pool, diving center.

SECRET HARBOUR BEACH HOTEL, 2H25 Estate Nazareth, Nazareth Bay, P.O. Box 7576, St. Thomas, USVI. Tel. 809/775-6550, or toll free 800/524-2250. Fax 809/775-1501. 60 suites (all with bath). A/C TV TEL **Transportation:** Vitran bus.

$ Rates (including continental breakfast): Winter, $235 studio double; $305 1-bedroom suite; $440 2-bedroom suite for up to four. Summer, $169 studio double; $199 1-bedroom suite; $290 2-bedroom suite for up to four. AE, MC, V. **Parking:** Free.

This all-suite resort is on the beach at Nazareth Bay, right outside Red Hook. The four contemporary buildings have a southwestern exposure and lie only a 20-minute ride from Charlotte Amalie. You'll think you've arrived at a South Seas island beach resort amid tall palms. Each unit has a private deck (or patio) and full kitchen. There are three kinds of accommodations: studio apartments with a bed-sitting-room area, patio, and dressing-room area; one-bedroom suites with a living/dining area, a separate bedroom, plus a sun deck; and the most luxurious, a two-bedroom suite with two baths and a private living room.

Dining/Entertainment: Tamarind by the Sea, on the beach, offers open-air dining, serving dinner daily from 6:30 to 10pm. The Secret Harbour Beach Café offers breakfast and lunch on an outdoor terrace or in the gazebo. Both restaurants have bars for drinks. A weekly manager's cocktail party for guests features local music, rum punches, and hors d'oeuvres.

Services: Babysitting, daily maid service.

Facilities: Five-star PADI dive center and water-sports facility on the beach, catamaran for sail charters, two all-weather tennis courts, fitness center, freshwater pool, and Jacuzzi.

STOUFFER GRAND BEACH RESORT, Smith Bay Rd., Rte. 38, P.O. Box 8267, St. Thomas, USVI 00801. Tel. 809/775-1510, or toll free 800/468-3571 in the U.S. Fax 809/775-3757. 254 rms, 36 suites. A/C MINIBAR TV TEL **Transportation:** Taxi.

$ Rates: Winter, $319–$439 single or double; from $595 suite. Summer, $219–$319 single or double; from $450 suite. MAP $65 per person extra. AE, DC, MC, V. **Parking:** Free.

Seven miles northeast of Charlotte Amalie, perched on a steep hillside above a 1,000-foot white sandy beach, this resort occupies 34 acres on the northeast shore of St. Thomas. Accommodations are in two separate areas, poolside and hillside. The two-story town house suites and one-bedroom suites have whirlpool spas, and all units are stylishly outfitted. Each accommodation has satellite color TV with HBO and Spectravision, a hairdryer, robe, safe, and an open balcony or patio.

Dining/Entertainment: You can enjoy beachfront breakfast, lunch and dinner at Baywinds, featuring continental and Caribbean cuisine. Dinner and an award-winning Sunday brunch are served in Smugglers Bar and Grill. Lighter fare is offered at the poolside snack bar. For cocktails, live entertainment, and dancing, there's the Baywinds Lounge.

Services: Babysitting, laundry, tropical garden tour, 23-hour room service, twice-daily chamber service, concierge, newspaper and coffee with wake-up call.

Facilities: Two swimming pools, free daily scuba and snorkel lessons, free Sunfish sailboats, kayaks, Windsurfers, snorkel equipment, on-site full-service dive shop, water-sports center (where you can arrange for day sails, deep-sea fishing and other excursions), six lit tennis courts, exercise facility, nearby 18-hole golf course, daily children's program, newsstand, gift shop, boutique, beauty salon.

BOLONGO BAY

There is a unique trio of resorts here, each one with a different character. Their facilities are interconnected by shuttle-bus service, and among the three, you'll find an attractive sampling of many of the diversions and pleasures of St. Thomas.

The three resorts include Bolongo Bay Beach and Tennis Club, Bolongo Bay Villas, and the Bolongo Limetree Beach Hotel. The same firm also operates Bolongo Elysian Beach Resort (see "East End," above).

The winner of several innkeeping awards since it was first established in 1974, this 34-acre complex was created by Dick and Joyce Doumeng. Today they are assisted by several of their children and a devoted staff. Families with children appreciate the complex's day-care center and a professionally supervised entertainment and restaurant center for children aged 3 to 12.

VERY EXPENSIVE

BOLONGO BAY BEACH & TENNIS CLUB, Bolongo Estate 50, P.O. Box 7337, Bolongo Bay, St. Thomas, USVI 00801. Tel. 809/779-2844, or toll free 800/524-4746. Fax 809/775-3208. 78 rms. A/C MINIBAR TV TEL **Transportation:** Vitran bus.

$ Rates (including continental breakfast): Winter, $180–$205 single; $190–$215 double. Summer, $135–$155 single; $145–$165 double. AE, DC, MC, V. **Parking:** Free.

Bolongo Bay is a unique property on St. Thomas—it's a resort complex with a beachside location where you stay in a comfortable accommodation with up-to-date amenities. After only 1 day here, you'll know why it's called "Club Everything." The 10-acre property has probably welcomed more honeymooners than any other hotel on the island. It was built in a series of interconnected bungalows in an arc that follows the shoreline of a 600-foot white sand beach studded with palm trees. Each unit has a private balcony, comfortably unpretentious furniture, and a private kitchenette. The social center is a cabaña-type bar, restaurant, and pool complex set near the edge of the beach. Water sports and an introductory scuba lesson, along with an all-day sail to St. John, are included in the rate. When booking, ask about special all-inclusive packages, or honeymoon or dive packages.

Dining/Entertainment: The restaurants include Lord Rumbottoms, specializing in prime ribs and steaks; Viola's Kitchen, featuring West Indian cuisine; and Coconut Henry's Smokehouse, the beach grill. Theme nights include West Indian Carnival Night, and occasional live entertainment is offered in winter.

Services: Open-air shuttle to town, supervised activities for children, babysitting.

Facilities: Swimming pool, snorkel gear, paddleboats, canoes, Sunfish sailboats, and St. Thomas Diving Center (see "Sports and Recreation," below).

BOLONGO BAY VILLAS, Estate Bolongo No. 50, P.O. Box 73371, St. Thomas, USVI 00801. Tel. 809/779-2844, or toll free 800/524-4746. Fax 809/775-3208. 70 suites. A/C MINIBAR TV TEL **Transportation:** Vitran bus.

$ Rates (including continental breakfast): Winter, mini-suite $225–$240 single, $235–$250 double; 1-bedroom suite, $265–$290 single, $275–$300 double; 2-bedroom suite for up to 4, $325–$350. Summer, mini-suite $165–$170 single, $175–$180 double; 1-bedroom suite, $185–$195 single, $195–$205 double; 2-bedroom suite for up to 4, $225–$250. AE, DC, MC, V. **Parking:** Free.

Adjoining the previously recommended Bolongo Bay Beach & Tennis Club (see above), this all-suite resort is one of the most luxurious on the island. It offers units with ocean or beachfront views, along with full kitchens and balconies. Other amenities include king-size or double beds, plus electronic safes. These units are suitable for couples or families wishing for privacy. The full resort privileges of Bolongo Bay Beach & Tennis Club, as well as their dining and entertainment offerings, services, and facilities, are available to guests who register here. Ask about the all-inclusive, honeymoon, or dive packages.

BOLONGO LIMETREE BEACH HOTEL, 100 Frenchman's Bay Estate, P.O. Box 7337, Frenchman's Bay Rd. (Rte. 30), St. Thomas, USVI 00801. Tel. 809/779-2844, or toll free 800/524-4746. Fax 809/774-3208. 84 rms. A/C TV TEL **Transportation:** Taxi.

$ Rates (including continental breakfast): Winter, $180–$195 single; $190–$204 double. Summer, $135–$150 single; $145–$160 double. AE, DC, MC, V. **Parking:** Free.

This resort, just 10 minutes from Charlotte Amalie, opens onto Frenchman's Cove. Its comfortable accommodations are in three-story villas set on two dozen beautifully landscaped acres. The spacious and comfortable accommodations are decorated in an island motif, and some contain sleeping lofts. Included in the rate are water sports, an introductory scuba lesson, and an all-day sail to St. John. All-inclusive packages are featured, along with honeymoon and dive packages (inquire when booking).

Dining/Entertainment: The resort is one of the major entertainment centers on the island, offering both Paradise One/Paradise Two nightclubs and Iggie's (see "Evening Entertainment," below). The hotel's Caribbean Lobster House features fresh locally caught lobster and a wide variety of local fish and shellfish. Iggie's serves light fare (see "Light and Casual Food," below). Live entertainment is offered in season, and the hotel features theme nights, such as West Indian Carnival Night.

Services: Open-air shuttle to Charlotte Amalie, babysitting.

Facilities: Exercise and workout room, swimming pool, Jacuzzi, two tennis courts, snorkel gear, paddleboats, canoes, Sunfish, and sailboats.

4. DINING

The cuisine in St. Thomas is among the best in the entire West Indies. Unfortunately, prices are high, and many of the best spots can be reached by taxi only. With a few exceptions, the finest and most charming restaurants aren't in Charlotte Amalie but are out on the island.

St. Thomas has a wide range of cuisines, including American as well as such other familiar cuisines as Mexican or Chinese. Try some of the local dishes, too, especially the fish, including "ole wife" and yellowtail. Cooked native style, the fish is served with a creole mixture of peppers, onions, and tomatoes. The best side dish is *fungi* (pronounced *foon*-gee), made with okra and cornmeal.

The best local soups are *bullfoot,* made with meat and vegetables and seasoned with herbs and spices, and *callaloo* made with ham hock, crab, and greens. Most main dishes consist of either fish, goat, pork, chicken, or conch. Local restaurants

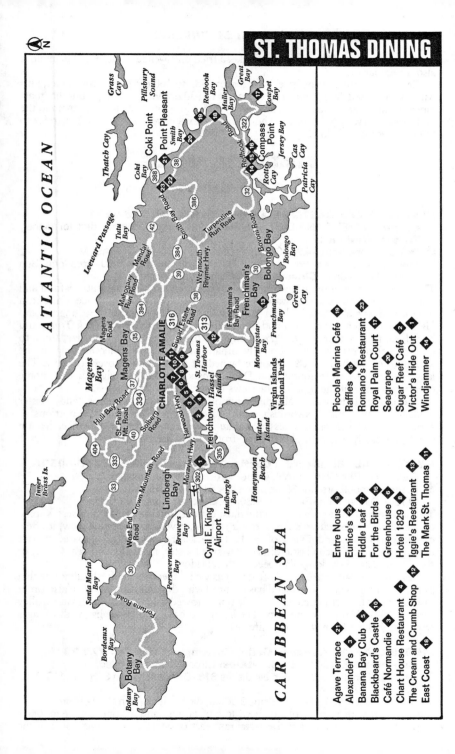

ST. THOMAS DINING

ATLANTIC OCEAN

CARIBBEAN SEA

Agave Terrace 21
Alexander's 3
Banana Bay Club 5
Blackbeard's Castle 10
Café Normandie 3
Chart House Restaurant 4
The Cream and Crumb Shop 12
East Coast 18

Entre Nous 9
Eunice's 22
Fiddle Leaf 7
For the Birds 16
Greenhouse 6
Hotel 1829 8
Iggie's Restaurant 13
The Mark St. Thomas 11

Piccola Marina Café 19
Raffles 15
Romano's Restaurant 17
Royal Palm Court 7
Seagrape 20
Sugar Reef Café 2
Victor's Hide Out 1
Windjammer 14

serve the most popular bread, johnnycake, a fried unleavened bread. Fried plantain is also a popular dish.

Restaurants rated "expensive" charge from $35 to $60 per person for dinner, plus wine. Those rated "moderate" can charge up to $30 or more for dinner, but the smart diner can also eat in most of them for only $25, plus wine, which places them in the budget category, at least for St. Thomas. For inexpensive meals under $25, refer to "Local Favorites," below.

CHARLOTTE AMALIE

EXPENSIVE

BLACKBEARD'S CASTLE, Blackbeard's Hill. Tel. 776-1234.
   Cuisine: AMERICAN/SEAFOOD. **Reservations:** Recommended for dinner.
   Transportation: Taxi.
$ **Prices:** Appetizers $4.75–$12; main dishes $16.50–$27.50. AE, MC, V.
   Open: Lunch Mon–Fri 11:30am–2:30pm; dinner daily 6:30–10:30pm; Sun brunch 11am–3pm. **Closed:** Mon for dinner in summer.

This elegant dining room in the previously recommended hotel presents seafood and nouvelle American cuisine. Awarded a trio of gold medals for ambience, Caribbean dishes, and overall food in local culinary contests, owners Bob Harrington and Henrique Konzen serve lunch and Sunday brunch with the *New York Times* and board games. In winter live jazz is enjoyed from Tuesday to Saturday, 8pm to midnight. Don't miss the elaborately ornate cast-iron chandelier hanging in the anteroom of the bar, which was once owned by the Delano-Roosevelt family. The laughing cherubs were found in a Danish manor house and given a new home overlooking one of the best harbor views on the island.

Specials include veal scaloppine; jumbo Gulf shrimp, scallops, and lobster medaillons; and grilled swordfish steak. Pastas are available in half portions as appetizers. Lunches, slightly less elaborate and about one-third the price, feature salads, delicately seasoned platters, and frothy rum-based drinks.

ENTRE NOUS, Bluebeard's Castle, Bluebeard's Hill. Tel. 776-4050.
   Cuisine: FRENCH/ITALIAN. **Reservations:** Recommended.
$ **Prices:** Appetizers $6–$9; main dishes $17–$27. AE, MC, V.
   Open: Dinner Mon–Sat 6:30–9:30pm. **Closed:** Sept.

This long-established restaurant in the most famous hotel of St. Thomas serves some of the island's finest cuisine. An open-air restaurant with a panoramic view, it offers candlelight dinners and a view of the harbor. Caesar salad will be prepared at your table, followed by such classic dishes as Maine lobster, medaillons of veal Oscar, or roast Long Island duckling flambéed with calvados.

Seafood specialties are heavily featured as well, especially the fresh salmon with a pink peppercorn sauce. The menu has changed with the times, and you can also order dishes low in fat. Of course, all that dieting is tossed aside when the dessert trolley arrives. Baked Alaska is a specialty. The hotel also has a good wine list, with vintages from everywhere from Italy to California.

FIDDLE LEAF, 31 Kongens Gade, Government Hill. Tel. 775-2810.
   Cuisine: AMERICAN. **Reservations:** Strongly recommended.
$ **Prices:** Appetizers $6–$9; main dishes $18–$27; lunch from $15. AE, DC, MC, V.
   Open: Lunch Mon–Fri 11:30am–2:30pm; dinner Tues–Sun 6:30–10pm.

Lushly filled with verdant plants, with lots of lattices and an open, contemporary Caribbean decor, this imaginative restaurant east of Main Street serves some of the most deliciously creative food on the island. Nestled next to Hotel 1829, it offers a menu that changes every week according to the availability of ingredients from the U.S. mainland. Especially good are the fresh fish, rack of lamb with pecan crust, sautéed shrimp West Indies, the flavorful salads sometimes prepared at tableside, and a succulent version of filet mignon. The dessert specialty is chocolate terrine with raspberry sauce. Every Friday and Saturday live piano music will accompany your meal.

HOTEL 1829, Kongens Gade. Tel. 776-1829.
 Cuisine: CONTINENTAL. **Reservations:** Recommended, but not accepted more than 1 day in advance.
$ **Prices:** Appetizers $5–$12.50; main dishes $23.50–$36.50. AE, DC, MC, V.
 Open: Dinner Mon–Sat 6–10pm.
Hotel 1829 (see "Accommodations," above) has some of the finest food in St. Thomas. Diners walk up the hill east of the post office and climb the stairs of this old structure, and then head for the attractive bar for a before-dinner drink. Dining is on a terrace or in the main room whose walls are made from ships' ballast and which is cooled by ceiling fans. The floor is made of 18th-century Moroccan tiles.

The cuisine has a distinctively European twist, with many dishes prepared and served from trolleys beside your table. For an appetizer, try assorted seafood cocktails, or one of the velvety-smooth soups such as cold cucumber or lobster bisque. Fish and meat dishes are usually excellent, and include such choices as filet of yellowtail, snapper amandine, roast rack of lamb with rosemary hollandaise, and pasta paella. The chateaubriand for two is a house specialty. Dessert might include an array of soufflés, such as chocolate, amaretto, and raspberry.

THE MARK ST. THOMAS, Blackbeard's Hill. Tel. 774-5511.
 Cuisine: CONTINENTAL. **Reservations:** Recommended.
$ **Prices:** Appetizers $4.75–$10; main dishes $17.25–$22.50. AE, DC, MC, V.
 Open: Dinner daily 5:30–10pm. **Closed:** Sun in summer.

⭐ This restaurant in the previously recommended inn has quickly become known as one of the finest in Charlotte Amalie. Guests dine on an open-air terrace in a room overlooking the harbor. Arrive early for a predinner drink in the hotel's Great Room. Built in 1785, the Mark was once a private residence for the many sea captains, traders, and merchants who passed through here.

The chef, among the finest on the island, uses the freshest available ingredients for his classic dishes. Begin with a selection of *tapas* (Spanish hors d'oeuvres), including such appetizers as cold Chinese noodles with sesame or a carrot blini with sour cream and caviar. Pan-fried crab cakes are also recommended. For a main dish, try roast game hen with mango chutney or braised red snapper filet with a corn and green papaya ragoût. Roast duck with a cassis sauce is also prepared. The wine list has a good selection of both Stateside and French vintages. White chocolate and pear mousse is the dessert specialty.

MODERATE

BANANA BAY CLUB, Windward Passage Hotel, Veterans Dr. Tel. 774-5200.
 Cuisine: INTERNATIONAL. **Reservations:** Not required. **Transportation:** Vitran bus.
$ **Prices:** Lunch appetizers $3–$5, lunch entrées $3.75–$8.50; dinner appetizers $3.50–$5.50, dinner entrées $9.75–$18.75. AE, DC, MC, V.
 Open: Lunch daily 11am–5pm; dinner daily 6:30–10pm.

FROMMER'S SMART TRAVELER: RESTAURANTS

VALUE-CONSCIOUS DINERS SHOULD CONSIDER THE FOLLOWING:

1. Daily specials or fixed price meals, which are often cheaper than the regular fare on the à la carte menu.
2. The cost of alcohol. Your tab will mount rapidly with liquor and wine, especially. Have your cocktails before happy hour ends (usually 7pm at most places).
3. A meal at a West Indian restaurant, such as Victor's Hide Out and Eunice's. These restaurants are invariably cheaper than the French/continental restaurants.
4. Having a light lunch of sandwiches and hamburgers at one of the many beach bars and cafés during the day and saving your big meal for the evening.
5. Whether service is included. Most restaurants add 10% to 15% to the bill, and there's no need to tip unless service has been very good.

At lunch, you'll sit near the splashing waters of the largest fountain in St. Thomas, in a sheltered atrium where the crowds, heat, and congestion of Charlotte Amalie will seem very far away. The conviviality of the nearby Atrium Bar adds energy and possible companionship. In the evening, guests enjoy the option of service within a stylish inner dining room.

The flavorful specialties include conch fritters, several different soups (including clam chowder), baby back ribs, sautéed conch, seafood platter, and filets of the catch of the day (usually red snapper and tuna). For dessert, many guests come here just to enjoy the chef's banana split.

GREENHOUSE, Veterans Dr. Tel. 774-7998.
Cuisine: AMERICAN. **Reservations:** Not required. **Transportation:** Vitran bus.
$ Prices: Appetizers $4–$6.75; main courses $4.25–$19. AE, MC, V.
Open: Breakfast daily 7–11am; lunch daily 11am–5pm; dinner daily 5–9:30pm.
Fronted with big windows which flood the plant-filled interior with sun, this all-purpose waterfront restaurant has a format which changes throughout the day. A breakfast menu of eggs, sausages, and bacon will cost from around $5. This segues into lunches and dinners that might include hamburgers, pastas, club sandwiches, fried fish filets, and a selection of jerked Jamaican meats. Appetizers range from St. Thomas crab cakes to gazpacho, followed by the fresh catch of the day, which depends on the weather and the season. The chef is also known for Caribbean house specialties, many of which owe a heavy debt to Jamaica. Happy hour, every day from 4:30 to 6:30pm, includes such half-priced libations as strawberry daiquiris and banana coladas. After 10pm the place devotes its energies to a nightlife venue (see "Evening Entertainment," below).

FRENCHTOWN

MODERATE

ALEXANDER'S, rue de St. Barthélemy, Frenchtown. Tel. 776-4211.

Cuisine: AUSTRIAN/ITALIAN. **Reservations:** Recommended. **Transportation:** Vitran bus.
$ Prices: Appetizers $5.25–$8.50; main dishes $11.50–$19. AE, MC, V.
Open: Lunch Mon–Sat 11:30am–2:30pm; dinner Mon–Sat 5:30–10pm.
Alexander's will accommodate you in air-conditioned comfort with picture windows overlooking the harbor. Named for its Austrian-born owner, Alexander Treml, the small restaurant offers Austrian specialties with flair. There's a heavy emphasis on seafood dishes, including conch schnitzel. Other dishes from the Middle European kitchen include a mouth-watering Wiener Schnitzel, Nürnberger Rostbraten, goulash, and homemade pâté. For dessert, you might try the homemade apple strudel or the richly caloric Schwarzwald torte. Midday meals consist of a variety of crêpes, quiches, and a daily chef's special.

At both lunch and dinner, the menu offers a selection of at least 15 different pasta dishes. The establishment's bar is open from 11:30am to midnight.

CAFE NORMANDIE, rue de St. Barthélemy, Frenchtown. Tel. 774-1622.
Cuisine: FRENCH. **Reservations:** Recommended. **Transportation:** Taxi.
$ Prices: Appetizers $8.50–$20; fixed-price dinner $28–$38. AE, MC, V.
Open: Dinner daily 6–10pm. **Closed:** Mon in summer.
The fixed-price meal offered here is one of the best dining values on the island: It begins with soup, although you have a choice of ordering an à la carte appetizer. Then you're served a salad and sorbet before your main course, which you select from specialties ranging from lobster Mornay to the poached catch of the day in white wine. The dessert special (not featured on the fixed-price meal) is their original chocolate fudge pie. The restaurant is air-conditioned, and the glow of candlelight makes it quite elegant. It's beautifully run, and the service is excellent. There is also a relaxed informality about the dress code, but you shouldn't show up in a bathing suit.

CHART HOUSE RESTAURANT, at the Admiral's Inn, Villa Olga, Frenchtown. Tel. 774-4262.
Cuisine: STEAKS. **Reservations:** Not required. **Transportation:** Taxi.
$ Prices: Appetizers $4.55–$8.75; main dishes $16.75–$24.25. AE, DC, MC, V.
Open: Dinner Sun–Thurs 5–10pm, Fri 5–11pm.
The stripped-down 19th-century villa that contains the Chart House was the Russian consulate during the island's Danish administration. It lies a short distance beyond the most densely populated area of Frenchtown village, but it has a completely separate management from the Admiral's Inn. The dining gallery is a spacious open terrace fronting the sea.

Cocktails start daily at 5pm, when the bartender breaks out the ingredients for his special drink known as a Bailey's banana colada.

The Chart House features the best salad bar on the island, with a choice of 30 to 40 items, which comes with the dinner. Menu choices range from chicken to Australian lobster tail. This chain is known for serving the finest cut of prime rib anywhere. For dessert, order the famous Chart House "mud pie."

SUGAR REEF CAFE, 17 Crown Bay. Tel. 776-4466.
Cuisine: SEAFOOD. **Reservations:** Not required.
$ Prices: Appetizers $4.50–$9.50; main dishes $12.50–$29.50. AE, MC, V.
Open: Lunch daily 11:30am–2:30pm; dinner daily 6–10pm.
Opening onto the East Gregerie Channel just west of Frenchtown, this restaurant is a good choice for a quiet afternoon of boat watching. Guests anchor at the mahogany bar beneath mulberry-colored ceiling beams and swirling fans in a breezy open-sided pavilion. Drinks are served here all day and often late into the night. Lunch is likely to

include a choice of deli sandwiches, a West Indian specialty of the day, and omelets. The dinner menu features such dishes as Caribbean lobster, sautéed veal medaillons with a whole-grain mustard sauce, grilled filet mignon, and the Sugar Reef fresh catch of the day. The chef is known for his dessert soufflés.

COMPASS POINT

MODERATE

FOR THE BIRDS, Scott Beach, near Compass Point, off Rte. 32. Tel. 775-6431.
   Cuisine: MEXICAN/SEAFOOD/BARBECUE. **Reservations:** Not required.
   Transportation: Taxi.
$ **Prices:** Appetizers $3.50–$8; main dishes $10–$30. AE, MC, V.
   Open: Lunch daily 11am–3pm; dinner daily 6–10:30pm.
Set in a green-roofed bungalow, this pleasant restaurant offers reasonably priced, well-prepared food in gargantuan helpings. A few steps from the restaurant's big windows, the surf and a sandy beach beckon. Spicy tempters include a dinner platter smothered with heaps of nachos or onion rings, a plate of the best baby back ribs on the island, filet mignon, and southern fried catfish. There's also a selection of such Mexican specialties as beef or chicken enchiladas, chimichangas, and burritos. Margaritas are huge, 46 ounces, and beer comes in mason jars. Entertainment, such as live rock and roll, is sometimes featured.

RAFFLES, 41 Frydenhoj, Compass Point, off Rte. 32. Tel. 775-6004.
   Cuisine: CONTINENTAL/SEAFOOD. **Reservations:** Recommended. **Transportation:** Taxi.
$ **Prices:** Appetizers $5–$8; main dishes $12–$22. AE, MC, V.
   Open: Dinner Tues–Sun 6:30–10:30pm.
Named after the legendary hotel in Singapore, this establishment is filled with tropical accents more evocative of the South Pacific than of the Caribbean. The furnishings include peacock chairs, wicker, and ceiling fans. A pianist plays Gershwin and Porter during dinner, and show time is 10:30pm—a little risqué but it's lots of fun. Dishes are organized on the menu into categories; you can choose from fresh seafood, beef, veal, lamb, chicken, and live Maine lobster. The fresh fish of the day is well prepared with various tasty sauces. The chef has also added Maryland soft-shell crabs to the menu. Raffles nestles beside the lagoon at Compass Point, 1 mile west of Red Hook.

WINDJAMMER RESTAURANT, 41 Frydenhoj, Compass Point, off Rte. 32. Tel. 775-6194.
   Cuisine: SEAFOOD/GERMAN. **Reservations:** Recommended. **Transportation:** Taxi.
$ **Prices:** Appetizers $3.75–$7.50; main dishes $11.75–$32.75. MC, V.
   Open: Lunch Mon–Sat 11:30am–5pm; dinner Mon–Sat 5–10pm. **Closed:** Sept.
The paneling and smoothly finished bar of this cozy place are crafted largely from thick slabs of island mahogany and illuminated by light streaming in from the open windows. After dark, the soft glow of oil lamps add a nautically romantic glow to a relaxed atmosphere with traces of tropical *Gemütlichkeit*. The restaurant lies within a seaport village 1 mile west of Red Hook, near the easternmost tip of the island.
   The extensive menu features more than 40 main dishes, many reflecting the restaurant's German heritage. These might include red snapper Adlon (boneless filet of snapper topped with shrimp and mushrooms) or *Jägertopf* (filet mignon served

with strips of veal, onions, mushrooms, and a red wine and cream sauce). Appetizers include escargots in garlic butter and veal soup. The classic desserts—key lime pie, a light and creamy cheesecake, chocolate rum cake (made with aged local rum), and apple strudel—are all homemade.

IN & AROUND RED HOOK

EXPENSIVE

ROYAL PALM COURT, Bolongo Elysian Beach Resort, 8-1 Estate Nazareth, Cowpet Bay. Tel. 775-1000.
   Cuisine: INTERNATIONAL. **Reservations:** Recommended. **Transportation:** Taxi.
$ **Prices:** Lunch appetizers $4–$9, lunch entrées $8.25–$10.50; dinner appetizers $4.25–$9.50, dinner entrées $20–$28. AE, DC, MC, V.
   Open: Lunch daily 11:30am–2:30pm; dinner daily 6:30–10pm.
Contained within the premises of this previously recommended luxury resort on the island, the cuisine, decor, and service of this restaurant succeeds more than any other in St. Thomas at creating a subtle, European-style glamour.
   The lunch menu lists pastas, exotic salads, soups, sandwiches, and brochettes of chicken or shrimp. Dinner is more of a culinary showcase for the talents of the chef, and might include a spinach-and-oyster chowder; a vegetarian mousse of the day; fricassee of monkfish garnished with scallops, crayfish, and Armagnac sauce; and medaillons of veal with lobster, white asparagus, and Pernod.

MODERATE

PICCOLA MARINA CAFÉ, 16-3 Smith Bay, Red Hook, Rte. 38. Tel. 775-6250.
   Cuisine: AMERICAN. **Reservations:** Required for dinner. **Transportation:** Red Hook bus.
$ **Prices:** Appetizers $4.95–$7.50; main dishes $12.50–$21. AE, MC, V.
   Open: Lunch Mon–Sat 11am–3pm; dinner daily 6–10pm; brunch Sun 11am–3pm.
Built on stilts over the water, within touching distance of one of the Caribbean's most varied assortment of yachts, this popular eatery has an open veranda, a popular bar, and enough business to fill every table on weekends. The menu includes various salads, from Caesar to Greek to a fresh antipasto primavera, an assortment of sandwiches, not to mention the charcoal-broiled hamburgers. Sunday brunch offers everything from the traditional eggs Benedict to flaky croissants filled with Canadian bacon. Fresh pasta dishes, such as Alfredo, carbonara, and pesto are on the menu, as are fresh fish, steak, chicken, and shrimp. To end a good meal, desserts include a homemade brownie special on Sunday and award-winning cheesecakes. All the food is homemade using only fresh ingredients.

INEXPENSIVE

EAST COAST, Red Hook Plaza, Rte. 38. Tel. 775-1919.
   Cuisine: CARIBBEAN. **Reservations:** Not required. **Transportation:** Red Hook bus.
$ **Prices:** Appetizers $3.75–$6.25; main dishes $7.50–$18.15. AE, MC, V.
   Open: Dinner daily 5:30–11pm. Bar daily 4:30pm–4am.
East Coast packs a Stateside and local crowd of sports fans into its pine-sheathed interior nightly to cheer their favorites playing on TV. What is not readily apparent is that the adjacent restaurant serves very good meals. Put your name on the list, and

enjoy a beer at the bar while waiting for a table. You can dine in a denlike haven or on an outdoor terrace in back. You might begin with a soup of the day, then follow with snapper native style or fresh Caribbean lobster. Habitués come for the fresh grilled catch of the day, often a game fish, such as wahoo. Live bands entertain on Saturday from 10:30pm to 2:30am.

SAPPHIRE BEACH

EXPENSIVE

SEAGRAPE, Sapphire Beach Resort & Marina, Rte. 38, Smith Bay Rd. Tel. 775-9750.
Cuisine: CONTINENTAL/AMERICAN. **Reservations:** Recommended. **Transportation:** Taxi.
$ Prices: Appetizers $4.95–$8.95; main dishes $13.95–$35. AE, DC, MC, V.
Open: Lunch daily 11am–3pm; dinner daily 6–10pm; brunch Sun 10:30am–3pm.
Counted among the finest dining rooms along the east coast of St. Thomas, Seagrape is open to the sea breezes of one of the most famous beaches in the Virgin Islands, Sapphire Beach. Its attractions include the accompanying sounds of the waves, a well-trained staff, and the fine quality of the food. The lunch menu includes the grilled catch of the day and freshly made salads; a children's menu is also offered. The dinner menu includes sautéed conch, pasta primavera, veal Seagrape (with shrimp and mushrooms), charbroiled chicken, a smoked Scottish salmon, and filet mignon. A variety of local fish and seafood is prepared nightly and served with fresh vegetables cooked to perfection. For dessert, the chef is rightly proud of his key lime pie. A steel band plays on Tuesday and Friday from 8 to 11pm, and the Sunday brunch offers such delectable dishes as tortellini Alfredo and french toast Grand Marnier.

NORTH COAST

EXPENSIVE

ROMANO'S RESTAURANT, 97 Smith Bay Rd. Tel. 775-0045.
Cuisine: ITALIAN. **Reservations:** Recommended. **Transportation:** Vitran bus.
$ Prices: Appetizers $7.95; main dishes $18.95–$26.95. AE, MC, V.
Open: Dinner Mon–Sat 6:30–10:30pm.
Located on the flatlands near Coral World, this restaurant is skillfully decorated with exposed brick and well-stocked wine racks like you'd find in a *trattoria* in the North of Italy. This recent and sophisticated creation of New Jersey–born Tony Romano, the chef-owner, is considered the best and most exciting Italian restaurant in St. Thomas, specializing in the flavorful and herb-laden cuisine that some diners yearn for after a constant diet of Caribbean cooking. Specialties include linguine con pesto; penne pianello with mushrooms, prosciutto, and pine nuts; osso buco; scaloppine marsala; and broiled salmon. Another specialty is veal sweetbreads with mushrooms, brandy peppercorns, and cream. All desserts are made on the premises.

SPECIALTY DINING

DINING WITH A VIEW

AGAVE TERRACE, Point Pleasant Resort, Estate Smith Bay No. 4. Tel. 775-4142.
Cuisine: CARIBBEAN. **Reservations:** Recommended. **Transportation:** Taxi.

$ Prices: Appetizers $4.50–$9; main dishes $14.50–$38. AE, MC, V.
Open: Dinner daily 6–10pm.

Perched high above a steeply inclined and heavily forested hillside on the eastern tip of St. Thomas, this restaurant offers a sweeping panorama, and a romantic mood that's hard to beat. In addition, the regular jazz concerts presented every Tuesday and Thursday night draw many visitors.

The house-special drink is a Desmond Delight, invented by the establishment's career bartender (Desmond), a combination of Midori, rum, pineapple juice, and a secret ingredient.

Following one or more of these, you might opt for dinner. The house appetizer is an Agave sampler prepared for two, which includes portions of crabmeat, conch fritters, and lobster chinola. For a main course, the preferred shellfish dish is the chef's specialty, lobster cardinale, served with a lobster-flavored cream and fresh tomato sauce on a bed of angelhair pasta. Many diners opt for the catch of the day, which the chef can prepare seven different ways. A children's menu is available for $7. There is an extensive wine list.

LOCAL FAVORITES

EUNICE'S, 66-67 Smith Bay, Rte. 38. Tel. 775-3975.
 Cuisine: WEST INDIAN/AMERICAN. **Reservations:** Recommended at dinner.
 Transportation: Red Hook bus.
 $ Prices: Appetizers $3.75–$7.95; main dishes $9.95–$27.95; fixed-priced dinner $14.95; fixed-price lunch $7.50. AE, MC, V.
 Open: Lunch Mon–Sat 11am–4:30pm; dinner daily 6–10pm.

 Eunice's, one of the best known of St. Thomas's West Indian restaurants, has evolved over the years from a simple shack into a modern building. A mix of construction workers, locals, and tourists from nearby Stouffer's Grand Beach Hotel crowd into its confines for generous platters of island food.

A concoction called a Queen Mary (a combination of tropical fruits laced with

---

Ⓕ FROMMER'S COOL FOR KIDS: RESTAURANTS

Seagrape *(see p. 84)*. Kids delight in being taken to Sapphire Beach, where they not only enjoy the wide sands and palm trees of the beach but are served a special menu. If they're guests of the hotel and are 12 or under, they dine free.

Eunice's *(see p. 85)*. Eunice's likes children, and everybody seems to have a good time here. This place offers a safe introduction to West Indian cooking. Kids like the fishburgers, the conch fritters, the sweet potato pie, and, everybody's favorite, key lime pie.

Iggie's *(see p. 86)*. If there is one place on the island where kids like to go, it's this spot at Limetree Beach (see Bolongo Bay accommodations, above). Here they munch on Iggie's wings (spicy Buffalo wings), Iggie's nachos, and many types of burgers (garnished with everything from Monterey Jack cheese to guacamole), along with a "basket o' fries."

dark rum) is a favorite throughout the late morning and afternoon. Dinner specialties include conch fritters, broiled or fried fish, sweet potato pie, and a number of chalkboard specials that are usually served with *fungi*, rice, or fried plantain. Local lobster, when available is considered a delicacy, and *callaloo* soup, "stew mutton," and *souse* are also featured. For lunch try a fishburger, a sandwich, or one of the daily specials, such as Virgin Islands pork or mutton. Key lime pie is a favorite dessert.

VICTOR'S HIDE OUT, 32A Sub Base, off Rte. 30. Tel. 776-9379.
  Cuisine: WEST INDIAN/AMERICAN. **Reservations:** Recommended. **Transportation:** Call for directions or take a taxi. It's a bit tricky to find at night.
  $ Prices: Appetizers $3.50–$7.95; main dishes $9.95–$25.95. AE, MC, V.
  Open: Lunch Mon–Sat 11:30am–4pm; dinner daily 5–10pm.

Victor Sydney's restaurant has some of the strongest West Indian flavor and some of the best seafood and local dishes on the island. First you must find it, though—it truly is a hideout. Perched on a hilltop, this is a large, airy, concrete-sided restaurant with spectacular views. It features such dishes as conch chowder, fresh lobster Montserrat style (in a creamy sauce) or grilled in the shell, and juicy barbecued ribs. Try the coconut, custard, or apple pie.

SUNDAY BRUNCH

ROYAL PALM COURT, Bolongo Elysian Beach Resort, 8-1 Estate Nazareth, Cowpet Bay. Tel. 775-1000.
  Cuisine: INTERNATIONAL. **Reservations:** Recommended. **Transportation:** Taxi.
  $ Prices: Buffet, $21. AE, DC, MC, V.
  Open: Sun 11am–3pm.

An exquisite Sunday brunch buffet is offered weekly at this previously recommended deluxe hotel. Items include roast meats, omelets, smoked fish, soups, fresh vegetables, eggs Benedict, freshly prepared seafood dishes, European-style pâtés, a sumptuous salad bar, tropical fruits, imported cheeses, and a delectable dessert table. You dine to keyboard sounds.

SEAGRAPE, Rte. 38, Smith Bay Rd. Tel. 775-6100.
  Cuisine: INTERNATIONAL. **Reservations:** Recommended. **Transportation:** Taxi.
  $ Prices: Sun brunch from $15. AE, DC, MC, V.
  Open: Sun 10:30am–3pm.

Acclaimed as one of the finest in St. Thomas, the Seagrape's Sunday brunch affords a chance to enjoy not only good food but also the sea. Various egg dishes are offered, including the eternal Sunday brunch favorite, eggs Benedict with a zesty hollandaise. You can also order a number of the chef's "Sunday favorites," including Grand Marnier french toast, Belgian waffles topped with fresh fruit, even tortellini Alfredo. A jazz band entertains.

LIGHT & CASUAL FOOD

IGGIE'S RESTAURANT, Bolongo Limetree Beach Hotel, Frenchman's Cove, Frenchman's Bay Rd. (Rte. 30). Tel. 779-2844.
  Cuisine: AMERICAN. **Reservations:** Not required. **Transportation:** Taxi.
  $ Prices: Appetizers $4.50–$6.50; burgers and sandwiches $8–$12; main dishes $11–$22. AE, DC, MC, V.
  Open: Lunch daily noon–3pm; dinner daily 6:30–10pm.

DID YOU KNOW . . . ?

- In 1825, the last pirate was hanged at St. Thomas.
- St. Thomas was a base for blockade runners and privateers sympathetic to the Confederate cause in the Civil War.
- The U.S. Senate in 1870 rejected a treaty signed with Denmark agreeing to pay $7.5 million for the U.S. Virgins.
- The U.S. Virgin Islanders celebrate more holidays than anywhere else in the U.S.—23.
- Charlotte Amalie was named after a queen of Denmark.
- A Jewish synagogue in Charlotte Amalie is the oldest in the U.S., and still maintains its sand floors.
- Locally made products from St. Thomas are not taxable.
- For centuries, St. Thomas had the largest slave auctions in the Caribbean Basin.

Set beneath an enormous white gazebo, with giant TV screens showing sports or great moments from the history of rock and roll, this place has indestructible furniture, lots of electronic action, and a crowd of aggressively informal clients who don't mind if children are present. The menu is geared to the kinds of hands-on food that kids like (burgers, oversize sandwiches, pastas). Adults order such sudsy tropical drinks as an Iggie's Queen (coconut cream, crème de Noya, and rum) or the "Ultimate Kamikazi."

For more on the electronics of this particular restaurant, see "Evening Entertainment," below.

PICNIC FARE & WHERE TO EAT IT

Because of the dozens of restaurants and beachside cabanas selling hamburgers and beer, many would-be picnickers tend to forgo advance picnic arrangements in favor of a quick beachside bite followed by a snooze on the sands. Ideal spots are the sands of Magens Bay Beach, Drake's Seat, and any of the secluded high-altitude panoramas along the island's western end.

You can, however, create a successful picnic with the culinary expertise of **The Cream and Crumb Shop,** Building 6, Havensight Mall (tel. 774-2499). Located at the point where most cruise ships dock for daytime excursions into St. Thomas, this cheerful modern shop is easy to miss amid the crush of tax-free jewelers and perfume shops that surround it.

The shop sells some of the best pizza on the island ($2.25 a slice) although more practical for take-out might be one of the thickly layered deli sandwiches ($4.50 to $6.50), or salads such as shrimp, chicken, potato, or crabmeat. You can also get freshly baked pastries, four different kinds of yogurt (piña colada is perfect), and 18 different kinds of deliciously fattening ice cream. Hours are Monday to Saturday from 6:30am to 6pm.

5. ATTRACTIONS

The color and charm of the Caribbean come vividly to life in the waterfront town of **Charlotte Amalie,** capital of St. Thomas, where most visitors begin their sightseeing of the small island. In days of yore, seafarers from all over the globe flocked to this old-world Danish town, as did pirates and members of the Confederacy, who used the port during the American Civil War. St. Thomas was also the biggest slave market in the world.

The old warehouses once used for storing pirate goods still stand. Nowadays they mostly house shops. In fact, the main streets called "Gade" here (in honor of their Danish heritage) are now a virtual shopping mall and are usually packed. Sandwiched among these shops are a few historic buildings, most of which can be covered on foot in about 2 hours.

All of the historic buildings of major importance can easily be covered on a walking tour of Charlotte Amalie (see below). Before starting your tour, stop off in the so-called Grand Hotel, near Emancipation Park. No longer a hotel, it contains, along with shops, a visitor's center (tel. 774-8784).

WALKING TOUR — CHARLOTTE AMALIE

Start: King's Wharf.
End: Waterfront.
Time: 2½ hours.
Best Time: Any day between 10am and 5pm.
Worst Time: When a cruise ship is in port.

Begin your tour along the eastern harborfront at:

1. **King's Wharf,** site of the Virgin Islands Legislature, housed in the apple green military barracks, which dates from 1874. From here walk away from the harbor up Fort Pladsen to:
2. **✪ Fort Christian,** dating from 1672. Named after the Danish king Christian V, the structure has been everything from a governor's residence to a jail. Many pirates were hanged in the courtyard of the fort. Some of the cells have been turned into the Virgin Islands Museum, which displays some minor Native American artifacts. It's open Monday through Friday from 8am to 5pm and from 1 to 5pm on Saturday. Admission is free. Continue walking up Fort Pladsen to:
3. **Emancipation Park,** where a proclamation freeing African slaves and indentured European servants was read on July 3, 1848. Facing the north side of the park is the:
4. **Grand Hotel,** where a visitor's center dispenses information. When this hotel was launched in 1837, it was considered a rather grand address, but it later fell into decay, finally closing in 1975. Its former guest rooms upstairs have been turned into offices and a restaurant. Northwest of the park, at main street and Tolbod Gade, stands the:
5. **Central Post Office,** displaying murals by Stephen Dohanos, who became famous as a *Saturday Evening Post* cover artist. From the post office, walk east along Norre Gade to Fort Pladsen, to the:
6. **Frederik Lutheran Church,** built between 1780 and 1793. The original Georgian-style building, financed by a free black parishioner, Jean Reeneaus, was rebuilt in 1825 after a fire, and rebuilt again in 1870 after it was damaged in a hurricane. Exiting the church, walk east along Norre Gade to Lille Taarne Gade. Turn left (north) and climb to Kongens Gade (King Street), passing through a neighborhood of law firms, to:
7. **✪ Government House,** the administrative headquarters for all the Virgin Islands. It's been the center of official life in the islands since it was built—around the time of the American Civil War. Visitors are allowed on the first two floors, Monday through Saturday from 8am to noon and 1 to 5pm. Some paintings by former resident Camille Pissarro are on display, as are works by other St.

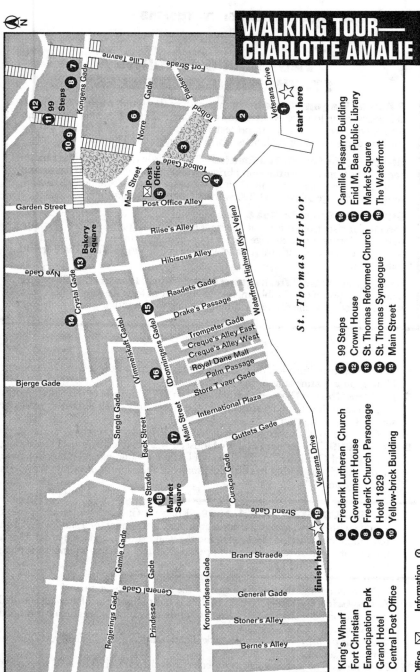

WALKING TOUR—CHARLOTTE AMALIE

N

St. Thomas Harbor

⭐ **start here**

⭐ **finish here**

Street labels:
Veterans Drive
Lille Tavnne
Fort Strade
Kongens Gade
Norre Gade
Toldbod Plaasen
Toldbod Gade
Main Street
Post Office Alley
Garden Street
Riise's Alley
Hibiscus Alley
Bakery Square
Raadets Gade
Nye Gade
Crystal Gade
Drake's Passage
Trompeter Gade
Creque's Alley East
Creque's Alley West
Royal Dane Mall
Palm Passage
Store T vaer Gade
International Plaza
Guttets Gade
Bjerge Gade
(Vimmelskaft Gade)
(Dronningens Gade)
Snegle Gade
Back Street
Main Street
Curaçao Gade
Waterfront Highway (Kyst Vejen)
Veterans Drive
Torve Strade
Market Square
Gamle Gade
General Gade
Kronprindsens Gade
Strand Gade
Brand Straede
General Gade
Stoner's Alley
Berne's Alley
Regierings Gade
Prindesse Gade

Legend:
1. King's Wharf
2. Fort Christian
3. Emancipation Park
4. Grand Hotel
5. Central Post Office
6. Frederik Lutheran Church
7. Government House
8. Frederik Church Parsonage
9. Hotel 1829
10. Yellow-brick Building
11. 99 Steps
12. Crown House
13. St. Thomas Reformed Church
14. St. Thomas Synagogue
15. Main Street
16. Camille Pissarro Building
17. Enid M. Baa Public Library
18. Market Square
19. The Waterfront

Post Office ⊠   Information ⊘

FROMMER'S FAVORITE
ST. THOMAS EXPERIENCES

A Day at Magens Beach In the north of the island, Magens Bay Beach is a spectacular loop of white sand, stretching about half a mile along calm waters with two peninsulas to protect it. It has a flat, sandy bottom, and for sunning and swimming it alone is worth the trip to St. Thomas.

Shopping in Charlotte Amalie To this little island in the West Indies cargo ships from all over the world bring an array of merchandise to dazzle and delight the shopper. The merchandise looks even more tempting to U.S. residents who are allowed $1,200 worth of purchases duty free.

Sunset at Drake's Seat Few views in all the West Indies equal the spectacular vista from this point, where the old English pirate himself is said to have sat, plotting a safe passage for his ships coming in from the Atlantic. It's a wide-angle view of Charlotte Amalie with the entire Virgin Island chain spread before you.

Sailing on Your "Yacht for a Day" Virgin Islanders run the biggest charter business in the Caribbean, taking visitors out for a day on the high seas, with snorkeling, picnics, and swimming adding to the fun.

Thomian artists. Turn left on Kongens Gade. Directly to the left of Government House, on the same side of the street, stands:

8. **Frederik Church Parsonage,** dating from 1725, and one of the oldest houses on the island. It is the only structure in the Government Hill district to retain its simple 18th-century lines.

      Continue to walk west along Kongens Gade until you reach:

9. **Hotel 1829.** The former Lavalette House, it was designed by one of the leading merchants of Charlotte Amalie. This is a landmark building and a hotel of great charm and character that has attracted many of the island's most famous guests over the years.

REFUELING STOP **Hotel 1829,** Kongens Gade, provides the perfect veranda with a view, ideal for a drink at midday but perfect for a sundowner. You may fall in love with the place, abandon the walking tour, and stick around for a dinner—it's that special. Its bar is open daily from 10am to midnight, serving drinks for $2.75 and up.

      Next door (still on the same side of the street), observe the:

10. **Yellow-Brick Building** from 1854. It was built in what local architects called "the style of Copenhagen." You can go inside the building, as part of it is filled with shops.

      At this point, you can double back slightly on Kongens Gade if you'd like to climb the famous:

11. **99 Steps.** The steps, which were erected in the early 1700s, take you to the summit of Government Hill, from where you'll see the 18th-century:

12. **Crown House,** immediately to your right on the south side of the street. This

was a stately home that was the residence of two of the past governors of the Virgin Islands. Here the rich and privileged lived in the 1700s, surrounded by Chinese wall hangings, a crystal chandelier from Versailles, and carved West Indian furniture. It was also the home of von Scholten, the Danish ruler who issued a proclamation of emancipation in 1848.

Walk back down the steps and continue right along Kongens Gade, then down a pair of old brick steps until you reach Garden Street. Across the way you'll pass the Straw Factory (see "Savvy Shopping," below). Go right on Garden Street and take a left onto Crystal Gade. On your left, at the corner of Nye Gade and Crystal Gade you'll see:

13. St. Thomas Reformed Church, formerly Dutch and dating from 1844. Designed like a Greek temple, much of its original structure has been preserved intact.

Continue up Crystal Gade. On your right (north side), you'll come to:

14. St. Thomas Synagogue, the oldest synagogue in continuous use under the American flag. It still maintains the tradition of sand on the floor, commemorating the exodus from Egypt. Erected in 1833 by Sephardic Jews, it was built of local stone along with ballast brick from Denmark and mortar made of molasses and sand. It is open to visitors from 9am to 4pm Monday to Friday.

Retrace your steps to Raadets Gade and turn south toward the water, crossing the famous Vimmelskaft Gade or "Back Street" of Charlotte Amalie. Continue along Raadets Gade until you reach:

15. Main Street (Dronningens Gade), the most famous shopping street of St. Thomas and its major artery. Turn right and walk along Main Street until you come to the mid-19th-century:

16. Camille Pissarro Building, on your right, at the Amsterdam Sauer Jewelry Store. Pissarro, a Spanish Jew who became one of the founders of French Impressionism, was born in this building as Jacob Pizarro in 1830. Before moving to Paris and becoming involved with some of the greatest artists of his day, he worked for his father in a store along Main Street.

Continuing along Main Street, you will pass on your right:

17. Enid M. Baa Public Library, the former von Bretton House, dating from 1818. Keep heading west until you reach:

18. Market Square, officially known as Rothschild Francis Square, at the point where Main Street intersects Strand Gade. This was the center of a large slave-trading market before the emancipation was proclaimed. It is an open-air fruit and vegetable market today, selling, among other items, *genips* (break open the skin and suck the pulp off a pit). The wrought-iron roof came from Europe, and at the turn of the century covered a railway station. It's open Monday through Saturday, with Saturday its busiest day.

If the *genip* doesn't satisfy you, take Strand Gade down to:

19. The Waterfront (Kyst Vejen), where you can purchase a fresh coconut. The vendor will whack off the top with a machete, so you can drink the sweet milk from its hull. Here you'll have an up-close preview of one of the most spectacular harbors in the West Indies, which is usually filled with cruise ships.

DRIVING TOUR — ST. THOMAS

Start: Fort Christian.
Finish: Magens Bay Beach.
Time: 2½ hours.

Best Time: Sunday, when traffic is lightest.
Worst Time: Wednesday and Saturday, when traffic is heaviest.

Begin at Fort Christian in the eastern part of Charlotte Amalie and head west a-long the Waterfront. To your left you'll see cruise ships anchored offshore and on your right will be all the stores that make Charlotte Amalie the shopping mall of the Caribbean. Continue on Route 30 and pass the Cyril E. King Airport on your left. As the road forks toward the airport, keep right along Route 30, which runs parallel to the airport where you'll have a very close view of jumbo jets from the United States landing.

At about 2.4 miles from Fort Christian the modern complex on your right will be:

1. **The University of the Virgin Islands,** which is the major university in all the Virgin Islands. It is a modern complex with beautifully landscaped campus grounds. Continue along until you reach:
2. **Brewers Bay** on your left, with its good sand beach. You may want to park near here and go for a swim, as this is considered one of the more desirable beaches on the island.

   Continue 3.8 miles west, climbing uphill through scrub country along a hilly drive past junction with Route 301. This far west Route 30 is called:
3. **Fortuna Road,** considered one of the most scenic areas of St. Thomas, with panoramic views of the water and offshore islands on your left. Along the way will be parking areas where you can pull off and enjoy the view. The one on Bethesda Hill is particularly spectacular. The names of the districts you pass through—Bonne Esperance and Perseverance—come from the old plantations that used to stand here. The area is now primarily residential. At Bordeaux Hill you descend sharply, and the road narrows until you come to a dead end.

   At this point, turn around and head back east along Route 30. The road is badly marked at this point, and you'll probably need the *Official Road Map of the United States Virgin Islands.* Turn left and head northeast at the junction with Route 301. You will come to the junction of:
4. **Crown Mountain Road,** the most scenic road in the Virgin Islands. Turn left at this junction onto Route 33. The road will sweep northward before it makes an abrupt switch to the east. You will be traversing the most mountainous heartland of St. Thomas. Expect hairpin turns during your descent. You'll often have to reduce your speed to 10 miles an hour, especially in the Mafolie district. The road will eventually lead to the junction of Route 37, where you should go left, but only for a short distance, until you reach the junction of Route 40. At one point Routes 37 and 40 become the same highway. But when they separate turn right and stay on Route 40. This will take you to:
5. **Drake's Seat,** the legendary perch where Sir Francis Drake is said to have figured out the best routes for the colonial European powers to take their ships from the Atlantic into the Caribbean Sea. Continue left onto Route 35. The road will veer northwest. Follow it all the way to:
6. **Magens Bay Beach,** hailed as one of the most beautiful beaches in the world. Here you'll find an array of activities and can arrange Sunfish rentals, glass-bottom paddleboats, and windsurf rentals. There is a full array of lounge chairs, changing facilities, showers, and lockers. There are also picnic tables.

REFUELING STOP **Magens Bay Bar & Grill,** Magens Bay Beach (tel. 775-4669), is an ideal place for light meals on this heart-shaped beach. The snack

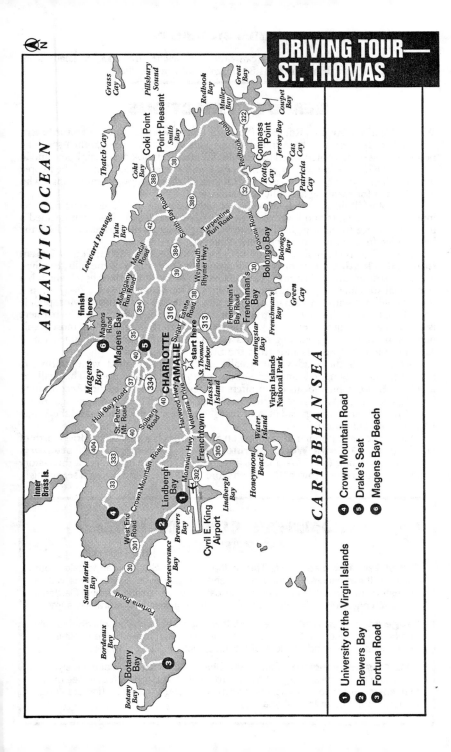

DRIVING TOUR—
ST. THOMAS

N

ATLANTIC OCEAN

Grass Cay

Thatch Cay

Leeward Passage

Pillsbury Sound

Coki Point
Point Pleasant

Redhook Bay

Muller Bay

Great Bay

Coupet Bay

Compass Point

Jersey Bay

Cas Cay

Patricia Cay

Rotto Cay

Redhook

Smith Bay

Coki Bay

Tutu Bay

Mandal Road

Mahogany Run Road

Turpentine Run Road

Bovoni Road

Bolongo Bay

Frenchman's Bay

Frenchman's

Green Cay

Weymouth Rhyner Hwy.

Frenchman's Bay Road

Morningstar Bay

Estate Road

Smith Bay Road

finish here

Magens Bay

Magens Bay

Magens Road

CHARLOTTE
AMALIE

start here

St. Thomas Harbor

Sugar Estate Road

Harwood Hwy.

Veterans Drive

Hassel Island

Water Island

Virgin Islands National Park

CARIBBEAN SEA

Hull Bay Road

St. Peter Mt. Road

Solberg Road

Moravian Hwy.

Frenchtown

Honeymoon Beach

Lindbergh Bay

Crown Mountain Road

West End 301 Road

Brewers Bay

Perseverance Bay

Cyril E. King Airport

Lindbergh

Inner Brass Is.

Santa Maria Bay

Fortuna Road

Bordeaux Bay

Botany Bay

Botany Bay

38
388
42
386
39
384
316
313
35
40
37
334
40
404
333
33
30
302
305
30
32
322

1 University of the Virgin Islands

2 Brewers Bay

3 Fortuna Road

4 Crown Mountain Road

5 Drake's Seat

6 Magens Bay Beach

bar overlooks the beach. You can order sandwiches from $3.75, salads from $3.95, and soft drinks from $1.85. Pizza is sold by the slice.

NEARBY ATTRACTIONS

West of Charlotte Amalie, Route 30 (Veterans Drive) will take you to **Frenchtown.** (Turn left at the sign to The Admiral's Inn.) This was settled by a French-speaking people who were uprooted when the Swedes invaded and took over their homeland in St. Barts. They were known for wearing *cha-chas* or straw hats. Many of the people who live here today are the direct descendants of those long-ago immigrants, who were known for speaking a distinctive patois.

This colorful village, many of whose residents engage in fishing, contains many interesting restaurants and taverns. Now that Charlotte Amalie has been deemed a dangerous place to be at night, Frenchtown has picked up the business, and it's the best choice for nighttime dancing, entertainment, and drinking.

West of Charlotte Amalie, Harwood Highway (Route 308) will lead you to **Crown Mountain Road,** a scenic drive opening onto the best views of the hills, beaches, and clear seas around St. Thomas. Eventually, you arrive at a former hotel which is a traditional stopping-off point. Mountain Top, Crown Mountain (tel. 774-5760), is a modern building with a restaurant and bar, plus some two dozen shops. Most people come here to enjoy the view and sip the world-famous banana daiquiris. The bar here is said to have invented them! It is generally considered to be one of the most scenic perches in St. Thomas, opening onto a view of Sir Francis Drake Channel, which separates the U.S. Virgin Islands from the British Virgin Islands.

Farther down the road you'll usually see tour buses filled with cruise-ship passengers converging on another scenic mountain lookout spot. This will be **Drake's Seat,** which locals claim offers the best view on the island. According to local legend, Sir Francis Drake sat there and charted the channels and passages of the Virgin Islands. You have spread at your feet the entire sweep of almost all the Virgin Islands, both U.S. and British.

One of the most popular attractions on St. Thomas is a 20-minute drive north of St. Thomas. **✪ Coral World Marine Park & Underwater Observatory,** Route 6, Coki Point (tel. 775-1555), is a marine complex that features a three-story underwater observation tower 100 feet offshore. Through windows you'll see sponges,

---

 FROMMER'S COOL FOR KIDS: ATTRACTIONS

Coral World *(see p. 94)* This is *the* place on St. Thomas to take your children. It's a hands-on experience—children can even shake hands with a starfish at the Touch Pond. Later they can discover exotic Marine Gardens, where 20 aquariums showcase the Caribbean's incredible natural treasures.

Magens Bay Beach *(see p. 95)* If you can introduce your children to only one beach in the entire Caribbean, make it this one. It's one of the finest in the world, with white sand and lots of facilities, including picnic tables.

***Atlantis* Submarine** *(see p. 98)* Children thrill to this unique underwater adventure in "space age air." They dive to depths of up to 150 feet to see exotic fish, spectacular sea gardens, coral formations, and unusual marine creatures. Children must be at least 4 years old.

deep-sea flowers, fish, and coral—underwater life in its natural state. In the Marine Gardens Aquarium, saltwater tanks display everything from sea horses to urchins. One 80,000-gallon reef tank features exotic marine life. Another tank is devoted to predators, with circling sharks and giant moray eels, among other creatures. Entrance is through a waterfall of cascading water.

The latest addition to the park is a semisubmarine which lets you enjoy the panoramic view and the "down under" feeling of a submarine without ever leaving the ocean's surface.

Coral World has also developed its own snorkeling and diving programs to take advantage of adjacent Coki Beach. Coral World will provide the instructors and all necessary equipment. Complimentary lockers and showers are available.

The marine park also contains the Tropical Terrace Restaurant, duty-free shops, and a tropical nature trail. The complex is open daily from 9am to 6pm. Admission is $14 for adults, and $9 for children.

ORGANIZED TOURS

An **"Island Safari"** is conducted Monday through Saturday. Reservations can be made through hotel activities desks or through the reception desk at all hotels. There seems to be no one outfit with a monopoly on giving these tours. A van is sent to pick you up (usually around 9am), and you're taken on a panoramic tour of Charlotte Amalie with the mandatory stopovers at Drake's Seat and Mountain Top for its banana daiquiris and panoramic view of the Virgin Islands. Cost is $25 per person for a 2-hour tour.

6. SPORTS & RECREATION

Chances are, your hotel will be right on the beach, or very close to one, and this is where you'll anchor for most of your stay, perhaps occasionally going out in a Sailfish or Hobie Cat. Incidentally, all beaches in the Virgin Islands are public.

In addition to beaches, St. Thomas offers one of the biggest sporting programs in the West Indies, everything from golf to boating, from scuba diving to deep-sea fishing.

BEACHES

Most of the beaches of St. Thomas lie from 2 to 5 miles from Charlotte Amalie.

NORTH SIDE

Magens Bay   I've already extolled the glories of this beach, located 3 miles north of the capital. One of the world's most beautiful beaches, it charges 50¢ admission for adults and 25¢ for children. Changing facilities are available, and snorkeling gear and lounge chairs can be rented. This beach of white sand, administered by the government, is half a mile long and lies between two mountains. There is no public transportation to reach it. From Charlotte Amalie, take Route 35 north all the way. The gates to the beach are open daily from 6am to 6pm. After four o'clock you should use insect repellent to protect yourself from mosquitoes and sand flies.

Coki Beach   Located in the northeast near Coral World, Coki Beach is good, but overcrowded whenever cruise ships are in port. Snorkelers and scuba divers are attracted to this popular beach, with its abundance of reef fish. So are pickpockets, so protect your valuables. Lockers can be rented at Coral World next door. It is absolutely forbidden to remove coral or marine life from the water. Most people take a taxi from the center of Charlotte Amalie. An East End bus runs to Smith Bay, letting you off at the gate to Coral World and Coki Beach.

Stouffer Grand Beach On the north side is one of the island's most beautiful beaches, with the previously recommended luxury hotel in the background. Many water sports are available at this palm-lined beach of white sand, opening onto Smith Bay in the vicinity of Coral World. The beach lies right off Smith Bay Road (Route 38) east of Charlotte Amalie. It's reached by taxi from Charlotte Amalie.

SOUTH SIDE

Morningstar At this beach near Frenchman's Reef Hotel, about 2 miles east of Charlotte Amalie, you can appear in your most daring swimwear, as this is the premier gathering spot on the island for bikini wearers (and watchers). You can also rent sailboards, sailboats, snorkeling equipment, and lounge chairs. The beach is reached by a cliff-front elevator at Marriott's Frenchman's Reef Beach Resort, which also owns the adjoining Marriott's Morning Star Resort. Because of its proximity to town, many residents of Charlotte Amalie use this beach, and the east side of the beach is often filled with young people who work in the hotels and restaurants of St. Thomas at night, occupying their time during the day on the beaches. There is no public transportation to the beach, but it's only a short taxi ride from Charlotte Amalie.

Limetree Beach Set against a backdrop of sea grape trees and shady palms, Limetree lures those who want a serene spread of sand where they can mix suntanning with feeding hibiscus blossoms to iguanas. Snorkeling gear, lounge and beach chairs, and towels can be rented. Cool drinks are served, including a Limetree green piña colada. There is no public transportation, but the beach can easily be reached by taxi from Charlotte Amalie.

Brewers Bay One of the most popular beaches, Brewers Bay lies in the southwest part of the island, near the University of the Virgin Islands. This beach of white coral sand is almost as long as the beach at Magens Bay. Students from the nearby university often come here for a swim between classes. Light meals and drinks are served along the beach. It's not good for snorkeling, however. From Charlotte Amalie, take the Fortuna bus heading west. Get off at the edge of Brewers Bay, across from the Reichhold Center, the cultural center of St. Thomas.

Lindbergh Beach With lifeguard, toilet facilities, and a bathhouse, Lindbergh is used extensively by the locals, who sometimes stage political rallies here as well as carnival parties. It lies at the Island Beachcomber Hotel. Drinks, such as piña coladas, are served on the beach. It is not good for snorkeling. Take the Fortuna bus route west from Charlotte Amalie.

EAST END

Secret Harbour Small and special, Secret Harbour lies near a number of condos whose owners frequent the beach. With its white sand, coconut palms and tranquil waters, it is a cliché of Caribbean charm. Many residents of St. Charlotte Amalie visit on the weekends because of its proximity to town, so it is at its most crowded then. No public transportation stops here, but it's an easy taxi ride east of Charlotte Amalie in the direction of Red Hook.

Sapphire Beach   One of the finest beaches in St. Thomas is Sapphire Beach, popular with windsurfers. A large reef is found close to the fine, white-coral-sand shore, and there are good views of offshore cays and St. John. It is set against the backdrop of one of the most desirable hotels and condominiums in St. Thomas, Sapphire Beach Hotel, where you can lunch or order drinks if you wish. Snorkeling gear and lounge chairs can be rented. To reach it, take the East End bus from Charlotte Amalie via Red Hook. Get off at the entrance to Sapphire Bay.

SPORTS

BOATING

The biggest charter-boat business in the Caribbean is conducted by Virgin Islanders. In St. Thomas most of the business centers around the Red Hook and Yacht Haven marinas.

Perhaps the easiest way to go out to sea is to charter "your yacht for the day" from **Yacht Nightwind,** Red Hook (tel. 775-4110 24 hours a day), for only $85 per person. You're granted a full-day sail with champagne buffet lunch and open bar aboard this 50-foot yawl. You're also given free snorkeling equipment and instruction. Operators Stephen and June Marsh have taken visitors out since 1977. If you're interested, ask them about two- or three-bedroom villas for rent on the beach.

New Horizons, Suite 237, Red Hook Plaza (P.O. Box 16), Red Hook (tel. 775-1171), offers windborne excursions amid the cays and reefs of the Virgin Islands. This two-masted 60-foot ketch was built in 1969 in Vancouver. It has circumnavigated the globe and has been used as a design prototype for other boats.

Owned and operated by former Vancouverites Tim and Sue Krygsveld, it contains a hot-water shower, serves a specialty drink called a New Horizons Nooner (its melon-liqueur base seems color-coordinated with the sea), and carries a complete line of snorkeling equipment for adults and children. A full-day excursion, with a "hot buffet Italian al fresco" and an open bar, costs $85 per person. Excursions depart every day, weather permitting, from the Sapphire Beach Club Marina. Call ahead for reservations and information. Children aged 2 to 12, who must be accompanied by an adult, pay half price.

My Way (tel. 776-7751) is a 35-foot Pearson sloop that sails to the uninhabited island of Hans Lollick for $65 per person, including everything. Snorkeling equipment and instruction are provided. There's an all-day bar, and you'll have lunch on a deserted beach. Sailings leave from the north side of St. Thomas. Only four to six guests are taken and guests are picked up free at their hotels.

True Love, P.O. Box 7595 (tel. 775-6547), is a sleek 54-foot Malabar schooner, used during the filming of *High Society* starring Bing Crosby and Grace Kelly. It sails at 9:30am from Sapphire Beach Club Marina and costs $75 per person. Bill and Sue Beer have sailed it since 1965. You can join one of the captain's snorkeling classes and later enjoy one of Sue's gourmet lunches with champagne.

If you want something more elaborate, you can go bareboating, that is rent a craft where you're the captain. You must first prove that you can handle the craft. If you'd like everything done for you, a fully crewed yacht with a captain at your service is the way to go on a charter. Either type of charter rental is available through **Avery's Boathouse,** P.O. Box 5248, Veterans Drive Station, St. Thomas, USVI 00803 (tel. 776-0113).

Rafting Adventures, Maritime Services International, 82 Red Hook Center, St. Thomas, USVI 00802 (tel. 809/779-2032), has been called "the most exciting boat trip in the Caribbean." Both half- and full-day tours are featured, and they visit such islands as St. John and Jost Van Dyke (the latter in the BVI). Snorkel expeditions are featured to remote islands in both the U.S. and British islands. Departures are daily from both St. Thomas and St. John, costing $85 for a full day's expedition (call for details).

A major attraction is the **Atlantis submarine,** which takes you on a 1-hour voyage to depths of 150 feet, unfolding a world of exotic marine life. You'll gaze on coral reefs and sponge gardens through 2-foot windows on the air-conditioned 65-foot-long sub, which carries 46 passengers. You take a surface boat from the West Indies Dock, right outside Charlotte Amalie, to the submarine, which lies near Buck Island (the St. Thomas version, not the more famous Buck Island near St. Croix). Divers swim with the fish and bring them close to the windows for photos. The fare is $74 per person; children 4 to 12 pay half fare (ages under 4 not permitted). The *Atlantis* operates daily from November through April and only Monday through Saturday from May through October. Reservations are imperative. For tickets, go to the Havensight shopping mall, Building 6, or call 776-5650 for reservations.

DEEP-SEA FISHING

The U.S. Virgins have very good deep-sea fishing—some 19 world records have been set in recent years (eight for blue marlin). Sportfishing is offered on the **Fish Hawk** (tel. 775-9058). Capt. Al Petrosky of New Jersey sails from Fish Hawk Marina Lagoon at the East End on his 43-foot diesel-powered craft fully equipped with rods and reels. All equipment (but no lunch) is included in the rate of $350 per half day for up to six passengers. A full-day excursion, depending on how far the boat goes out, ranges from $700 to $800.

GOLF

On the north shore, **Mahogany Run,** at the Mahogany Run Golf & Tennis Resort, Mahogany Run Road (tel. 775-5000), is an 18-hole, par-70 course. Designed by Tom and George Fazio, this is considered one of the most beautiful courses in the West Indies, rising and dropping like a roller coaster on its journey to the sea where cliffs and crashing sea waves are the ultimate hazards at the 13th and 14th holes. Greens fees depend on the time of year, from $60 per 18 holes between January and April 1 to $33 July through September. A cart is mandatory, costing $10 for 9 holes or $15 for 18 holes.

SCUBA DIVING & SNORKELING

With 30 spectacular reefs just off St. Thomas, the U.S. Virgins are rated as one of the "most beautiful areas in the world" by *Skin Diver* magazine.

St. Thomas Diving Club, Bolongo Bay Beach and Tennis Club (P.O. Box 7337), St. Thomas, USVI 00801 (tel. 809/776-2381), is a full-service, PADI five-star center, considered the best on the island. If you're a resident at Bolongo Bay Resorts (see "Accommodations," above), you get such extras as a sail on the club's 52-foot *Heavenly Daze* to St. John, if you stay 7 or more nights. An open-water certification course, including four scuba dives, costs $330. An advanced open-water certification course, including five dives that can be accomplished in 2 days, costs $275. Every Thursday participants are taken on an all-day scuba excursion that includes a dive to the wreck of RMS *Rhone* in the British Virgin Islands. This two-tank dive costs $150. You can enjoy snorkeling for $22.

Another good bet for dive operations is **Joe Vogel Diving Co.,** P.O. Box 6577, St. Thomas, USVI 00804 (tel. 775-7610). The oldest certified dive school in the Caribbean, in operation since 1960, is conveniently located in central Charlotte Amalie at the Galleon House Hotel on Government Hill. Dean Johnson, owner, is a NAUI instructor-trainer, and offers quality scuba instruction from a "no experience required introductory dive" to scuba instructor certification. Advanced classes, rescue diver, dive master, and crossover courses are offered at this dive training center.

Dive In, Sapphire Beach Resort & Marina, Smith Bay Road, Route 38 (tel. 775-6100), is a well-recommended and complete diving center, offering some of the finest diving services in the U.S. Virgin Islands. These include professional instruction for all levels, daily beach and boat dives, custom dive packages, underwater photography and videotapes, snorkeling trips, and a full-service PADI dive center. An introductory resort course costs $55, and an open-water certification course, with four dives, goes for $350. A six-dive pass costs $185. It's especially convenient for those staying at hotels on the East Side.

TENNIS

St. Thomas has many courts lit for night play. Outstanding ones are at the **Bolongo Bay Beach and Tennis Club,** Bolongo Bay (tel. 779-2844), which has four courts, two of which are lit until 10pm. It is free to members and hotel guests only, except for lessons, which cost $16 per half hour and are available to anyone.

At **Frenchman's Reef Tennis Courts** (tel. 776-8500, ext. 444), four courts are available and lights stay on until 10pm. Nonguests pay $10 per half hour per court.

At the famous **Bluebeard's Castle,** Bluebeard's Hill (tel. 774-1600), nonguests are charged $4 per hour for a court.

WINDSURFING

This increasingly popular sport is available at the major resort hotels and at some public beaches, including Brewers Bay, Morningstar Beach, and Limetree Beach. Stouffer Grand Beach Resort (tel. 775-1510), Smith Bay Road, Route 38, is the major hotel offering windsurfing. Cost is from $15 per hour.

7. SAVVY SHOPPING

The $1,200 duty-free allowance makes every purchase a double bargain. If you go over the limit duty is charged at a flat rate of 5% up to $1,000 rather than the 10% imposed on goods from other countries. You can send as many gifts as you want to family or friends duty free—but not more than one per day up to $100. These items do not have to be declared on your exemption.

Some well-known brand names have been known to offer savings of up to 60% off Stateside prices. To be realistic, though, you often have to plow through a lot of junk to find the savings. You need to know the price back home of the item involved to determine if you are in fact making a savings. Having sounded that warning, I'll survey some St. Thomas shops where I have found good buys. There are lots more that you can discover on your own.

Most of the shops, some of which occupy former pirate warehouses, are open Monday to Saturday from 9am to 5pm. Some stores open Sunday and holidays if a cruise ship is in port. Note: Friday is the biggest cruise-ship visiting day at Charlotte Amalie (I once counted eight at once), so try to avoid shopping then.

Recently, the town leaders ordained that it was illegal for most street vendors to ply their trades outside of a designated area called "Vendor's Plaza," at the corner of Veterans Drive and Tolbod Gade. Hundreds converge at 7:30am, remaining there usually no later than 5:30pm, Monday through Saturday. (Very few remain in place on Sunday, unless a cruise ship is scheduled to arrive.) Their protection from the elements usually derives from oversized parasols. The only exception to this strictly maintained ordinance are the food vendors, who are permitted to sell on sidewalks outside of Vendor's Plaza.

BEST BUYS & WHERE TO FIND THEM

Nearly all the major shopping in St. Thomas is done along the harbor at Charlotte Amalie. Cruise-ship passengers mainly shop the **Havensight Mall** where they disembark, lying at the eastern edge of Charlotte Amalie. The principal shopping street is called **Main Street** or Dronningens Gade (its old Danish name). North of this street is another merchandise-loaded street called **Back Street** or Vimmelskaft.

Many shops are also spread along the **Waterfront Highway** (also called Kyst Vejen). Between these major streets or boulevards are a series of side streets, walkways, and alleys, each filled with shops. Major ones include Tolbod Gade, Raadets Gade, Royal Dane Mall, Palm Passage, Storetvaer Gade, and Strand Gade.

All the major stores in St. Thomas are located by number on an excellent map in the center of a publication, *St. Thomas This Week,* distributed free to all arriving plane and boat passengers.

If you want to combine a little history with shopping, go into the courtyard of the old Pissarro Building entered through the archway off Main Street. The Impressionist painter lived here as a child, and the old apartments have been turned into a warren of interesting shops.

Best buys include china, crystal, perfumes, jewelry (especially emeralds), Haitian art, fashions, and especially wooden specialties. Cameras and electronic items, based on my experience, are not the good buys they're reputed to be.

St. Thomas is perhaps the finest place in all the Caribbean for discounts in porcelain. Look for the imported patterns for the biggest savings, but even Stateside brands may be purchased for 25% off the retail price of the mainland.

Purchasing brand name watches is one of the reasons some visitors come to St. Thomas, as value here is considered excellent.

All of these stores recommended below can be reached on foot along the streets directly in the center of Charlotte Amalie.

A lot of the stores don't have street numbers, or don't display them, so look for their signs instead. All of the signs are prominent.

IN THEIR FOOTSTEPS

Camille Pissarro (1830–1903) The dean of the French Impressionist painters was the most famous resident ever born on the island of St. Thomas. Attracted by the work of Camille Corot and, later, Gustave Courbet, Pissarro moved in a lofty artistic circle of friends that included Monet, Cézanne, and Renoir. He painted landscapes and scenes of rural life, and also some portraits.

• **Birthplace:** Danish St. Thomas, July 10, 1830, son of Jewish parents of French/Spanish extraction.

• **Residences:** The Pissarro Building, off Main Street in Charlotte Amalie; Paris.

• **Resting Place:** Paris.

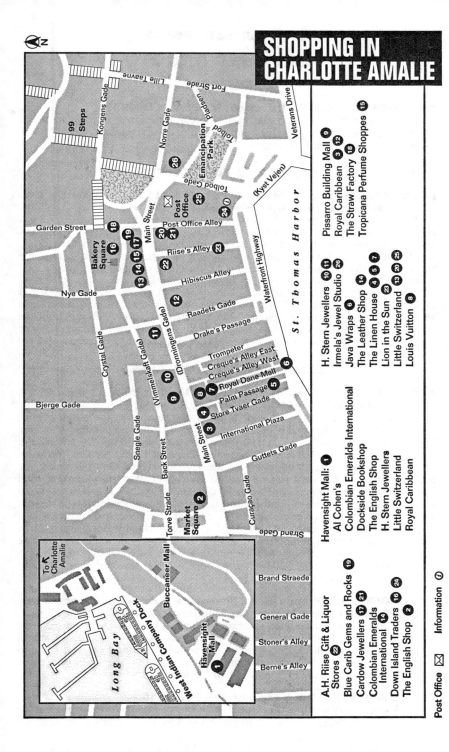

SHOPPING IN CHARLOTTE AMALIE

Pissarro Building Mall 9
Royal Caribbean 3 12
The Straw Factory 18
Tropicana Perfume Shoppes 15

H. Stern Jewellers 10 11
Irmela's Jewel Studio 26
Java Wraps 6
The Leather Shop 14
The Linen House 4 5 7
Lion in the Sun 23
Little Switzerland 13 20 25
Louis Vuitton 8

Havensight Mall: 1
Al Cohen's
Colombian Emeralds International
Dockside Bookshop
The English Shop
H. Stern Jewellers
Little Switzerland
Royal Caribbean

A.H. Riise Gift & Liquor Stores 22
Blue Carib Gems and Rocks 19
Cardow Jewellers 17 21
Colombian Emeralds International 14
Down Island Traders 16 24
The English Shop 2

Post Office ⊠   Information ⑦

SHOPPING A TO Z

BOOKSTORES

DOCKSIDE BOOKSHOP, Havensight Mall. Tel. 774-4937.
The best supply of books is found at this store near the cruise ships dock, east of Charlotte Amalie. The shop has the best selection of books on island lore, as well as numerous light and serious reading selections.

CAMERAS & ELECTRONICS

ROYAL CARIBBEAN, 33 Main St. (tel. 776-4110); 23 Main St. (tel. 776-5449); and Havensight Mall (tel. 776-8890).
This is the largest camera and electronics store in the Caribbean. Since 1977 it has offered good values in cameras and electronic equipment, including all accessories. The store carries such top brands as Minolta, Nikon, Pentax, Canon, Olympus, Leica, and Ricoh, several of which have special camera packages. Royal Caribbean is the authorized dealer of Sony, Panasonic, and AIWA, with a complete selection of their products. They also have good buys in Seiko, Movado, Baume & Mercier, Corum, Fendi, Concord and Swatch watches, Mikimoto pearls, Dupont and Dunhill 14- and 18-karat gold jewelry for both men and women, and gift items, such as Mont Blanc and Cross pens, Swiss army knives, and NOA figurines by Lladró. At Royal Caribbean all customers are given one 5-function digital watch free with the purchase of $50 or more. They also give a $50 value coupon with the purchase of any camera.

CHINA, CRYSTAL & WATCHES

A. H. RIISE GIFT & LIQUOR STORES, 37 Main St. at A. H. Riise Gift & Liquor Mall. Tel. 776-2303, or toll free 800/524-2037.
Displayed in a beautifully restored 18th-century Danish warehouse that extends from Main Street to the waterfront is an unusually wide and fine selection of quality imported merchandise. Special attention is paid to the collection of fine jewelry and watches from Europe's leading craftspeople, including Patek Philippe, Vacheron Constantin, Hublot, Gucci, Movado, Omega, and Tag-Heuer. Featured among the many internationally known name brands in the china and crystal department are Waterford, Lalique, Daum, Baccarat, Wedgwood, Royal Crown Derby, Royal Doulton, Royal Copenhagen, and Lladró figurines. Also available are Crabtree & Evelyn and Scarborough products, liquor, tobacco, and duty-free art including a wide selection of Caribbean prints and note cards. A. H. Gift & Liquor Stores also boasts a vast selection of fragrances for men and women, as well as cosmetics. Every purchase is backed by a 60-day unconditional guarantee. For brochure and toll-free-shop-by-phone service, call 800/524-2037 9am to 5pm Atlantic standard time, Monday through Saturday except major holidays.

THE ENGLISH SHOP, Main St., at Market Sq. (tel. 774-3495, or toll free 800/524-2013) and Havensight Mall (tel. 776-3776).
The English Shop has a wide selection of china, crystal, and figurines from the world's top makers. Fine Limoges, Royal Doulton, Noritake, Royal Worcester, Spode, Coalport, and Haviland china represent only a small portion of the many brands carried. Crystal includes Stuart, Edinburgh, Gobel, and several Irish-blown pieces, and you can choose figurines from a wide range of well-known makers.

LITTLE SWITZERLAND, 5 Main St. Tel. 776-2010.
With stores in downtown Charlotte Amalie and one on the dock at Havensight Mall, Little Switzerland is known as the premier watch retailer in the Caribbean. They

are the exclusive agent for many famous brands including Audemars Piguet, Bertolucci, Eterna, Kreiger, Memosail, Rado, Rolex, Sector, Swiss Army, Tiffany, Zodiac, and the famous Little Switzerland line of high-fashion watches. You will also find such names as Baume & Mercier, Omega, Raymond Weil, and Tag-Heuer. The shop carries only Swiss-made watches. Also offered is an extensive selection of 14K and 18K gold, colored stone, and diamond jewelry from Europe and Asia as well as a beautiful collection of "private label" Little Switzerland jewelry.

Little Switzerland has the finest names in china and crystal including Ansley, Atlantis, Baccarat, Caithness, Christofle, Daum, Gallo, Herend, Hutschenreuther, Kosta Boda, Lalique, Marcolinh, Orrefors, Rosenthal, Royal Albert, Royal Crown Derby, Royal Doulton, Villeroy & Boch, Waterford, and Wedgwood; figurines from D'Argenta, David Winter, Goebel-Hummel, Lladró, and Swarovski; and flatware by Christofle, Jean Couzon, Retroneu, Rosenthal, and WMF. Little Switzerland has branched out elsewhere in the Caribbean, with locations also in St. Croix, St. Martin, St. Barthélemy, Antigua, Aruba, and Curaçao, as well as St. Kitts and Nevis.

CLOTHING

COKI, Compass Point. Tel. 775-6560.

Coki stands outside Charlotte Amalie in the "East End" in the midst of a little restaurant row, so you might want to combine a gastronomic tour with a shopping expedition. From the store's expansive cutting boards come some of the most easy-to-wear cotton clothes in the Virgin Islands. You'll see pieces of canvas or handwoven Madras cotton being turned into the kind of chic resortwear suitable for yachting, beaching, or hanging out. Throughout the year the shop is open Wednesday through Monday from 9am to 9pm.

LION IN THE SUN, A. H. Riise Alley. Tel. 766-4203.

This is one of the most sophisticated clothing stores on the island. Patrons shop here for the collection of designer chic casual apparel and accessories. Whether it's tanks, T's, shorts, pants, or skirts, this store is likely to have what you're looking for. It has a men's department as well. The owner is firm about prices as marked—no bargaining here.

GIFTS & CRAFTS

DOWN ISLAND TRADERS, at the Waterfront (tel. 776-4641) and Bakery Sq., Back St. (tel. 774-4265).

An aroma of spices will lead you to these original native markets, which have an attractive array of spices, teas, seasonings, candies, jellies, jams, and condiments, most of which are packaged from natural Caribbean products. The owner carries a line of local cookbooks, as well as silk-screened T-shirts and bags, Haitian metal sculpture, handmade jewelry, Caribbean folk art, and children's gifts.

JAVA WRAPS, 24 Palm Passage, on the Waterfront. Tel. 774-3700.

Charlotte Amalie's Java Wraps is all white tiles with traditional Javanese matting decorated with exotic Balinese wood carvings on the walls. Locals and tourists alike buy the hand-batiked resortwear line specializing in shorts, shirts, sundresses, and children's clothing. Java Wraps is known for its sarong pieces and demonstrates tying them in at least 15 different ways.

JEWELRY

BLUE CARIB GEMS AND ROCKS, 2 Back St. Tel. 774-8525.

For a decade the owners prospected for gemstones all over the world, and the stones have been brought directly from the mine to you. The raw stones are cut and polished and then fashioned into jewelry by the lost-wax process. On one side of the premises you can see the craftspeople at work, and on the other side, their finished products, including such handsomely set stones as larimar, the sea/sky-blue-patterned variety of pectolite found only in the Caribbean. A lifetime guarantee is given on all handcrafted jewelry. Since the items are locally made, they are duty free and are not included in the $1,200 exemption. Incidentally, this establishment also provides emergency eyeglass repair.

CARDOW JEWELERS, 39 Main St. Tel. 776-1140.

Often called the Tiffany's of the Caribbean, Cardow Jewelers boasts the largest selection of fine jewelry in the world. This fabulous shop, where more than 20,000 rings are displayed, offers savings because of its worldwide direct buying, large turnover, and duty-free prices. Unusual and traditional designs are offered in diamonds, emeralds, rubies, sapphires, and Brazilian stones, as well as pearls and coral. Cardow has a whole wall of Italian gold chains, and also featured are antique coin jewelry and Piaget watches.

COLOMBIAN EMERALDS INTERNATIONAL, Havensight Mall. Tel. 774-2442.

The Colombian Emerald stores are renowned throughout the Caribbean for offering the finest collection of Colombian emeralds, both set and unset. In addition to jewelry, the shop stocks some of the world's finest watches, including Raymond Weil and Seiko.

H. STERN JEWELLERS, Havensight Mall. Tel. 776-1939.

Colorful gem and jewel creations are offered at Stern's locations in St. Thomas—three on Main Street, one at the Havensight Mall above, and branches at Bluebeard's Castle, Stouffer Grand Beach Resort, and Marriott's Frenchman's Reef. Stern gives worldwide guaranteed service, including a 1-year exchange privilege.

IRMELA'S JEWEL STUDIO, in the Old Grand Hotel, Main St. Tel. 774-5875, or toll free 800/524-2047.

Irmela's has made a name for itself in the highly competitive jewelry business in St. Thomas. Here the jewelry is unique, custom-designed by Irmela and handmade by her studio or imported from around the world. Irmela has the largest selection of cultured pearls in the Caribbean, including freshwater Biwa and South Sea pearls. Choose from hundreds of clasps and pearl necklaces. Irmela has a large selection of unset stones, such as rubies, sapphires, emeralds, and unusual ones, including tanzanite and alexandrite. The diamond collection includes every shape and size. The studio has designed and produced a Virgin Islands Gold Piece, a commemorative coin minted in pure gold with the American eagle and the inscription of the Virgin Islands on it.

LEATHER GOODS

THE LEATHER SHOP, INC., 1 Main St. Tel. 776-0290.

Here you'll find a good selection from these Italian designers—Fendi, Bottega Veneta, De Vecchi, Prima Classe, Furla, and Il Bisonte. There are many styles of handbags, belts, wallets, briefcases, and attaché cases, as well as all-leather luggage from Land. The traditional Indian molas of Colombia and Panama, which are still stitched entirely by hand, have been incorporated into sophisticated leather handbags.

LOUIS VUITTON, 24 Main St., at Palm Passage. Tel. 774-3644.

For fine leather goods, you can't beat Louis Vuitton, where the complete line by the world-famous French designer is available, including suitcases, handbags, wallets, and other accessories.

LINENS

THE LINEN HOUSE, 7A Royal Dane Mall. Tel. 774-8117.
The Linen House is considered to be one of the best stores for linen in the West Indies. You'll find a wide selection of place mats, decorative tablecloths, and many hand-embroidered goods. There are many high-fashion styles. Other branches are at A. H. Riise Mall (tel. 774-0469) and Havensight Mall (tel. 774-0868).

LIQUOR

AL COHEN'S, Long Bay Rd. Tel. 774-3690.
In Al Cohen's big warehouse at Havensight, across from the West Indies Company dock, where cruise-ship passengers come in, you can purchase discount liquor, fragrances, T-shirts, and souvenirs. Your purchases are delivered free to the airport or your ship.

A. H. RIISE LIQUORS, 34 Main St. (tel. 774-6900) and Havensight Mall (tel. 774-6900).
This store has almost every brand of liquor worth mentioning, along with a well-stocked supply of cigarettes and cigars. Fine ports, vintage Madeiras, rare cognacs and Armagnacs, and even "island flavor" favorites are sold here. The store will package your purchases for delivery to the airport or cruise ship.

PERFUMES

TROPICANA PERFUME SHOPPES, 2 and 14 Main St. Tel. 774-0010, or toll free 800/233-7948.
These two shops are near the Emancipation Park post office. The first is billed as the largest parfumerie in the world. Behind its rose-colored facade, it offers all the famous names in perfumes and cosmetics, including Pierre Cardin and Chanel for women and men. Men will also find Europe's best colognes and aftershave lotions here. When you return home, you can mail-order these same fragrances by taking advantage of Tropicana's toll-free number.

STRAW ARTICLES

THE STRAW FACTORY, 2A Garden St. Tel. 774-4849.
A short stroll from Post Office Square is the island's largest selection of straw hats, from classic Panamas to beachcomber bargains. The wide variety of handcrafted items includes straw baskets of every size and description, and hand-carved, brightly painted parrots and fish. The shop also has a big selection of handbags in straw and fabric, big and small, and a wide choice of sportswear. Also check their large assortment of dollar souvenirs.

SILK SCREENING

JIM TILLETT, Tillett Gardens, Tutu. Tel. 775-1929.
A visit to the art gallery and craft studios of Jim Tillett is a sightseeing expedition. The Tillett compound was converted from a Danish farm called "Tutu," and the Tillett name conjures up high-fashion silk-screen printing by

the famous Tillett brothers, who for years had their exquisite fabrics used by top designers and featured in such magazines as *Vogue* and *Harper's Bazaar*. After creating a big splash in Mexico, Jim Tillett settled in St. Thomas. At his compound nearby, you can visit the adjoining workshop where silk screening will be in progress.

There is an art gallery, which has an abundance of maps, paintings, sculpture, and graphics made by local artists. Mr. Tillett created a series of maps on fine cotton canvas that have been a best-selling item. Shopping tip: Buy a square of florid Tillett fabric and frame it when you return; it will make a vivid wall hanging.

Arts Alive Fairs are held in the Tillett Gardens three times a year—in autumn, spring, and summer. These fairs give local artists a showcase for their work, and offer crafts demonstrations. Other events include puppet shows for children, steel bands, calypso music, and dancing—folk, tap, ballet, and modern.

To reach Jim Tillett, take Route 38 east from Charlotte Amalie.

8. EVENING ENTERTAINMENT

St. Thomas has more nightlife than any other island in the Virgins, either U.S. or British, but it's not as extensive as you might think. The big hotels, such as Marriott's Frenchman's Reef Beach Resort and Bluebeard's offer the most varied programs.

After a day of sightseeing and shopping in the hot West Indies sun, many visitors are content to stay at their hotels in the evening, perhaps listening to a local fungi band. Big-time, big-name entertainment doesn't exist here.

There are reasons for that. Charlotte Amalie is no longer the rocking, swinging town it used to be at night. Many of the dark streets are considered dangerous, and muggings are frequent—so visitors have relatively abandoned it, except for a few places, such as the Greenhouse. Much of the action has shifted to Frenchtown, which is not big on nightclubs, but which does have the best restaurants and bars if you want a "communal" village for your drinking and dining.

Another problem is drinking and driving along badly lit and badly marked roads. If you're stuck at a distant resort hotel, it might not be worth the trouble to drive to some little hot spot.

There are infrequent cultural performances (see below), but most of the action is listening or dancing to a local band at your hotel.

THE PERFORMING ARTS

REICHHOLD CENTER FOR THE ARTS, University of the Virgin Islands, Brewers Beach. Tel. 774-8475.

This artistic center, considered the most visible and sophisticated in the Caribbean, lies west of Charlotte Amalie. Call the theater or check with the tourist office to see if one of the frequent performances is offered at the time of your visit.

Its lobby displays a frequently changing exhibition of paintings and sculptures by Caribbean artists, for which there is no charge for viewing.

The theater itself is a Japanese-inspired amphitheater set into a natural valley, with seating space for 1,200. The smell of gardenias adds to the pleasure of the frequent performances. The stage is used for presentations by several different repertory theaters of music, dance, and drama.

Prices: $15–$20.

Open: Performances begin at 8 or 8:30pm (call the theater). **Transportation:** Taxi or Vitran bus.

THE CLUB & MUSIC SCENE

IGGIE'S BOLONGO, Limetree Beach Hotel, Frenchman's Bay Rd., Frenchman's Bay. Tel. 779-2844.

⭐ During the day, Iggie's gazebo-inspired premises function as an informal open-air restaurant serving hamburgers, fries, and pasta. After dark, however, it turns into the most electronically sophisticated nightclub in St. Thomas, part of a trio of clubs that make Limetree one of the leading nightlife complexes on the island.

The secret is a complicated electronic device from Japan called a karaoke machine. The orchestrations of hundreds of highly singable pop songs are played while members of the audience, urged on by a talented and affable master of ceremonies, enjoy a temporary center stage as lead singer. To encourage the "famous for 5-minutes star," an array of tropical drinks help lubricate the participant's vocal cords. And, incidentally, Iggie's is named after the club's mascot iguanas.

Admission: Free. **Prices:** Drinks $4.

Open: Daily 9am–1am. **Transportation:** Taxi.

PARADISE ONE/PARADISE TWO, Bolongo Limetree Beach Hotel, Frenchman's Bay Rd., Frenchman's Bay. Tel. 779-2844.

Located on an elevated covered terrace near the lobby of the Bolongo Limetree Beach Resort Hotel, these twin nightclubs are separated by a quasi-soundproof glass wall. Guests move freely from one to another of the areas.

Paradise One is a disco, with recent music imported from New York, Los Angeles, and Paris, and refreshing breezes wafting in from the balcony.

Paradise Two has sit-down tables and a live West Indian, calypso, or reggae band. Drinks and sea breezes flow, conversation grows, and the combination of live and electronic music, with easy passage between the settings, contributes to a good time. The house drink is a Club Lime Tree. It's frozen, green, soothing, and potent.

Admission: $12 (allows entrance to both clubs). **Prices:** Drinks $4.

Open: Mon–Sat 10pm–2am.

THE TOP OF THE REEF, Marriott's Frenchman's Reef Beach Resort, Flamboyant Point. Tel. 776-8500.

This previously recommended hotel is the best entertainment center on the island. Some of the best acts are featured at The Top of the Reef, emphasizing the sights and sounds of the Caribbean. "Calypso Carnival" is a fast-paced revue of island talent, culture, and music. A native menu is served along with the show, which offers two performances nightly, at 7:30pm and again at 9:30pm.

Admission: $38 per person for dinner and show; $25 per person for two drinks and show.

Open: Mon–Sat 6:30–10:30pm.

BLUEBEARD'S CASTLE HOTEL, Bluebeard's Hill. Tel. 774-1600.

Overlooking the pool and yacht harbor, the Dungeon Bar at Bluebeard's offers piano-bar entertainment nightly and is a popular gathering spot for both residents and visitors. You can dance to a combo from 8pm to midnight Thursday and from 8pm to 1am Saturday. On Monday there's a steel band. Other nights a piano player entertains. Drink specialties are named after Bluebeard himself—Bluebeard's wench, cooler, and ghost.

Admission: Free. **Prices:** Drinks $2.50–$4.50.

Open: Sun–Fri 11am–midnight, Sat 11am–1am.

EPERNAY, rue de St. Barthélemy, Frenchtown. Tel. 774-5348.

Located adjacent to Alexander's Restaurant, this watering hole adds a European touch to the neighborhood. Within a color scheme of gray, black, and peach, you can order glasses of at least six different brands of champagne, and vintage wines by the glass ($5 and up). No main courses are served, but a list of appetizers ($6 to $10) seems tailor-made to accompany the flavors of the wine, such as sushi, fresh oysters, caviar, and a tempting array of desserts.

Open: Mon–Sat 4pm–2am. **Transportation:** Taxi.

COURTYARD BAR, Windward Passage Hotel, Veterans Dr. Tel. 774-5200.

You'd never know that the roar of Charlotte Amalie's coastal boulevard lies just outside the Courtyard Bar. Soothed by the sound of water splashing from a massive concrete fountain, and sheltered within the comforting enclosure of a semisecluded cabaña, you can enjoy such drinks as a "Paradise" (rum with cream of coconut, grenadine, and three kinds of fruit juices).

Prices: Drinks $3.25.
Open: Daily 10:30am–midnight.

GREENHOUSE, Veterans Dr. Tel. 774-7998.

Set directly on the Waterfront, this bar and restaurant is one of the few nightlife venues recommended in Charlotte Amalie. Each night a different entertainment is featured, ranging from oldies night to rock and roll. Wednesday night is a big blast.

Admission: $3 Wed and Fri, including first drink; other nights free. **Prices:** Beer $2.50; meals from $15.
Open: Daily 7am–2am.

ANDIAMO RISTORANTE CLUB Z, 41 Contant Rd., Rte. 33. Tel. 776-4655.

This famous nightspot lies a 5-minute drive west of Charlotte Amalie. Profiting from a sweeping panoramic view over the capital, the former Great House on Contant Hill attracts a young, urban crowd. Patrons come here to dine or to enjoy after-dinner dancing. An Italian-American cuisine is served in either the bistro or the main dining room. You might begin with a warm spinach salad studded with Gorgonzola, followed by veal medaillons cooked with wild mushrooms. A variety of pastas, even pizza, are featured. On Thursday and Friday from 5 to 8pm, you can order all the drinks you want, served with hors d'oeuvres, costing only $10 for men or $5 for women. On those same evenings, from 7 to 9pm, two persons can order dinner for the cost of one meal. Every night (except Tuesday), live music begins at 10pm. The action then shifts from the restaurant to the Club Z nightclub.

Admission: $5 cover charge Fri, $10 Sat; otherwise free. **Prices:** Dinners from $28; drinks from $4.
Open: Restaurant Wed–Mon 6:30–11pm; club Wed–Mon 10pm–4am.

WALTER'S II, 3 Trompeter Gade. Tel. 774-5025.

This is the most recommendable of the several remaining clubs in Charlotte Amalie. Located about a hundred yards from the island's famous synagogue within a clapboard town house built around 1935, it was established by Nevis-born Walter Springette. The cellar bar, Ronnie's Place, features an intimate atmosphere with music from the 50s, 60s, and 70s.

Admission: Free. **Prices:** Drinks $3.
Open: Daily 5pm–4am.

9. NETWORKS & RESOURCES

Most of the networks and resources that exist in larger places, such as Los Angeles, London, or Paris simply aren't available on a small West Indian island such as St.

Thomas. There are no rape crisis centers, counseling for gay men or lesbians, or even many student services.

FOR STUDENTS

St. Thomas is generally considered an expensive destination for students, with no discount opportunities for them. Students tend to pass through St. Thomas en route to St. John's famous campsites or the one at Tortola in the British Virgin Islands.

Students seeking economical lodgings for one night or longer in Charlotte Amalie should try **Bunkers' Hill,** 9 Commandant Gade (tel. 774-8056). You'll be in the center of town, near the bars and nightlife of Frenchtown, and you'll avoid expensive taxi rides to the island's East End.

Other than at the Greenhouse, the most reasonably priced food in Charlotte Amalie is served at that familiar chain favorite, **Arby's Bar and Restaurant,** 29-30 Main St. (tel. 776-5150).

FOR GAY MEN & LESBIANS

St. Thomas might be the most cosmopolitan of the Virgin Islands, but it is no longer the "gay paradise" it was in the 1960s and 1970s. The Caribbean action has shifted now mainly to San Juan. The major gay scene in the U.S. Virgins is in Frederiksted on St. Croix (see Chapter 6).

That doesn't mean that gay men and lesbians aren't attracted to St. Thomas. They are, but many of the clubs that used to cater exclusively to them are gone. What is available today are pockets of gay men and women who attend predominantly straight establishments.

These places include such previous recommendations as Blackbeard's Castle, The Mark St. Thomas, Hotel 1829, and even the Greenhouse on Veterans Drive.

FOR WOMEN

St. Thomas is not an ideal place for single women travelers. Sexual harassment can be a problem in certain bars in Charlotte Amalie, where few single women would want to be alone at night anyway. Any of the major resort hotels is safe.

Women might enjoy participating in one of the all-women sailing groups that use St. Thomas as a port of departure (see "Alternative/Adventure Travel," Chapter 2).

Jane's International, 2603 Bath Ave., Brooklyn, NY 11214 (tel. 718/266-2045), links potential travel companions with each other, has no age limit, and charges no fees for the service. Jane La Corte also functions as a full-service travel agent and a part-time "matchmaker."

Many women traveling alone prefer to go on an organized tour arranged by **Singleworld,** 402 Theodore Fremd Ave., Rye, NY 10580 (tel. 914/967-3334, or toll free 800/223-6490). About half its clients are women, and shared accommodations can be arranged through its travel packages, which greatly cuts down on expenses.

10. AN EASY EXCURSION

The fourth-largest of the U.S. Virgins, **Water Island** is only half a mile long and about a half- to 1-mile wide; its highest elevation is only 300 feet above sea level. Its nearest point is about ⅜-mile from St. Thomas.

Visitors travel here to spend the day on **Honeymoon Beach,** swimming, snorkeling, sailing, waterskiing, or just sunbathing on the palm-shaded beach. Lunch and drinks are available at the beach bar.

A ferry runs daily from 7am to midnight between Water Island Dock and the Sub Base at St. Thomas. It's a 7-minute ride and costs $3.50 each way. For information, phone 774-1207.

CHAPTER 5

THE U.S. VIRGIN ISLANDS: ST. JOHN

About 3 to 5 miles east of St. Thomas, across a glistening and turquoise-colored channel known as Pillsbury Sound, St. John rises verdantly out of the waters of the Atlantic. Only 7 miles long and 3 miles wide, it has a total landmass of some 20 square miles, making it the smallest of the three main U.S. Virgins. It is also the least densely populated.

Under the Danish regime, its surface was subdivided into parcels for development by plantation owners. A number of slave rebellions and a decline in the feasibility of economically producing sugar here ended that idea forever.

In 1917, the island was purchased by the U.S. Government from the Danes. In the 1940s, word of the island's rare beauty circulated widely through yachting circles and among developers in the U.S.

Today St. John (unlike some other U.S. Virgins) is truly pristine, a state of affairs rigidly enforced by the U.S. Park Service. Thanks to the efforts of Laurance Rockefeller, who purchased large tracts of its acreage and donated them as a gift to the American people, its shoreline waters as well as more than half of its landmass comprise the Virgin Islands National Park.

St. John is ringed with a rocky coastline that forms crescent-shaped bays, white sand beaches, and an array of bird and wildlife that is the envy of ornithologists and zoologists around the world. The island contains miles of serpentine hiking trails, whose edges are dotted with spectacular views and the ruins of 18th-century Danish plantations. At scattered intervals, there are mysteriously geometric petroglyphs incised into boulders and cliffs. Of unknown age and origin, they have never been deciphered.

The pleasures and beauties of St. John are not limited to land. The boating world seeks out its dozens of sheltered coves for anchorages, swimming, and extended vacations. The hundreds of coral gardens that surround St. John's perimeter are protected as rigorously as the land surfaces by the National Park Service. Any attempt

WHAT'S SPECIAL ABOUT ST. JOHN

Beaches
- ☐ Trunk Bay—wide and long—one of the most beautiful beaches in the West Indies.
- ☐ Caneel Bay, site of the famous Rockresort, with its string of seven beaches that stretch around Durloe Point to Hawksnest Caneel.
- ☐ Cinnamon Bay, site of one of the best campsites in the Caribbean.
- ☐ Maho Bay, largest beach on the north shore, once the site of an old sugar plantation.
- ☐ Hawksnest Bay—great for a beach party, with its white sand, picnic tables, and charcoal grills.

Ace Attractions
- ☐ Cruz Bay, the capital, a stage-set version of a little West Indian village, with pastel-painted houses.
- ☐ Annaberg Ruins, site of a Danish sugar mill and plantation from the early 1700s.

National Park
- ☐ The Virgin Islands National Park— 9,500 acres of land filled with historical sites.
- ☐ National park trails, including a 2½-mile section that goes by petroglyphs carved into boulders by mysterious people of the past.

to damage or remove coral from these waters is punishable with large and strictly enforced fines.

The island's status as a national park does not preclude the presence of well-maintained roads, a scattering of hotels and restaurants, and a small commercial center (Cruz Bay) on the island's western tip. Growth and commercial development on the island is limited to the parcels of privately owned land that are not part of the National Park.

Despite the unspoiled beauty of much of St. John, the island does contain most of the services that are necessary for modern tourism, including a sampling of restaurants, car-rental kiosks, yacht-supply facilities, hotels, and campgrounds. Cinnamon Bay is the most famous campsite in the Caribbean, founded by the National Park Service in 1964.

One of the most fun things to do on St. John is to rent an open-sided car to drive around its tortuous perimeter. Panoramas are endlessly variable, dramatically steep, and richly tinted with tones of forest green and turquoise, liberally accented with flashes of silver and gold from the strong and clear sunshine. Snorkelers, scuba divers, hill climbers, sailing enthusiasts, and underwater photographers alike all benefit from the island's unique status as one of the National Park Service's greatest resources.

1. ORIENTATION

ARRIVING

BY BOAT

The easiest and most popular way to reach St. John is by **ferryboat,** which leaves from the Red Hook landing on St. Thomas (trip time: 20 minutes). Beginning at

6:30am daily, boats depart every hour. The last ferry back to St. Thomas shoves off from Cruz Bay, St. John at 11:15pm. With such frequent departures, even cruise-ship passengers anchored in Charlotte Amalie for only a short time can visit St. John for a quick island tour and perhaps a picnic and a swim at one of its fine sandy beaches, and return in time for dinner. The one-way fare is $3 per adult, $1 for children under 12. Schedules can change without notice, so call 809/776-6282, for more information.

To reach the ferry, you can take an **open-air shuttle** to Red Hook Monday through Saturday from the Market Square in Charlotte Amalie. The fare is $3 per person each way.

Water-taxi service is available 24 hours a day for about $40 for two people, but it should be negotiated in advance. Call 809/775-6501.

It's also possible to board a boat directly at the Charlotte Amalie waterfront for $7 one way; the ride takes 45 minutes. The first boat departs St. Thomas at 9am, and the last one to leave Cruz Bay heading for Charlotte Amalie is at 5:15pm.

Also, a **launch service** leaves from National Park Dock at Red Hook on St. Thomas for the dock at Caneel Bay at St. John. The one-way fare is $9 per person, $12 to Charlotte Amalie.

TOURIST INFORMATION

The **St. John Tourist Office** (tel. 776-6450) is located near the Battery, a 1735 fort a short walk from where the ferry from St. Thomas docks. Get whatever information you are seeking about St. John here, and pick up a free map of the island, which colorfully and graphically illustrates where everything is located inside Cruz Bay. On the back is a map of the little island itself, illustrating the major roads and the location of all the main attractions, including some restaurants, beaches, and campsites.

2. GETTING AROUND

Your 20-minute ferry ride from St. Thomas will take you to **Cruz Bay,** the capital of St. John, which seems a century removed from the life you left behind. There are no cruise ships here, no array of milling shoppers—St. John is definitely sleepy and that's why many people like it. Don't come here looking for street addresses, as they don't exist. In fact, Cruz Bay is so small its streets are without names. It is sufficient to write Cruz Bay, St. John, U.S. Virgin Islands, on any mail to St. John.

Cruz Bay has a few shops, the Mongoose Junction shopping center (definitely worth a visit, a scattering of restaurants, and a small park. After a stroll around it, seek out the natural attractions of the island. Some claim St. John is the most beautiful island in the Caribbean.

BY BUS OR TAXI

The **bus** service runs from Cruz Bay to Maho Bay and stops at Caneel and Cinnamon bays. The one-way bus fare is $3.50 for adults.

IMPRESSIONS

[St. John has] the most superb beaches and view of any place I've seen, and [is] the most beautiful island in the Caribbean.
—LAURANCE ROCKEFELLER

The most popular way to get around St. John is by **surrey-style taxi.** If you want to go from the ferry-landing dock to Trunk Bay, the cost is about $7.50 for two passengers. Between midnight and 6am fares are increased by 40%.

BY CAR OR JEEP

The extensive stretches of St. John's national park have kept the edges of the island's roads undeveloped and uncluttered, with some of the most breathtaking vistas anywhere. Because of these views, many visitors opt to rent a vehicle (sometimes with four-wheel drive) to tour the island. Unless you have luggage which should probably be locked away in a trunk, you might consider one of the open-sided, Jeep-like vehicles which allow a maximum view of the surroundings and a minimum of plush accessories. Sturdy, informal, and endlessly ventilated, with manual transmissions, they are arguably among the most fun of the several available options on the island. Because of the island's relatively limited facilities, most renters need a car for only a day or two.

One excellent source is **Budget Rent-a-Car** (tel. 776-7575, or toll free 800/527-0700). It operates from a kiosk beside Route 104, a 3-minute drive from Cruz Bay's ferryboat piers. Arriving passengers head for the company's pierside kiosk, where an employee will complete some paperwork and arrange for the immediate delivery to the dock of any vehicle. At Budget, both conventional and four-wheel-drive vehicles begin at $55 a day during high season (slightly less in summer), with unlimited mileage included. Collision-damage insurance costs around $5 a day, although renters will still be responsible for the first $500 worth of repair costs in the event of an accident. Renters must be between 25 and 65 years of age.

Gasoline at Budget and at most of the island's other car-rental agencies is not provided in the cost of the rental. You're likely to be delivered a car with an almost-empty tank, just enough to get you to one of the island's two gas stations, or at best, a half-empty tank. (At presstime, a third gas station on the island dispensed gas only to government vehicles.) *Warning:* Because of the distance between gas stations, it's never a good idea to drive around St. John with less than half a tank of gas.

Hertz (tel. 776-6412, or toll free 800/654-3001) also rents vehicles from its office in Cruz Bay. Priced between $60 and $80 per day, a rental requires the presentation of a major credit card. Drivers must be at least 25 years old. Hertz has a more comprehensive insurance policy than Budget, offering a collision-damage waiver at $10 per day that charges no deductible in the event of an accident.

Also available on St. John are the services of **Avis Rent-a-Car** (tel. 776-6374, or toll free 800/331-2112), at Cruz Bay. Drivers must be 25 or older for any rental. At presstime, Avis charged more than either of its competitors, between $90 and $100 a day in winter (a bit less in summer) for each of its cars. A collision-damage waiver costs $12 a day, the price of which eliminated any financial responsibility in the event of an accident.

PARKING

No problem on St. John. Parking is abundantly available in most places. Hotels don't charge for parking.

DRIVING RULES

Remember to drive on the left! Otherwise, follow posted speed limits, which are generally very low, and traffic signs, which are the same as on the U.S. mainland.

BY SCOOTER

At presstime, no business offered this type of rental. They are legal, however, and if you ask at the ferry dock you may be directed to one of the locals who will rent you one for the day. Expect to spend $30 to $40 a day in summer and $40 to $50 a day in winter, with the payment of a $300 cash deposit required. Note, again, that there is no one to call or no office to go to.

ON FOOT

Walking is the only way to explore Cruz Bay and Mongoose Junction, but you'll need a taxi, scooter, motorcycle, or rented car to go to some of the faraway beaches or hidden pockets of beauty on the island. The national park has countless hiking trails, and most of its more interesting sections can be explored on foot.

FAST *ST. JOHN*

American Express See "Fast Facts: St. Thomas," Chapter 4.

Area Code 809. You can dial direct from the U.S.

Babysitting There is no central agency. Make arrangements through your hotel.

Business Hours Banking hours are Mon–Thurs 9am–2:30pm, Fri 9am–2pm and 3:30–5pm. Typical business hours are Mon–Fri 9am–5pm, Sat 9am–1pm. Stores are open Mon–Fri 9am–5pm, Sat 9am–1pm.

Car Rentals See "Getting Around," above.

Climate See "When to Go," Chapter 2.

Currency See "Information, Entry Requirements, and Money," Chapter 2.

Currency Exchange Go to a branch of Chase Manhattan Bank, Cruz Bay (tel. 776-6881).

Dentists See "Fast Facts: St. Thomas," Chapter 4.

Doctor Call 922 for a medical emergency. Otherwise, go to St. John Myrah Keating Smith Community Health Clinic, 3B Sussanaberg (tel. 776-6400).

Drugstores Go to St. John Drugcenter Inc., Boulon Shopping Center, Cruz Bay (tel. 776-6353). The staff here not only fill prescriptions, but sell film.

Electricity 110 to 115V, 60 cycles, as in the mainland U.S.

Emergencies Police, 915; ambulance, 922; fire, 921.

Etiquette St. Johnians tend to be a bit conservative. Save the skimpy swimwear for the beach, and cover up when patronizing public places, such as restaurants, hotel lobbies, or when shopping at Mongoose Junction.

Holidays See "When to Go," Chapter 2.

Hairdresser Try Decisions A Hair Salon, Mongoose Junction (tel. 776-6962).

Laundry Try Inn Town Laundromat, Cruz Bay (tel. 776-7449), open Mon–Fri 8:30am–5:30pm, Sat 8am–4pm. It's drop-off service only.

Liquor Laws Persons must be at least 21 years of age to patronize bars or purchase liquor in St. John.

Mail Postage rates are the same as on the U.S. mainland.

Maps See "Tourist Information," above.

Newspapers and Magazines Copies of U.S. mainland newspapers, such as *The New York Times* and *The Miami Herald* arrive daily and are for sale at Mongoose Junction, Caneel Bay, and Hyatt. The latest copies of *Time* and

Newsweek are also for sale. Complimentary copies of *Here's How: St. Thomas & St. John* contain many helpful hints. It is the official guidebook of the St. Thomas and St. John Hotel Association, and is available at the tourist office (see above) and at various hotels.

Photographic Needs To purchase film on St. John, go to the St. John Drug center Inc. (see "Drugstores," above). However, to have film developed, you'll have to take it to St. Thomas (see "Fast Facts: St. Thomas," Chapter 4).

3. ACCOMMODATIONS

The number of accommodations on St. John is limited, and that's how most people would like to keep it. Your choices range from an elegant tropical haven to a no-frills campsite.

Prices are often slashed in summer, from 30% to 60%. But in winter, expect to spend from $305 to $570 in a double room rated "very expensive." Condo rentals, which are always EP, are judged "expensive" if two persons pay from $295 per day, but moderate at $170 (for two). (See "Where to Stay," Chapter 3, for an explanation of the abbreviations AP, CP, EP, and MAP.) Inns around Cruz Bay are considered "inexpensive" if they offer either standard rooms or efficiencies (with small kitchens) for $50 to $95 per day. Campgrounds (see below) are the most economical way to live on St. John.

For tips on saving money on accommodations, see "Frommer's Smart Traveler: Hotels," Chapter 4.

LUXURY RESORTS

CANEEL BAY, INC., Virgin Islands National Park, St. John, USVI 00831. Tel. 809/776-6111, or toll free 800/223-7637. Fax 809/776-2030. 171 rms (all with bath). MINIBAR **Transportation:** Taxi.

$ Rates (including EP): Dec 20–Mar, $320–$570 single or double. Off-season, $200–$380 single or double. MAP $65 per person extra. AE, DC, MC, V. **Parking:** Free.

The style of this Rockresort isn't flashy—its beauty is subtle and conservative, appreciated by a discerning (and usually wealthy) clientele. Caneel Bay itself is the first to admit that for a certain kind of client, the resort is a dream come true; for others, it simply wouldn't be appropriate as their fantasy vacationland. It was established upon the rolling seaside acreage of a sugar plantation with stone-sided mills and towers that today are heavily weighted with cascading bougainvillea. The site was deliberately and personally selected by Laurance Rockefeller for its seven spectacular beaches, its array of convenient yacht anchorages, and its 170-acre location next to land that he eventually donated to the U.S. government for use as a national park.

Conscious decisions were made for an environment where families could fraternize quietly in elegant but not overly decorated settings of uncluttered charm. Tennis courts are deliberately not illuminated for nighttime play, accommodations contain no telephones or TVs, and bungalows lie far from their neighbors.

ST. JOHN ACCOMMODATIONS

ATLANTIC OCEAN

CARIBBEAN SEA

Coral Bay

VIRGIN ISLANDS NATIONAL PARK

Bays and geographic features:
East End Bay, Privateer Bay, Round Bay, East End, Haulover Bay, Salt Pond Bay, Lameshur Bay, Reef Bay, Fish Bay, Rendezvous Bay, Chocolate Hole, Great Cruz Bay, Leinster Bay, Francis Bay, Mabo Bay, Cinnamon Bay, Trunk Bay, Peter Bay, Jumbie Bay, Trunk Bay, Hawksnest Bay, Caneel Bay

Hills and peaks:
Blackrock Hill, Nancy Hill, More Hill, Leinster Hill, Minna Hill, Ajax Peak, King Hill, Bordeaux Mtn., Camelberg Peak, Mamey Peak, Gifft Hill, Peter Peak, Margaret Hill, Roman Hill, Great Hill

Roads and places:
East End Road, Centerline Road, King Hill Road, Bordeaux Mtn. Road, Northshore Road, Centerline Road, Peter Peak, Gifft Hill Road, CRUZ BAY, Southside Road, Mongoose Junction, Caneel Hill

Hurricane Hole

Route markers: 4, 10, 107, 20, 10, 3, 20, 2, 10, 104, 6, 5, 1, 10, 7, 8, 9, 11

Accommodations legend

Caneel Bay **1**
Cinnamon Bay Campground **2**
Cruz Inn **11**
Estate Zootenvaal **4**
Gallows Point Suite Resort **7**
Hyatt Regency St. John **5**
Inn at Tamarind Court **10**
Lavender Hill Estates **8**
Maho Bay **3**
Raintree Inn **9**
Virgin Grand Villas **6**

Dining/Entertainment: See "Dining," below, for descriptions of the Caneel Bay Beach Terrace Dining Room and The Sugar Mill. Nightly entertainment is offered in the Caneel Bay Bar beneath the soaring ceiling of a stone-and-timber pavilion.

Services: An array of scheduled garden tours, fishing expeditions, diving excursions to offshore wrecks, deep-sea fishing, free snorkeling lessons, tennis lessons, babysitting, valet, laundry.

Facilities: Full-service dive shop and water-sports activities desk, 11 tennis courts, free use of Sunfish sailboats and Windsurfers, swimming pools, seven beaches.

HYATT REGENCY ST. JOHN, Great Cruz Bay, St. John, USVI 00831.
Tel. 809/776-7171, or toll free 800/233-1234. Fax 809/775-3858. 285 rms (all with bath). A/C MINIBAR TV TEL **Transportation:** Taxi.

$ Rates: Winter, $305–$495 single or double. Summer, $175–$275 single or double. Mandatory MAP $55 per person extra. AE, DC, MC, V. **Parking:** Free.

The Hyatt, the splashiest and most immediately impressive hotel on St. John, sits on 34 acres of what used to be scrub forest on the southeast side of the island. The 13 cedar-roofed postmodern buildings have ziggurat-shaped angles, soaring ceilings, large windows, and an overall style that seems inspired by Aztec, Egyptian, or neocolonial models. Herringbone-patterned brick walkways connect the gardens (where 400 palms were imported from Puerto Rico) with the beach and the most unusual swimming pool in the Virgin Islands.

Each of the stylish accommodations contains fan-shaped windows, curved ceilings, unusual but pleasing dimensions, and a softly vibrant color scheme of rose and mauve.

Dining/Entertainment: One of the leading dining choices is Chow Bella (see "Dining," below). The Café Grand serves breakfast and dinner, featuring a buffet at both times. The Spanish Grill draws the lunch crowd, with its barbecues and island drinks. The Splash Bar is open daily from 11am to midnight and entertainment is often presented in season.

Services: Round-trip transfers from St. Thomas airport, supervised activities program for children.

Facilities: 11,000 square-foot swimming pool, six lit tennis courts, 1,200-foot beach, water sports, spa and health club.

VIRGIN GRAND VILLAS, Great Cruz Bay, St. John, USVI 00830. Tel.
809/775-3856, or toll free 800/356-5890. Fax 809/779-4760. 43 villas. A/C MINIBAR TV TEL **Transportation:** Taxi.

$ Rates (including EP): Winter, $370 terrace suite for 2; $450 1-bedroom loft; $600 2-bedroom townhome; $850 3-bedroom pool villa. Summer, $186 terrace suite for 2; $248 1-bedroom loft; $600 2-bedroom townhome; $850 3-bedroom villa. AE, MC, V. **Parking:** Free.

The buildings here were designed in the same postmodern style as the nearby Hyatt Regency, and guests within its premises have easy access and signing privileges at the Hyatt Regency's bars, restaurants, and sports facilities.

The villas lie across the road from the hotel and were begun in 1986. Each of the units is technically a privately owned condominium, and all but a handful are rented out to vacationers when the owners are not in residence. The decor of each unit is postmodern, like the hotel itself (marble floors, tile patios, Italian lacquered furniture). Full chamber service is only once a week, although towel changes and garbage collection are daily. A fully equipped kitchen in each unit keeps the cost of a vacation down.

Each unit contains a washing machine and dryer, microwave oven, and cooking equipment. Although guests at the villas are free to use the hotel's beaches and swimming pool, they also have their own pool separate from the one used by the hotel.

CONDOS

EXPENSIVE

GALLOWS POINT SUITE RESORT, P.O. Box 58, Cruz Bay, St. John, USVI 00831. Tel. 809/776-6434, or toll free 800/776-7229. Fax 809/776-6520. 60 units (all with bath). **Transportation:** Taxi.

$ Rates: Winter, $250–$275 single or double. Summer, $140–$155 single or double. Extra person $25. AE, DC, MC, V. **Parking:** Free.

Clustered on top of one of the rocky headlands in the harbor of Cruz Bay, these condominiums were stylishly patterned after an 18th-century Danish manor house. Their clapboards, lattices, fan-shaped windows, panoramic porches, and louvered French doors are all stained the same shade, and are softened with verdant landscaping. Each of the 15 villas is divided into four units, the most desirable of which are the two top-floor units. These have massive exposed beams of Canadian cedar, yards and yards of planking, sleeping lofts, and comfortable tropical furniture.

The two ground-floor units have lower ceilings, sunken living rooms, and wooden decks facing the water. Each has a ceiling fan, comfortable tropical furniture, and a kitchenette with dishwasher, refrigerator, microwave, cutlery, and dishes. None of them has telephones, or air conditioning. A few contain TVs, and residents without TV can rent one from the reception desk.

LAVENDER HILL ESTATES, P.O. Box 8306, Cruz Bay, St. John, USVI 00831-8306. Tel. 809/776-6969. Fax 809/776-6969. 8 units (all with bath). TV TEL **Transportation:** Taxi.

$ Rates: Winter, $210 1-bedroom unit; $260 2-bedroom unit. Summer, $125 1-bedroom unit; $150 2-bedroom unit. MC, V. **Parking:** Free.

This outfit offers some of the best condominium values on the island, with a swimming pool with a lounging deck and a tropical setting. It is a short walk to the shops, markets, restaurants, and safari buses of Cruz Bay. The rates are midway between the campgrounds and inns and the upscale properties of Virgin Grand and Caneel Bay. The units overlook Cruz Bay Harbor, and each one has a spacious central living/dining area opening onto a tiled deck, along with a fully

---

ⒻFROMMER'S COOL FOR KIDS: HOTELS

Hyatt Regency St. John *(see p. 118).* This hotel has more for kids than any other on the island, including a supervised activities program for ages 3 to 15 during the summer months, winter weekends, and certain holiday periods. A special children's menu is available in the restaurants.

Lavender Hill Estates *(see p. 119).* Families often save money by staying at one of these condos with a swimming pool. Meals can be prepared in each of the condo's fully equipped kitchen units. Children under 12 stay free; others are charged $25 extra per night.

Cinnamon Bay Campground *(see p. 121).* Tents or cottages with cooking gear—families have a choice here. They can even rent a bare site on a beachside campground. The National Park Service is the host.

Maho Bay *(see p. 121).* The tents here are really like small canvas houses, with kitchen areas and sun decks. In this laid-back hideaway, children can be taught how to become more aware of the environment.

equipped kitchen and one or two bedrooms. Laundry facilities are available. Units are furnished in an attractive modern Caribbean style.

MODERATE

CARIBBEAN VILLAS & RESORTS MANAGEMENT CO. INC., P.O. Box 458, St. John, USVI 00831. Tel. 809/776-6152, or toll free 800/338-0987. A/C **Transportation:** Taxi.

$ Rates: Most less than $200 per night (Cruz Views 2-bedroom unit for four costs $210 in winter, $170 in summer). Private homes more expensive. Children under 6 stay free in parents' room. No credit cards. **Parking:** Free.

Caribbean Villas, the island's biggest company, manages five small to medium-size resorts, all of which were constructed in the last few years. These affordable accommodations cater to families with children. Properties include Gift Hill, Battery Hill, Cruz Views, Cruz Bay Villas, and Pastory Estates, the last a 12-unit resort condo on a private hill about a 5-minute drive from Cruz Bay. Caribbean Villas also manages 30 private homes, with from 2 to 6 bedrooms, renting for $200 to $1,500 per night, with pools, Jacuzzi, and views.

ESTATE ZOOTENVAAL, Hurricane Hole, St. John, USVI 00830. Tel. 809/776-6321, 216/861-5337 in the continental U.S. Fax 809/776-6321. 4 cottages. **Transportation:** Taxi.

$ Rates: Year-round, cottage $1,000–$1,250 weekly for two; $175–$220 daily for two. Extra person $35–$50. No credit cards. **Parking:** Free.

Located within the boundaries of the U.S. national park at the edge of a horseshoe-shaped bay, which local mariners know is usually safe from hurricanes, Estate Zootenvaal is a good choice for urban escapees. Consisting of cement-sided villas and a two-bedroom house, it sits within earshot of the waves on the grounds of a former private estate called Zootenvaal. The accommodations have designer interiors with muted colors and all have fully equipped kitchens, Danish flatware, and Arzberg china. Chamber service can be arranged at an extra cost on an as-needed basis. The private beach is known for its good snorkeling.

BUDGET INNS

Let's face it: Except for the campgrounds recommended below, the tab at most of the establishments on St. John is far beyond the pocketbook of the average traveler. If you're willing to settle for few frills, the following places can provide a low-cost holiday on St. John.

CRUZ INN, P.O. Box 566, Cruz Bay, St. John, USVI 00831. Tel. 809/776-7688, or toll free 800/666-7688. Fax 809/776-7449. 14 rms (5 with bath and kitchen).

$ Rates (including continental breakfast): Winter, $50 double without bath; $65–$85 efficiency. Summer, $45 double without bath; $60–$75 efficiency. Extra person $15. Housekeeping units require a 3-day minimum stay. AE, MC, V. **Parking:** Free.

This low-priced accommodation overlooking Enighed Pond is a bit of a walk from the Cruz Bay ferry dock. Seven of the guest rooms are in the main building and share two baths; each has an overhead fan and either a double or twin beds. Other accommodations are housed in efficiencies and apartments in the complex. Five of the units have cooking facilities. The inn has a convivial bar and offers weekly entertainment. Tennis courts are available nearby.

INN AT TAMARIND COURT, P.O. Box 350, Cruz Bay, St. John, USVI 00831. Tel. 809/776-6378, or toll free 800/221-1637. 20 rms (13 with bath), 1 apt., 1 suite.

$ Rates (including continental breakfast): Winter, $48 single without bath; $73 double with bath; $98 apt.; $108 suite. Summer, $38 single without bath; $63 double with bath; $88 apt.; $98 suite. AE, MC, V. **Parking:** Free.

Right outside Cruz Bay but still within walking distance of the ferryboat dock, this modest establishment consists of a small hotel (where rooms have been renovated) and an even simpler West Indian inn. Baths at the inn are shared, whereas within the hotel, all rooms have private bath. The establishment's social life revolves around its courtyard bar.

RAINTREE INN, P.O. Box 566, Cruz Bay, St. John, USVI 00831. Tel. 809/776-7449, or toll free 800/666-7449. Fax 809/776-7449. 11 rms (all with bath). A/C

$ Rates: Winter, $70 double; $95 efficiency. Summer, $50 double; $75 efficiency. Efficiencies require a 3-day minimum. MC, V. **Parking:** Free.

One block from the ferry stop, next to the Catholic church, the Raintree Inn has simple double rooms with high ceilings. Linen, towels, and soap are supplied upon request. Three of the rooms have full kitchen, and two twins are in a carpeted loft. A small deck is attached. The inn adjoins a reasonably priced restaurant next door, The Fish Trap. Laundry service is available on the premises.

CAMPGROUNDS

CINNAMON BAY CAMPGROUND, P.O. Box 720, Cruz Bay, St. John, USVI 00831. Tel. 809/776-6330, or toll free 800/223-7637. Fax 809/776-6458. 111 units (none with bath). **Transportation:** Safari bus from Cruz Bay.

$ Rates: Winter, $79 cottage for two; $62 tent; $14 bare site. Summer, $53 cottage for two; $40 tent; $13 bare site. Breakfast $6 extra. AE, MC, V. **Parking:** Free.

Established by the National Park Service in 1964, this is the most complete campground in the Caribbean. Located on the north coast of the island, the site is directly on the beach, amid thousands of acres of tropical vegetation. You have a choice of three accommodations—tent, cottage, or bare site. At the campsites, only bare necessities are provided. The tents are permanently affixed to wooden platforms measuring 10 by 14 feet. Cottages have 15 by 15 feet cement floors, and consist of a cross-ventilated shelter with two concrete walls and two screens. They each contain four twin beds, and two cots can be added. Each additional occupant is charged $10. Those renting both the tents and the showers get free use of a two-burner propane gas stove, cooking utensils, cutlery, plates, and cups. Linen is changed weekly. Lavatories, showers, a grocery store, and a cafeteria (serving $12 dinners) are all located nearby. Camping here for more than a 2-week period in any given year is illegal.

Management of this campground is handled by Rockresorts.

MAHO BAY, P.O. Box 310, Cruz Bay, St. John, USVI 00831. Tel. 809/776-6226, or toll free 800/392-9004; 212/472-9453 in New York. Fax 212/816-6210. 113 tent cottages (none with bath). **Transportation:** Maho Bay shuttle.

$ Rates: Mid-Dec to Apr, $80 tent cottage for two; minimum stay of 7 nights required. May to mid-Dec, $55 tent cottage for two; no minimum stay required. $10 extra for each additional occupant over 16; $7 extra for each additional occupant 15 and younger. No credit cards. **Parking:** Free.

Maho Bay is an interesting concept in ecology vacationing, where you get close to nature, but with considerable comfort. The deluxe campground, an 8-mile drive from Cruz Bay, is set in the Virgin Islands National Park. To preserve the existing ground cover, all 113 tent cottages are on platforms above a thickly wooded slope. Utility lines and pipes are hidden under wooden boardwalks and stairs.

The tent cottages are covered with canvas and screens. Each unit has two movable twin beds, a couch, electric lamps and outlets, a dining table, chairs, a propane stove, and an ice chest (cooler). That's not all—you're furnished linen, towels, cooking and eating utensils. There's a store where you can buy supplies. You can do your own cooking, although you can eat at the camp's outdoor restaurant. Guests share communal bathhouses.

Maho Bay has an open-air Pavilion Restaurant, which always serves breakfast and dinner. Lunches are offered in winter, and the international dinner menu is changed nightly depending on what food is fresh. Both meat and vegetarian selections are offered. The Pavilion also functions as an amphitheater and community center where various programs are featured. A new Pavilion, higher up the hill with spectacular views of the ocean, is also used for a community center as well as special occasions such as weddings and group meetings. The camp has an excellent water-sports program.

4. DINING

St. John has some posh pockets for dining, particularly at Caneel Bay and Hyatt Regency St. John, but it also has some West Indian places with lots of local color and flavor. Many of the restaurants here command high prices, but you can lunch almost anywhere for reasonable rates. Dinner is considered a bit of an event here, since there's not much organized entertainment anywhere.

Prices are considered "expensive" if restaurants charge from $40 to $65 per person for dinner without wine. Those viewed as "moderate" charge from $22 to $35 for dinner. Anything under $20 is "inexpensive." Most of the places in this category are "inexpensive" if you order the less costly items on the menu, although Caribbean lobsters and steak always cost more.

For tips on saving money when dining, see "Frommer's Smart Traveler: Restaurants," Chapter 4.

LUXURY DINING AROUND THE ISLAND
EXPENSIVE

CANEEL BAY BEACH TERRACE DINING ROOM, Caneel Bay Hotel. Tel. 776-6111.
Cuisine: INTERNATIONAL/SEAFOOD. **Reservations:** Required for dinner.
Transportation: Taxi.
$ Prices: Lunch buffet $22 per person; dinner appetizers $6–$12.50, dinner main courses $27–$38; fixed-price dinner $55. AE, DC, MC, V.
Open: Lunch daily 11:30am–2:30pm, dinner daily 7–9pm.
This is the main dining room for the Caneel Bay resort. Located beneath the soaring ceiling of a gazebo-inspired pavilion set midway between the beach and the hotel's reception desk, the Beach Terrace Dining Room serves richly laden buffets at lunch, and more formal à la carte and fixed-price dinners. Men are requested to wear jackets for dinner (especially between November and May).

Although the menu changes nightly according to the available ingredients, your meal might include poached oysters with a sauce of roast fennel and garlic, fresh figs with prosciutto, rack of lamb with green peppercorn sauce, grilled grouper with a roast red pepper sauce, and such desserts as a gingered floating island with an English cream sauce.

LE CHATEAU DE BORDEAUX, Junction 10, Centerline Rd., Bordeaux Mountain. Tel. 776-6611.

Cuisine: FRENCH/CARIBBEAN. **Reservations:** Recommended. **Transportation:** Taxi.
$ **Prices:** Appetizers $6–$8; main dishes $17–$25. DC, MC, V.
Open: Dinner Mon–Sat, two nightly seatings from 5:30–6:30pm and from 7:45–8:45pm.

Set 5 miles east of Cruz Bay near the geographical center of the island, close to one of its highest points, this restaurant is known for its eastward-facing vistas and some of the best high-altitude views in St. John. Although an ice-cream kiosk sells sundaes and milk shakes throughout the day, most visitors patronize the place for its evening allure. Then, amid a Victorian decor with lace tablecloths, you can enjoy such dishes as banana-papaya conch fritters; saffron-flavored pastas; West Indian seafood chowder; chicken and seafood paella; roasted rack of lamb with a Dijon and honey-nut crust, served with a shallot and port wine sauce; and a changing array of cheesecakes, among other desserts. The specialty drink is a passion fruit daiquiri.

CHOW BELLA, Hyatt Regency St. John, Great Cruz Bay. Tel. 776-7171.
Cuisine: ASIAN/ITALIAN. **Reservations:** Recommended. **Transportation:** Taxi.
$ **Prices:** Appetizers $4–$8.50; pastas $14–$18; main dishes $18.50–$26.50. AE, DC, MC, V.
Open: Dinner daily 6–9:30pm.

Everything about Chow Bella is a direct import from the most sophisticated food and design experts of California, with liberal doses of managerial razzmatazz added by Hyatt Hotels. Its hypermodern marble tables are placed one floor above the most dramatic lobby in the Caribbean, with views of an architectural style inspired by ancient Egypt or Mesopotamia. Piano music filters from a spotlit dais in the restaurant to the lobby below, as scents from the hotel's gardens filter upward.

The cuisine mingles the traditions of Italy and the Far East in amusing and innovative ways. Menu selections include *farfalle agli asparagi* (bowtie pasta with asparagus and parmesan) accompanied by a platter of Thai pork and Japanese eggplant.

ELLINGTON'S, Gallows Point, Cruz Bay. Tel. 776-7166.
Cuisine: CONTINENTAL. **Reservations:** Required.
$ **Prices:** Appetizers $4–$10; main dishes $10–$25. AE, MC, V.
Open: Breakfast daily 8–11am; dinner daily 6–10pm.

By far one of the most stylish and exciting independent restaurants on St. John, Ellington's is set near the neocolonial villas of Gallows Point. Its putty-colored exterior has the double staircase, fan windows, louvers, and low-slung hip roof of an 18th-century Danish manor house. Drop in for a drink on the panoramic upper deck featuring the finest view of sunsets over St. Thomas anywhere.

The establishment is named after a local radio announcer, raconteur, and mystery writer, whose real estate developments helped transform St. John into a stylish enclave for the American literati of the 1950s and 60s. Named Richard "Duke" Ellington, he entertained his friends, martini in hand, around a frequently photographed table that is currently used in the sunset lounge. Ellington's dining room is very open and is lavishly adorned with tropical hardwoods. Breakfast is served daily from 8 to 11am. The dinner menu changes daily to accommodate the freshest offering of the sea. Some favorites include conch fritters, swordfish scampi, coconut shrimps with passion fruit dipping sauce, chilled mango soup, chicken Martinique, baked scallops à la duke, and whatever fresh fish the sea has to offer including wahoo, tuna, and mahimahi.

PARADISO, Mongoose Junction. Tel. 776-8806.
Cuisine: ITALIAN. **Reservations:** Recommended.

$ Prices: Appetizers $5-$8; main dishes $16.95-$24.95. AE, MC, V.

Open: Dinner daily 6-10:30pm. Bar daily 4:30pm-midnight.

The most talked-about restaurant on St. John is located among the catwalks and lattices of the island's most interesting shopping center, Mongoose Junction. The decor includes lots of brass, glowing hardwoods, and nautical antiques. Paradiso has what might be the most beautiful bar on the island. Its crafted from mahogany, purpleheart, and angelique.

Menu items include an array of pastas, Caesar salads, a platter of smoked seafood, baked stuffed sole with a lobster cream sauce, lobster fra diavolo (with seafood and red chilies), and a selection of daily specials whose availability depends on their arrival that day from the U.S. mainland. The house drink is Redbeard's Rum, the bartender's version of plantation punch.

THE SUGAR MILL, in the Caneel Bay Hotel. Tel. 776-6111.

Cuisine: INTERNATIONAL. **Reservations:** Recommended. **Transportation:** Taxi.

$ Prices: Fixed-price all-you-can-eat buffet $55 per person. AE, DC, MC, V.

Open: Dinner (buffet only) Tues-Sat 7-9pm.

This is the most attractive restaurant in St. John, thanks to a lavish upgrading in 1990. It provides an opportunity for nonresidents to visit one of the most legendary resorts of the Caribbean, the Caneel Bay refuge, carved out of primeval forests in the 1950s by Laurance Rockefeller.

It lies behind the bougainvillea-covered tower of an 18th-century sugar mill, where ornamental ponds with water lilies fill former crystallization pits for hot molasses. A flight of stairs leads to a monumental circular dining room, with a wraparound veranda, sweeping views of an immaculate park, and a design that reminds some diners of the underview of a very upscale umbrella. In the center rises the stone column that horses and mules once circumambulated while crushing the sugar cane stalks.

From a brass-accented exposed kitchen come such specialties as peach daiquiris and one of the most lavish buffet tables on the island. Both the theme and the ingredients of the table change nightly, but might feature apricot-ginger soup, a seafood bar of shellfish, grilled kingfish with essence of tomato, grilled lobster tail, lamb chops, steaks, and an array of desserts.

MODERATE

CAFE ROMA, Cruz Bay. Tel. 776-6524.

Cuisine: ITALIAN. **Reservations:** Not required.

$ Prices: Appetizers $2.75-$8; main dishes $9.50-$15.50. AE, MC, V.

Open: Dinner daily 5-10pm.

Diners climb a flight of concrete steps to reach this rustic Italian restaurant and pizza parlor. You may want to arrive early and have a strawberry colada, then enjoy a selection of pastas or veal and chicken dishes. Ask about their "white pizza," made without tomato sauce. Italian wines are sold by the glass or bottle, and you can end the evening with an espresso.

MONGOOSE RESTAURANT, CAFE, AND BAR, Mongoose Junction. Tel. 776-7586.

Cuisine: INTERNATIONAL. **Reservations:** Not required.

$ Prices: Lunch appetizers $3-$3.50; salads, burgers, and sandwiches $5-$9; dinner appetizers $5-$9; main dishes $6-$25. AE, DC, MC, V.

Open: Breakfast daily 8:30-11:30am; lunch daily 11:30am-5:30pm; dinner daily 5:30-10pm. Bar daily 11am-midnight.

Some visitors compare the soaring interior design here to a large Japanese birdcage, because of the strong vertical lines and the 25-foot ceiling. Set among trees and built

N

ST. JOHN DINING

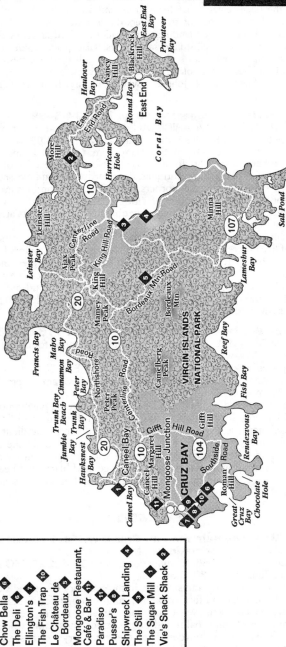

Café Roma ◆ 9
Caneel Bay Terrace
  Dining Room ◆ 1
Chow Bella ◆ 6
The Deli ◆ 6
Ellington's ◆ 1
The Fish Trap ◆ 10
Le Château de
  Bordeaux ◆ 5
Mongoose Restaurant,
  Café & Bar ◆ 11
Paradiso ◆ 11
Pusser's ◆ 8
Shipwreck Landing ◆ 4
The Still ◆ 3
The Sugar Mill ◆ 4
Vie's Snack Shack ◆ 2

above a stream, it's a lot like a structure you might find in northern California. Some guests perch at the open-centered bar for a drink and sandwich, while others sit on an adjacent deck where a canopy of trees filters the tropical sunlight. The bar offers more than 20 varieties of frothy island-inspired libations, priced at about $4 to $5 each. Lunches include soups, well-stuffed sandwiches, salad platters, burgers, and pastas. Dinner is more formal, with such specialties as grilled steaks, fresh catch of the day, surf and turf, seafood creole, and island fish cakes. This establishment's Sunday brunch is mobbed with St. Johnians, who make eggs Benedict ($7) the most popular dish.

PUSSER'S, Wharfside Village, Cruz Bay. Tel. 774-5489.
   Cuisine: INTERNATIONAL/CARIBBEAN. **Reservations:** Recommended.
 $ **Prices:** Appetizers $4.95–$8.95; main dishes $12.95–$24.95. AE, MC, V.
   Open: Mon–Sat 11:30am–10pm, Sun 9am–5pm. **Closed:** 2 weeks in Sept.
More than any other place in St. John, Pusser's re-creates the days of the English clipper ships, with English maritime antiques, dark hardwood, and masses of polished brass jutting out from unexpected corners. Its two levels combine a pub with a sophisticated store selling its own line of clothing and gift items. Its veranda high above the shoreline of Cruz Bay is immediately obvious to newcomers arriving via the ferryboat from St. Thomas.

The establishment (now a chain throughout the Caribbean) is named after the famous blend of five different rums that the Royal Navy served its sailors for 300 years. At tables near the bar, you can order traditional English dinner pies, including one made with steak and ale. Also try Cajun barbecued chicken, crab ravioli, lobster medaillons, or New York strip steak. Pusser's famous frozen "mud pie" is the most popular dessert, followed by "Pusser's Coffee," roasted coffee with Pusser's Rum and a bit of brown sugar and whipped cream.

THE STILL, 10-19 Estate Carolina, Coral Bay. Tel. 776-6866.
   Cuisine: CONTINENTAL. **Reservations:** Recommended for dinner and parties of more than six. **Transportation:** Taxi.
 $ **Prices:** Appetizers $4–$9; main dishes $12–$22. AE, MC, V.
   Open: Lunch Mon–Sat 11am–3:30pm; dinner daily 5:30pm–10pm; brunch Sun 10:30am–3:30pm.
This relatively undiscovered restaurant is housed in a timbered pavilion on the water of Coral Bay. Its breezy location and extensive frozen-drink menu offer a relaxing respite from beach activities. Quiet evenings provide romantic, candlelit dining. Try Caribbean conch fritters or blackened mahimahi at lunch. At night the fare is more elaborate, and includes items such as baked Brie with mango chutney and toasted almonds, coconut shrimp with mango mustard sauce, and blackened beef with sour cream horseradish sauce. Main dishes include shrimp in lime honey sauce, steak au poivre, and fresh fish.

INEXPENSIVE

THE FISH TRAP, in the Raintree Inn, Cruz Bay. Tel. 776-9817.
   Cuisine: SEAFOOD. **Reservations:** Not required.
 $ **Prices:** Appetizers $2.95–$6.75; main courses $8.95–$22.95. MC, V.
   Open: Dinner Tues–Sun 4:30–9:30pm.
In this previously recommended inn standing in the center of the island's capital, The Fish Trap enjoys both local and foreign patronage. It's known for its seafood (a wide selection), but also caters to the vegetarian and burger crowd as well. In a tropical setting in the midst of coconut palm and banana trees, most diners begin with the conch fritters or the Fish Trap chowder. Then they might try a tasty seafood combo, blackened sea scallops, or shrimp Palermo (with olive oil, garlic, and parsley). All desserts are prepared fresh in the kitchen daily.

SHIPWRECK LANDING, 34 Freeman's Ground, Rte. 107, Coral Bay. Tel. 776-8640.
    Cuisine: SEAFOOD/CONTINENTAL. **Reservations:** Not required. **Directions:** 8 miles east of Cruz Bay on the road to Salt Pond Beach.
$ **Prices:** Appetizers $3.50–$6.75; main courses $11.25–$16.25. MC, V.
    Open: Restaurant daily 11am–10pm. Bar daily 11am–11pm.

Run by Michael and Julie Young, this is an attractive place to head for after an island sightseeing tour. You dine amid palms and tropical plants on a veranda overlooking the sea. The intimate bar specializes in tropical frozen drinks, and the kitchen prepares such items as chicken Caribbean Bleu, blackened red snapper, and surf and turf, along with daily seafood specials. Some Mexican and Asian dishes are also served. Music is often featured on Tuesday night.

EAST END

BUDGET

VIE'S SNACK SHACK, East End Rd. Tel. 776-8033.
    Cuisine: WEST INDIAN. **Reservations:** Not required.
$ **Prices:** Appetizers $3.25; main courses $5–$6.50. No credit cards.
    Open: Daily 10am–5pm, but call first!

 The owner of this plywood-sided hut on the island's East End is one of the best local chefs in St. John. Her famous garlic chicken is considered the best on the island. She also serves conch fritters, johnnycakes, and coconut and pineapple tarts. While the place is open most days, it's wise to call first, since, Vie warns, "Some days, we might not be here at all." Vie's is about 12½ miles east of Cruz Bay.

PICNIC FARE & WHERE TO EAT IT

Most picnickers follow their fancies to mountain panoramas or low-lying semiconcealed beaches along the island's eastern end. If you don't care about privacy, a good spot is Trunk Bay, where the National Park Service maintains picnic tables.

    The best place to buy your picnic fixings is **The Deli,** at the Hyatt Regency St. John in Great Cruz Bay (tel. 776-7171). Decorated like a brightly painted West Indian cottage, it carries everything you'll need, including an array of international cheeses, sausages, and salamis, succulent fresh pastries, French bread, English crackers, pizza, and stuffed sandwiches. Virtually anything you can buy here can be wrapped for a picnic lunch, including wine from around the world.

Ⓕ **FROMMER'S COOL FOR KIDS: RESTAURANTS**

Café Roma (see p. 124) is a family favorite. Introduce your child to a "white pizza" made without tomato sauce.

Mongoose Restaurant (see p. 124). The best choice for children if you're visiting Cruz Bay. At this tropical stage setting, kids delight in the well-stuffed sandwiches and island fish cakes.

Pusser's (see p. 126). Families like this place for its succulent barbecued chicken, and no kid can resist its frozen "mud pie."

DID YOU KNOW . . . ?

- Caneel Bay, the chic Rockresort, was once the Pieter Duerloo plantation, where slaves revolted against white settlers.
- The mongoose was brought to St. John to kill rats. It has practically been adopted as the island mascot—watch for them darting across roads.
- St. John was once a volcano.
- The only Danes left on the former Danish colony of St. John are dogs.

5. ATTRACTIONS

ON YOUR OWN

I like to spend lots of time at **Cruz Bay,** where the ferry docks. In this West Indian village there are interesting bars, restaurants, boutiques, and pastel-painted houses. It's pretty sleepy, but it's pleasant after the fast pace of St. Thomas. The **Elaine I. Sprauve Museum** (tel. 776-6359), at Cruz Bay, isn't big, but it does contain some local artifacts and will teach you some of the history of the island. It's in the public library, and can be visited from 9am to 5pm Monday through Friday.

Most cruise-ship passengers dart through Cruz Bay and head for the island's biggest attraction, the ✪ **Virgin Islands National Park.** But before going to the park, you may want to stop at the Visitor's Center at Cruz Bay, which is open daily from 8am to 4:30pm. There you'll see some exhibits and learn more about what you can see in the park.

Today the Virgin Islands National Park is the only national park in the Caribbean. It totals 12,624 acres, including submerged lands and waters adjacent to St. John, and has a 20-mile trail system.

If time is limited, try to visit the **Annaberg Ruins,** Leinster Bay Road, where the Danes maintained a thriving plantation and sugar mill after 1718. It's located off North Shore Road east of Trunk Bay on the north shore. On certain days of the week (days vary) from 10am to 1pm, St. John islanders show you their own style of native cookery and explain basketweaving.

✪ **Trunk Bay** is considered one of the world's most beautiful beaches. It's also the site of one of the world's first marked underwater trails (bring your mask, snorkel, and fins). It lies to the east of Cruz Bay along North Shore Road. Beware of pickpockets.

Fort Berg (also called Fortsberg), at Coral Bay, dating from 1717, played a disastrous role during the 1733 slave revolt. The fort may be restored as a historic monument.

AN ORGANIZED TOUR

Park rangers conduct several different **national park tours** on St. John. You must make a reservation by calling 776-6330 for the 2½-mile Reef Bay Hike that enables you to explore old sugar mill ruins and the mysterious petroglyphs. Other conducted programs include shore walks, a 3-hour historic bus tour, snorkel tours, and informal evening lectures. For more information on these and other special programs, call 776-6201.

Another tour is offered by **Margie Brown-Boynes Enterprises,** Captain's Quarters 3GA in Cruz Bay (tel. 776-8293). On this tour you'll see the most charming hidden inlets and panoramic vistas on the island. Photographers appreciate the dozens of stops offering picture-postcard scenes. A tour of the land and waters ringing St. John costs about $30 per person.

The **St. John Taxi Association** (tel. 776-6060) conducts a historical tour of St. John, and includes a swim at Trunk Bay and a visit to the Caneel Bay resort, at a cost of $30 for two people. Depending on demand, tours depart Cruz Bay daily.

DRIVING TOUR — ST. JOHN

Start: Ferry docks in Cruz Bay.
End: Ferry docks in Cruz Bay.

Estimated Time: 3 to 7 hours, depending on beach time, bar stops, and pedestrian detours.

Worst Time: Any rainy day when you are likely to get stuck in the mud on bad roads.

Important Note: Before you begin this tour, make sure you have at least three-quarters of a tank of gas, since there are only two gas stations on St. John, one of which is often closed. The more reliable of the two stations is in the upper regions of Cruz Bay, beside Route 104. Ask directions when you pick up your rented vehicle. *Remember to drive on the left!*

Head out of Cruz Bay, going east on Route 20. Within about a minute, you'll pass the catwalks and verandas of:

1. Mongoose Junction. Considered a sightseeing attraction as well as a shopping emporium, it contains some unusual art galleries and jewelry shops. (See "Savvy Shopping," below.)

Two miles northeast of Cruz Bay, you'll see a pair of unmarked stone columns on your left, and an area of immaculate landscaping. This is the entrance to the island's most legendary resort:

2. Caneel Bay. Past the security guard, near the resort's parking lots, is an attractive gift shop, and a handful of bars and restaurants. In a mile, you'll see the first of many spectacular panoramic vistas. Along the entire trajectory, note the complete absence of billboards and electrical cables (a rule rigidly enforced by the National Park Service). In less than 3 miles, you'll come to:

3. Hawksnest Beach, whose palms and salt-tolerant wild figs are maintained by the National Park Service. Stop to read the ecological signs and perhaps wet your feet in the water. There are some squat toilets (with lots of flies) at this point if you need them. Continuing your drive, you'll pass, in this order, Trunk Bay, Peter Bay (private), and Cinnamon Bay, which all have sand, palm trees, and clear water. A few steps from the entrance to the Cinnamon Bay campground is a redwood sign marking the beginning of:

4. The Cinnamon Bay Trail. Laid out for hill climbers by the National Park Service, this is an optional 1.2-mile walk that takes about an hour. Its clearly marked paths lead through shaded forest trails along the rutted cobblestones of a former Danish road, past ruins of abandoned plantations.

A short drive beyond Cinnamon Bay is the sandy sweep of Maho Bay, whose borders contain one of the most upscale campgrounds in the Caribbean.

Shortly after Maho Bay, the road splits. Take the left fork, which merges in a few moments with an extension of Centerline Road. Off this road, on your left, will appear another NPS signpost marked DANISH ROAD, indicating a 5-minute trek along a potholed road to the ruins of an 18th-century school.

At the next fork, bear right, toward Annaberg. (Make sure you don't go toward Francis Bay.) You'll pass the beginning of a 0.8-mile walking trail to the Leinster Bay Estate, which leads to a beach said to be good for snorkeling. Within less than a minute, you'll reach the parking lot for the:

5. Annaberg Historic Trail. The historic highlight of this driving tour, the Annaberg Trail leads pedestrians within and around the ruined buildings of the best-preserved plantation on St. John. During the 18th and 19th centuries, the smell of boiling molasses and sweating slaves permeated the air here. The sea breezes have long ago taken away all but the painful memories of that era. About a dozen National Park Service plaques identify and describe each building within the compound. The walk around the grounds takes about 30 minutes. From a terrace near the ruined windmill, a map identifies the panorama to the north, naming such landmasses of the British Virgin Islands as Little Thatch, Tortola, Watermelon Cay, and Jost Van Dyke.

After your visit to Annaberg, retrace your route to its first major division, and take the left fork. Soon a road sign will identify your road as Route 20 east. Stay on this road, forking left whenever possible, until you come, after many bends in the road, to sandy bottomlands that contain an elementary school, a baseball field, and, on a hilltop, a simple barnlike building known as the:

6. Emmaus Moravian Church, with its yellow clapboards and red roof. (It's often closed to visitors.) Near its base yet another NPS walking trail begins (the 1½-mile Johnny Horn Trail), known for its panoramic views and steep hills. You will by now be about 12½ miles east of Cruz Bay.

The roads at this point are not very clearly marked. Do not drive beyond the elementary school below the church. That road, although beautiful, is long, and leads only to the barren and rather dull expanses of the island's East End. Instead, backtrack a very short distance to a cluster of signs that point to such restaurants as the Still and Shipwreck Landing. Follow these signs (i.e., head south) about a mile to:

7. Coral Bay. Claimed by the Danes in the 1600s, it still contains a crumbling stone pier that they used to unload their ships. It was also the site of the first plantation on St. John. Established in 1717 (and long ago abandoned) it predated the far better-developed facilities of Cruz Bay. Coral Bay was the site of a state visit by a princess of the Danish royal family in the early 1700s.

Considered by yachting enthusiasts one of the most desirable harbors anywhere, it shelters a closely knit community of boaters who moor and live on their yachts here between excursions to other parts of the Caribbean. Ringing its perimeter are a widely spaced handful of restaurants and bars.

REFUELING STOP 8. The Still, 10-19 Estate Carolina (tel. 776-6866). Contained within an open-sided timbered pavilion close to the emerald waters of Coral Bay, it provides shelter from the sun and open access to the trade winds blowing in from the sea. Its most famous drink? A Standstill Punch, a pink froth of three fruit juices, crème de cassis, and two different kinds of rum, priced at $3.50 each. Make sure the driver sticks to juices or soft drinks.

After your refueling stop, continue driving south beside Coral Bay, perhaps stopping in at another of the two or three shops and bars beside the road. (Shipwreck Landing, described in "Dining," above, is a good choice.)

After you pass Shipwreck Landing, the road is passable for only another 5 or 6 miles. If you want, you can sightsee for a few miles along the eastern coastline (there are some churches and houses along the way), but eventually you'll have to retrace your route.

(Conditions, of course, might have changed by the time you take this tour. Road signs on this end of the island are notoriously bad, so it's wise to ask directions at one of the Coral Bay bars, restaurants, or shops before making any firm conclusions about road conditions.)

Backtrack north along Coral Bay to a point near the Emmaus Moravian Church, which you'll see in the distance. At the cluster of restaurant signs, turn left onto Route 10 West (Centerline Road), which gives good high-altitude views in all directions as you follow it back toward Cruz Bay. (An alternate, although much steeper, way is Route 108, which merges later with Route 10 West.)

Within 7 or 8 miles, Route 10 merges with Route 104 (Gifft Hill Road) just after the island's only hospital, the St. John Myrah Keating Smith Community Health

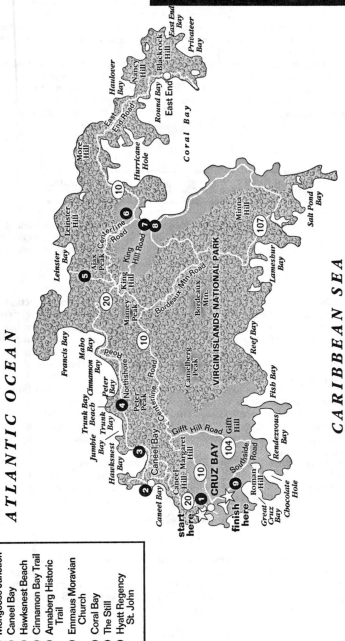

DRIVING TOUR—ST. JOHN

N

ATLANTIC OCEAN

CARIBBEAN SEA

Coral Bay

VIRGIN ISLANDS NATIONAL PARK

East End

East End Bay

Privateer Bay

Round Bay

Blackrock Hill

Nancy Hill

Haulover Bay

East End Road

More Hill

Hurricane Hole

Salt Pond Bay

Minna Hill

Leinster Hill

Leinster Bay

Centerline Road

King Hill Road

Ajax Peak

King Hill

Mamey Peak

Bordeaux Mtn Road

Bordeaux Mtn.

Lameshur Bay

Reef Bay

Camelberg Peak

Fish Bay

Francis Bay

Maho Bay

Cinnamon Bay

Peter Bay

Northshore Road

Peter Peak

Trunk Bay

Jumbie Beach

Trunk Bay

Hawksnest Bay

Caneel Bay

Caneel Bay

Caneel Bay Centerline Road

Gifft Hill Road

Gifft Hill

Rendezvous Bay

Caneel Hill

Margaret Hill

CRUZ BAY

Southside

Ronnan Road

Great Cruz Bay

Chocolate Hole

start here

finish here

10

20

20

10

10

6

7

8

5

4

3

2

1

9

104

107

① Mongoose Junction
② Caneel Bay
③ Hawksnest Beach
④ Cinnamon Bay Trail
⑤ Annaberg Historic Trail
⑥ Emmaus Moravian Church
⑦ Coral Bay
⑧ The Still
⑨ Hyatt Regency St. John

Clinic. Take Route 104, and begin one of the steepest descents with the greatest number of blind curves of your driving tour. (Use low gear whenever possible, and honk around blind curves.) When the land levels off, you'll see, on your left, the entrance to one of the most imaginative pieces of modern architecture on the island, the spectacularly postmodern:

9. Hyatt Regency St. John. If you're a gardening or architecture enthusiast, stop in for a look at a hotel whose inspiration included ancient Mesopotamia, colonial Denmark, and the coast of California. What makes all of this even more impressive is the fact that it was built upon land that was considered unusable swampland only a few years ago. A staff member will direct you to the hotel's scattering of bars (perhaps the Poolside Splash Bar) for a midafternoon quaff.

From here, your return to Cruz Bay involves only a short drive along Route 104, through a slightly urbanized periphery of private homes.

6. SPORTS & RECREATION

Don't visit St. John to play golf. Rather, anticipate some of the best snorkeling, scuba diving, swimming, fishing, hiking, sailing, and underwater photography in the Caribbean. The island is known for its coral-sand beaches, winding mountain roads, trails past old, bush-covered sugarcane plantations, and hidden coves.

BEACHES

✪ **Trunk Bay** on the northwest coast of the island, is the biggest attraction on St. John and a beach lover's find. Trouble is the word is out. It's likely to be overcrowded, and there are pickpockets. Against a backdrop of sea grape and palm, the beach has lifeguards, and offers rentals, such as snorkeling gear. Beginning snorkelers in particular are attracted to its underwater trail near the shore. Both taxis and safari buses meet the ferry as it docks at Cruz Bay from Red Hook on St. Thomas. Round-trip passage is provided to Trunk Bay, where most people seem headed.

As mentioned, **Caneel Bay,** the stamping ground of the rich and famous, has seven beautiful beaches on its 170 acres—but only one is open to the public. The campgrounds of **Cinnamon Bay** and **Maho Bay** (see "Accommodations," above) have their own beaches where forest rangers sometimes have to remind visitors to put their swimming trunks back on. Snorkelers find good reefs here, and changing rooms and showers are available.

Hawksnest Beach is a little gem of white sand, beloved by St. Johnians. The beach is a bit narrow, but beautiful, as filmmakers long ago discovered. Close to the road are barbecue grills, and there are portable toilets. Safari buses and taxis from Cruz Bay will take you along the North Shore Road.

SPORTS

HIKING

Hiking is popular here, and a network of trails covers the national park. However, I suggest a tour by Jeep first, just to get your bearings. At the Visitor's Center at Cruz Bay, ask for a free trail map of the park. It's best to set out with someone experienced in the mysteries of the island. Both **Maho Bay** and **Cinnamon Bay** conduct nature walks (see "Accommodations," above).

TENNIS

Caneel Bay (tel. 776-6111) has seven courts and a pro shop. The courts aren't lit at night and nonguests are not welcome. There are two public courts at Cruz Bay. **Hyatt**

Regency St. John, Great Cruz Bay (tel. 776-7171), has six tennis courts, all lit at night.

WATER SPORTS

The most complete line of water sports available on St. John is offered at the **Cinnamon Bay Watersports Center,** on Cinnamon Bay Beach (tel. 776-6330). Specializing in sailing, the staff charges $50 for a full day's outing ($30 for a half day) aboard the yacht *Gratia.* Snorkeling equipment and stopoffs at secluded reefs and uninhabited islands provide some of the most vivid underwater viewing in the region. Beer, sodas, and snorkeling equipment are included in the cost of the trip, but you must bring your own picnic lunch. If you're interested in snorkeling, you can make trips on the MV *Cinnamon Bay,* which circumnavigates St. John; it leaves at 9am and returns at 3pm Wednesday and Friday. You bring your own lunch. The cost is $35 per person. Also, the windsurfing here is some of the best anywhere. You can rent a board for $12 to $15 per hour or $35 to $40 for half a day. A 90-minute lesson costs $35.

Divers can ask about scuba packages at **Low Key Watersports,** Wharfside Village (tel. 776-7048). All wreck dives are two-tank, two-location dives. A one-tank dive costs $45 per person, with night dives going for $55. Snorkel tours are also available at $35 per person. The center uses its own custom-built dive boats and also offers and specializes in water-sports gear, including masks, fins, snorkels, and "dive skins." It also arranges day sailing charters and deep-sea sportfishing.

Cruz Bay Watersports, Cruz Bay (tel. 776-6234), is a PADI five-star diving center on St. John, offering daily dive trips year-round. Certifications can be arranged through a divemaster. This outfit uses dive boats certified by the Coast Guard to explore the gorgeous reefs, which range in depth from 30 to 80 feet. Two-tank reef dives costs $78, and a beginner's scuba course goes for $68. Night dives and wreck dives are also offered.

7. SAVVY SHOPPING

Compared to St. Thomas, the shopping on St. John isn't much, but what there is is interesting. The boutiques and shops of **Cruz Bay** are quite special. Most of the shops are clustered at **Mongoose Junction,** a woodsy area beside the roadway, about a 5-minute walk left (or northeast) from the ferry dock. In addition to having shops of merit, this avant-garde complex also has some good restaurants (see "Dining," above).

BAMBOULA, Mongoose Junction. Tel. 776-7699.
Bamboula has an unusual and very appealing collection of gifts from such destinations as Guatemala, Haiti, India, Indonesia, and Central Africa. Its exoticism is unexpected and very pleasant.

THE CANVAS FACTORY, Cruz Bay. Tel. 776-6196.
This shop produces its own handmade, rugged, and colorful canvas bags in the "factory" at Mongoose Junction. Their products range from canvas sailing hats to handsome luggage. Among the many items for sale is an extensive line of island-made 100% cotton clothing. They are also the Caribbean agent for Lee sailmakers.

THE CLOTHING STUDIO, Mongoose Junction. Tel. 776-6585.
At the Caribbean's oldest hand-painted-clothing studio (in operation since 1978) you can watch talented artists create original designs on fine tropical clothing, including swimwear, daytime and evening clothing, and articles for babies, children, men, and women. They ship worldwide.

D. KNIGHT & COMPANY, Cruz Bay. Tel. 776-7958.
This establishment is of interest to those who like fine cabinetry and tropical hardwoods. In an industrial building on the east side of Cruz Bay on Route 104, you'll find one of the finest collections of exotic woods in the Caribbean, including beautifully striated Brazilian angelique, red locust from Dominica, Burmese teak, ebony, black jacaranda, brownheart, greenheart, purpleheart, and rosewood. Shipping home large quantities will be a problem, but if you're just looking for a few boards for something you're rebuilding in your workshop, Mr. Knight can arrange shipping through the mail.

DONALD SCHNELL STUDIO, Mongoose Junction. Tel. 776-6420.
This working studio and gallery features one of the finest collections of handmade pottery, sculpture, and blown glass in the Caribbean. Especially noted for their rough-textured coral work, the artists here can be seen producing their crafts daily. Water fountains are a specialty item, as are lighting fixtures and signs. The coral pottery dinnerware is also unique and popular. Go in and discuss any particular design you may have in mind; they enjoy designing to please customers. The studio will mail works all over the world.

FABRIC MILL, Mongoose Junction. Tel. 776-6194.
This shop specializes in silk-screen and batik prints from around the world. You'll find home decorative and fabric accessories, unique sculpture, and unusual gift items.

PUSSER'S OF THE WEST INDIES, Wharfside Village, Cruz Bay. Tel. 774-5489.
Before you set sail for St. Thomas, pay a visit to Wharfside Village, just a few steps from the ferry dock, and explore this pastel complex of courtyards, alleys, and shady patios, with its boutiques, restaurants, fast-food joints, and bars.
Pusser's offers a large collection of classically designed old-world travel and adventure clothing along with unusual accessories. Clothing for women, men, and children is displayed, along with T-shirts carrying Pusser's colorful emblem. Nautical paintings and antiques are also displayed.

R AND I PATTON GOLDSMITHING, Cruz Bay. Tel. 776-6548.
R and I Patton Goldsmithing has been on the island since 1973. At the entrance to Mongoose Junction, it has a large selection of island-designed jewelry in sterling, gold, and precious stones.

THE SHOP AT CANEEL BAY, Caneel Bay Resort, Caneel Bay. Tel. 776-6111.
Its location within a palatial outbuilding on the manicured grounds of the most legendary resort on St. John almost guarantees both an upscale clientele and an upscale assortment of merchandise. Scattered over two rustically elegant floors are the usual drugstore items, books, sundries, and handcrafts you'd expect at a Caribbean resort hotel, as well as some unusual artworks and pieces of expensive jewelry. Also featured are racks of resort- and sportswear for men, women, and children.

8. EVENING ENTERTAINMENT

Bring a good book. St. John is no St. Thomas after dark, and everybody here seems to want to keep it that way. Most people are content to have a drink or two, a long leisurely dinner, and then head for bed.
Among the hotels, the **Hyatt Regency St. John** in season has the most activity, including live music for dancing. The crowd at **Caneel Bay** (especially the older guests, attracted to the place in winter) tends to be conservative, and likes to retire

early. There are sometimes island events, such as a fish fry—ask at the tourist office (see "Orientation," above).

Among the popular bars of Cruz Bay, **Pusser's** at Wharfside Village has the most convivial atmosphere. The **Caneel Bay Bar,** at the Caneel Bay resort (tel. 776-6111), open daily from 11am to 11:30pm, presents live music nightly from 8:30 to 11pm. The most popular drinks (from $4) include a Cool Caneel (local rum with sugar, lime, and anisette), and the trademark of the house, a Plantation Freeze (lime and orange juice with three different kinds of rum, bitters, and nutmeg). A drink here might be your most inconspicuous and cheapest way to visit the Caneel Bay resort.

CHAPTER 6

THE U.S. VIRGIN ISLANDS: ST. CROIX

At 84 square miles, St. Croix is the largest of the U.S. Virgin Islands. Columbus named it Santa Cruz (Holy Cross) when he stopped here November 14, 1493. Columbus anchored his ship off the north shore, but left soon after, driven away by the spears, arrows, and axes of the Caribs.

Despite the Caribs' efforts to the contrary, settlers began arriving—first the Dutch, who were driven out by the English, then the Spanish, who were kicked out by the French, who laid claim to the island in 1650.

The Danes purchased St. Croix in 1773, attracted to it because of its slave labor and sugarcane fields. This marked the golden era for both planters and pirates. However, the sugar boom ended with eventual slave uprisings, the introduction of the sugar beet in Europe, and the slave emancipation of 1848. Even though seven different flags have flown over St. Croix, it is the nearly 2½ centuries of Danish influence that you'll see throughout the island.

Today tourists flock to St. Croix for some of the best beaches in the Virgin Islands and its ideal weather. At its east end, which, incidentally, is the easternmost point of the United States, the terrain is rocky and arid. The west end is lusher, with a rain forest of mango and mahogany, tree ferns, and dangling lianas. Between the two extremes are rolling hills and pastures.

1. ORIENTATION

ARRIVING

BY PLANE

American Airlines (tel. toll free 800/433-7300) is currently the front-runner airline, with the most frequent and most reliable flights to St. Croix. From New York's JFK, a flight departs daily for the island early every morning, making only one touchdown (with no change of plane) in nearby St. Thomas. Passengers who prefer

WHAT'S SPECIAL ABOUT ST. CROIX

Beaches

☐ Cormorant Beach, 5 miles northwest of Christiansted, with some 1,200 feet of white sands and palm tree shade.

☐ Sandy Point, the biggest beach in the U.S. Virgin Islands, with shallow, calm waters.

☐ Cane Bay, adjoining Route 80 on the north shore—a favorite of snorkelers and divers attracted to its rolling waves and coral gardens, with a "dropoff wall."

Great Towns/Villages

☐ Christiansted, capital of St. Croix, a charming seaport filled with handsome 18th-century Danish Colonial buildings.

☐ Frederiksted, a gingerbread-studded monument to a long-ago mercantile prosperity.

Historic Buildings

☐ Government House, in Christiansted, former seat of the Danish governor-general with a courtyard evocative of old Europe.

☐ Fort Christiansvaern, built on the foundations of a 1645 French fortress, with fine harbor views from the battlements.

☐ Estate Whim Plantation Museum, a unique sugar plantation "Great House" that stands as a vestige of the plantation era.

---

later flights usually opt for one of the airline's many different connections from either JFK or Newark, New Jersey, through San Juan, Puerto Rico. (From San Juan, around eight American Eagle flights fly every day nonstop to St. Croix.)

There are also two daily flights to St. Croix from Miami, with one stop (but no change of plane) in St. Thomas.

Unless they transfer through Miami or San Juan, passengers from the Midwest and Middle South often transfer through American's hub in Raleigh-Durham, North Carolina. From Raleigh-Durham, a daily nonstop flight, as well as a daily one-stop flight (with a touchdown in St. Thomas but no change of plane) both continue on to St. Croix.

American's least expensive round-trip fare to St. Croix from any of its departure points is a SuperSaver fare, requiring a 14-day advance payment, a delay of between 3 and 30 days before activating the return portion, and a payment of a $25 penalty for any alterations in the itinerary. From New York, this sells for between $363 and $443 round-trip, depending on the season and the flight dates.

American is not alone in flying to St. Croix. **Delta** (tel. toll free 800/221-1212) offers daily flights to St. Croix from both Atlanta and Orlando. Flights usually touch down in St. Thomas before continuing on to St. Croix. From St. Croix, flights turn around and head back (nonstop) to their point of origin. Convenient connections are available through these two hubs from virtually anywhere on Delta's vast network. Prices are competitive, sometimes matching dollar for dollar those at American.

IMPRESSIONS

Fort Christiansvaern [Christiansted] contains only 20 living soldiers, of whom one is over 60, and the others are such drunkards that they cannot stand watch.
—DANISH GOVERNOR-GENERAL (1747)

Transit time, including ground time, to St. Croix from New York is 4 hours, from Chicago, 5½ hours, from Miami 3½ hours, and from the nearby island of Puerto Rico, 20 minutes.

A final reminder: Often, an airline can arrange discounted hotel accommodations in conjunction with air passage if both are booked simultaneously. Ask an airline reservations agent to explain the various options.

BY BOAT

There is no ferry from St. Thomas to St. Croix. However, many cruise ships stop over in St. Croix (see "Getting There," Chapter 2).

ISLAND LAYOUT

St. Croix has only two towns of any significance: Christiansted on the north-central shoreline, and Frederiksted in the southwest. The airport of St. Croix, Alexander Hamilton Airport, opens onto the south coast, lying directly west of the Hess Oil Refinery, the major industry on the island. There is no road that encircles the coast.

To continue east from Christiansted, take Route 82 or the East End Road. Route 75 will take you west from Christiansted, through the central heartland, all the way to the Hess Oil Refinery. Melvin H. Evans Highway, Route 66, runs along the southern part of the island. You can connect with this route in Christiansted and head west all the way to Frederiksted.

FREDERIKSTED

Frederiksted is so tiny that it's almost impossible to get lost. Most visitors head for the central historic district, where the Frederiksted Pier juts out into the sea. The two major streets, both of which run parallel to the water, are Strand Street and King Street. Farther back are Queen Street, Prince Street, Hospital Street, and New Street, the last of which runs beside the cemetery. These streets are crisscrossed by such side streets as Queen Cross Street, King Cross Street, Hill Street, and Market Street.

CHRISTIANSTED

The historic district—the only part of the capital of concern to most visitors—is in the center bordering Veterans Drive, which runs along the waterfront. The district is split by Kronprindsens Gade (Route 308), which runs completely through the district.

IN THEIR FOOTSTEPS

Alexander Hamilton (1755–1804) American statesman from the West Indies who served brilliantly in the American Revolution. He wrote many of the articles contained in the *Federalist Papers* and became Secretary of the Treasury to George Washington. He was noted for both his literary and oratorical skills.

- **Birthplace:** The British-held island of Nevis on January 11, 1755.
- **Residence:** St. Croix.
- **Final Days:** In a duel fought with Aaron Burr, Hamilton was mortally wounded and died July 12, 1804.

Kronprindsens Gade (also called Main Street) is connected to Veterans Drive by a number of shop-filled little streets, including Gutters Gade, Trompeter Gade, Raadets Gade. The Visitor's Information Center lies at the end of King Street (Kongens Gade) near the water.

Nearby Fort Christiansvaern also opens onto the water. The center of Christiansted can get very congested at times, and driving around is difficult because of the one-way streets. It is usually more practical to park your car and cover the relatively small district on foot. You will find open-air parking on both sides of Fort Christiansvaern.

FINDING AN ADDRESS In both Christiansted and Frederiksted, buildings are numbered consecutively on one side, stretching all the way to the limits of these towns. Then the numbers "cross the street" and begin numbering on the opposite side. That means that even and odd numbers appear on the same side of the street. The numbering system begins in Christiansted at the waterfront. In Frederiksted, the first number appears at the north end of town for streets running north-south. Numbering begins at the waterfront for streets running east-west.

2. GETTING AROUND

BY TAXI OR BUS

At the airport, you'll find official **taxi** rates posted; per-person rates require a minimum of two passengers; one passenger pays double the fares listed. Expect to pay about $5 per person from the airport to Christiansted and about $4.25 per person from the airport to Frederiksted. Because the cabs are unmetered, be sure to agree on the rate before you get in.

The **St. Croix Taxicab Association,** which offers door-to-door service, can be reached by calling 778-1088.

Taxi tours are the ideal way to explore the island. For one or two passengers, the cost is often $30 for 2 hours or $40 for 3 hours, but all fares have to be negotiated.

At present, there is no **bus** service for the island. However, there is a public van that goes from the center of Christiansted to the shopping centers in the center of the island or to Frederiksted for a cost of $1.

BY CAR, MOTORCYCLE, OR SCOOTER

This is a suitable means of exploring for some, but know that if you're going into "bush country," you'll find the roads very difficult. Sometimes the government smoothes them out before the big season begins, but in these climes they deteriorate rapidly.

St. Croix offers reasonable rates for its **car rentals.** Cars with automatic transmissions and air conditioning are easily available, even among some of the lowest-priced cars.

However, because of the island's higher than usual accident rates (which is partly the result of forgetfulness by some drivers about which side of the road to drive on) insurance costs are a bit higher than usual. **Budget** (tel. 809/778-9636, or toll free 800/472-3325), **Hertz** (tel. 809/778-1402, or toll free 800/654-3001), and **Avis** (tel. 809/778-9355, or toll free 800/331-2112) all maintain their headquarters at the island's airport, with kiosks near the baggage claim areas.

Each of the big three companies offers such cost-conscious vehicles as Suzuki Swifts or Ford Escorts with automatic transmission and air conditioning as their least expensive cars. At presstime, prices at all three of the companies (including unlimited mileage) range from between $199 and $225 per week. Of the three, the least expensive cars were offered by Budget ($199 per week), which required a reservation of 24 hours in advance. Of course, these prices can and probably will change before the time of your arrival on the island; it's best to phone around before you go.

Renters at all three companies must be between 25 and 70 years old, and present a valid driver's license and a credit card at the time of rental.

Collision-damage insurance can be arranged for an additional fee of between $11 and $12 a day, depending on the company. Considering the dangers, the bad lighting, and the unfamiliarity with left-hand driving, it's a wise investment. This advice does not necessarily apply if you pay for the rental with a credit card. In certain instances, your credit-card issuer might automatically have granted you collision-damage protection if you pay for the rental with the appropriate credit card. Verify coverage in advance directly with your credit-card issuer. Additional forms of supplementary insurance offered by each of the companies included personal accident insurance, which at presstime was priced at around $3.50 per day.

Remember to *drive on the left* and to take more precautions than usual because of the unfamiliarity of the roads. A 35 m.p.h. speed limit is called for in most rural areas, and certain parts of the major artery, Route 66, the Melvin H. Evans Highway, are 55 m.p.h. In towns and urban areas, the limit is 20 m.p.h.

You can rent motorcycles and scooters at **A & B Honda Motorcycles & Scooter Rentals,** 26 Bassin Triangle (tel. 778-8567), in Christiansted.

ON FOOT

St. Croix is too big to tour on foot, and you'll need a rented car or taxi to get about in lieu of the totally inadequate public transportation. The historic districts of Christiansted and Frederiksted, however, are relatively small and can only be explored adequately on foot.

FAST ST. CROIX

American Express The American Express travel representative is Southerland, Chandler's Wharf, Gallows Bay (tel. 773-9500).

Area Code The area code is 809. You can call direct from the U.S. mainland.

Banks Several major banks are represented in St. Croix. Most banks are open Mon–Thurs 9am–2:30pm and Fri 9am–2pm and 3:30–5pm. First Pennsylvania Bank has a branch at 12 King's St. (tel. 773-0440) in Christiansted.

Babysitters There is no central agency. Make arrangements through your hotel as far in advance as possible.

Bookstores The Writer's Block, 36C Strand St. (tel. 773-5101), in Christiansted, will supply you with a selection of titles to read on the beach or around the pool. Collage Book Café, 6 Company St. (tel. 773-0066), established in 1984, is a café and bookstore which many consider the finest on the island. It carries contemporary American, Caribbean, and international literature, a large selection of women's studies, self-help, and children's books, and prints, posters, cards, and calendars.

Business Hours Typical business hours are Mon–Fri 9am–5pm, Sat 9am–1pm.

Car Rentals See "Getting Around," above.

Climate See "Climate," Chapter 2.

Crime   At night, parts of Christiansted and Frederiksted are considered unsafe. Stick to the heart of Christiansted, exercise caution, and avoid wandering around Frederiksted at night.

Currency   See "Information, Entry Requirements, and Money," Chapter 2.

Customs   See "Information, Entry Requirements, and Money," Chapter 2.

Documents Required   See "Information, Entry Requirements, and Money," Chapter 2.

Dentist   Go to the Sunny Isle Medical Center, Sunny Isle (tel. 778-6356). Call first for an appointment.

Doctors   A good local doctor is Dr. Frank Bishod, Sunny Isle Medical Center (tel. 778-0069). Call for an appointment.

Drugstores   Try the Golden Rock Pharmacy, Golden Rock Shopping Center (tel. 773-0299), or People's Drugstore, Sunny Isle Shopping Center (tel. 778-5537), which has a more convenient branch at 1A King St. (tel. 778-7355) in Christiansted.

Embassies and Consulates   St. Croix has no embassies or consulates. Go to one of the local U.S. government agencies if you have a problem.

Emergencies   Police, 915; fire 921; ambulance, 922.

Eyeglasses   The best place to go is Southern Optical, Sunny Isle Professional Building, Sunny Isle (tel. 778-6565).

Etiquette   Cruzans tend to be fairly conservative about dress. When walking the streets or visiting public places such as restaurants, don't appear in skimpy swimwear.

Hairdressers   The best place is Spencer's Beauty, Hair & Health Spa, 14A La Grande Princesse (tel. 773-1000), in The Pink Building on Northside Road, Route 75, Christiansted. It's open Mon–Sat 9am–8pm. Call for an appointment. It has a fitness studio, a hair salon, a nail salon, a center offering skin and body care, even a lingerie boutique. All kinds of hair care, including textured perms, are also offered at Head Quarters, Caravelle Hotel, Queen Cross Street (tel. 773-2465), in Christiansted.

Hitchhiking   It isn't illegal, but it isn't commonly practiced. You'll probably wait a long time for a ride.

Holidays   See "When to Go," Chapter 2.

Hospitals   The principal facility is St. Croix Hospital, Estate Ruby (tel. 778-6311).

Information   The U.S. Virgin Islands Division of Tourism has offices in Christiansted at The Old Scalehouse, King Street (tel. 773-0495), and at the Customs House Building, Strand Street (tel. 772-0357), in Frederiksted.

Laundry   Try Tropical Cleaners & Launderers, 16–17 King Cross (tel. 773-3637), in Christiansted.

Liquor Laws   You must be at least 21 years of age to purchase liquor.

Lost Property   Go to the police station (see below).

Mail   Postal rates are the same as on the U.S. mainland.

Maps   Tourist offices provide free maps to the island. *St. Croix This Week,* which is distributed free to cruise-ship passengers and air passengers, has detailed maps of Christiansted, Frederiksted, and the island itself, pinpointing individual attractions, hotels, shops, and restaurants. If you plan to do extensive touring of the island, purchase *The Official Road Map of the U.S. Virgin Islands,* available in island bookstores.

Newspapers and Magazines   Newspapers, such as *The Miami Herald,* are flown into St. Croix daily. St. Croix also has its own newspaper, *St. Croix Avis. Time* and *Newsweek* are widely sold as well. Your best source of local information is *St. Croix This Week,* which is distributed free by the tourist offices.

Photographic Needs   V.I. Express Photo, 2A Strand St. (tel. 773-2009), in Christiansted, offers 1-hour photo finishing. You might also try Fast Foto, 1116 King St. (tel. 773-6727), Christiansted.

Police   The Police Headquarters (tel. 915) is on Market Street in Christiansted.
Post Office   The U.S. Post Office is on Company Street (tel. 773-3586) in Christiansted.

Radio and TV   Local radio stations include WVGN-105FM and WJKC Isle 95 FM. The local television station is WSVI-TV Channel 8.

Religious Services   Places of worship in Christiansted include Lutheran Church Lord God of Saboath, 52 King St. (tel. 773-1320), and St. Paul's Episcopal Church, 28 Prince St. (tel. 772-0818). In Frederiksted, St. Patrick's Catholic Church is at 5 Prince St. (tel. 772-0138).

Restrooms   There are few public ones, except at the major beaches and airport. Most people use those in commercial establishments, which, technically, businesses have a right to reserve for customers. In Christiansted, the National Park Service maintains some within the public park beside Fort Christiansvaern.

Safety   St. Croix is safer than St. Thomas. Possessions should never be left unattended, especially on the beach. Exercise extreme caution at night around Christiansted and Frederiksted. Avoid night strolls along beaches or drives along little-used roads.

Shoe Repair   Go to Rodriguez Shoe Repair, Bassin Triangle (no phone).

Taxis   Summon a taxi by calling 778-0599 or 778-1088.

Telephone, Telex, and Fax   A local call at a phone booth costs 25¢. You can dial direct to St. Croix from the mainland by using the 809 area code. Omit the 809 for local calls. The bigger hotels will send telex and fax, or you can go to the post office (see above).

Tipping   As a general rule, it is customary to tip 15%. Most hotels add a 10% to 15% surcharge to cover service. When in doubt, ask.

Water   Water is generally considered safe, but you are asked to conserve. If you have a delicate stomach, stick to bottled water.

Yellow Pages   See "Fast Facts: The U.S. Virgin Islands," Chapter 3.

3. ACCOMMODATIONS

The charming old waterfront inns are at Christiansted, and the deluxe resorts lie mainly along the North Shore. You can also stay at a former plantation, or in a unit in a condo complex. Rates for the most part are steep, and all rooms are subject to a 7.5% tax.

Hotels considered "very expensive" charge from $185 to $325 for a double room in winter. Hotels ranked "moderate" on their higher price scales charge from $95 to $156 a night for a double room. But nearly all of these so-called "moderate" places have less desirable rooms that begin at around $85 a night, which would definitely make them "inexpensive." "Inexpensive" hotels offer doubles for $79 to $85.

In summer, St. Croix is filled with bargains, as hotels slash prices about 20% to 50%.

For an explanation of the abbreviations AP, CP, EP, and MAP, see "Where to Stay," Chapter 3.

For tips on saving money on accommodations, see "Frommer's Smart Traveler: Hotels," Chapter 4.

NORTH SHORE
VERY EXPENSIVE

BUCCANEER, P.O. Box 25200, Rte. 82 (East End Rd.), Estate Shoys,

Gallows Bay, St. Croix, USVI 00824. Tel. 809/773-2100, or toll free 800/223-1108. Fax 809/773-0010. 150 rms (all with bath). A/C TEL
$ Rates (with EP): Winter, $175–$315 single; $184–$325 double. Summer, $130–$200 single; $140–$210 double. Breakfast $10 extra. AE, DC, MC, V.
Parking: Free.

⭐ Two miles east of Christiansted, this large, family-owned resort has been in operation since 1948. Its 240 acres contain three of the island's best beaches.

The property was once a cattle ranch and a sugar plantation, and its first estate house, dating from the mid-17th century, stands near a freshwater swimming pool. Pink and patrician, the hotel offers a choice of accommodations in its main building or in one of the beachside properties. The baronially arched main building has a lobby opening toward a few terraces, with a sea vista on two sides, and Christiansted to the west. The interiors of the accommodations effectively use modern construction materials and tropical furnishings to provide fresh, comfortable bedrooms, which range from "deluxe" to "standard."

Dining/Entertainment: Breakfast and dinner are served at the Terrace Dining Room and at The Little Mermaid Restaurant. Lunch is also served at The Mermaid and The Grotto, where hamburgers and hot dogs are available. The hotel's gourmet restaurant, Brass Parrot is recommended separately. There is entertainment nightly at the Terrace Lounge, with a variety of music ranging from Jimmy Hamilton's jazz to island steel drums.

Services: Best sports program on St. Croix, trips arranged to Buck Island.

Facilities: Swimming pool, eight championship tennis courts, 18-hole golf course, 2-mile jogging trail.

CORMORANT BEACH CLUB, 4126 La Grande Princesse, St. Croix, USVI 00820. Tel. 809/778-8920, or toll free 800/548-4460. Fax 809/778-9218. 34 rms, 4 suites (all with bath). A/C TEL
$ Rates (with EP): Winter, $260 single; $285 double; $385 suite; Summer, $135 single; $160 double; $260 suite. AE, DC, MC, V. **Parking:** Free.

⭐ Surrounded by king palms on a 12-acre site about 3 miles northwest of Christiansted on Route 75, this sumptuous resort strikes a perfect balance between seclusion and accessibility. Long Reef, one of the better-known zoological playgrounds of the Caribbean, lies a few hundred feet from the hotel's sandy beachfront. The hotel's social center revolves around a wood-sheathed and high-ceilinged clubhouse, whose walls were removed for a firsthand taste of the salty air. Off the central core are a well-stocked library, the largest freshwater pool on St. Croix, and a tastefully airy dining room, where half a dozen large fan-shaped windows offer a view of the beach.

Accommodations are in well-maintained outbuildings. Each contains a spacious bath, a tasteful decor of cane and wicker furniture, and bouquets of seasonal flowers. Much of the success of the place is because of its manager, Larry Bathon, whose charm and welcome make you feel that you've made "the right choice" in resorts. In winter, children under 5 are politely discouraged.

Dining/Entertainment: Dinners, served à la carte, are elegantly lighthearted affairs, featuring California cuisine and costing about $30 per person. The food is perhaps the best on the island (see "Dining," below). Weekly steel bands and dance combos are regularly featured. You can stay here on the CBC meal plan (Cormorant Beach Club), including a gourmet breakfast, complete lunch, and all drinks until 5pm for only $37.50 per person. The AIP (All-Inclusive Plan) adds to that an open dinner menu and all beverages until closing for $77.50 per person. Thursday night is Caribbean Grill Night with a buffet and entertainment, and Sunday brunch is rated the best on the island.

Services: Laundry; arrangement for golf, horseback riding, sailing, and scuba diving.

Facilities: Freshwater swimming pool, two tennis courts, snorkeling, croquet, library just off the lobby.

EAST END

VERY EXPENSIVE

VILLA MADELEINE, P.O. Box 3109, Gallows Bay, St. Croix, USVI 00822. Tel. 809/773-8141, or toll free 800/548-4461. Fax 809/773-7515. 3 1-bedroom villas, 40 2-bedroom villas (all with bath). A/C TV TEL
$ Rates (with EP): Winter, $320 1-bedroom villa for two; $420 2-bedroom villa for four. Summer, $225 1-bedroom villa; $325 2-bedroom villa. Breakfast $10 extra. AE, DC, MC, V. **Parking:** Free.

Villa Madeleine was built in 1990 on a 6½-acre plot of some of the most desirable land on the island, about 8 miles east of Christiansted, at the pinnacle of the rocky spine that divides the east end of the island into north- and south-facing watersheds. Its focal point is a newly built Great House whose Chippendale balconies and foursquare proportions recall the Danish colonial era. The richly landscaped property is dotted with serpentine paths and flowering shrubbery.

Villas are completely detached pale-yellow structures with their own pools. Thanks to the sloping terrain, each villa is hidden from the others and contains a well-equipped kitchen, a four-poster bed, marble bathrooms, and an elegant decor. Beach lovers willingly travel one-third of a mile to the nearest beach.

Children under 12 years of age are discouraged.

Dining/Entertainment: Café Madeleine, a sophisticated restaurant (see "Dining," below), a piano bar with nautical accessories and a billiard table.

Services: Concierge, room service, daily chamber and pool service, laundry, babysitting.

Facilities: Small library with writing tables, mini-boutique, game room for cards and billiards, access to nearby tennis courts.

CHRISTIANSTED

MODERATE

ANCHOR INN, 58A King St., Christiansted, St. Croix, USVI 00820. Tel. 809/773-4000, or toll free 800/524-2030. Fax 809/773-4408. 31 units (all with bath). A/C MINIBAR TV TEL
$ Rates (with EP): Winter, $119–$134 single; $141–$156 double; $163–$178 triple. Summer, $79–$90 single; $98–$109 double; $118–$129 triple. Breakfast $5 extra. AE, DC, MC, V. **Parking:** Free.

One of the few hotels on the waterfront, the Anchor Inn is set in a quiet courtyard close to such historic buildings as Government House and the Old Danish Customs House. It's also right in the heart of the shopping belt. The space is so compact and intimate you might not expect it holds 31 units, each with refrigerator, radio, and a small porch. A few larger units (without porches) have king- and queen-size beds. Furnishings are conventional but warm. Directly on the waterfront is a sun deck and small swimming pool, as well as the Anchor Inn's own boardwalk, where catamarans and glass-bottom boats operate daily to Buck Island. There are also deep-sea fishing boats, a scuba-dive shop, and honeymoon and family package tours. Antoine's Restaurant & Bar is on the hotel's second level, overlooking the historic harbor.

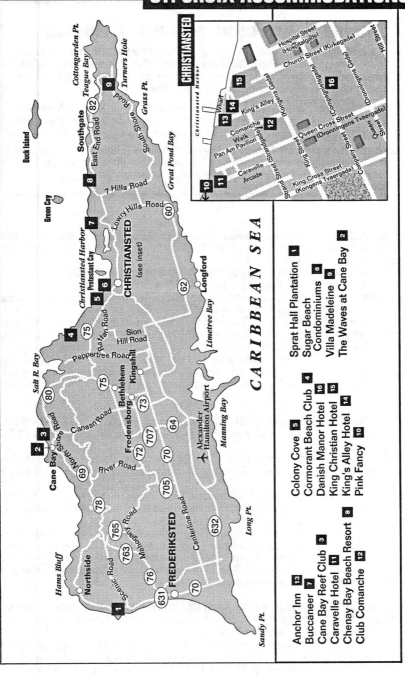

ST. CROIX ACCOMMODATIONS

CHRISTIANSTED

Hospital Street (Hospitalgade)
Church Street (Kirkegade)
Hill Street
King's Alley
Comanche Walk
Pan Am Pavilion
Caravelle Arcade
King Cross Street (Kongens Tvaergade)
King Street
Queen Cross Street (Dronningens Gade)
Company Street (Compagniets Gade)
Queen Street
Strand Street (Strandgade)
Kongens Gade
Wharf
Christiansted Harbor

Buck Island
Green Cay
Cottongarden Pt.
Teague Bay
Turners Hole
Southgate
East End Road
Grass Pt.
South Shore Road
Great Pond Bay
7 Hills Road
Lowry Hills Road
Christiansted Harbor
Protestant Cay
CHRISTIANSTED (see inset)
Longford
Limetree Bay
Salt R. Bay
Cane Bay
Peppertree Road
Rattan Road
Sion Hill Road
North Shore Road
Canaan Road
Bethlehem
Kingshill
Fredensborg
River Road
Scenic Road
Melbourne Road
Northside
Hams Bluff
FREDERIKSTED
Centerline Road
Alexander Hamilton Airport
Manning Bay
Long Pt.
Sandy Pt.

CARIBBEAN SEA

Sprat Hall Plantation **1**
Sugar Beach Condominiums **6**
Villa Madeleine **9**
The Waves at Cane Bay **2**

Colony Cove **5**
Cormorant Beach Club **4**
Danish Manor Hotel **16**
King Christian Hotel **15**
King's Alley Hotel **14**
Pink Fancy **10**

Anchor Inn **13**
Buccaneer **7**
Cane Bay Reef Club **3**
Caravelle Hotel **11**
Chenay Bay Beach Resort **8**
Club Comanche **12**

ⓕ FROMMER'S COOL FOR KIDS: HOTELS

Anchor Inn (see p. 144). This is a good choice for families who don't want to spend money on a rental car. Right in the heart of Christiansted, this hotel lets children under 12 stay free in a room with their parents. It's directly on the waterfront from where boats operate to Buck Island.

Colony Cove (see p. 149). Families can set up housekeeping here with their own kitchens and clothes washer and dryer. It's near a beach and also has a swimming pool. Children cost $20 a day in a unit with their parents.

Chenay Bay Beach Resort (see p. 149). This is ideal for families with children. You have your own cottage with kitchenette overlooking the Caribbean, with both a swimming pool and a fine beach nearby.

CARAVELLE, 44A Queen Cross St., Christiansted, St. Croix, USVI 00820. Tel. 809/773-0687, or toll free 800/524-0410. Fax 809/778-7004. 43 rms (all with bath). A/C TV TEL
$ Rates: Winter, $110–$120 single; $120–$130 double. Summer, $80–$90 single; $90–$100 double. Breakfast $6 extra. AE, DC, MC, V. **Parking:** Free.
The biggest of the hotels in the historic core, Caravelle, between Church and King Cross Streets, usually caters to a clientele of international businesspeople who prefer to be near the center of town. There's an Andalusian-style fountain in the lobby, and the restaurant, Banana Bay Club, is a few steps away. Many resort activities, such as sailing, deep-sea fishing, snorkeling, scuba, golf, and tennis, can be arranged at the reception desk. A swimming pool and sun deck face the water, and all the shopping and activities of the town are close at hand. Accommodations, which are generally spacious and comfortably furnished, are priced according to their views.

CLUB COMANCHE, 1 Strand St., Christiansted, St. Croix, USVI 00820. Tel. 809/773-0210, or toll free 800/524-2066. 43 rms (all with bath). A/C TV TEL
$ Rates (with EP): Dec 15 to mid-Apr, $70–$145 single or double. Mid-Apr to Dec 14, $60–$98 single or double. Breakfast $6 extra. AE, V. **Parking:** Public lot off King St.
Club Comanche lives up to my idea of what a West Indian inn should really be like. Right on the Christiansted waterfront, the main house is old, but has been completely adapted to modern tastes in its remodeling. It's quite charming.
Some of the bedrooms have slanted ceilings with handsomely carved four-poster beds, old chests, and mahogany mirrors. Reached by a covered bridge, a newer addition passes over a shopping street to the waterside. Some rooms are in the poolside and harborfront buildings. There is a waterfront refreshment bar, where you can order drinks and watch yachts come in to dock.

DANISH MANOR HOTEL, 2 Company St., Christiansted, St. Croix, USVI 00820. Tel. 809/773-1377, or toll free 800/524-2029. Fax 809/773-1913. 37 rms (33 with bath), 2 suites. A/C TV TEL
$ Rates: Winter, $59 single without bath; $79–$89 single or double with bath; from $135 suite. Summer, $49 single without bath; $59 single or double with bath; from $95 suite. Breakfast $6 extra. AE, DC, MC, V. **Parking:** Public lot off King St.

Built around an old Danish courtyard and a freshwater pool, Danish Manor is located right in the heart of town between King and Queen Streets. An L-shaped three-story addition stands in the rear of the hotel. The spacious rooms have balconies and ceiling fans, and all units overlook the courtyard dominated by an ancient mahogany tree.

KING CHRISTIAN HOTEL, 59 King's Wharf, P.O. Box 3619, Christiansted, St. Croix, USVI 00822. Tel. 809/773-2285, or toll free 800/524-2012. Fax 809/773-9411. 38 rms (all with bath). A/C TV TEL
$ Rates: Winter, $90–$120 single; $95–$130 double. Summer, $75–$90 single; $80–$97 double. AE, DC, MC, V. **Parking:** Public lot off King St.

One of the finest innkeepers on the island, Betty Sperber, owns this pink hotel on the harborfront in the center of Christiansted. The 24 front rooms have two double beds or one king-size bed, a refrigerator, a room safe, and a private balcony overlooking the harbor. Fourteen no-frills economy-wing rooms have either two single beds or one king-size bed, but no view or balcony.

You can relax on the sun deck, shaded patio, or in the freshwater pool. The staff will make arrangements for golf, tennis, horseback riding, and sightseeing tours, and there's a beach just a few hundred yards across the harbor, reached by ferry. Mile Mark Charters water-sports center offers daily trips to Buck Island's famous snorkeling trail as well as a complete line of water sports. Special events are organized on request. The hotel is also the headquarters of Dive St. Croix, operating a 46-foot dive boat (see "Sports and Recreation," below).

Also on the premises is the Chart House, one of the best restaurants on St. Croix, noted for its salad bar and steaks. It's an easy walk to several nearby cafés that serve breakfast.

KING'S ALLEY HOTEL, 57 King St., Christiansted, St. Croix, USVI 00820. Tel. 809/773-0103, or toll free 800/843-3574. Fax 809/773-4431. 23 rms (all with bath). A/C TV TEL
$ Rates (with EP): Winter, $74–$128 single; $84–$140 double. Summer, $60–$105 single; $73–$116 double. AE, DC, MC, V. **Parking:** Public lot off King St.

The King's Alley Hotel stands at water's edge, near Christiansted Harbor's yacht basin. The hotel is furnished with a distinct Mediterranean flair, and many of its units overlook its swimming pool terrace, which is surrounded by tropical plants. The galleries opening off the bedrooms are almost spacious enough for entertaining. All the rooms have twin or king-size beds. The Marina Bar features nightly entertainment by the pool, and right outside your door are boutiques and restaurants. Breakfast can be ordered if you walk over to one of the nearby cafés.

PINK FANCY, 27 Prince St., Christiansted, St. Croix, USVI 00820. Tel. 809/773-8460, or toll free 800/524-2045. Fax 809/773-6448. 12 units (all with bath). A/C TV TEL
$ Rates (including continental breakfast): $75 single; $90 double. Extra person $15. Children under 12 stay free in parents' room. MC, V. **Parking:** Free on street.

The oldest part of this unique, private four-building complex in downtown Christiansted is a 1780 Danish town house, now one of the historic places of St. Croix. Years ago the building was a private club for wealthy planters. Fame came when Ziegfeld Follies star Jane Gottlieb opened it as a hotel in 1948. In the 1950s, the hotel became a mecca for writers and artists, attracting, among others, Noël Coward. Built on different levels, the efficiency rooms are clustered around the swimming pool and have ceiling fans; nine have air conditioning. Units are known by estate names, such as "Sweet Bottom" and "Upper Love." Other than the complimentary breakfast, and a 24-hour complimentary bar, you're on your own for meals. This is the only hotel in the U.S. Virgin Islands that maintains year-round rates.

FREDERIKSTED

MODERATE

SPRAT HALL PLANTATION, Rte. 58, P.O. Box 695, Frederiksted, St. Croix, USVI 00841. Tel. 809/772-0305, or toll free 800/843-3584. 14 units (all with bath). A/C TV

$ Rates (including continental breakfast): Winter, $110 single in servants' quarters; $120 double in servants' quarters; $150 single or double no-smoking room in Great House; $140 2-room suite in private cottage with kitchenette for one or two (without breakfast). Summer, $70–$80 single in servants' quarters; $80–$90 double in servants' quarters; $130 single or double no-smoking room in Great House; $110 2-room suite in private cottage with kitchenette for one or two (without breakfast). AE. **Parking:** Free.

This resort 1 mile north of Frederiksted is the oldest plantation "great house" in the Virgin Islands, and the only French plantation house left intact. Dating from the French occupation of 1650 to 1690, it's set on 20 acres of grounds, with private white sandy beaches. The plantation has room for about 40 people, depending on how many guests use the cottage units, which all have radios.

The units in the Great House have been designated for nonsmokers because of the value of the antiques. A carefully upgraded annex originally built in the 1940s for farmhands, is known today as the servants' quarters. Within it, each unit has comfortable furnishings and a view of the sea. Room service is available to guests in either the Great House or servants' quarters. If you want privacy, you might choose one of the redecorated one-bedroom cottages, with front porches for lounging or outdoor dining. There is full chamber service daily, and guests have a choice of suites with king-size, double, or twin beds.

You can be sure of warm hospitality and good food, either at the Beach Restaurant at lunch or in the Sprat Hall Plantation restaurant (see "Dining," below). On the grounds is the best equestrian stable in the Caribbean (see "Sports and Recreation," below). The Hurd and Young family run the operation, and offer hiking and birdwatching, as well as snorkeling, swimming, and shore fishing. Jetskiing and waterskiing can be arranged.

SELF-SUFFICIENT UNITS AROUND THE ISLAND

MODERATE

CANE BAY REEF CLUB, P.O. Box 1407, Kingshill, St. Croix, USVI 00851. Tel. 809/778-2966, or toll free 800/253-8534. 9 suites.

$ Rates: Winter, $110–$150 single or double. Summer, $70–$95 single or double. Extra person $15 a night. MC, V. **Parking:** Free.

Since 1975, Carl Seiffer has run one of the little gems of the island, offering 9 large-size suites, each with a living room, a full kitchen, a bedroom, a bath, and a balcony overlooking the water. Trade winds make air conditioning unnecessary, although two units contain it, and the decor is breezy tropical, with cathedral ceilings, overhead fans, and Chilean tiles. The location is on the north shore of St. Croix, about a 20-minute taxi ride from Christiansted. The hotel fronts a rocky beach near The Waves at Cane Bay (see hotel recommendation below). Guests from everywhere introduce themselves around the pool, and local rum drinks are served at the patio bar.

The hotel's dining choice is the No Name Bar & Grille, where a sample dinner menu always includes grilled fresh fish (perhaps dolphin, wahoo, swordfish, or halibut). Other dishes might include an old-fashioned pot roast or various stir fries. When available, fresh stuffed lobster is prepared.

CHENAY BAY BEACH RESORT, P.O. Box 24600, Rte. 82, East End Rd., Chenay Bay, St. Croix, USVI 00824. Tel. 809/773-2918, or toll free 800/548-4457. Fax 809/773-2918. 50 cottages (all with bath). A/C TEL
$ Rates (with EP): Winter, $160–$175 single or double. Summer, $135 single or double. Extra person $25. AE, MC, V. **Parking:** Free.

This resort, with a rustic and casual ambience, is nestled on a beachside of 30 acres; Chenay Bay, 4 miles east of Christiansted, is one of the island's finest beaches for swimming, snorkeling, and windsurfing. Each of the West Indian–style cottages, new or newly renovated, contains a fully equipped kitchenette and ceiling fan, and most have air conditioning. The establishment, owned and managed by hotel veterans of the Caribbean, Richard and Vicki Locke, houses the Mistral Windsurfing Center of St. Croix. The Beach Bar and Grille is open for casual dining daily from 9am to 9pm. A freshwater pool overlooks the Caribbean, and there are two tennis courts.

Rates include free tennis, snorkeling, kayaks, floating mats, twice-weekly entertainment, and daily shuttles to the grocery store. You might be interested in one of their package rates. For example, a 4-night package with a 2-day car rental and two dinners at local restaurants is priced at $665 per person off-season, rising to $825 per person in winter. Tariffs are based on double occupancy.

COLONY COVE, 3221 Estate Golden Rock, St. Croix, USVI 00820. Tel. 809/773-1965, or toll free 800/828-0746. Fax 809/773-5397. 60 rms (all with bath). A/C TV TEL
$ Rates: Winter, $225 single or double. Summer, $150 single or double. Extra person $20. AE, MC, V. **Parking:** Free.

Of all the condo complexes of St. Croix, this one, located about 1 mile west of Christiansted, is perhaps the most like a full-fledged hotel. It's next to a palm-dotted beach and is composed of a quartet of buff-colored three-story buildings with angular facades surrounding an oval-shaped swimming pool. Each unit contains a clothes washer and dryer, a kitchen, an enclosed veranda or gallery, ceramic-tile floors, two air-conditioned bedrooms, and a pair of bathrooms. The complex also has a good restaurant and two tennis courts.

SUGAR BEACH CONDOMINIUMS, 3245 Estate Golden Rock, St. Croix, USVI 00820. Tel. 809/773-5345, or toll free 800/524-2049. Fax 809/773-1359. 46 units (all with bath). A/C TEL
$ Rates: Winter, $150–$200 studio or 1-bedroom unit for two; $250 2-bedroom unit for four; $300 3-bedroom unit for six. Summer, $90–$120 studio or 1-bedroom unit for two; $150 2-bedroom unit for four; $200 3-bedroom unit for six. AE, MC, V. **Parking:** Free.

These modernized, one-, two-, and three-bedroom apartments are strung along 500 feet of sandy beach on the north coast, off North Shore Road. When you tire of the sand, you can swim in the freshwater pool nestled beside a sugar mill, where rum was made three centuries ago. Under red-tile roofs are the apartments with enclosed balconies to provide privacy. All units open toward the sea, are tastefully decorated, and have completely equipped kitchens. Chamber service is extra. The property has two Laykold tennis courts, and the Carambola golf course is a few minutes away.

THE WAVES AT CANE BAY, P.O. Box 1749, Kingshill, St. Croix, USVI 00851. Tel. 809/778-1805, or toll free 800/545-0603. Fax 809/778-1805. 12 units (all with bath). A/C TV

$ Rates: Winter, $120–$175 single or double. Summer, $75–$100 single or double. AE, DC, MC, V. **Parking:** Free.

Ⓢ This intimate and tasteful property, run by Suzanne and Kevin Ryan, is 8 miles east of the airport, midway between the island's two biggest towns. It sits on a narrow but well-landscaped plot of oceanfront property on Cane Bay, the heart of some of the best scuba and snorkeling on the island. Accommodations rise in angular two-story units with screened-in verandas almost directly above the ocean. The Ryans welcome their guests as part of their extended family, hosting cocktail parties on their waterside terrace, and adding many homelike touches to their guests' accommodations.

Each accommodation is high-ceilinged, with fresh flowers, a well-stocked kitchen, a private library, and thick towels; some are air conditioned. A two-room villa next to the main building has a large oceanside deck. The establishment's social center is a beachside bar ringed with stone and coral. Don't overlook the possibility of a game of golf or tennis at nearby Carambola. A full PADI dive center operates on the property, providing everything from rented tanks to individual scuba lessons. An all-you-can-eat barbecue dinner is featured one night a week for $12 per person.

4. DINING

Don't limit yourself to your hotel for dining. Head for one of the island's many independently owned restaurants—they are among the best in the Caribbean.

Restaurants considered "expensive" charge from $40 for a meal; those ranked "moderate" ask from $20 to $25, and anything under that is considered "inexpensive." In all cases, drinks are extra.

For tips on saving money on dining, see "Frommer's Smart Traveler: Restaurants," Chapter 4.

NORTH SHORE

MODERATE

BRASS PARROT, in the Buccaneer, Rte. 82 (East End Rd.), Estate Shoys. Tel. 773-2100.
 Cuisine: INTERNATIONAL. **Reservations:** Recommended. **Directions:** Leave Christiansted heading east (there's only one road that goes this way); turn left at the pink-and-white entrance about 2 miles out from town.
 $ Prices: Appetizers $5.50–$9.50; main dishes $14.50–$23.50. AE, DC, MC, V.
 Open: Dinner Thurs–Mon 6:30–9:30pm.
Set in the pink "great house" in this leading resort, the Brass Parrot is one of the most elegant restaurants on the island. Views open onto the sea, as well as onto the lights of Christiansted. In air-conditioned comfort, this restaurant remains popular with locals and visitors alike. The chef specializes in seafood, but there are plenty of other choices on the menu, backed up by an extensive and reasonably priced wine list. One specialty is a Jamaican seafood fire pot (a soup), made with clams, crab, and a whole crayfish flavored with cilantro, lemongrass, ginger, and hot Cruzan peppers. Curried lobster is a favorite opening salad. You might follow with Bobwhite quail breasts served with a Thai peanut sauce, or orange roughy, a fish with an almost crablike flavor, served with a creamy ginger lime sauce. The best steaks and chops are flown down from Chicago. No smoking is allowed inside the restaurant, and slacks and collared shirts are required for men.

CORMORANT BEACH CLUB RESTAURANT, 4126 La Grande Princesse. Tel. 778-8920.

Cuisine: CONTINENTAL/CARIBBEAN. **Reservations:** Required. **Directions:** Take Rte. 75, 3 miles northwest of Christiansted.

$ Prices: Appetizers $5–$12; main courses $17–$28; Caribbean grill night $32; Sun brunch $22. AE, DC, MC, V.

Open: Lunch daily 11am–2pm; dinner daily 6:30–9:30pm; brunch Sun 11:30am–2:30pm.

This restaurant could easily provide you with your most elegant and best dining experience on St. Croix. Enjoy a sea breeze and listen to the swaying palm trees as you dine in a restaurant on the beach. Entertainment is featured on Thursday evening—a taste of the Caribbean with steel drum, calypso, and limbo dancers. Steel-drum music continues throughout the weekend until Sunday brunch (see "Specialty Dining," below).

Chef Jeff Fratianne (member of the Chaine des Rôtisseurs and president of the Virgin Islands Chef's Association), offers an artful combination of continental and Caribbean cuisine. Sample his caviar of eggplant with sautéed escargots or shrimp in a Pernod flambé. You might follow with grouper Oscar, locally caught grouper served with lobster medaillons and asparagus tips in a passion fruit hollandaise. Choose from an extensive menu of homemade desserts and dessert wines.

INEXPENSIVE

OSKAR'S BAR AND RESTAURANT, 4A La Grande Princesse, Rte. 75. Tel. 773-4060.

Cuisine: CONTINENTAL. **Reservations:** Not required. **Transportation:** Taxi.

$ Prices: Appetizers $2.50–$3; main courses $7–$13. No credit cards.

Open: Lunch Mon–Sat 11am–2:30pm; dinner Mon–Sat 6–9pm.

Set within a simple concrete building just west of Christiansted, this good, inexpensive restaurant is often filled when other, better-known (and more expensive) establishments are empty. It was established in 1974 by Oskar Bütler, an expatriate Swiss, who freely admits to never having changed his highly successful menu since he opened the restaurant. After beginning with soup, try the special of the day, such as roast pork with gravy, accompanied by mashed potatoes and corn. To go continental, you may prefer bratwurst with sauerkraut, or even filet mignon. To finish your repast, why not Black Forest cake?

EAST END

EXPENSIVE

CAFE MADELEINE, Gallows Bay. Tel. 778-7377.

Cuisine: ITALIAN. **Reservations:** Recommended.

$ Prices: Appetizers $6–$10; pasta $15–$30; main courses $21–$28. AE, DC, MC, V.

Open: Dinner daily 6–9:30pm.

Contained within the colonial-inspired great house that was built by the Roncari family in 1990, Café Madeleine, 8 miles east of Christiansted, offers a mountaintop panorama of both the north and south sides of the island, a lavish decor created by a battalion of hardworking decorators, and a choice of either indoor or terrace dining. Don't overlook a before-dinner drink at the mahogany-trimmed bar before your meal, where a scale model of a Maine schooner, bolted against mahogany paneling, creates a private club aura.

The cuisine is inspired by the recipes of northern Italy, with a generous dose of highly experimental nouvelle cuisine thrown in as well. Menu choices might include baked artichoke hearts, oysters Mario, filet of red snapper milanese, breast of pheasant with capers and lemon, veal scallopini alla Madeleine, and some of the most unusual pastas in the world, including a version of key lime fettuccine with raspberry sauce or a wild mushroom ravioli.

MODERATE

DUGGAN'S REEF, East End Rd., Teague Bay. Tel. 773-9800.
   Cuisine: CONTINENTAL/CARIBBEAN. **Reservations:** Required for dinner.
   Directions: Take Rte. 82 7 miles east of Christiansted; park in the public lot near the public beach at Teague Bay.
   $ Prices: Lunch salads and sandwiches $4.50–$8; main courses $14.50–$29. AE, MC, V.
   Open: Lunch daily noon–3pm; dinner daily 6–9:30pm. Bar daily 11am–11:30pm.
Set only 10 feet from the still waters of Reef Beach, and open to the sea breezes, Duggan's Reef is an ideal perch for watching the Windsurfers and Hobie Cats careening through the nearby waters. The restaurant, owned for more than 10 years by Boston-born Frank Duggan, is considered the most popular in St. Croix—all visitors seemingly dine here at least once during their stay on the island. At lunch, a simple array of salads, crêpes, and sandwiches is offered. At night a more elaborate menu contains the popular house specialty—Duggan's Caribbean lobster pasta and Irish whiskey lobster. Other choices include veal piccata and rack of lamb.

THE GALLEON, East End Rd., Green Cay Marina, 50 Estate Southgate. Tel. 773-9949.
   Cuisine: FRENCH/ITALIAN. **Reservations:** Recommended.
   $ Prices: Appetizers $4.50–$12; main courses $13.50–$25; Sun brunch $13–$15. AE, MC, V.
   Open: Dinner daily 6–10pm; brunch Sun 10am–2pm. **Closed:** Sun–Mon in summer.
Overlooking the ocean on Route 82, 5 minutes east of Christiansted, the Galleon enjoys a fine reputation—and deservedly so. The best cooking of northern Italy and France is offered at this casual but elegant spot, including osso buco, just as good as that served in Milan. Freshly baked bread, two fresh vegetables, and rice or potatoes accompany main dishes. The menu always includes at least one local fish, such as wahoo, tuna, grouper, swordfish, snapper, or dolphin. If you prefer the classics, you might order a perfectly done rack of lamb carved at your table. Chilled soup, fruit salads, and croissants complement any meal. Music from a baby grand accompanies your dinner.

CHRISTIANSTED

EXPENSIVE

KENDRICKS, 52 King St. Tel. 773-9199.
   Cuisine: CONTINENTAL. **Reservations:** Recommended.
   $ Prices: Appetizers $6.50–$9.50; main courses $15–$26. AE, MC, V.
   Open: Dinner Mon–Sat 6–10pm. **Closed:** June.
This fine restaurant is housed in a 19th-century brick building in the heart of town. Climb a flight of brick stairs to the second-floor dining room, which has a view of old Christiansted with the distant sea beyond the rooftops. David and Jane Kendrick's menu might include such appetizers as artichoke heart filled with scallops on a bed of lemon cream sauce or one of the soups, perhaps chilled pear and

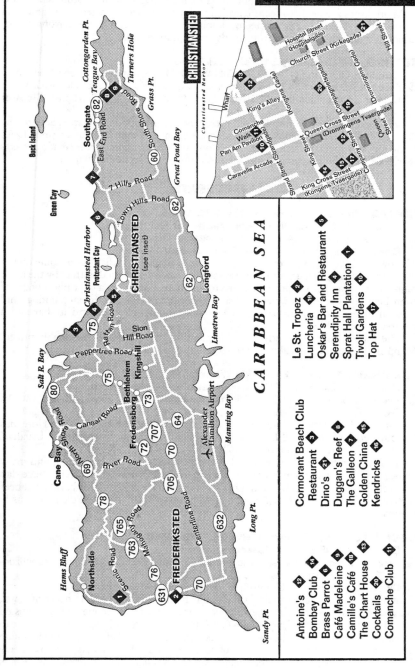

ST. CROIX DINING

CHRISTIANSTED

CARIBBEAN SEA

Le St. Tropez ◆ 2
Luncheria ◆ 19
Oskar's Bar and Restaurant ◆ 5
Serendipity Inn ◆ 4
Sprat Hall Plantation ◆ 1
Tivoli Gardens ◆ 10
Top Hat ◆ 17

Cormorant Beach Club
Restaurant ◆ 3
Dino's ◆ 21
Duggan's Reef ◆ 8
The Galleon ◆ 7
Golden China ◆ 15
Kendricks ◆ 16

Antoine's ◆ 12
Bombay Club ◆ 14
Brass Parrot ◆ 6
Café Madeleine ◆ 9
Camille's Café ◆ 18
The Chart House ◆ 13
Cocktails ◆ 20
Comanche Club ◆ 11

watercress. There's always a selection of pasta, including homemade stuffed manicotti. Main dishes are likely to feature grilled rack of lamb with roasted garlic and fresh thyme sauce, roasted pecan-crusted pork loin à la O'Brien with ginger mayonnaise, or grilled filet of fish with fresh fruit salads and lemon butter.

TOP HAT, 52 Company St. Tel. 773-2346.
   Cuisine: CONTINENTAL/SCANDINAVIAN. **Reservations:** Recommended.
$ **Prices:** Appetizers $4.50–$10; main courses $14.50–$30. AE, DC, MC, V.
   Open: Lunch Tues–Fri 11:30am–2pm; dinner Mon–Sat 6–10pm. **Closed:** June–Oct.

On the second floor of a restored old merchant's house opposite Market Square, the Top Hat has been operated by Scandinavians Bent and Hanne Rasmussen since 1970. Look for daily specials, such as fresh seafood. A good selection of homemade desserts is offered, and the changing menu is backed up by a selection of wines.

MODERATE

BOMBAY CLUB, 5A King St. Tel. 773-1838.
   Cuisine: INTERNATIONAL. **Reservations:** Not required.
$ **Prices:** Appetizers $4–$7; main courses $9–$15. AE, MC, V.
   Open: Restaurant daily 11am–10pm. Bar daily 11–1am.

The owners have managed to squeeze much miscellany into what has become one of the most enduring restaurants in Christiansted. Concealed from the street by the brick foundations of an 18th-century planter's town house, it includes a large photograph of John Lennon near the entrance, and such other ornaments as original paintings and tropical plants. You enter through a low stone tunnel that leads to its bar and a courtyard with tables.

The food, while not overly fancy, is plentiful, flavorful, and reasonably priced. Menu items include the catch of the day, veal dishes, beef filet, and pasta.

THE CHART HOUSE, 59 King's Wharf. Tel. 773-7718.
   Cuisine: STEAKS/SALADS. **Reservations:** Recommended.
$ **Prices:** Appetizers $4.50–$8.75; main courses $16.25–$25.95. AE, DC, MC, V.
   Open: Dinner daily 6–10pm.

This nautically decorated restaurant on the wharf under the King Christian Hotel has a classy decor of varnished hardwoods, polished brass, and wicker chairs. Usually I don't like chain restaurants, but the Chart House is an exception.

To begin with, the Chart House has the best salad bar on the island, and many come here just for that. I always order their celebrated prime rib, which is a huge slab of carefully seasoned meat. You might prefer instead their lobster, or barbecued beef ribs. Regardless, try their baked potato; it's a palate-pleaser. The mud pie is also justly renowned.

COCKTAILS, 54B Company St. Tel. 773-4243.
   Cuisine: SURF & TURF. **Reservations:** Not required.
$ **Prices:** Lunch salads, sandwiches, and platters $2.50–$8; dinner appetizers $3–$5; dinner main courses $8–$22. AE, DC, MC, V.
   Open: Lunch daily 11:30am–5pm; dinner daily 5–10:30pm.

Contained within a century-old Danish-built building in the historic heart of town, this establishment is one of the newest restaurant and nightlife venues in Christiansted (see "Evening Entertainment," below). Within its raftered dining areas, guests can order cost-conscious lunches that include hamburgers, salads, and grilled minute steaks, accompanied by a wide array of such frozen drinks as banana or strawberry daiquiris, or margaritas. Evening meals feature a similar array of drinks, as well as dishes like surf and turf, stuffed pork chops, stuffed mahimahi, lobster, and a variety of seafood.

COMANCHE CLUB, 1 Strand St. Tel. 773-2665.
Cuisine: WEST INDIAN/CONTINENTAL. **Reservations:** Recommended.
$ **Prices:** Appetizers $3.50–$10.50; main dishes $7.50–$14.75. AE, V.
Open: Breakfast daily (Nov–May only) 7–10am; lunch daily 11:30am–2:30pm; dinner daily 6–11pm.

One of the most popular restaurants on the island is the relaxed yet elegant Comanche. The specialties are eclectic—there's everything from fish and conch chowder to shark cakes. Each night a different special is featured. There's also a good selection of Cruzan dishes—one for every night of the week. Typical of these is a plate of fish cakes served with seasoned rice. Desserts include a caramel flan with rum sauce.

DINO'S, 4C Hospital St. Tel. 778-8005.
Cuisine: ITALIAN. **Reservations:** Required.
$ **Prices:** Appetizers $4.25–$8; main courses $12–$18.50. AE.
Open: Dinner Mon–Sat 6–10pm.

This Mediterranean-style bistro is housed in a 200-year-old brick building, and has two different sections: an air-conditioned interior and an open-air terrace. Begin with one of the homemade pasta dishes, then go on to veal piccata or perhaps breast of duck. A specialty is steak Dino, made with wild mushrooms and a flavoring of balsamic vinegar. Most guests end their meal with a luscious Italian dessert and cappuccino.

GOLDEN CHINA, 28 King Cross St. Tel. 773-8181.
Cuisine: CHINESE. **Reservations:** Recommended, especially on weekends.
$ **Prices:** Appetizers $1–$5.50; main courses $9.50–$12.50. AE, MC, V.
Open: Lunch Mon–Fri 11am–5pm; dinner daily 5–10:30pm.

Within a vividly lacquered decor of red, white, green, and black, Golden China serves food as fine as that enjoyed in the Chinatowns of New York or San Francisco. It's particularly fun to get a group of six couples and arrange for the special Chinese banquet. Diners in smaller groups will still enjoy many Hunan and Szechuan specialties. Each dish is prepared to order, and only the finest-quality ingredients are used. Specialties include a puu-puu platter for two, and Peking duck.

LUNCHERIA, Apothecary Hall Courtyard, 2111 Company St. Tel. 773-4247.
Cuisine: MEXICAN. **Reservations:** Not required.
$ **Prices:** Appetizers $4–$6.75; main courses $4.25–$7.50. No credit cards.
Open: Mon–Fri 11am–9pm, Sat noon–9pm.

In a historic courtyard in the center of town, this Mexican restaurant offers some of the best dining values on the island. You get the usual array of tacos, tostadas, burritos, nachos, and enchiladas. Specialties include chicken fajitas, enchiladas verde, and *arroz con pollo* (spiced chicken with brown rice). Daily specials feature both low-calorie and vegetarian choices, and the chef's refried beans are lard free. Whole-wheat tortillas are offered. Check the board for daily specials, and know that the salsa bar is complimentary, ranging from mild to hot sauce, plus jalapeños.

SERENDIPITY INN, Mill Harbour Condominiums, Mill Harbour. Tel. 773-5762.
Cuisine: INTERNATIONAL. **Reservations:** Required for dinner and Sun brunch.

$ Prices: Appetizers $4.50–$5.75; main courses $14.50–$19.50. AE, DC, MC, V.
Open: Lunch daily 11am–3pm; dinner daily 6:30–9:30pm; brunch Sun 10:30am–2:30pm. Bar daily 11am–midnight.

This beach and poolside restaurant lies just west of Christiansted, in the Mill Harbour Condominiums. Surrounded by iron gates and brick walls, the restaurant offers a spacious courtyard fronting the lagoon. At lunch you can enjoy light fare such as homemade soups, freshly made salads, and sandwiches. Daily specials are regularly featured. On Friday night a barbecue, including chicken and ribs, along with salad, costs only $10. For dinner, begin with lobster bisque or stuffed mushrooms, then try the chef's fresh catch of the day, seafood pasta, or perhaps veal piccata. On Saturday a steak-and-lobster grill is featured. Sunday brunch costs about $20.

TIVOLI GARDENS, 39 Strand St., upstairs in the Pan Am Pavilion. Tel. 773-6782.
  Cuisine: INTERNATIONAL. **Reservations:** Recommended after 7pm.
$ Prices: Appetizers $3.50–$7; main courses $10.50–$20. AE, MC, V.
  Open: Lunch Mon–Fri 11:15am–2:30pm; dinner daily 6–9:30pm.

This large second-floor porch festooned with lights affords the same view of Christiansted Harbor that a sea captain might have. This well-known local rendezvous, run by Gary Thomson, has white beams, trellises, and hanging plants that evoke its namesake, the pleasure gardens of Copenhagen. The menu lists everything from escargots provencale to a goulash inspired by a recipe concocted in the days of the Austro-Hungarian Empire. The Thai curry is excellent. For dessert, those in the know order a wicked, calorie-laden chocolate velvet cake. Often there is live music and dancing from 7pm.

IN & AROUND FREDERIKSTED

MODERATE

LE ST. TROPEZ, Limetree Court, 67 King St., Frederiksted. Tel. 772-3000.
  Cuisine: FRENCH/MEDITERRANEAN. **Reservations:** Recommended.
$ Prices: Appetizers $4.50–$6; main courses $12.50–$22. AE, MC, V.
  Open: Mon–Sat 11am–9pm.

André and Danielle Ducrot operate this cozy bistro, where lunch folds into dinner without interruption. Vaguely capturing the atmosphere of Provence, they offer such luncheon fare as croque-monsieur, quiche, and crêpes, along with a selection of homemade soups and fresh salads. They are known for their brochettes (fish, poultry, or meat), and a changing array of French specialties at night.

SPRAT HALL PLANTATION, Rte. 58. Tel. 772-0305.
  Cuisine: CARIBBEAN/CONTINENTAL. **Reservations:** Required for dinner.
  Directions: From Frederiksted, head 1½ miles north on Rte. 58.
$ Prices: Appetizers $3.50–$4; main courses $19–$24. No credit cards.
  Open: Lunch daily noon–2:30pm; dinner Mon–Sat 7:30–8:15pm.

Even if you don't stay at this previously recommended plantation house (see "Accommodations," above), you might want to call the managers/owners of Sprat Hall, Mark and Judy Young, to tell them you'd like to come by for dinner. One of the finest restaurants on the island (and recommended in *Gourmet* magazine), it has been feeding satisfied guests for years. The place is equally famous for its status as the oldest plantation great house in St. Croix.

Appetizers include homemade soups and fresh salads from the plantation's gardens. Main courses might be conch in sherry-butter sauce, loin of pork in a wild orange sauce, grilled steak, and frequently changing preparations of local fish. Clients are requested to dress with decorum. No jeans or T-shirts, please.

Lunches are less formal, served almost directly on the white sands of a ¼-mile beach amid the encircling lattices of the hotel's gazebo-inspired Beach Club. Specialties include a Caribbean-inspired assortment of such dishes as a basket of pumpkin fritters, conch salad, sandwiches, and a succulent version of curried chicken with coconut and raisins.

SPECIALTY DINING

For **dining with a view,** you can't beat Antoine's, 58A King St. (tel. 773-0263), on King's Wharf. It became famous when it was known as the Anchor Inn Restaurant and Bar, and today it is better than ever. From your dining perch on the second floor of the covered terrace you'll have a spectacular view of the marina and the historic harbor of Christiansted.

The menu includes a wide variety of alpine dishes, such as Austrian Gulaschsuppe and knockwurst salad, plus fresh local seafood, Caribbean and Maine lobster, shrimps and scallops, and a number of Cruzan dishes, such as callaloo and fish chowder. Appetizers cost $3 to $8, and main courses go for between $11.50 and $28.50. The bar is known for its more than 35 frozen drinks, and for having the largest selection of beers on the island. Live entertainment is provided in season. Antoine's is open daily for lunch from 11am to 2:30pm and for dinner from 6 to 10pm. Credit cards (AE, MC, and V) are welcome.

For ✪ **Sunday brunch,** try the Cormorant Beach Club Restaurant, 4126 La Grand Princesse (tel. 779-8920), open from 11:30am to 2pm. You'll enjoy an array of delicious dishes for $22 for adults, $16 for children. Sample such dishes as Cruzan-style fish, West Indian curried lamb, shrimp salad, salade niçoise, barbecued ribs, eggs Benedict, salmon mousse, and johnnycakes. Wash it all down with a mimosa or a glass of champagne. A steel-drum band entertains.

A **local favorite** is the New York deli–style Camille's Café, 53B Company St. (tel. 773-2985). Formerly called the Ritz Café, Camille's is a favorite gathering place for locals. Its brick walls and beamed ceilings were part of the original 18th-century house. Fresh daily salad specials are featured, as are soups and sandwiches. Appetizers go for $3 to $3.95 and main courses are $7.95 to $12.95. The fixed-price dinner at $13 is one of the best dining values in Christiansted. Camille's is open Monday through Saturday from 7:30am to 10pm. Reservations are not needed.

Camille's is also a good place to buy **picnic fare.** Sandwiches (from $4) include a crunchy vegetarian delight, chicken salad, salami, and other deli favorites, and all come with garnishes. The special "Buck Island Lunch," named after an ideal spot for a picnic (see "An Easy Excursion," below), is ready to be picked up at 7:30am.

5. ATTRACTIONS

Many like to explore St. Croix on a **taxi tour** (tel. 778-1088), which for a party of two costs from $35 to $45 for 4 hours. The fare should be negotiated in advance.

Check with your hotel desk to see if you can go on an organized tour. These operate according to demand, with fewer summer departures than winter. A typical 4-hour tour costs $20 per person, and many are conducted at least three times a week during the winter season. Tours usually go through old Christiansted, and visit the Botanical Gardens, Whim Estate House, a rum distillery, the rain forest, the St. Croix

DID YOU KNOW . . . ?

- Columbus, "the first tourist," to St. Croix, was driven away by a rain of arrows by the Carib Indians.
- Under FDR's New Deal, the federal government produced a rum here called "Government House." FDR designed the label himself.
- Alexander Hamilton once worked in a hardware store on St. Croix.

Leap mahogany workshop, and the site of the ill-fated Columbus landing at Salt River. Call **Travellers' Tours,** Alexander Hamilton Airport (tel. 778-1636), for more information.

CHRISTIANSTED

This picture-book harbor town of the Caribbean is an old Danish port in the process of being handsomely restored. Located on the northeastern shore of the island, on a coral-bound bay, the town is filled with Danish buildings, most erected by prosperous merchants in the booming mercantile days of the 18th century. Built of solid stone, these red-roofed structures are often washed in pink, ocher, or yellow; their walls are so thick that the buildings keep cool. The whole area around the harborfront has been designated as a historical site, supervised by the National Park Service.

WALKING TOUR — CHRISTIANSTED

Start: Visitors' Bureau.
Finish: Christiansted harborfront.
Time: 1½ hours.
Best Time: Any day 10am to 4pm.
Worst Time: Monday to Friday 4 to 6pm.

Begin your tour at:

1. **The Visitors' Bureau,** a yellow-sided building with a cedar-capped roof near the harborfront. It was originally built as The Old Scalehouse in 1856 to replace a similar, older, structure which burned down. In its heyday, all taxable goods leaving and entering Christiansted's harbor were weighed here. The scales which once stood here could accurately weigh barrels of sugar and molasses weighing up to 1,600 pounds each.

   In front of the Scalehouse is one of the most charming squares in the Caribbean, whose old-fashioned asymmetrical allure is still evident despite the masses of cars.

   With your back to the Scalehouse, turn left and walk through the parking lot to the foot of the white-sided gazebo-inspired band shell that sits in the center of a park named after Alexander Hamilton. The yellow-brick building with the ornately curved brick staircase is the:

2. **Old Customs House** (headquarters of the National Park Service). The gracefully proportioned 16-step staircase was added as an 1829 embellishment to an older building. (There are public toilets on the ground floor.)

   Continue climbing the hill to the base of the yellow-painted:

3. **Fort Christiansvaern.** Considered the best-preserved colonial fortification in the Virgin Islands, it is maintained as a historic monument by the National Park Service. Its original four-sided star-shaped design followed the most sophisticated military planning of its era.

   Exit from the fort, and head straight down the tree-lined path toward the most visible steeple in Christiansted. It caps the appropriately named:

4. **Steeple Building** (Church of Lord God of Sabaoth), completed in 1753 as St. Croix's first Lutheran church, and embellished with a steeple in 1794–96. The

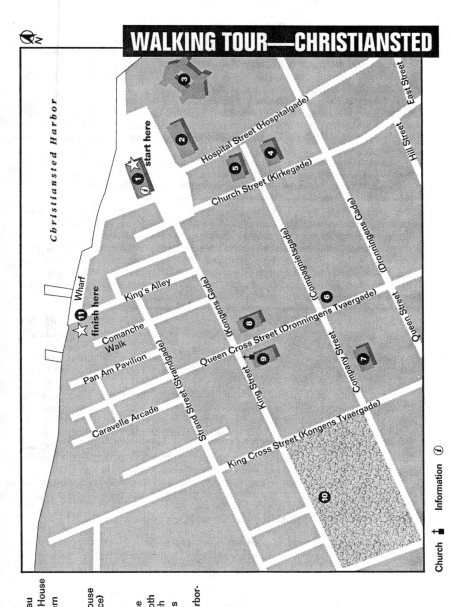

WALKING TOUR—CHRISTIANSTED

Christiansted Harbor

N

Hospital Street (Hospitalgade)

Church Street (Kirkegade)

King's Alley

Comanche Walk

Pan Am Pavilion

Caravelle Arcade

Strand Street (Strandgade)

Kongens Gade)

Queen Cross Street (Dronningens Tvaergade)

King Street

Compagnietsgade)

(Dronningens Gade)

Queen Street

Company Street

King Cross Street (Kongens Tvaergade)

East Street

Hill Street

Wharf

start here

finish here

1 The Visitors' Bureau
2 The Old Customs House
3 Fort Christiansvaern
4 Steeple Building
5 West Indies and
   Guinea Warehouse
   (U.S. Post Office)
6 Luncheria
7 Hendricks Square
8 Government House
9 Lord God of Sabaoth
   Lutheran Church
10 Limprecht Gardens
    and Memorial
11 Christiansted's harbor-
    front

Church   Information

building was deconsecrated in 1831, and served at various times as a bakery, a hospital, and a school. A museum devoted to local history is inside.

Across Company Street from the Steeple Building is a U.S. Post Office. The building that contains it was built in 1749 as:

5. The West Indies and Guinea warehouse. It was once three times larger than today, and included storerooms and lodgings for staff. Go to the building's side entrance, on Church Street, and enter the rear courtyard if the iron gate is open. For many years this was the site of some of the largest slave auctions in the Caribbean.

From the post office, retrace your steps to Company Street and head west for 1 block. On your left you'll pass the entrance to Apothecary Hall, 2111 Company St., which contains a charming collection of shops and restaurants.

REFUELING STOP If you'd like to pause for refreshment, try **6. Luncheria,** Apothecary Hall Courtyard, 2111 Company St. (tel. 773-4247). Housed in an extension of an 18th-century building, the bar's tables are grouped in a courtyard shaded by trees. The owners are considered the margarita specialists of the island, stocking more types or tequila (15 plus) than any other bar in the neighborhood. Most margaritas cost from $3 each. Specializing in Mexican fare, Luncheria serves burritos, enchiladas, and tacos, as well as daily specials and vegetarian meals.

Exit Apothecary Hall and turn left onto Company Street. Cross Queen Cross Street (*Dronningens Tvergade*). Half a block later, you'll arrive at the island's largest outdoor market:

7. Hendricks Square (Christian "Shan" Square), rebuilt in a timbered 19th-century style after the 1989 hurricane. Fruits and vegetables are sold here Monday to Saturday from 7am to 6pm.

Retrace your steps half a block along Company Street, and turn left onto Queen Cross Street. Head downhill toward the harbor, walking on the right-hand side of the street. Within half a block you'll reach an unmarked arched iron gateway, set beneath an arcade. If it's open, enter the charming gardens of:

8. Government House. Evocative of Europe, they contain a scattering of very old trees, flowerbeds, and walkways. The antique building that surrounds the gardens was formed from the union of two much older town houses in the 1830s.

Exit the same way you entered, turn right, and continue your descent of Queen Cross Street. At the first street corner (King Street), turn left, and admire the neoclassical facade of the:

9. Lord God of Sabaoth Lutheran Church, established in 1734.

Continue walking southwest along King Street. Within 2 blocks is:

10. The Limprecht Gardens and Memorial. For 20 years (1888–1908) Peter Carl Limprecht served as governor of the Danish West Indies. Today, an occasional chicken pecks at seedlings planted near a Danish-language memorial to him.

After the park, retrace your steps to King Cross Street, and go left. One very short block later, turn right onto Strand Street, which contains some interesting stores, including at least two different shopping arcades. The streets will narrow, and the pedestrian traffic will be more congested. Pass beneath the overpass belonging to a popular bar and restaurant, the Club Comanche.

Continue down the meandering curves of King's Alley and within 1 block you'll be standing beside:

11. Christiansted's harborfront, where you can end your tour by strolling on the boardwalk of the waterside piers.

FREDERIKSTED

This old Danish town at the western end of the island, about 17 miles from Christiansted, is a sleepy port town that comes to life only when a cruise ship docks at its shoreline.

Frederiksted was destroyed by a fire in 1879, and the citizens rebuilt it, using wood frame and clapboards on top of the old Danish stone and yellow-brick foundations.

Most visitors begin their tour at russet-colored **Fort Frederick,** next to the pier. Some historians claim that this was the first fort to sound a foreign salute to the U.S. flag, in 1776. It was here on July 3, 1848, that Governor-General Peter von Scholten emancipated the slaves in the Danish West Indies. The fort, at the northern end of Frederiksted, has been restored to its 1840 look. You can explore the courtyard and stables, and an exhibit area has been installed in what was once the Garrison Room.

Just south of the fort, the **Customs House,** is an 18th-century building with a 19th-century two-story gallery. Here you can go into the **Visitor's Bureau** and pick up a free map of the town.

Nearby, privately owned **Victoria House,** Market Street, is a gingerbread-trimmed structure built after the fire of 1879. In the rebuilding, some of the original 1803 structure was preserved.

Along the waterfront Strand Street is the **Bellhouse,** once the Frederiksted Public Library. One of its owners, G. A. Bell, ornamented the steps with bells. The house today is an arts and crafts center and a nursery. Sometimes a local theater group presents dramas here.

Other buildings of interest include the **Danish School,** Prince Street, which was adapted in the 1830s into a building designed by Hingelberg, a well-known Danish architect. Today it's the police station and Welfare Department.

Two churches are of interest: **St. Paul's Episcopal Church,** 28 Prince Street, was founded outside the port in the late 18th century; the present building dates from 1812; **St. Patrick's Catholic Church,** on Prince Street, was built in the 1840s.

AROUND THE ISLAND

North of Frederiksted you can drop in at **Sprat Hall,** the island's oldest plantation, or else continue along to the rain forest, which covers about 15 acres, including the 150-foot-high **Creque Dam.** Mahogany trees and yellow cedar grow in profusion, as

FROMMER'S FAVORITE ST. CROIX EXPERIENCES

Sundowners at Club Comanche (see p. 146). The sun deck at Club Comanche, a hotel in Christiansted, provides one of the most panoramic vistas in the Caribbean. The drinks are good, too.

Snorkeling on Buck Island (see p. 172). The crystal clear water and white coral sand of this national park has two major underwater trails for snorkeling along the reef. For more serious divers, there are labyrinths and grottoes.

Playing Golf at Carambola (see p. 166). Like playing golf in a tropical garden. It's the site of "Shell's Wonderful World of Golf."

do wild lilies. The terrain is private property, but the owner lets visitors go inside to explore. Most people want to see the jagged estuary of the northern coastline's **Salt River,** but other than bird life there, there isn't much to see. This is where Columbus landed for a brief moment before being driven off by Caribs.

ST. GEORGE VILLAGE BOTANICAL GARDEN OF ST. CROIX, Kingshill. Tel. 772-3874.

Just north of Centerline Road, 4 miles east of Frederiksted at Estate St. George, is a veritable Eden of tropical trees, shrubs, vines, and flowers. Built around the ruins of a 19th-century sugarcane workers' village, the garden is a feast for the eye and the camera—from the entrance drive bordered by royal palms and bougainvillea to the towering kapok and tamarind trees. Restoration of the ruins is a continuing project. Two sets of workers' cottages provide space for a gift shop, restrooms, a kitchen, and an office; these have been joined together with a Great Hall, which is used by the St. Croix community for various functions. Other completed projects include the superintendent's house, the blacksmith's shop, the Orchid and Fern House, and various smaller buildings used for a library, a plant nursery, workshops, and storehouses.

Self-guided walking tour maps are available at the entrance to the Great Hall.

Admission: $3 adults, $1 for children 12 or under. Donations are welcome.

Open: Tues–Sat 9am–4pm. **Transportation:** Taxi.

CRUZAN RUM FACTORY, West Airport Rd. Tel. 772-0799.

This factory distills the famous Virgin Islands rum, which is considered by residents to be the finest in the world. Guided tours depart from the visitors' pavilion; call for reservations and information.

Admission: Free.

Open: Tours Mon–Fri 8:30–11:15am and 1–4:15pm.

ESTATE WHIM PLANTATION MUSEUM, Centerline Rd. Tel. 772-0598.

About 2 miles east of Frederiksted, this museum was restored by the St. Croix Landmarks Society and is unique among the many sugar plantations whose ruins dot the island of St. Croix. This great house is different from most in that it is composed of only three rooms. With 3-foot-thick walls made of stone, coral, and molasses, the house is said by some to resemble a luxurious European chateau. Also on the premises is a typical woodworking shop, kitchen, gift shop, and a reproduction of a typical town apothecary. The ruins of the plantation's sugar-processing plant, complete with restored windmill, remain.

Admission: $5 adults, $1 children.

Open: Tues–Sat 10am–4pm.

DRIVING TOUR —— EAST ST. CROIX

Start: Buccaneer.
Finish: Fort Christiansvaern.
Time: 1½ hours.
Best Time: Early morning or late afternoon.
Worst Time: Any evening after 5pm.

Head east from Christiansted on Route 75. (Some maps and some residents refer to this as East End Road.) Within a few miles, it will change its markings to Route 82. If you get confused at any time during this tour, remember to keep the ocean always on your left.

Landmarks you'll pass on your way out of town will include Gallows Point and:

N

CARIBBEAN SEA

CARIBBEAN SEA

Buck Island

Green Cay

Protestant Cay

East Pt.

Cottongarden Pt.

Teague Bay

Turners Hole

Southgate

Grass Pt.

Robin Bay

East End Road

South Shore Road

Great Pond Bay

7 Hills Road

Lowry Hills Road

CHRISTIANSTED

start here

finish here

Longford

82

60

60

75

624

62

62

3

2

4

1

5

1 Buccaneer
2 Green Cay Marina
3 Mountaintop Eyrie
4 Hartmann's Great Pond
5 Fort Christiansvaern

1. Buccaneer, a hotel where you might want to return for one of the nightly musical performances that are among the best on the island.

Suddenly, the landscape will open onto verdant countryside. Cows graze peacefully on a rolling landscape that may remind you of the Scottish lowlands. Accompanying the cows are tickbirds, which feed on ticks buried in the cows' skin. An occasional traffic mini-jam might form as herds of goats cross the road. Continue driving and you'll pass:

2. Green Cay Marina, identified by a road sign, which you might want to visit to admire the yachts bobbing at anchor, or perhaps have a swim nearby at beautiful Chenay Bay. Nearby monuments include the Southgate Baptist Church, and a handful of stone towers that once housed the gear mechanisms of windmills that crushed the juice from sugarcane.

As vistas unfold, scatterings of bougainvillea-covered private villas will appear near sparkling combinations of sea, verdant earth, and sky.

About 7 miles along the route from Christiansted, you'll see the:

3. Mountaintop eyrie of the island's most prominent socialite, the Contessa Nadia Farbo Navarro, the Romanian-born heiress to a great fortune. This opulent castle is the most outrageously unusual, most prominent, and most talked-about villa on St. Croix. Understandably, its privacy is rigidly maintained.

A couple of miles farther, you'll reach one of the most popular windsurfing beaches in St. Croix, Teague Bay. This is a good spot to take a break.

REFUELING STOP For a break, **Duggan's Reef,** East End Road, Teague Bay (tel. 773-9800), offers flavorful lunches, more formal dinners, fruit daiquiris, and a bar only 10 feet from the waves. Many guests claim this is the best way to experience windsurfing without getting on a sailboard. See "Dining," above, for details.

After your stop, continue driving east along Route 82 to the area that most residents consider the most peaceful and dramatic on the island. It is especially beautiful at sunset, when the vistas are highlighted and the sun is against your back.

At Knight Bay, near the eastern tip of the island, turn right onto Route 60 (South Shore Road), and head west. One of the several lakes you'll pass is:

4. Hartmann's Great Pond (also known as Great Pond), a favorite of nesting seabirds. The sea vistas and the rolling grasslands are spectacular.

Route 60 merges with Route 624 a short distance north of Great Pond. Fork left

---

 FROMMER'S COOL FOR KIDS: ATTRACTIONS

Fort Christiansvaern (see p. 158) Children are taken through dungeons and around battlements, and even shown how soldiers of olden days fired a cannon.

St. George Village Botanical Garden of St. Croix (see p. 162) Kids delight in wandering in this sunny spot built around the ruins of a sugarcane workers' village from the 1800s.

Buck Island (see p. 172) The boat ride to Buck Island's 850 mostly underwater acres is often the highlight of a child's visit to St. Croix. Equally appealing are the island's white sandy beaches, its profuse wildlife, and the picnic you've brought along.

onto Route 624, and, a short distance later, right onto Route 62 (Lowry Hill Road). You travel the mountainous spine of the island through districts named after former farms, such as Sally's Fancy, Marienhøj, and Boetzberg.

Within 2 miles, Lowry Hill Road merges with Route 82 again. Fork left, and follow it as it turns into Hospital Gade and leads to the center of Christiansted. To your right will appear:

5. Fort Christiansvaern, as you pull into the parking lot in front of Christiansted's tourist office (Old Scalehouse).

6. SPORTS & RECREATION

BEACHES

While beaches are the big attraction in St. Croix, getting to them from Christiansted, the center of most of the hotels, isn't always easy. It can also be expensive, especially if you want to go back and forth every day.

In Christiansted, if you want to beach it, take the ferry to the **Hotel on the Cay,** which occupies its own tiny island in the middle of the harbor. There you'll find a sandy bottom, a bar, restaurant facilities, and Windsurfers.

Cramer Park, at the northeast end of the island, is a special public park operated by the Department of Agriculture. Lined with sea grape trees, the beach also has a picnic area, a restaurant, and a bar.

I highly recommend **Cane Bay** and **Davis Bay**—they're the kind of beaches you'd expect to find on a Caribbean Island (with palms, white sand, good swimming, and snorkeling). Cane Bay, which adjoins Route 80 on the north shore, attracts snorkelers and divers with its rolling waves, coral gardens, and dropoff wall. Davis Bay, which doesn't have any reefs to block the ocean swells, draws bodysurfers and has an alluring white sand beach. Changing facilities aren't available. It's off the South Shore Road (Route 60), in the vicinity of the Carambola Beach Resort.

Windsurfers like **Reef Beach,** opening onto Teague Bay along Route 82, a half-hour ride from Christiansted. Food can be ordered at Duggan's Reef. On Route 63, a short ride north of Frederiksted, **Rainbow Beach** lures people with its white sand and ideal snorkeling conditions. In the same vicinity, also on Route 63, about 5 minutes north of Frederiksted, **La Grange** is another good beach. Lounge chairs can be rented, and there's a bar nearby.

At the **Cormorant Beach Club** (see "Accommodations," above), about 5 miles west of Christiansted, some 1,200 feet of white sands are shaded by palm trees. Since a living reef lies just off the shore, snorkeling conditions are ideal. **Grapetree Beach** offers about the same footage of clean white sand on the eastern tip of the island (Route 60). Follow the South Shore Road to reach it. Water sports are popular here.

Buccaneer Beach, 2 miles east of Christiansted, is another beach awaiting the explorer.

Sandy Point, lying directly south of Frederiksted, has the largest beach in all of the U.S. Virgin Islands. Its waters are shallow and calm, perfect for swimming. Sandy Point juts out from southwestern St. Croix like a small peninsula. It is reached by taking the Melvin Evans Highway (Route 66) west from the Alexander Hamilton Airport.

SPORTS

FISHING

The fishing grounds at Lang Bank are about 10 miles from St. Croix. Here you'll find kingfish, dolphin fish, and wahoo. Using light-tackle boats gliding along the reef, you'll probably turn up jack or bonefish. At Clover Crest, in Frederiksted, Cruzan anglers fish right from the rocks.

Serious sports fishers can board the *Ruffian,* a 41-foot Hatteras convertible, available for half- or full-day charters with bait and tackle included. It's anchored at St. Croix Marina, Gallows Bay. Reservations can be made during the day by calling 773-7165, or 773-0917 at night.

GOLF

St. Croix has the best golf in the U.S. Virgins. In fact, guests staying on St. John and St. Thomas often fly over for a day's round. On the island are two 18-hole golf courses. ✪ **Carambola Golf Course** (tel. 778-5638), on the northeast side of St. Croix, was designed by Robert Trent Jones, who called it "the loveliest course I ever designed." The course, formerly Fountain Valley, looks like a botanical garden with its bamboo, saman trees, and palms in many varieties. Its collection of par-3 holes is known to golfing authorities as the best in the tropics. The course record at Carambola, site of "Shell's Wonderful World of Golf," is 66, set by Tom Kite in 1987. Greens fees are $50 for 18 holes. The rental of a golf cart is mandatory at $12 and $18.

The other major course is at the **Buccaneer** (tel. 773-2100, ext. 738), 2 miles east of Christiansted (see "Accommodations," above). The Buccaneer is a challenging 6,200-yard, 18-hole course that allows the player to knock the ball over rolling hills right to the edge of the Caribbean. The vistas are truly spectacular. Nonguests who reserve pay $24 greens fees, and $12 for a cart. A golf pro is available for lessons, and there is a pro shop.

The Reef (tel. 773-8844) is a popular 3,100-yard course, charging greens fees of $12, with carts for $12 and $18. On the east end of the island, the course is at Teague Bay. It's longest hole is a 579-yard par 5.

HORSEBACK RIDING

Specializing in nature tours, ✪ **Jill's Equestrian Stables,** Sprat Hall Plantation, Route 58 (tel. 722-2880), is the largest equestrian stable in the Virgin Islands. Set on the sprawling grounds of the island's oldest plantation great house, it's operated by Paul Wojcie and his wife, Jill Hurd, one of the daughters of the establishment's original founders. The stables are known throughout the Caribbean for the quality of the horses and the beautiful trail rides through the forests, past ruins of abandoned 18th-century plantations and sugar mills, to the tops of the scenic hills of St. Croix's western end. All tours are accompanied by operators who give a running commentary on island fauna, history, and riding techniques. Beginners and experienced riders alike are welcome.

A 2-hour trail ride costs $50 per person, with discounts granted to residents staying at Sprat Hall Plantation. Tours usually depart at 10am and 4pm, with slight seasonal variations on this theme. Reservations at least 3 days in advance are important from December through April.

SNORKELING & SCUBA

Spectacular sponge life, black-coral trees (considered the finest in the West Indies), and steep dropoffs into water near the shoreline have made St. Croix a diver's mecca.

Buck Island, with an underwater visibility of more than 100 feet, is the site of the nature trail of the underwater national monument, and it's the major diving target (see "An Easy Excursion," below). All the minor and major travel agencies offer scuba and snorkeling tours to Buck Island.

Divers also like to go to **Pillar Coral,** with its columns of coral spiraling up to 25 feet and **North Cut,** one of the tallest, largest coral pinnacles in the West Indies. **Salt**

River Dropoff, plunges to depths of well over 1,000 feet, as does **Davis Bay Dropoff,** with its unique coral and rock-mound structures twisted into grotesque shapes.

Dive St. Croix, 59 King's Wharf (tel. 773-3434, or toll free 800/523-DIVE), operates the 46-feet dive boat *Betty Ann.* The staff offers complete instructions from resort courses through full certification, as well as night dives, underwater photography, and rentals of underwater cameras. A resort course, including all equipment, and a one-tank boat dive, is $55. A two-tank boat dive for the certified diver goes for $65.

V. I. Divers, Ltd., Pan Am Pavilion, Suite 11, 1102 Strand St., Christiansted (tel. 773-6045, or toll free 800/544-5911), is a PADI five-star dive center established in 1971. *Skin Diver* magazine called its offerings one of the "ten top dives in the Caribbean." An introductory resort course costs $65, with a two-dive boat tour going for $60.

TENNIS

Some authorities rate the tennis at the previously recommended **Buccaneer** (tel. 773-2100, ext. 736) as the best in the West Indies. The eight courts, two of which are lit for night games, are open to the public. Nonguests pay $7 per person per hour. You must call to reserve a court. A tennis pro is available for lessons, and there is also a pro shop.

A notable selection of courts is also found at the **Carambola Golf Club** (tel. 778-5638), which has five clay courts, two of which are lit for night games. Open to the public, it charges $23 per hour for nonguests, around $30 at night. You must call to reserve. Both a pro shop and a tennis pro for lessons are available.

WINDSURFING

The best place for this increasingly popular sport is the **Tradewindsurfing Water Sports Center** (tel. 773-2035), located on a small offshore island in Christiansted Harbor and part of the Hotel on the Cay. They give lessons and are open daily from 9:30am to 3:30pm. Renting a sailboat costs $20 to $25 for 2 hours.

---

7. SAVVY SHOPPING

CHRISTIANSTED

In Christiansted, where the core of my shopping recommendations are found, the emphasis is on hole-in-the-wall boutiques, selling one-of-a-kind merchandise. Handmade items are popular. Of course, the same duty-free stipulations, as outlined earlier, apply to your shopping selections in St. Croix.

Knowing it can't compete with Charlotte Amalie, Christiansted has forged its own creative statement in its shops, and by reputation it has now become the "chic spot for merchandise" in the Caribbean. All the shops are easily compressed into half a mile or so. On a day's tour (or half day) you'll be able to inspect much merchandise before making your purchases.

SHOPPING A TO Z

Art and Miscellanies

AMERICAN WEST INDIA COMPANY, 1 Strand St. Tel. 773-7325.

Occupying the two floors of a circa 1733 town house in downtown Christiansted, the American West India Company offers a broad collection of luxury products actually made in the Caribbean. Included are artwork from Haiti, gourmet foods, limited-production rums and liqueurs, sea island cotton clothing, T-shirts with unique Caribbean designs, ceramic figurines, island-made jewelry, and much more.

Fashion

JAVA WRAPS, Strand and King Sts. Tel. 773-3770.

From the East Indies to the West Indies, Java Wraps is famous throughout the Caribbean for hand-batik women's, men's, and children's resortwear. A kaleidoscope of colors and prints are showcased in stores filled with Dutch colonial antique furniture and Javanese antiquities, all for sale. Old chests are filled with home accessories such as hand-quilted bedcovers, batik bed linens, napkins, and place mats. Every day brings a Dorothy Lamour show as the salespeople demonstrate the wrapping and tying of beach pareos and sarongs. You could continue your treasure hunt throughout the islands in the other Java Wraps stores in St. Thomas, St. Maarten, Anguilla, Grand Cayman, and Aruba.

Gifts

MANY HANDS, in the Pan Am Pavilion. Tel. 773-1990.

Many Hands is devoted exclusively to Virgin Islands handcrafts. Children get a lot of attention here, as there's an assortment of custom-made clothing for children along with stuffed toys. The merchandise includes West Indian spices and teas, shellwork, stained glass, hand-painted china, ceramics, and handmade jewelry. Be sure to see their collection of local paintings and their year-round "Christmas tree."

ONLY IN PARADISE, 5 Company St. Tel. 773-0331.

This spacious air-conditioned store offers a choice assortment of gifts, such as art glass, linens, real and costume jewelry, and decorative items, as well as pearls—cultured, freshwater, or baroque. Its boutique, out back in a secluded courtyard, offers leather goods and cotton lingerie.

THE ROYAL POINCIANA, Strand St. Tel. 773-9892.

This is probably the most interesting gift shop on St. Croix, the creative statement of Stacy Lee Wood, an upstate New York–born entrepreneur who has made a career out of promoting island herbs and balms. Within a decor like that of an antique apothecary shop, you'll find such Caribbean-inspired items as hot sauces, seasoning blends for gumbos, island herbal teas, Antillean coffees, a scented array of soaps, toiletries, lotions, and shampoos, and museum-reproduction greeting cards and calendars.

Jewelry

COLOMBIAN EMERALDS, 43 Queen Cross St. Tel. 773-1928.

Colombian Emeralds specializes in stunning emeralds. In addition, there are rubies and diamonds and a large selection of other gemstones, including ametrine, blue topaz, opals, and amethyst. The staff will show you their large range of 14-karat gold jewelry, along with the best buys in watches, including Seiko quartz, Omega, and Porsche.

PEGASUS JEWELERS, 58 Company St. Tel. 773-6926.

Both a trusted retail outlet and a workshop, Pegasus specializes in diamonds, gold, and gemstones. They offer earrings, pendants, bracelets, and many one-of-a-kind pieces; tariffs are based on the fluctuating price of gold. They also have a varied selection of handcrafted gold, diamond, pearl, and coral jewelry. The shop also offers the finest collection of antique coins on the island.

Liquor

THE SPIGOT LIQUOR STORE, 59 King's Wharf. Tel. 778-8400.

Located in the King Christian Hotel building, this is the place to go for fine beverages and snack foods. The owners will advise you on how much you can take back home with you in the liquor, liqueur, wine, and champagne line. Many times the prices here are so low that you will still get a bargain even if you go over the U.S. Customs limit and have to pay duty. You can have everything packed in easy-to-carry boxes and delivered to your hotel ready for you to take home. If you're making a trip to Buck Island from the dock next to the shop, you can purchase grocery items for a picnic, as well as beer and soda. Cigarettes are also sold here.

Perfume

ST. CROIX PERFUME CENTER, 53 King St. Tel. 773-7604, or toll free 800/225-7031.

You'll find the largest duty-free assortment of men's and women's fragrances in St. Croix, usually at 30% below Stateside prices. For a minimum shipping charge of $5, this store will ship perfumes anywhere in the world. For purposes of duty-free expedition to the U.S., each shipment should be for your personal use and be valued at less than $100.

VIOLETTE BOUTIQUE, in the Caravelle Arcade, 38 Strand St. Tel. 773-2148.

This small department store, carrying worldwide lines of perfume and luxury goods, stocks exclusive fragrances and hard-to-find bath lines. They also have the latest in Cartier, Fendi, Seiko, Pequignet, Gucci, and Yves St. Laurent watches. A wide selection of famous cosmetic names are featured, and Fendi has its own area for bags and accessories.

Sportswear

ISLAND SPORT, Club Comanche, Strand St. Tel. 773-5010.

This store offers championship sportswear collections from Izod for men and women, along with casual resortwear from Renny and lighthearted seaside prints from Boscali for women. It also sells Ken Done's whimsical bright swimwear, along with coverups, beachwear, jewelry, accessories, towels, and some of the best St. Croix T-shirts for adults and kids on the island.

POLO RALPH LAUREN FACTORY STORE, 52C Company St. Tel. 773-4388.

Here you'll find Ralph Lauren sportswear for men and women priced at less than what you pay Stateside. Some of the fashions might be from previous seasons, and others might be unsold inventories from mainland stores, but amid the racks of inventory, you can often find good buys.

Toys

LAND OF OZ, 2126 Company St. Tel. 773-4610.

This is one of the most enchanting stores for children in the Caribbean, lying opposite Market Square Mall. Owner Margha Feehan says the store is for children of all ages. Variety is the keynote of this establishment, with emphasis on unusual items from around the world. Some 3,000 items are in stock. Shipping is available.

AROUND THE ISLAND

If you're touring western St. Croix, in the vicinity of Frederiksted, you might want to stop off at the following offbeat shops.

ST. CROIX LEAP, Mahogany Rd., Rte. 76. Tel. 772-0421.
In this open-air shop, you can see stacks of rare and beautiful wood being tastefully fashioned into various objects. It is a St. Croix Life and Environmental Arts Project, dedicated to the natural environment through manual work, conservation, and self-development. The end result is a fine collection of Cruzan mahogany serving boards, tables, wall hangings, clocks, and so on. St. Croix Leap is 5 miles from Christiansted, 2 miles up Mahogany Road from the beach north of Frederiksted. Large mahogany signs and sculptures flank the driveway. Bear to the right to reach the woodworking area and gift shop. For inquiries, write to Leap, P.O. Box 245, Frederiksted, St. Croix, USVI 00841-0245. Open daily from 8am to 4pm.

WHIM GIFT SHOP, in the Estate Whim Plantation Museum, Centerline Rd. Tel. 772-0598.
Be sure to browse through this museum gift shop east of Frederiksted. Their selection appeals to a wide age spectrum. Many of the goods are imported, but many are Cruzan made, and some are specially crafted for the Whim shop. When you buy something, you contribute to the upkeep of the museum and the grounds.

8. EVENING ENTERTAINMENT

St. Croix doesn't have the sophisticated nightlife of St. Thomas, nor would its permanent residents want it. To find the action, you might have to hotel- or bar-hop.
If he's playing, The man to seek out is Jimmy Hamilton, Duke Ellington's "Mr. Sax." He and his quartet are a regular feature of St. Croix nightlife. Ask at your hotel if he is appearing.
Also try to catch a performance of the **Quadrille Dancers,** the big treat of St. Croix. Their dances are little changed since plantation days: The women wear long dresses, white gloves, and turbans, and the men are attired in flamboyant shirts, sashes, and tight black trousers. When you've learned their steps, you're invited to join the dancers on the floor. Ask at your hotel if and where they are performing.

THE PERFORMING ARTS

ISLAND CENTER, Sunny Isle. Tel. 778-5272.
This 1,100-seat theater ½ mile north of Sunny Isle continues to attract big-name entertainers to St. Croix. Its program is widely varied, ranging from jazz, nostalgia and musical revues, to plays from Broadway, such as *The Wiz.* Consult *St. Croix This Week* or call the center to see what's being presented. The Caribbean Community Theatre and Courtyard Players perform regularly.
Admission: Tickets $12–$25.
Open: Call the theater for performance times. **Transportation:** Taxi.

THE CLUB & MUSIC SCENE

THE TERRACE LOUNGE, Buccaneer, Estate Shoys. Tel. 773-2100.
Contained within a satellite lounge of the main dining room of one of St. Croix's most upscale hotels, the Terrace Lounge welcomes some of the Caribbean's finest entertainers, such as Jimmy Hamilton, who used to play with Duke Ellington. Guests of the Buccaneer pay only for their drinks. The house specialty is a Caribbean Sunset. The music is wide ranging—jazz, calypso, reggae, Stateside contemporary.

Admission: $4 nonguests. **Prices:** Drinks $4.
Open: Daily 8–11pm. **Transportation:** Taxi.

CORMORANT BEACH CLUB BAR, 4126 La Grande Princesse. Tel. 778-8920.

One of the most romantic bars on the island sits near the sands of the beach of La Grande Princesse, near the entrance to this previously recommended hotel northwest of Christiansted. Guests sit at tables overlooking the ocean, or around an open-centered mahogany bar whose perimeter is defined by the open-air supports of an enlarged gazebo enhanced with wicker love seats, comfortable chairs, and soft lamp lighting. After their drinks, you can move into the adjacent restaurant (see "Dining," above) for dinner.

Excellent tropical drinks are mixed here, such as the house specialty, a Cormorant cooler, made with champagne, pineapple juice, and Triple Sec.
Prices: Drinks from $3.50.
Open: Daily 5pm–"whenever."

COCKTAILS, 54B Company St. Tel. 773-4243.

Although much of its function is devoted to an all-day restaurant, after 9:30pm the open-air rear courtyard here hosts some of the most talked-about musical groups on the island. These alternate with musical gigs from the U.S. mainland, as well as occasional bouts of live comedy acts. As the establishment's name would imply, a commodious bar area serves a large array of cocktails.
Prices: Drinks from $3.50.
Open: Daily 11:30am–10:30pm.

HONDO'S BACKYARD/HONDO'S NIGHTCLUB, 53 King St. Tel. 778-8103.

Pass through the bar to join the activity in the fenced-in courtyard. On simple picnic tables in the open air, beer and rum punches flow freely, accompanied by such Tex-Mex or Stateside food as nachos, hamburgers, tacos, grilled chicken or ribs, and meat-loaf platters.

Some clients eventually drift upstairs to Hondo's Nightclub (more frequently referred to simply as Hondo's), which is also fun.
Admission: $3 disco. **Prices:** Platters $4.75–$6.75; drinks $2.75.
Open: Hondo's Backyard Mon–Sat 11:30am–midnight, Hondo's Nightclub Mon–Sat 8pm–3am.

---

9. NETWORKS & RESOURCES

FOR STUDENTS & ENVIRONMENTALISTS

ST. CROIX ENVIRONMENTAL ASSOCIATION, 6 Company St. Tel. 773-1989.

Although the schedules of its events and tours vary widely according to staff availability and public demand, this is the most visible environmentalist group on St. Croix. They coordinate movements to restrict development in environmentally or culturally sensitive areas, help reforest the island, wage a major recycling and antilitter campaign, and conduct ongoing public education programs.

Among their offerings are field trips and lectures on environmental issues, usually priced at $10 per person, with additional contributions gratefully accepted. Every spring they organize nighttime ecology tours to the western tip of St. Croix (Sandy Point) during the hatching season for the island's leatherback turtles. There are frequent Saturday 1-hour boat tours to the biggest estuary on St. Croix, the northern coast's Salt River, where birds and marine life thrive. The association disseminates information only for St. Croix, not for St. John or St. Thomas.

FOR GAY MEN & LESBIANS

The only gay scene of any significance is in Frederiksted, on the western shore of the island. Life is relatively quiet here, and the gay scene is subdued. Gay men or lesbians mainly come here to relax and rest and enjoy the beaches—not to indulge in any frenzied nightlife.

Two or three inns in Frederiksted are popular with gays, although the clientele in all of these is mixed, attracting both gays and nongays.

The best of these hotels is **King Frederik on the Beach Hotel,** Frederiksted Beach, P.O. Box 1908, Frederiksted 00840 (tel. 772-1205, or toll free 800/524-2018), a small hotel lying half a mile from the town's shopping and dining. It offers 13 bedrooms, all with kitchenettes, private baths, and chamber service. In winter, a single or double ranges from $105 to $180 daily, lowered in summer to $65 to $110 (either single or double). Coffee and a continental breakfast are provided free, and the in-house patio restaurant provides more substantial breakfasts (at an extra charge) for guests who want them. The hotel accepts major credit cards.

10. AN EASY EXCURSION

The crystal-clear water and the white coral sand of **Buck Island,** 1½ miles off the northeast coast of St. Croix, are legendary. Only ⅓-mile wide and 1 mile long, the island and much of its offshore reef has been administered by the National Park Service since 1948, much to the delight of environmental groups. Even the endangered brown pelicans produce their young here, and marine life in the outlying waters is thriving.

Today, the park covers about 850 acres of land and water surface. The island contains picnic tables, barbecue pits, and a hiking trail through tropical vegetation. Facilities include restrooms and a small room in which you can change your clothes. Offshore, there are two underwater trails for snorkeling above the coral, amazing schools of fish, and many other much deeper labyrinths and underwater grottoes for more serious divers. Among the attractions are "forests" of elkhorn coral and thousands of colorful reef fish.

Small boats ferry snorkelers, divers, and nature enthusiasts between St. Croix and Buck Island for $35 to $45 for a full day. A half-day trip costs $20 to $30 per person, usually with snorkeling equipment provided.

Mile Mark Watersports, in the King Christian Hotel, 59 King's Wharf (P.O. Box 3045), Christiansted, St. Croix, USVI 00820 (tel. 773-2628), offers twice-daily tours to the aquatic wonders of Buck Island. They offer two ways to reach the reefs. One is aboard a glass-bottom boat departing twice daily from a point in front of the King Christian Hotel from 9:30am to 1pm and 1:30 to 5pm, costing $25 per person. All snorkeling equipment is included. A more romantic journey is aboard one of the company's wind-powered sailboats, which, for $35 per person, offers the sea breezes and the thrill of wind power to reach the reef. A full-day tour in the company's 40-foot catamaran can take up to 20 participants on a tour to Buck Island's reefs. Included in the tour are a West Indian barbecue picnic on the isolated sands of Buck Island's beaches, complimentary rum punches, and plenty of opportunities for snorkeling. Offered daily from 10am to 4pm, the cost is $40 for adults and $25 for children under 14.

Captain Heinz, P.O. Box 2881, Christiansted, St. Croix, 00820. (tel. 773-3161 or 773-4041), is an Austrian-born skipper with some 20 years of sailing experience. His trimaran, *Teroro II,* leaves Green Cay Marina "H" Dock at 9am and 2:30pm, never filled with more than 24 passengers, who pay $35 per person. All gear and safety equipment are provided. The captain sailed the first *Teroro* across the Atlantic, and he's not only a skilled sailor, but is also a considerate host. He will even take you around the *outer* reef, which the other guides do not, for an unforgettable underwater experience.

![CHAPTER 7]

THE BRITISH VIRGIN ISLANDS

- **WHAT'S SPECIAL ABOUT THE BRITISH VIRGIN ISLANDS**
- **DID YOU KNOW . . . ?**
1. **ANEGADA**
2. **JOST VAN DYKE**
3. **MARINA CAY**
4. **PETER ISLAND**
5. **TORTOLA**
6. **VIRGIN GORDA**
7. **MOSQUITO ISLAND**
8. **GUANA ISLAND**

In the northeast corner of the Caribbean, about 60 miles east of Puerto Rico, the British Virgin Islands consist of some 40 islands, although granted, some are no more than rocks or spits of land. Only a trio of the British Virgins are of any significant size—Virgin Gorda (Fat Virgin), Tortola (dove of peace), and Jost Van Dyke. These islands, craggy and volcanic in origin, are just 15 air minutes from St. Thomas. There is regularly scheduled ferry service between St. Thomas and Tortola as well.

With its small bays and hidden coves, once havens for pirates, the British Virgin Islands are considered by the yachting set to be among the world's loveliest cruising grounds. Even though there are predictions that mass tourism is on the way, these islands are still a paradise for escapists.

The smaller islands have such colorful names as Fallen Jerusalem and Ginger. Norman Island is said to have been the prototype for Robert Louis Stevenson's *Treasure Island*. On Deadman Bay, a barren islet, Blackbeard marooned 15 pirates and a bottle of rum, which gave rise to the ditty.

Note: The British Virgin Islands use the U.S. dollar as their form of currency. British pounds are not accepted.

GETTING THERE

Your gateway to the BVI will most likely be either Tortola or Virgin Gorda, which has the most hotels and services. If you're going to any of the other islands, make sure you carry adequate stocks of prescribed medicines or other items you need, because supplies and services in these islands tend to be severely limited or nonexistent.

Before you go, you can obtain **information** about the British Virgin Islands from the **BVI Tourist Board,** 370 Lexington Ave., Suite 416, New York, NY 10017 (tel. 212/696-0400, or toll free 800/835-8530), or from the **BVI Tourist Board,** 1686 Union St., San Francisco, CA 94123 (tel. 415/775-0344, or toll free 800/232-7770). In Canada, contact **BVI Information Office,** 801 York Mill Rd., Suite 201, Don Mills, ON M3B 1X7 (tel. 416/283-2235).

BY PLANE

There are no direct flights from North America to Tortola, but you can make easy connections through San Juan, St. Thomas, or St. Croix.

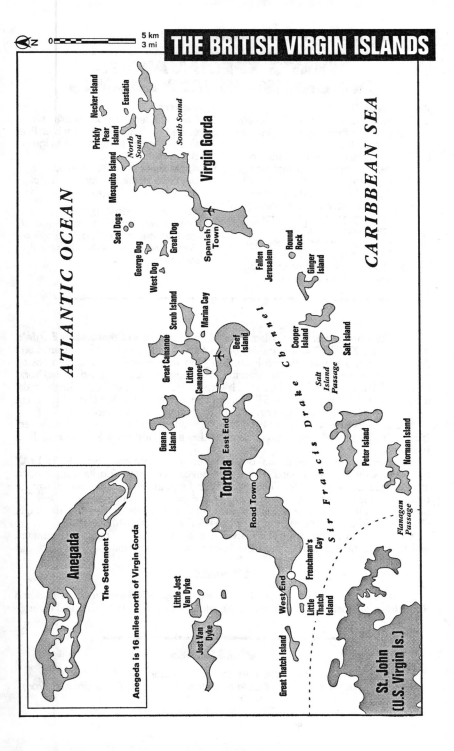

THE BRITISH VIRGIN ISLANDS

ATLANTIC OCEAN

CARIBBEAN SEA

Necker Island

Eustatia

Prickly Pear Island

Mosquito Island

North Sound

South Sound

Virgin Gorda

Seal Dogs

George Dog

West Dog

Great Dog

Spanish Town

Round Rock

Fallen Jerusalem

Ginger Island

Scrub Island

Marina Cay

Great Camanoe

Little Camanoe

Beef Island

Cooper Island

Salt Island

Guana Island

Tortola

East End

Sir Francis Drake Channel

Salt Island Passage

Road Town

Peter Island

Normal Island

Frenchman's Cay

Flanagan Passage

West End

Little Thatch Island

St. John (U.S. Virgin Is.)

Little Jost Van Dyke

Jost Van Dyke

Great Thatch Island

5 km
3 mi
0

N

Anegada

The Settlement

Anegada is 16 miles north of Virgin Gorda

WHAT'S SPECIAL ABOUT
THE BRITISH VIRGIN ISLANDS

Ace Attractions
☐ Guana Island, containing the richest fauna known for an island of its size in the West Indies.
☐ Sage Mountain National Park, on Tortola, with the highest mountain in the Virgin Islands (1,780 feet).
☐ The Baths, Virgin Gorda, clusters of massive prehistoric rocks forming cool, inviting grottoes, ideal for swimming and snorkeling.
☐ The wreck of the RMS *Rhone*, off Salt Island, a royal mail steamer from 1867—the most celebrated dive site in the West Indies.

Beaches
☐ Cane Garden Bay, on Tortola, which some beach aficionados rank as fine as St. Thomas's celebrated Magens Bay Beach.
☐ Apple Bay (also called Cappoon's Bay), the surfer's favorite, west of Road Town on Tortola.

Great Towns/Villages
☐ Road Town, capital of Tortola and of the BVI, center for "stocking up" on everything for those heading for the remote islands.

Your best bet to reach Beef Island/Tortola is to take one of **American Eagle's** (tel. toll free 800/433-7300) four daily flights from American's most important Latin American hub, San Juan, Puerto Rico. San Juan receives dozens of daily nonstop flights from throughout North America, including Boston, Toronto, New York, Chicago, Miami, and Raleigh-Durham, North Carolina. Some schedules might make a flight on American Airlines to St. Thomas easier than to San Juan, in which event American Eagle will carry passengers from St. Thomas on to Tortola.

Sunaire Express (tel. 809/495-2480) flies daily from St. Thomas to both Beef Island (Tortola) and Virgin Gorda. Sunaire also flies daily from St. Croix to Beef Island.

Another choice, if you're on one of Tortola's neighboring islands, is **LIAT** (Leeward Islands Air Transport). This Caribbean carrier flies to Tortola from St. Kitts and Antigua, St. Maarten, St. Thomas, and San Juan, in small planes not known for their frequency or careful scheduling. LIAT does not maintain its own toll-free number, so all reservations are made through travel agents or through the larger U.S.-based airlines which connect with LIAT hubs. Call 809/462-0701.

Flying time to Tortola from San Juan is 30 minutes; from St. Thomas, 15 minutes; and from the most distant of the LIAT hubs (Antigua), 60 minutes.

BY BOAT

You can go from Charlotte Amalie (St. Thomas) by **public ferry** to West End and Road Town on Tortola, a 45-minute voyage along Sir Francis Drake Channel through

IMPRESSIONS
Question: Where are the British Virgin Islands?
Answer: I have no idea, but I should think that they are as far as possible from the Isle of Man.
—SIR WINSTON CHURCHILL

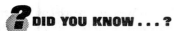

- Richard Humphreys, a Tortola-born man, founded the first black university in the United States.
- William Thornton, a BVI citizen, designed the U.S. Capitol Building.
- As late as 1869, the steamship *Telegrafo* was held in Tortola and officially charged with piracy.
- Tortola in 1756 had 181 white men and 3,864 slaves—about 21 slaves to each planter.
- In 1831 free blacks living in the BVI were accorded the full legal rights of British subjects.
- The wreckage of the HMS *Nymph*, which sank off Road Town in 1783, was discovered in 1969.
- In the late 1960s the British foreign secretary offered the BVI for sale to the United States.
- In 1752 the BVI was the major Caribbean supplier of cotton to Britain.

the islands. Services making this run include **Native Son** (tel. 495-4617), **Smith's Ferry Service** (tel. 494-4430), and **Inter-Island Boat Services** (tel. 776-6597).

GETTING AROUND

BY PLANE, BUS, OR BOAT

Once on the islands, you can fly between Tortola and Virgin Gorda on **Sunaire Express** (tel. 495-2480). The flight takes only 5 minutes.

In Tortola, **Smith's Ferry** (tel. 44430) and **Speedy's Fantasy** (tel. 55240) operate ferry links to the Virgin Gorda Yacht Club (½ hour). The **North Sound Express** (tel. 42746), near the airport on Beef Island, has daily connections to the Bitter End Yacht Club on Virgin Gorda. **Peter Island Boat** (tel. 42561) also shuttles between Road Town on Tortola and Peter Island at least seven times a day.

Bus service exists only on Tortola and Virgin Gorda. See the specific section on each island (below) for further details.

1. ANEGADA

The most northerly and isolated of the British Virgins, 30 miles east of Tortola, Anegada (pop. 250) has more than 500 wrecks lying off its notorious Horseshoe Reef. It's different from the other British Virgins in that it's a coral-and-limestone atoll, flat, with a 2,500-foot airstrip. At its highest point, its landmass reaches a height of only 28 feet; Anegada hardly appears on the horizon if you're sailing to it, which helps to explain why it has always been so notoriously dangerous to sailing craft. It is 11 miles long and 3 miles wide.

Many of the inhabitants of Anegada have looked unsuccessfully for the legendary hidden treasure on such sunken ships as the *Paramatta*, which has rested on the sea bottom for more than a century.

At the northern and western ends of the island are some good beaches, which might be your only reason for coming here. This is a remote little corner of the Caribbean: Don't expect any frills, and be prepared to put up with some hardships, such as mosquitoes. The island is home to many species of plants and wildlife including wild orchids and the rare Anegada rock iguana.

GETTING THERE & GETTING AROUND

Sunaire Express (tel. 52480) provides an easy connection to Virgin Gorda and Anegada from Tortola, a short hop. You can also come by boat; call **Speedy's** (tel. 55240).

Limited **taxi** service is available on the island—not that you will have many places to go. Round-trip fares from the Anegada Reef Hotel to West End Beach cost $6 per person, $7 per person to North Shore. From the Anegada Reef Hotel to the village costs $8 per person round-trip.

WHERE TO STAY & DINE

The Anegada Reef Hotel is the only major accommodation on the island. Neptune's Treasure, below, rents tents to stay in overnight.

ANEGADA REEF HOTEL, Setting Point, Anegada, BVI. Tel. 809/495-8002. Fax 809/495-9362. 12 rms (all with bath). A/C **Transportation:** Hotel shuttle.

$ Rates (with AP): Winter, $155 single; $215 double. Summer, $130 single; $205 double. No credit cards.

The Anegada Reef Hotel is one of the most remote places in this guide, and guests who stay here are in effect "hiding out." It is a favorite of the yachting set, who enjoy the hospitality provided by Lowell Wheatley. He offers large rooms with private porches opening onto the beach. Inshore and deep-sea fishing (also bonefishing), along with diving and snorkeling, are possible.

On party nights, Mr. Wheatley brings in a fungi band or he hosts a barbecue on the beach. If you're going over for the day, you can order lunch at the beach bar. At night, the barbecued lobster is a favorite. If you plan to dine at the Reef, make a reservation early, dinner costs from $22 and is served at 7:30pm nightly.

NEPTUNE'S TREASURE, between Pomato and Saltheap Points. VHF Ch. 16 or 68, or radio 4-3111.

Cuisine: SEAFOOD. **Reservations:** Recommended. **Transportation:** Taxi.

$ Prices: Breakfast from $5; fixed-priced lunch $6; fixed-price dinner $10–$20. No credit cards.

Open: Daily 8am–9pm.

While on the island, you may want to visit this seaside restaurant run by the Soares family, who serve fresh fish and fresh lobster that they catch themselves. The family is helpful in explaining how to explore the island. Live combos entertain Thursday. The family also rents tents with single or double air mattresses. You can take a taxi to one of their sandy beaches and go snorkeling along their reefs.

Note: The restaurant doesn't have a telephone. In its place is a radio contact number (which the boating set employs).

2. JOST VAN DYKE

This rugged island (pop. 130) on the seaward (west) side of Tortola, was probably named after a Dutch settler. On the south shore of this 4-square-mile mountainous island are some good beaches, at White Bay and Great Harbour. The island has only a handful of places to stay, but has several dining choices, as it's a popular stopover point not only for the yachting set but for many cruise ships. Peace and tranquillity will only be found if the cruise ships aren't here.

In the 1700s, a Quaker colony settled here to develop sugarcane plantations. One of the colonists, William Thornton, won a worldwide competition to design the Capitol in Washington, D.C. Smaller islands surround the place, including little Jost Van Dyke, the birthplace of Dr. John Lettsom, founder of the London Medical Society.

GETTING THERE

Guests heading for the Sandcastle Hotel or Sandy Ground fly first to Beef Island. From the airport, they take a taxi over the narrow bridge to West End or Road Town on Tortola; or they can take a ferry to West End from St. Thomas. At West End, a private launch picks up visitors (who must make arrangements to be met when booking their hotel reservations) and transports them to the Sandcastle or Sandy Ground.

Those not staying on the island but who'd like to go over for a day-trip can go on **Jost Van Dyke Ferry Service** (tel. 52775 for reservations). It operates a regularly scheduled daily ferry service, departing West End, Tortola, at 7:30am Monday through Friday, 8am Saturday, and 9:30am Sunday.

WHERE TO STAY

Very casual types should consider the simple accommodations offered by Rudy's Mariner's Rendezvous restaurant, listed below.

THE SANDCASTLE, White Bay, Jost Van Dyke, BVI. Tel. 809/775-5262.
Fax 809/775-5262. 4 units (all with bath). **Transportation:** 20-minute private motor-launch trip from St. Thomas.
$ **Rates** (with AP): Winter, $235 single; $295 double. Apr 15–Dec 14, $175 single; $235 double. MC, V.

A perfect retreat for escapists, this four-villa colony has octagonal-shaped cottages surrounded by flowering shrubbery and bougainvillea. Nestled among the palms, individual cottages take advantage of the tropical breezes and profit from every inch of the view. This is a small, personalized place, catering to only a handful of guests.

You're allowed to mix your own drinks at the beachside bar, the Soggy Dollar, and keep your own tab. Visiting yachting people often drop in here for a while, enjoying the beachside informality and ordering a drink called a Painkiller. See below for information about the dining room.

In the guest book you'll find this endorsement: "I thought places like this only existed in the movies." For reservations and information from the U.S., call or write The Sandcastle, Suite 237, Red Hook Plaza, St. Thomas, USVI 00802 (tel. 809/771-1611).

SANDY GROUND, East End, Jost Van Dyke, BVI. Tel. 809/494-3391. Fax
809/495-9379. 8 villas (all with bath). **Transportation:** Private water taxi from Tortola.
$ **Rates** (weekly): Winter, $1,150 double; extra person $150. Summer, $750 double; extra person $100. No credit cards.

Built on a 17-acre hill site on the northeastern part of Jost Van Dyke, Sandy Ground offers villas with self-sufficient housekeeping units of the type you might see along Spain's Costa del Sol. The complex rents two- and three-bedroom villas. One of my favorites, constructed on a cliff, seems to hang about 60 or so feet over a good beach. If you've come all this way to reach this tiny outpost, you might as well stay a week, which is the way the rates are quoted. The airy villas are each privately owned, and each unit is fully equipped with refrigerators and stoves. You'll be directed to a store on Jost Van Dyke where you can purchase groceries. The managers help guests with boat rentals and water sports.

WHERE TO DINE

ABE'S BY THE SEA, on Little Harbour. Tel. 59329.
Cuisine: WEST INDIAN. **Reservations:** Recommended for groups of five or more. **Directions:** As you approach the harbor by private motor launch or boat from Tortola, you'll see Abe's on your right.
$ **Prices:** Appetizers $3; main courses $12–$30. No credit cards.

Open: Lunch daily noon–3pm; dinner daily 7:30–9:30pm.

At this local bar and restaurant on Little Harbour, the cook knows how to please the sailors with a menu of fish, boiled lobster, conch, spareribs, and chicken. Prices are low, and a fungi band entertains. The main course is accompanied by peas, rice, green salad or coleslaw, and dessert. On Wednesday night in season, Abe's has a festive pig roast. Friday is barbecue night, costing $18 per person.

RUDY'S MARINER'S RENDEZVOUS, Great Harbour, Jost Van Dyke, BVI. Tel. 59282.
    Cuisine: WEST INDIAN. **Reservations:** Required by the afternoon.
$ Prices: Dinners $15–$25. No credit cards.
    Open: Dinner daily 7pm–1am.

Rudy's serves good food and plenty of it. A welcoming drink awaits the captain, and the food that follows is simply prepared and inexpensive. Conch is usually available, and a catch of the day is featured—sometimes lobster. There are three simple rooms for rent, with eight beds. Kitchenettes are provided, and there is hot and cold running water. In winter, with MAP, a single costs $75 daily; a double, $150; a triple, $180; and a quad, $220. In summer, also with MAP, the single rate is $55 daily, $100 in a double, $130 in a triple, and $180 in a quad. Rudy's is at the western end of Great Harbour.

THE SANDCASTLE, on White Bay. Tel. 55262.
    Cuisine: CONTINENTAL. **Reservations:** Required for lunch by 11am, for dinner by 4pm. **Transportation:** 20-minute private motor-launch trip from Tortola.
$ Prices: Dinner from $30; lunch $18. MC, V.
    Open: Lunch daily, seating at 1:30pm; dinner daily, seating at 7:30pm.

The restaurant of this previously recommended hotel serves food which has often been frozen. Lunch is served in the open-air dining room, while lighter fare and snacks are available at the Soggy Dollar Bar. Dinner is by candlelight, featuring five courses, including such typical dishes as duck à l'orange, chicken tarragon, and grouper piccata. Meals are served with seasonal vegetables and fresh pasta, along with a variety of salads and homemade desserts.

3. MARINA CAY

Near Beef Island, Marina Cay is a tiny private islet of 6 acres. Its claim to fame is that it was the setting for the Robb White book *Our Virgin Isle,* which was made into a film, with Sidney Poitier and John Cassavetes.

The island lies only 5 minutes away by **launch from Trellis Bay,** adjacent to Beef Island International Airport.

WHERE TO STAY

MARINA CAY HOTEL, Marina Cay, P.O. Box 76, Road Town, Tortola, BVI. Tel. 809/494-2174. Fax 809/494-4775. 12 units (all with bath). **Transportation:** Private launch from Beef Island.
$ Rates (with MAP): Winter, $250–$395 double. Summer, $140–$340 double. AE, MC, V.

This small cottage hotel, opened in 1960 and extensively renovated, still has its original charm and conviviality. It houses guests in chalets, villas, and A-frames, all doubles overlooking a reef and the Sir Francis Drake Channel, dotted with islands. Marina Cay is a tropical garden, with frangipani, almond, tamarind, hibiscus, oleander, and bougainvillea in abundance. Dining is casual, with a good cuisine featuring continental and West Indian dishes. Activities include snorkeling on adjacent Mother Turtle Reef, sailing on Sunfish, Windsurfers, and the J-24 sloop, scuba diving (with certification courses taught by a resident divemaster), castaway picnics on secluded beaches, and deep-sea fishing.

4. PETER ISLAND

Half of this 1,050-acre island, with its good marina and docking facilities, is devoted to the yacht club described below. The other part is deserted. Beach facilities are found at palm-fringed Deadman Bay, which faces the Atlantic but is protected by a reef. All goods and services are at the hotel.

The island is so private that except for an occasional mason at work about the only creature you'll encounter will be an iguana or a feral cat whose ancestors were abandoned generations ago by shippers (the cats are said to have virtually eliminated the rodent population).

GETTING THERE

A complimentary hotel-operated ferry, **Peter Island Boat** (tel. 4-2561), picks up any overnight guest who arrives at the Beef Island airport. It departs from the pier at Trellis Bay, near the airport, and requires a 45-minute crossing. Other boats depart 8 or 9 times a day from the CSY Dock in Road Town, for a 20- to 30-minute crossing. Passengers must communicate their needs to the hotel several hours in advance of their arrival or departure.

WHERE TO STAY & DINE

VERY EXPENSIVE

PETER ISLAND RESORT AND YACHT HARBOUR, Peter Island (P.O. Box 211, Road Town, Tortola), BVI. Tel. 809/494-2561, or toll free 800/346-4451. Fax 809/494-2313. 50 rms; 1 4-bedroom villa, 3 2-bedroom villas. A/C MINIBAR TEL **Transportation:** See above.

$ Rates (with EP): Winter, $305–$425 double; summer, $225–$350 double. MAP $65 per person extra. Hawk's Nest Villas (with AP): Winter, $575–$795 double; summer, $500–$725 double. Crow's Nest villa (with AP): Winter, $3,500 for eight; summer, $2,500 for eight. AE, MC, V.

This tropical island comprising 1,800 acres is the home of Peter Island Resort and is solely dedicated to island guests and yacht owners who moor their craft here. After the 1989 hurricane, the facilities and marina were meticulously restored and reopened in 1991. The island's tropical gardens and hillside are bordered by five private beaches.

The resort contains 30 units facing Sprat Bay and Sir Francis Channel (oceanview rooms), and 20 larger units on Deadman Bay Beach (beachfront). Designed with a blend of casual elegance, the rooms include a terrace balcony, ceiling fan, coffee maker, clock radio, hairdryer, and bathrobes. The "Crow's Nest," a luxurious, four-bedroom villa, overlooks the harbor and Deadman Bay and features a private swimming pool, hot tub, full kitchen, maid, gardener, personal steward, and island vehicle. The "Hawk's Nest" is three two-bedroom villas situated on a tropical hillside.

Dining/Entertainment: Tradewinds Restaurant serves breakfast and dinner—five-star gourmet cuisine—throughout the year in fine Caribbean tradition. For a more casual setting, Deadman's Beach Bar and Grill serves sandwiches and salads beside the ocean. The main bar, Drakes Channel Lounge, is also open throughout the day and evening.

Services: Room service, laundry, massage, babysitting, guest launch transport to/from Beef Island airport.

Facilities: Fitness center, gift shop, freshwater pool, four tennis courts (two lit for night play), scuba-diving base, library, spa, conference facility, complete yacht marina; complimentary use of Sunfish, snorkeling gear, Windsurfers, and 19-foot Squib day-sailers.

5. TORTOLA

On the southern shore of this 24-square-mile island is **Road Town,** a sprawling village and the capital of the British Virgin Islands. The landfill at Wickhams Cay, a 70-acre town center development and marina in the harbor, has brought in a massive yacht-chartering business and has transformed the sleepy capital into a bustling, sophisticated center.

The entire southern coast, including Road Town, is characterized by rugged mountain peaks with yellow cedar and frangipani, among other foliage. On the northern coast are white sandy beaches, banana and mango trees, and clusters of palms.

The **BVI Tourist Board** (tel. 809/494-3134) is in the center of Road Town near the ferry dock, lying south of Wickham's Cay. It is open Monday through Friday from 9am to 5pm.

GETTING THERE

Close to Tortola's eastern end is **Beef Island,** the site of the main airport for passengers arriving in the British Virgins. The tiny island is connected to Tortola by the one-lane Queen Elizabeth Bridge.

GETTING AROUND

BY TAXI

Taxis meet every arriving flight. Your hotel can also call you a taxi. The fare from the Beef Island airport to Road Town is $5 per person, maybe more (fares must be negotiated). To call a taxi in Road Town, dial 42322; in Beef Island, 52378.

BY CAR

Because of the volume of tourism to Tortola, it's recommended that you reserve your rental car in advance, especially in winter. A handful of local companies rent cars, but because of the more lenient refund policies in case of billing errors, damage disputes, or insurance claims, I recommend using one of the U.S.-based giants, even if the cost is slightly higher. On Tortola, the well-recommended **Budget** is at 11 Wickhams Cay, Road Town (tel. 809/494-5151, or toll free 800/527-0700). **Avis** maintains offices opposite the police headquarters in Road Town (tel. 809/494-3322, or toll free 800/331-2112). **Hertz** (tel. 809/495-4405, or toll free 800/654-3001) has offices outside of Road Town, on the island's West End, near the ferryboat landing dock.

All three companies require that renters be at least 25 years old. Also required is the presentation of a valid driver's license, and the purchase of a temporary government-ordained BVI driver's license (which the car-rental company can sell you for $10; it's valid for 3 months).

At presstime, Budget charged $180 per week for its least expensive car, a Nissan Sentra, a simple but peppy car with manual transmission suitable for four passengers and—in a pinch—up to five. For an extra $30 a week, the same model was available with automatic transmission. A collision-damage waiver, eliminating all but $600 worth of financial responsibility in the event of an accident, cost an additional $6 per day. A 5% government tax was extra. Rates at the other two companies were competitive.

These rates will almost certainly change before your departure. Call the companies for last-minute price adjustments at least 36 business hours before your intended pickup.

Remember to *drive on the left.* Because the island roads are notoriously dim at night, with few if any lines marking the shoulder of the sinuous and narrow roads, nighttime driving can be frightening. It's a good idea to hire a taxi to take you to that difficult-to-find restaurant or nightspot.

BY BUS

Scato's Bus Service operates from the north end of the island to the west end, picking up passengers who hail it down. Fares for a trek across the island cost from $3 to $3.50.

BY BICYCLE & MOPED

You'll find single and tandem bicycles for rent at **Hero's Bicycle Rental,** Pasea Estate, Tortola (tel. 43536). Bicycles cost $10 to $25 per day, and scooters go for $30. Be forewarned that the terrain is rugged.

WHAT TO SEE & DO

No visit to Tortola is complete without a trip to ✪ **Mount Sage,** Ridge Road, a national park rising 1,780 feet. Here on its slopes you'll find traces of a primeval rain forest and you can enjoy a picnic overlooking neighboring islets and cays. The mountain is reached by heading west from Road Town.

Before you head out, go by the tourist office and pick up a copy of a little brochure

IN THEIR FOOTSTEPS

Sir Francis Drake (1543–96) English navigator and explorer famous for defeating the Spanish Armada in 1588, and viewed as a notorious pirate throughout many sections of the Caribbean. Arriving in the Caribbean as the young captain of *The Judith,* this favorite of Elizabeth I brought the swashbuckling adventures of the Elizabethan age to the Virgin Islands. That channel is now named after him. He was the first Englishman to circumnavigate the globe.

• **Birthplace:** Near Tavistock, England.
• **Residences:** He spent most of his life aboard ship, often in the Caribbean.
• **Resting Place:** Drake died aboard ship off Porto Bello January 27, 1596, and was buried at sea.

called *Sage Mountain National Park*. It has a location map, indicating directions to the forest (where there is a car park) and an outline of the main trails through the park.

Covering 92 acres, the park was established in 1964 to protect the remnants of Tortola's original forests not burned or cleared during the island's plantation era. From the parking lot, a trail leads to the main entrance to the park. The two main trails to choose from are the Rain Forest Trail and the Mahogany Forest Trail.

An organized tour may be your best way to see Tortola. **Travel Plan Tours,** Waterfront Plaza, Road Town (tel. 4-2872), will pick you up at your hotel (a minimum of four people is required) and take one to four persons on a 2½-hour tour of the island for $50.

A **taxi tour** lasting 2½ hours costs $50 for one to three people. To call a taxi in Road Town, dial 42322; in Beef Island, 52378.

A DRIVING TOUR OF TORTOLA'S WEST END

Start: Harbour Drive, in the center of Road Town.
Finish: Harbour Drive, in the center of Road Town.
Time: 2 hours, not counting stops.
Best Time: Any day before 5:30pm.
Worst Time: Sunday, when many places close.

If you arrived on the island by plane, you landed at Beef Island's airport, on the island's northeastern tip. You probably viewed much of the topography of the island's East End en route to your hotel. This tour, therefore, concentrates on the West End, site of some of the lovelier beaches and vistas. Begin your tour at:

1. **Wickhams Cay,** site of the densest concentration of shops and restaurants of Road Town. Less carefully planned than many other Caribbean capitals, Road Town seems at first glance to be a scattered sprawl of modern buildings which form a crescent along the harborfront and up the hillsides. At Wickhams Cay, however, some of the town's charm might become more clear to you.

   From Road Town, head southwest along the coastal road, passing the capital's many bars and restaurants. These will include Pusser's, The Paradise Pub, and the local Struggling Man Restaurant. St. Paul's Episcopal Church (established 1937) and the Faith Tabernacle Church are other landmarks you'll pass.

   Less than 2 miles away, on your left, is the sandy peninsula containing:
2. **Nanny Cay Hotel and Marina.** There's an attractive restaurant here (Pegleg Landing; see "Where to Dine," below) and an opportunity to view some very fine yachts bobbing at anchor.

   Along the same road, 2½ miles southwest of Road Town, spectacular views open on your left, combinations of sea and land that form the 5-mile-wide Sir Francis Drake Channel, beloved of yachters throughout the world. You'll now enjoy a frequently curving expanse of uncluttered road, one of the loveliest on the island, whose coastline is dotted with rocks, cays, inlets, and verdant uninhabited offshore islands.

   The crumbling antique masonry on the right side of the road (look through the creeping vegetation) is the ruins of a stone prison built by the English for pirates and unruly slaves. Lush St. John, on the opposite side of the channel, will appear across the distant channel.

   Keeping the water constantly on your left, you'll come to the unpretentious hamlet of:
3. **West End and the pier at Soper's Hole.** Yachters and boaters report to the immigration and Customs officer stationed here. Turn left over the hamlet's only bridge to:

4. Frenchman's Cay, where there's a charming view and, to the west, Little Thatch Island.

Retrace your route toward Road Town, but at the first major intersection, turn left, up Zion's Hill. This road's most prominent landmark, tucked into a hollow in the hillside, is the:

5. Zion Hill Methodist Church. Charming in its rural isolation, with a devoted local following, it's one of many churches dotting the island.

You'll soon be driving parallel to the island's northern coast, site of many of its least developed beaches, with evocative names like Apple Bay, Little and Great Carrot Bays, and Ballast Bay. Stop at any of them (and swim or snorkel wherever it looks safe; if in doubt, ask a local), and continue to enjoy the glittering vistas. Churches you'll pass along the way include the Methodist Church of Carrot Bay and the Seventh-day Adventist Church of Tortola.

REFUELING STOP On the island's north coast, **Quito's Gazebo** is at Cane Garden Bay. Owned by Quito Rymer, one of the island's best musicians (who usually runs things), it serves piña coladas (either "virgin" or laced with liberal quantities of Callwood's local rum) from an enlarged gazebo built almost directly above the waves.

After Quito's the road will cut inland, climbing dramatically through forests and fields, always with a sweeping view unfolding behind you. Soon, you'll be forced to make a turn. Fork left, and continue for a short distance along the rocky spine that runs down the length of the island. A sign will point to a platform offering one of the finest views on Tortola:

6. SkyWorld. This eagle's-nest aerie has survived the most vicious hurricanes, and offers unparalleled views of the entire island, as well as a succulent array of food and drink. Many visitors return to SkyWorld for a candlelit dinner. A small observatory near SkyWorld's parking lot has a memorial plaque you might want to read.

After SkyWorld, continue east for about 1 mile, forking right whenever possible. After the second right fork, the road will descend, passing houses, churches, suburbs, and schools, and eventually join the main road running beside the waterfront at Road Town.

WHERE TO STAY

Many of the island's hotels are small, informal family-run guesthouses offering only the most basic of amenities. Others are more elaborate, offering a full range of resort-related facilities. None of them, however, are as big, splashy, and all-encompassing as the hotels in the U.S. Virgin Islands, although many of the island's repeat clients seem to like that just fine.

Note: All rates given within this chapter are subject to a 10% service charge and a 7% government tax on the room.

Hotels judged "very expensive" charge from $230 to $290 a night for two persons. Hotels rated "expensive" ask for $195 to $275 per night in a double, and those ranked "moderate" charge from $140 to $190 a night for a double. In "inexpensive" hotels, charges begin at $95 per night in a double. All the tariffs quoted are high season (winter) rates. In summer, reductions ranging from 20% to as much as 60% are granted.

For an explanation of the abbreviations AP, CP, EP, and MAP, see "Where to Stay," Chapter 3.

For tips on saving money on accommodations, see "Frommer's Smart Traveler: Hotels," Chapter 4.

VERY EXPENSIVE

SUNSET HOUSE, Cane Garden Bay, West End, P.O. Box 263, Road Town, Tortola, BVI. Tel. 809/494-2550. Fax 809/494-5866. 5 rms (all with bath). TEL

$ Rates (including breakfast): Year-round, $210 single; $230–$275 double; $500–$1,200 per day for the entire villa, depending on the season and the number of occupants. AE, MC, V. **Parking:** Free.

Built in 1988 on a bluff overlooking the southern end of a mile-long stretch of one of the best beaches on the island, the Sunset House provides five-star views any time of the day. Shortly after its construction, its first occupant was Princess Alexandra, cousin to Britain's Queen Elizabeth. With its views, its staff, and its layout of lattices and balconies, this is, quite simply, about as good as it gets in the BVI.

Rooms are rented individually whenever the house is not rented as a block to a group of friends. One fully equipped kitchen is available, and the size of the staff varies with the needs of the rental. Four-course meals can be prepared for $20 to $35 per person if advance notice is given.

EXPENSIVE

LONG BAY HOTEL, P.O. Box 433, Road Town, Long Bay, West End, Tortola, BVI. Tel. 809/495-4252, or toll free 800/729-9599. Fax 809/495-4677. 82 units (all with bath). A/C TEL **Transportation:** Taxi.

$ Rates (with MAP): Winter, $195–$290 double; $375 cottage for four. Summer, $155–$225 double; $240 cottage for four. AE, MC, V. **Parking:** Free.

Located on the northwest shore, about 10 minutes from the West End, this low-rise hotel complex is set in a 50-acre estate near the water. Escapists who want a faraway corner of a half-forgotten island come here. Regular and superior suites and cottages are available in a wide range of styles, shapes, and sizes. Accommodations are scattered up the side of a hill planted with shrubbery. Cottages come with two bedrooms (suitable for four guests), a bath and shower, a kitchen, and a living room overlooking the ocean. Beachfront deluxe rooms and cabanas, many benefiting from a massive rebuilding and upgrading following the 1989 hurricane, are set at the edge of the white sands overlooking the ocean.

Dining/Entertainment: The beach restaurant (within the stone ruins of a former distillery and sugar mill) offers breakfast and lunch, as well as informal à la carte suppers with delectable desserts. The Garden Restaurant serves dinner by reservation only, and the food is excellent.

Services: Room service, laundry, babysitting.

Facilities: Oceanside saltwater swimming pool, beach house.

MODERATE

FRENCHMAN'S CAY HOTEL, P.O. Box 1054, West End, Tortola, BVI. Tel. 809/495-4844, or toll free 800/235-4077. Fax 809/495-4056. 9 villas (all with bath). A/C **Transportation:** Taxi.

$ Rates: Winter, $180 1 bedroom for two; $270 2 bedroom for four. Summer, $108 1 bedroom for two; $162 2 bedroom for four. Extra person $10. Breakfast $5–$9 extra. AE, MC, V. **Parking:** Free.

This luxury resort is on the windward side of the little island of Frenchman's Cay that is connected to Tortola by a bridge. Its location provides year-round cooling breezes and panoramic views of the Sir Francis Drake Channel and the outer Virgins. Set on 12 acres of handsomely landscaped waterfront land, the hotel has one- and two-bedroom detached villas, elegantly furnished, each with a shady terrace, a full kitchen, a dining room, and a sitting room. The two-bedroom villas have two full baths.

Dining/Entertainment: The Clubhouse Restaurant and lounge bar, overlooking the freshwater pool, between the beach and the tennis court, is open to the public daily for breakfast from 8 to 10:30am, with lunch from 11:30am to 2:30pm, and dinner from 6:30 to 9pm. The restaurant features Caribbean and continental cuisine.
Facilities: Day sails, scuba diving, fishing tours, horseback riding, and windsurfing can be arranged along with island tours and car rentals.

THE MOORINGS/MARINER INN, P.O. Box 139, Wickhams Cay, Road Town, Tortola, BVI. Tel. 809/494-2332, or toll free 800/535-7289 for reservations. 39 rms, 2 suites (all with bath). A/C TV TEL **Transportation:** Taxi.
$ Rates (with EP): Winter, $130 single; $140 double; $180 suite. Summer, $75–$85 single or double; $110 suite. Breakfast $11 extra. AE, MC, V. **Parking:** Free.
The Caribbean's only complete yachting resort, this 8-acre complex provides not only support facilities and service but also shoreside accommodations, lanai hotel rooms, a dockside restaurant, Mariner Bar, a swimming pool, a tennis court, a beach club, a gift shop, and a dive shop that has underwater video cameras available for rent. Rooms are spacious and all have kitchenettes. The inn is outfitted with 100 sailing yachts, some worth around $500,000.

NANNY CAY RESORT & MARINA, Nanny Cay, P.O. Box 281, Road Town, Tortola, BVI. Tel. 809/494-4895, or toll free 800/786-4753. Fax 809/833-3318. 41 rms (all with bath). A/C MINIBAR TV TEL **Transportation:** Taxi.
$ Rates (with EP): Winter, $150 standard studio single or double; $170 deluxe studio single or double. Summer, $90 standard studio single or double; $110 deluxe studio single or double. Extra person $15. Breakfast $11 extra. AE, MC, V. **Parking:** Free.
Occupying a 25-acre site adjoining a 210-slip marina, the Nanny Cay is located 1½ miles southwest of the center of Road Town and 10 miles from the airport. It offers rooms and studios with sitting areas, fully equipped kitchenettes, ceiling fans, and private balconies opening onto a view of the water, the marina, or the gardens. Accommodations, decorated in a West Indian motif, contain two big double or queen-size beds, along with many extras. Some of the accommodations are arranged around lushly overgrown courtyards; others are on a strip of sandy land facing the distant end of the marina. When booking, ask about the hotel's package deals—for everybody from divers to honeymooners. Built on stilts above the marina, the Pegleg Landing Restaurant serves both lunch and dinner daily, featuring international dishes with a Caribbean flair. More casual food is offered at the Plaza Restaurant.

PROSPECT REEF RESORT, P.O. Box 104, western end of Road Town, Tortola, BVI. Tel. 809/494-3311, or toll free 800/356-8973 for reservations. Fax 809/494-5595. 131 units (all with bath). TEL **Transportation:** Taxi.
$ Rates (with EP): Winter, $140–$190 single or double; $370 2-bedroom villa for four. Summer, $80–$117 single or double; $229 2-bedroom villa for four. Continental breakfast $5 extra. AE, MC, V. **Parking:** Free.
British-owned Prospect Reef is the largest resort in the British Virgin Islands. Built on a coral reef with panoramic views of Sir Francis Drake Channel, it offers attractive modern buildings on 15 tastefully landscaped acres opening onto a small private harbor. Initially designed as condominiums, there are unique studios, town houses, and villas in addition to guest rooms. All include private balconies or patios; larger units have kitchenettes, good-size living and dining areas, plus separate bedrooms or sleeping lofts. Thirty-nine rooms are air-conditioned while others are cooled by ceiling fans and the constant trade winds. Food at the hotel's Upstairs Restaurant, offering a combination of continental specialties and island favorites, was praised by

Gourmet magazine. Count on spending about $30 a person at dinner, more if you order wine and lobster. Light meals are served on the terrace of the Harbour Café or around the Seapool Bar and Grill. There's a pool to swim in, another to dive in, plus spectacular sand terraced sea pools for snorkeling or just fish-catching. Six tennis courts are available. There's a health-and-fitness center and a pitch-and-putt course. Guest services can fill you in on what's available from the harbor—day sailing, snorkeling, scuba diving, and sportfishing.

THE SUGAR MILL, P.O. Box 425, Apple Bay, Tortola, BVI. Tel. 809/495-4355, or toll free 800/462-8834. Fax 809/495-4696. 20 units (all with bath), 1 2-bedroom villa. **Transportation:** Taxi.

$ Rates (with EP): Mid-Dec to mid-Apr, $140–$205 single; $150–$215 double; $230–$245 triple; $245 quad; $475 2-bedroom villa. Summer, $110–$150 single; $120–$160 double; $175 triple; $190 quad; $355 2-bedroom villa. Breakfast $5–$10 extra. AE, MC, V. **Parking:** Free.

Surrounded by lush foliage above the northwest shore of Tortola, this resort is a small inn of character with an acclaimed restaurant. Built on the site of a 300-year-old sugar mill, the cottage colony sweeps down the hillside to its own little beach, with jasmine, avocados, citrus trees, gardenias, bougainvillea, mangoes, bananas, pineapples, and sugar apples brightening the grounds. The estate is owned by Jeff and Jinx Morgan, formerly of San Francisco, who write about travel, food, and wine.

Comfortable apartments climb up the hillside, and at the center is a circular swimming pool. The accommodations are contemporary and well planned, ranging from cottages to suites, all self-contained with kitchenettes and private terraces with views. Ceilings are sloped, and you can keep the sea breezes moving by turning on the ceiling fan. Four of the units are suitable for families of four.

Lunch is served down by the beach, and dinner is served in the old Sugar Mill Restaurant, whose stone walls are decorated with Haitian paintings (see "Where to Dine," below). Breakfast is offered on the terrace. The bars are open all day, and snorkeling equipment can be used free.

TREASURE ISLE HOTEL, P.O. Box 68, Pasea Estate, east end of Road Town, Tortola, BVI. Tel. 809/494-2501, or toll free 800/334-2435 for reservations. Fax 809/494-2507. 39 rms, 2 suites (all with bath). A/C TEL **Transportation:** Taxi.

$ Rates (with EP): Winter, $140 single; $155 double; $215 suite. Summer, $80 single; $90 double; $125 suite. Breakfast $7–$11 extra. AE, MC, V. **Parking:** Free.

The most centrally located resort hotel on Tortola, Treasure Isle was built at the eastern edge of the capital, 1 mile from the center, on 15 acres of steeply inclined hillside overlooking the coastal road and a marina. The large and sunny bedrooms occupy two-storied angular buildings built along landscaped terraces. Other buildings on the site are condominiums.

Adjoining the hotel's free-form swimming pool area is a covered pavilion reminiscent of a West Indian clapboard-covered house. Overlooking the harbor, it serves barbecue, carvery items, an à la carte menu, and—every Wednesday—one of the best-known West Indian buffets on the island, complete with music and dancing.

The hotel has a thoughtful staff, and a fully equipped dive facility. Daily excursions are offered to nearby beaches, reefs, and secluded islands.

INEXPENSIVE

FORT BURT HOTEL, Fort Burt, Road Town, Tortola, BVI. Tel. 809/494-2587. 7 rms (all with bath). A/C

$ Rates: Winter, $80 single; $150 double. Summer, $45 single; $100 double. English breakfast $7 extra. AE, MC, V. **Parking:** Free.

Ⓢ Covered with flowering vines, Fort Burt rents rooms, but devotes most of its energy to its popular pub and restaurant, which are recommended below. Built in 1960 upon the ruins of a 17th-century Dutch fort, the rooms are set at a higher elevation than any others in Road Town, offering views from their private terraces to the waterfront below. Simple, sun-flooded and cozy, they require treks to the nearest beach, but in many ways, they have a colonial charm and freewheeling conviviality.

SEBASTIANS ON THE BEACH, P.O. Box 441, Little Apple Bay, West End, Tortola, BVI. Tel. 809/495-4212. Fax 809/495-4466. 26 rms (all with bath). MINIBAR **Transportation:** Taxi to West End.
$ Rates (with EP): Winter, $100–$170 single; $110–$180 double. Summer, $55–$100 single; $65–$110 double. Extra bed $15. MAP $35 per person extra. AE, MC, V.

Ⓢ This turquoise hotel is centered around one of the most pleasant restaurants and bars on the island, which serves as its reception area, social center, and hangout zone. Built in the early 1960s, and set on a half-acre of beachfronting land, it is a favorite of informal clients who prefer to don a swimsuit and remain that way the rest of the day. Children are especially welcome.

Each room contains a ceiling fan and a refrigerator. Eight of them face the sea.

VILLAGE CAY HOTEL, Wickhams Cay, Road Town, Tortola, BVI. Tel. 809/494-2771. Fax 809/494-2773. 20 rms (all with bath). A/C TV TEL
$ Rates: Winter, $95–$125 single or double. Summer, $75–$95 single or double. Breakfast $7 extra. AE, DC, MC, V. **Parking:** Free.

Village Cay is the most centrally located full-service lodging facility in the British Virgin Islands. Set in the heart of Road Town, all rooms have been recently refurbished and many directly overlook a marina filled with yachts from around the world. The dockside restaurant here is open from 7am to 11pm daily, serving breakfast, lunch, and dinner 7 days a week. Entertainment is featured during winter season.

Anything you need is available within a 5-minute walk of the premises, including ferry service to other islands, secretarial services for traveling business clients, or taxi service to anywhere on Tortola.

WHERE TO DINE

Most guests dine at their hotels, but if you are feeling more adventurous, try one of my suggestions below.

Restaurants considered "very expensive" charge from $45 a meal. Those rated "expensive" ask around $30 to $35 for dinner, and those judged "moderate" cost from $20 to $25 for a meal. Anything $16 or under is considered "inexpensive."

EXPENSIVE

THE CLOUD ROOM, Ridge Road. Tel. 42821.
Cuisine: CONTINENTAL. **Reservations:** Required. **Transportation:** Private pickup from your hotel.
$ Prices: Appetizers $11–$19; main courses $22–$28. AE, MC, V.
Open: Nov–May, dinner Mon–Sat 7:30–9:30pm.
The Cloud Room provides a unique dining experience in Tortola. This restaurant and bar sits at the top of Butu Mountain, overlooking Road Town. When Weather

permits, which is practically every day of the year, the roof slides back, allowing you to dine under the stars. Unfortunately the road here is bad and there's no place to park, so the owner, Paul Wattley, prefers to arrange to pick you up when you make your reservation for dinner. The selection includes juicy sirloin steaks, fresh fish in season, shish kebab (the house specialty), and shrimp in creole sauce.

MODERATE

THE APPLE, Little Apple Bay. Tel. 54437.
  Cuisine: WEST INDIAN. **Reservations:** Recommended. **Transportation:** Taxi.
  $ Prices: Appetizers $3.25–$8; main courses $14–$30. AE.
  Open: Dinner Tues–Sun 4–11pm. **Closed:** Sept–Oct.
You get West Indian fare with flair at this place on the northwest coast of Tortola, which opens onto charming Little Apple Bay. Diners can begin with the bartender's special drink, a Virgin "souppy" made with soursop juice (from the famous Caribbean fruit) and rum, among other ingredients. Later, you can select from an array of seafood dishes, including whelks (large marine snails) in garlic butter, conch BVI style, or the catch of the day steamed and served with a creole sauce. Call Liston Molyneaux, a native Tortolian, for a reservation. He will feed you well. In winter local entertainment is offered from 7 to 10pm on Wednesday and Sunday.

BRANDYWINE BAY RESTAURANT, Brandywine Estate. Tel. 52301.
  Cuisine: FLORENTINE/CARIBBEAN. **Reservations:** Required.
  Transportation: Taxi.
  $ Prices: Appetizers $6–$13; main courses $19–$26. AE, MC, V.
  Open: Dinner Mon–Sat 6:30–9:30pm. **Closed:** Aug–Oct.
On the south shore, 3 miles east of the center of Road Town, this restaurant is set on a cobblestone garden terrace and overlooks Sir Francis Drake Channel.
    Chef Davide Pugliese and his wife, Cele McLachlan, have earned a reputation in Tortola for their outstanding Florentine and Caribbean food. Davide changes his menu daily, based on the availability of fresh produce. Typical dishes include beef carpaccio, homemade lobster ravioli, and his own special calves' liver with cassis. When available, pheasant and venison might also be featured. Try his homemade mozzarella with fresh basil and tomatoes.

CAPTAIN'S TABLE, Inner Harbour Marina, Wickhams Cay. Tel. 43885.
  Cuisine: CARIBBEAN/FRENCH. **Reservations:** Required at dinner.
  $ Prices: Lunch appetizers $3.50, main dishes $8–$12; dinner appetizers $8–$15, main dishes $18–$25. AE, DC, MC, V.
  Open: Lunch Mon–Fri noon–2:30pm. Winter, dinner daily 6:30–9pm; Summer, dinner Mon–Sat 6–9pm.
This cool pocket of elegance is contained within a pastel-colored, low-slung building that was originally built as a disco in the early 1980s. Seating is available within a clean, high-ceilinged and spacious dining room, but the more desirable tables are on a waterfront veranda with cane chairs and furnishings.
    Lunch choices might include a salad of smoked salmon with asparagus, "wings of fire" (chicken wings in creole sauce), and sautéed flying fish. Dinner specialties might include linguine with seafood, stuffed crab, garlic-stuffed saltwater mussels, lobster pulled from the restaurant's holding tank, and several kinds of local fish, blackened and served with Cajun sauce. Kir Royale (champagne with crème de cassis) is a fine apéritif.

FORT BURT RESTAURANT AND PUB, Fort Burt, Road Town. Tel. 42587.

Cuisine: CONTINENTAL. **Reservations:** Recommended for dinner.
$ **Prices:** English breakfast $7; lunch platters, sandwiches, and salads $3.50–$12; dinner appetizers $5–$10; dinner main courses $18–$30. AE, MC, V.
Open: Breakfast daily 7:30–10am; lunch daily noon–2:30pm; dinner daily 7:30–10pm. Bar open Sun–Fri 10am–midnight, Sat 10am–3am.
This restaurant was built upon rocks mortared together in the 17th century with lime and molasses by the Dutch and the French. Lunches offer a selection of soups, salads, grilled fish, and sandwiches. Dinners are candlelit and more elaborate, with such dishes as fresh asparagus with aïoli sauce, Scottish smoked salmon, grilled Dover sole with lime butter, pepper steak, and roast duck with orange and tarragon sauce.

MARINER INN RESTAURANT/MOORINGS, Wickhams Cay. Tel. 42332.
Cuisine: FRENCH/CARIBBEAN. **Reservations:** Recommended.
Transportation: Taxi.
$ **Prices:** Appetizers $5–$6.50; main dishes $16–$23. AE, MC, V.
Open: Lunch daily noon–3pm; dinner daily 6:30–9:30pm.
This is one of the more sophisticated restaurants in the BVI, attracting a nautically minded crowd. Its open-air tables overlook the Moorings Marina lying east of Road Town. At lunch you can drop in and enjoy light food at the Marina Inn Bar, including sandwiches, hamburgers, roti, and chef's salad. At night the candlelit dinners are more elegant, featuring such dishes as steak au poivre, scallops in a creamy sauce, and lobster Virgin Islands style.

SKYWORLD RESTAURANT, Ridge Rd. Tel. 43567.
Cuisine: INTERNATIONAL. **Reservations:** Recommended for dinner. **Transportation:** Taxi.
$ **Prices:** Appetizers $4–$8.75; main courses $6.50–$22; 6-course dinner $34. AE, MC, V.
Open: Lunch daily 11:30am–2:30pm; dinner daily 6:30–9pm. **Closed:** Sept.
SkyWorld is all the rage and it is certainly the worthiest excursion on the island, lying up "Joe's Hill," a mile north of Road Town. The route is signposted. At one of the loftiest peaks on Tortola, a breezy 1,337 feet, it offers views of both the U.S. and British Virgins. The french fries and onion rings have been praised by *Gourmet* magazine, and many consider the conch fritters the best on the island. Guests enjoy the view at lunch and dinner, when an elegant, classic French-inspired menu is offered. Main dishes include smoked scallops, rack of lamb, and fresh local fish grilled to order. You can finish with a dish of homemade tropical ice cream.

SUGAR MILL RESTAURANT, Apple Bay. Tel. 54355.
Cuisine: CALIFORNIA/CARIBBEAN. **Reservations:** Required.
Transportation: Taxi.
$ **Prices:** Fixed-priced menu $35; lunch from $20. AE, MC, V.
Open: Lunch daily noon–2pm; dinner daily 7–8:30pm.
Here you'll dine in an informal room that was once a 300-year-old sugar mill (see "Where to Stay," above). Haitian paintings decorate the stone walls near big copper basins once used for distilling rum and now filled with tropical flowers. Your hosts are Jeff and Jinx Morgan, who know a lot about food and wine: Together they write a monthly column, "Cooking for Friends" for *Bon Appétit*. They have also cowritten a cookbook. One of their most popular creations is curried banana soup.
Before you go to the dining room, I suggest a visit to the gazebo-inspired bar, open-air in the true West Indian fashion. Jinx Morgan supervises the dining room, where specialties might include seafood creole, lobster crêpes, and a cold rum soufflé. Everything here is homemade, including many island specialties. Ingredients for the crisp salads come mostly from the hotel's extensive herb and vegetable garden. The

small menu changes each evening. Lunch can be ordered by the beach at the second restaurant, Islands, where dinner is also served daily from 6:30 to 8:30pm, December through May. Islands features Caribbean specialties. Try "jerk" ribs or stuffed crabs.

INEXPENSIVE

CHOPSTICKS, Little Denmark Building, Waterfront Dr., Road Town. Tel. 43616.
   Cuisine: CHINESE/CARIBBEAN. **Reservations:** Not required.
$ **Prices:** Appetizers $3–$7.50; main dishes $7.70–$18. No credit cards.
   Open: Mon–Sat 11am–11pm, Sun 5–11pm.
Set in a West Indian cottage amid the sprawl of central Road Town, opposite Cable and Wireless, Chopsticks has only a scattering of picnic tables, simple chairs, a bartop, and the smallish kitchen where the chef-owner will take your order. Specialties, written on a blackboard posted on the front veranda, change frequently according to the availability of the ingredients. They might include almond chicken with ginger-garlic soy sauce and various stir-fried dishes. The chef-owner is German, but the dishes are mainly Chinese. Local dishes are served as well. Food is cooked to order, and a take-out service is available.

MRS. SCATLIFFE'S RESTAURANT, Carrot Bay. Tel. 54556.
   Cuisine: WEST INDIAN. **Reservations:** Required before 5:30pm for dinner.
   Transportation: Taxi.
$ **Prices:** Lunches from $16; 4-course fixed-priced dinner $25. No credit cards.
   Open: Lunch Mon–Fri noon–2:30pm; dinner daily 7–8:30pm.
For the best and most authentic West Indian cuisine (with an international touch), check out this restaurant. Mrs. Una Scatliffe offers meals on the open-air deck of her island home, and some of the vegetables come right from her garden. Begin with one of the best daiquiris on the island, made from fresh tropical fruit, while munching a breadfruit stick. Next you'll be served a soup, perhaps spicy papaya, which will be followed by curried goat or "ole wife" fish, perhaps chicken in a coconut shell. After dinner, the devoutly religious Scatliffe family often entertains with a fungi-band performance (Monday to Saturday only).

PARADISE PUB, Fort Burt Marina, Harbour Rd. Tel. 42608.
   Cuisine: INTERNATIONAL. **Reservations:** Not required.
$ **Prices:** Lunch appetizers $3–$4, main dishes $5–$8; dinner appetizers $5–$7, main dishes $9–$22. AE, MC, V.
   Open: Daily 8:30am–1 or 3am, depending on business.
Contained within a low-slung timbered building on a narrow strip of land between the coastal road and the southern edge of Road Town's harbor, this establishment has a grangelike interior and a rambling veranda, built on piers over the water. Many of the island's sports teams celebrate here after their victories. The pub also attracts the island's "boat people." In inventory are more than 25 different kinds of beer. Live entertainment begins at 10pm. If you're here for a meal, you can order Bahamian fritters, Paradise mushrooms (stuffed with ricotta, mozzarella, and parmesan and covered with marinara sauce), also Caesar or Greek salads, pasta, four kinds of steaks, and burgers. The chef also prepares a "catch of the day."

PEGLEG LANDING, Nanny Cay Hotel and Marina, Road Town. Tel. 44895.
   Cuisine: INTERNATIONAL. **Reservations:** Not required.
$ **Prices:** Lunch appetizers $5.50–$7.50, main courses $8–$14; dinner appetizers $5.75–$8, main courses $10–$26. AE, MC, V.
   Open: Lunch daily 11:30am–2pm; dinner daily 7–9:30pm.
Lying 1½ miles southwest of Road Town, this restaurant was built in 1980,

overlooking the yachts of the Nanny Cay Marina. You'll find accents of stained glass, mastheads from old clipper ships, lots of rustic paneling, and a nautical state of mind enhanced by the views and breezes from the sea. Specialties include sautéed breast of chicken in a champagne-and-orange sauce, charbroiled New York strip steak with mushrooms, and fresh filets of fish.

PUSSER'S LANDING, Frenchman's Cay, West End. Tel. 54554.
   Cuisine: CARIBBEAN/ENGLISH PUB/MEXICAN. **Reservations:** Not required. **Transportation:** Taxi.
   $ Prices: Appetizers $4–$9; main dishes $15–$25; lunch $6–$8.75. AE, MC, V.
   Open: Lunch daily 11:30am–2:30pm; dinner daily 6:30–9:30pm.
This second Pusser's (see below) is even more desirably located in the West End, opening onto the water. Here you can choose a well-prepared dinner, including fresh grilled fish, or select some English-inspired dishes, perhaps a classic shepherd's pie with a potato crust. In a nautically inspired setting, begin with a hearty bowl of fresh soup with seasonal ingredients and follow it with filet mignon, West Indian roasted chicken, or a filet of swordfish. "Mud pie" is the classic dessert. Happy hour is daily from 5 to 6:30pm.

PUSSER'S LTD., Main St., Road Town. Tel. 43897.
   Cuisine: CARIBBEAN/ENGLISH PUB/MEXICAN. **Reservations:** Recommended.
   $ Prices: Appetizers $3–$7.50; main courses $4.50–$7.95. AE, MC, V.
   Open: Daily 9:30am–midnight.
The complete lunch and dinner menu here includes old-style English shepherd's pies, New York deli–style sandwiches, and even Mexican fare in the evening. *Gourmet* magazine asked for the recipe for its chicken-and-asparagus pie. It also serves John Courage draft ale. Of course, the drink to have here is the famous Pusser's Rum, the same blend of five West Indian rums that the Royal Navy has served for more than 300 years.

SEBASTIANS ON THE BEACH, West End. Tel. 54212.
   Cuisine: INTERNATIONAL. **Reservations:** Not required. **Transportation:** Taxi.
   $ Prices: Breakfast $6; lunch sandwiches, burgers, salads, and platters $3.50–$8; dinner appetizers $2.50–$5.50; dinner main dishes $11.50–$32. AE, MC, V.
   Open: Breakfast daily 7–11am; lunch daily noon–4pm; dinner daily 6:30–9:30pm. Bar daily 10am–10:30pm.
The wooden tables and rush-buttoned chairs here are scattered, Polynesian style, beneath a rustic yet comfortable pavilion near an accommodating bar, a few feet from the waves of the island's West End. Sun lovers sit within the open courtyard nearby. A lunch menu of burgers, sandwiches, and salads is replaced in the evening with a more elaborate choice of food. Then, specialties include a selection of fresh fish and lobster, dolphin in an island creole sauce or lime butter, and grilled steaks.

BUDGET

HARBOUR CAFE, Prospect Reef Resort, Drake's Hwy. Tel. 43311 (ext. 229).
   Cuisine: INTERNATIONAL. **Reservations:** Not accepted.
   $ Prices: Sandwiches, platters, and salads $4–$13; breakfast omelets $5. AE, MC, V.
   Open: Daily 7am–1am.
Its greatest attraction is its location 1 mile west of the center of Road Town beside the smallest and perhaps the most charming marina in Road Town. Order your meal at the counter, then carry it to one of the picnic tables, which are sheltered from the sun but

not from the breezes blowing off the water. The simple setting here keeps the prices down, and the food—especially breakfast—is plentiful and good. Specialties include lobster or beef crêpes, fried filets of fish, lobster or crabmeat salads, sandwiches, burgers, and a house drink that combines several kinds of rum into a lethal combination known as a Painkiller. The place is especially popular at breakfast, when eight different kinds of "rooster omelets" draw the yachting and construction-worker crowd.

SPORTS & RECREATION
BEACHES

Beaches rarely tend to be crowded on Tortola unless a cruise ship arrives. You can rent a car or a Jeep to reach these beaches, or else take a taxi (but arrange for a return at an appointed time to pick you up). There is no public transportation.

The finest beach is **Cane Garden Bay,** which some aficionados have compared favorably to the famous Magens Bay Beach on the north shore of St. Thomas. Cane Garden Bay lies directly west of Road Town, up and down some steep hills, but it's worth the effort.

Surfers like **Apple Bay,** lying to the west of Road Town. A hotel here, Sebastians (see "Where to Stay," above), caters to a surfing crowd. January and February are the ideal time for visits.

Brewers Bay, site of a campground, lies northwest of Road Town. Both snorkelers and surfers are attracted to this beach.

Smugglers Cove is at the extreme western end of Tortola, lying opposite the offshore island of Great Thatch. At this point you will be very close to the American island of St. John, directly south of Smugglers Cove. Sometimes this beach is also known as Lowre Belmont Bay. Snorkelers also like this beach.

Long Bay Beach is on Beef Island, east of Tortola, and the site of the major airport. It is reached by taking the Queen Elizabeth Bridge. Long Bay is approached by going along a dirt road to the left before you come to the airport. From Long Bay you'll have a good view of Little Camanoe, one of the rocky offshore islands around Tortola.

SPORTS

Boating The best place for this is the **Moorings,** P.O. Box 139, Wickhams Cay, Road Town, BVI (tel. 42331, or toll free 800/535-7289) (this 8-acre waterside resort is also recommended under "Where to Stay," above). This place, along with a limited handful of others, makes the British Virgins the cruising capital of the world. Charlie and Ginny Cary started the first charter service in the BVIs. You can choose from their fleet of sailing yachts, which can accommodate up to four couples in comfort and style. Depending on your skill and inclination, you can arrange a bareboat rental (with no crew), a fully crewed rental with a skipper, a staff, and a cook, or any variation in between. Boats usually come equipped with a portable barbecue, snorkeling gear, dinghy, linens, and galley equipment.

The Moorings has an experienced staff of mechanics, electricians, riggers, and cleaners. In addition, if you're going out on your own, you'll get a thorough briefing session about Virgin Island waters and anchorages.

Horseback Riding **Shadow's Ranch,** Todman's Estate (tel. 42262), offers horseback riding through Sage Mountain National Park or down to the shores of Cane Garden Bay. Call for details.

Scuba Divers in the BVI are attracted to Anegada Reef, the site of many shipwrecks, including the *Paramatta* and the *Astrea*. The one dive site in the British Virgins that lures them over from St. Thomas is the wreckage of the RMS *Rhone,* which sank in 1867 near the western point of Salt Island. *Skin Diver* magazine called this "the world's most fantastic ship wreck dive." It teems with beautiful marine life and coral formations, and was featured in the motion picture *The Deep*.

For a good swimmer interested in taking his or her first dive under careful supervision, try **Baskin in the Sun** (tel. 45854, or toll free 800/233-7938). This well-equipped five-star outfit, established in 1969, is the best choice in Tortola. There are two locations: Prospect Reef Resort (near Road Town) and Soper's Hole, at the island's West End. The establishment offers a resort course for beginners, which includes lessons in a pool and a one-tank reef dive lasting a full afternoon. The cost is $95. The operators provide expeditions to many dive sites, including the RMS *Rhone,* and have a solid working knowledge of the best offshore dive sites.

Underwater Safaris (tel. 43235, or toll free 800/537-7032) takes you to all of the best sites, including not only the RMS *Rhone,* but "Spyglass Wall" and "Alice in Wonderland." Its offices, "Safari Base," are located in Road Town and its "Safari Cay" office lies on Cooper Island. Get complete directions and information when you call. The center, connected with the Moorings, offers a complete PADI training facility. An introductory resort course and one dive costs $85, and an open-water certification, with 4 days of instruction and four open-water dives, goes for $360.

Snorkeling   Marina Cay off Tortola's East End is known for its good snorkeling beach. I also recommend the one at Cooper Island, across Sir Francis Drake Channel. Underwater Safaris (see above) leads dive and snorkel expeditions to both sites frequently, weather permitting.

SHOPPING

Most of the shops in the BVI are on Main Street, in Road Town on Tortola. British goods are imported without duty, and the wise shopper will be able to find some good buys among these imported items, especially in English china. In general, store hours are 9am to 4pm Monday through Friday and 9am to 1pm on Saturday.

THE COCKLE SHOP, Main St., Road Town. Tel. 42555.
    Here you'll find a wide range of souvenirs and gift items, maps, charts, T-shirts, books, games, film, and a large selection of the famous English-made Wedgwood china.

PUSSER'S COMPANY STORE, Main St. and Waterfront Rd., Road Town. Tel. 42467.
    Pusser's is both a long, mahogany-trimmed bar accented with many fine nautical artifacts and a souvenir store selling T-shirts, postcards, and upmarket gift items. Pusser's Rum is one of the best-selling items here.

SUNNY CARIBBEE HERB AND SPICE COMPANY, Main St., Road Town. Tel. 42178.
    In a lovely old West Indian building that was the first hotel on Tortola is a store that specializes in Caribbean spices, seasonings, teas, condiments, and handcrafts. Most of the products are blended and packaged on the island. You can buy two world-famous specialties here: West Indian hangover cure and Arawak love potion. A Caribbean cosmetics collection, Sunsations, is also available, including herbal bath gels, West Indian bay rum, island perfume, and the like. In the art gallery at Sunny Caribbee you'll find an extensive collection of original art, prints, metal sculpture, and many other Caribbean crafts. A branch location of Sunny Caribbee is located at SkyWorld Restaurant (see "Where to Dine," above).

LITTLE DENMARK, Main St., Road Town. Tel. 42455.
    Little Denmark is your best bet for famous names in gold and silver jewelry and china such as Spode and Royal Copenhagen. Here you'll find many of the well-known

designs from Scandinavian countries. The store also offers jewelry made in the BVI, a collection of watches, and even a large selection of fishing equipment.

SALLY BELL'S, Main St. Tel. 44670.

If you need some casual wear during your stay, or some accessories, drop in at Sally Bell's. All the fashions here are imported; many items are from Europe or Indonesia.

EVENING ENTERTAINMENT

Ask around and find out which hotel has entertainment on any given evening. Steel bands and fungi or scratch bands appear regularly, and nonresidents are usually welcome. Pick up a copy of *Limin' Times,* usually available at your hotel, which lists local events.

BOMBA'S SURFSIDE SHACK, Cappoon's Bay. Tel. 54148.

The oddest, most memorable, and most uninhibited nightlife venue on the island sits on a 20-foot-wide strip of unpromising coastline near the West End.

By anyone's standards, this is the "junk palace" of the island, covered with Day-Glo graffiti, and laced into a semblance of coherence with wire, rejected odds and ends of plywood, driftwood, and abandoned rubber tires.

Despite its makeshift appearance, the shack has all the electronic amplification anyone would need to create a really great party, which is exactly what happens every night from the first rum punch "until the last person is drunk and ready to go home." The place is at its wildest Wednesday and Sunday nights, when there's live music and an all-you-can-eat barbecue. The once-a-month "Full Moon" parties, assisted with an herbal tea brewed on the islands, are legendary.

Admission: Free. **Prices:** Bomba punch $3; beer $2; Wed and Sun barbecue $7 per person.

Open: Daily 10am–midnight (or later).

SPYHOUSE BAR, Treasure Isle Hotel, eastern end of Road Town. Tel. 42501.

This is one of the most popular bars on the island, lying in a little house designed with Haitian gingerbread and a sunken bar, set on a terrace overlooking the swimming pool and faraway marina facilities of this popular hotel (see "Where to Stay," above). Its specialties include "Treasure Trove" (Bailey's Irish Cream, brandy, crème de cacao, and milk) and "Virgin Decider" (vodka, gin, brandy, Benedictine, and pineapple juice).

Prices: Drinks $2.50–$4.

Open: Daily 5–11:30pm.

MOORINGS/MARINER INN, Wickhams Cay. Tel. 42332.

This inn (see "Where to Stay," above) contains the preferred watering hole for some of the most upscale yacht owners in the islands. Open to a view of its own marina, and bathed in a dim and flattering light, the place is urbanized, nautical, and relaxed. A fungi band sometimes accompanies the highly sociable drinking.

Admission: Free. **Prices:** Drinks $3.50.

Open: Daily 11am–11pm.

AN EASY EXCURSION TO CANE GARDEN BAY

If you've decided to risk everything and navigate the roller-coaster hills of the BVI, you need a destination. **Cane Garden Bay** is one of the choicest pieces of real estate on the island, long ago discovered by the sailing crowd. Its white sandy beach with sheltering palms is a cliché of Caribbean charm, but it's sometimes crowded with cruise-ship passengers.

WHERE TO DINE

QUITO'S GAZEBO, Cane Garden Bay. Tel. 54837.
Cuisine: CONTINENTAL/WEST INDIAN. **Reservations:** Not required. **Transportation:** Taxi.
$ Prices: Lunch platters, sandwiches, and salads $3.50–$7.50; dinner appetizers $4–$7; dinner main courses $10–$15. No credit cards.
Open: Lunch Tues–Sun 11am–3pm; dinner Tues–Sun 6:30–9:30pm. Bar open Tues–Sun 11am–midnight.

Owned by Quito Rymer, one of the island's most famous and acclaimed musicians, this is the most popular of the several restaurants located along the shoreline of Cane Bay. Quito himself performs after dinner on Tuesday, Thursday, Friday, Saturday, and Sunday. Set directly on the sands of the beach, and designed like an enlarged gazebo, it serves frothy rum-based drinks priced at from $4 each (ask for the house version of a piña colada, or a Bushwacker made with four different kinds of rum). Lunch is served to a beach-loving crowd, and includes sandwiches, salads, and platters. Evening meals are more elaborate, and might include conch or pumpkin fritters, mahimahi with a wine-butter sauce, a conch dinner with (Callwood) rum sauce, chicken rôti, and steamed local mutton served with a sauce of island tomatoes and pepper.

RHYMER'S, Cane Garden Bay. Tel. 54639.
Cuisine: SEAFOOD. **Reservations:** Not required. **Transportation:** Taxi.
$ Prices: Appetizers $3.50–$7; main courses $13–$19. AE, MC, V.
Open: Daily 8am–9:30pm.

Rhymer's is the place to go for food and entertainment. Skippers of any kind of craft are likely to stock up on supplies here. Conch and whelk show up regularly on the bill of fare as well as beer and refreshing rum drinks. If you're tired of fish, maybe James will make you some of his barbecued spareribs. On some nights a steel-drum band entertains, and maybe host James Rhymer himself will show you what a limbo dance is all about! You can rent Sunfish and Windsurfers, and ice and freshwater showers are available (towels are for rent, too).

6. VIRGIN GORDA

The second-largest island in the cluster of British Virgins, Virgin Gorda is 10 miles long and 2 miles wide, with a population of some 1,400. It is 12 miles east of Road Town and 26 miles from St. Thomas.

In 1493, on his second voyage to the New World, Columbus named the island Virgin Gorda or fat virgin, after the mountain framing the island, which looks like a protruding stomach. Seen from a boat, its shape has also been compared to that of a pregnant woman lying on her back.

The island was a fairly desolate agricultural community until Laurance S. Rockefeller established the resort of Little Dix in the early 1960s, following his success with St. John and Caneel Bay in the 1950s.

He envisioned a "wilderness beach," where privacy and solitude reigned, and he literally put Virgin Gorda on the map. Other major hotels followed in the wake of Little Dix, but privacy and solitude still reign supreme among visitors to the island.

In 1971 the Virgin Gorda Yacht Harbour opened, accommodating 120 yachts. It is operated by Little Dix Bay Hotel, a Rockresort.

GETTING THERE & GETTING AROUND

Speedy's Fantasy (tel. 55240) operates a ferry service between Road Town and Virgin Gorda; the ferry makes several trips daily (½ hour).

Frequent air service (approximate flying time is 50 minutes) is provided from San Juan, Puerto Rico, to Virgin Gorda by **Sunaire Express** (tel. 809/495-2480). **American Eagle** (tel. toll free 800/433-7300) also flies in from St. Thomas.

There are so few roads on the island that detouring from any of them will almost never prevent you from quickly recovering the thread of your itinerary.

An aerial view of the island shows what looks like three bulky masses connected by two very narrow isthmuses. The most northeasterly of these three masses (which contains two of the most interesting hotels) is not even accessible by road at all, requiring a ferryboat transit from more accessible parts of the island.

One possibility for exploring Virgin Gorda by car is to drive from southwest to northeast along the island's rocky and meandering spine. This route will take you to The Baths (in the extreme southeast), Spanish Harbour (near the middle), and eventually, after skirting the mountainous edges of Gorda Peak, the most northwesterly tip of the island's road system, near North Sound. There, a cluster of houses and a mini-armada of infrequently scheduled ferryboats depart and arrive from Biras Creek and The Bitter End Yacht Club.

Independently operated open-sided **"safari buses"** run along the main road. Holding up to 14 passengers, these buses charge from $3 per person to transport a passenger, say, from The Valley to The Baths.

FAST FACTS

American Express   The local representative is Travel Plan, Virgin Gorda Yacht Harbour (tel. 55586).

Laundry and Dry Cleaning   Stevens Laundry & Dry Cleaning, near the Virgin Gorda Yacht Harbour (tel. 55525), is open daily from 8am to 9pm.

Photographic Needs   Try Kysk Tropix, Virgin Gorda Yacht Harbour (tel. 55636).

Services and Supplies   In Spanish Town, opposite Beef Island, stands the Yacht Harbour Shopping Centre where you can stock up on supplies and find various services. The shopping complex contains a supermarket, ice-cream parlor, a pub, a wine and liquor store, a dive shop, a bakery, a Laundromat, a drugstore, and a boutique.

WHAT TO SEE & DO

The northern side of Virgin Gorda is mountainous, with one peak reaching 1,370 feet. However, the southern half is flat, with large boulders appearing at every turn. The best **beaches** are at Spring Bay, Trunk Bay, and Devil's Bay.

Among the places of interest, **Coppermine Point** is the site of an abandoned copper mine and smelter. Because of loose rock formations, it can be dangerous, and you should exercise caution if you explore it. Legend has it that the Spanish worked these mines in the 1600s; however, the only authenticated document reveals that the English sank the shafts in 1838 to mine copper.

✪ **The Baths** are on every visitor's list, and the area is known for its snorkeling. Equipment can be rented on the beach. These are a phenomenon of tranquil pools and caves formed by gigantic house-size boulders. As these boulders toppled over one another, they formed saltwater grottoes, suitable for exploring. The pools among the boulders around The Baths provide excellent places for swimming.

The **Devil's Bay National Park** can be reached by a trail from the Baths Roundabout. The walk to the secluded coral sand beach takes about 15 minutes through a natural setting of boulders and dry coastal vegetation.

The Baths and surrounding areas are part of a proposed system of parks and protected areas for the BVI. The protected area encompasses 682 acres of land, including sites at Little Fort, Spring Bay, The Baths, and Devil's Bay on the east coast.

The best way to see the island if you're over for a day-trip is to call Andy Flax at

Fischers Cove Beach Hotel (tel. 55252). He runs **Virgin Gorda Tours Association,** which will give you a tour of the island for about $45 for one to three persons. The tour leaves twice daily. You can be picked up at the ferry dock.

Kilbrides Underwater Tours (tel. 59638, or toll free 800/932-4286) is located at the Bitter End Resort at North Sound. The outfit is one of the recipients of the prestigious NOGI awards for diving education, the Oscar of the diving industry. Today Kilbrides offers the best diving in the BVI at more than 40 dive sites, including Anegada Reef, the wreck of the *Chikuzen*, and the ill-fated RMS *Rhone*. Prices range from $70 to $90 for a two-tank dive on one of the coral reefs. Tanks and weighted belts are supplied at no charge, and videos of your dives are available.

WHERE TO STAY

VERY EXPENSIVE

LITTLE DIX BAY HOTEL, P.O. Box 70, Virgin Gorda, BVI. Tel. 809/495-5555, or toll free 800/223-7637. Fax 809/495-5661. 102 units (all with shower). **Transportation:** Free hotel shuttle bus from Virgin Gorda Airport.
$ Rates (with EP): Winter, $390–$540 single or double. Summer, $190–$270 single or double. MAP $65 per person extra. AE, DC, MC, V. **Parking:** Free.

An embodiment of understatement in luxury, this resort, launched in 1964, is set discreetly along a crescent-shaped private bay on a 500-acre preserve in the northwest corner of the island. It has the same quiet elegance as its fellow Rockresort, Caneel Bay on St. John in the U.S. Virgins. All rooms, built in woods of purpleheart, mahogany, locust, and ash, have private terraces with a view of the sea or the gardens. Some units are two-story rondavels raised on stilts to form their own breezeways. The decor is contemporary with all the conveniences. Trade winds come through louvers and screen walls and are circulated by ceiling fans. There is no air conditioning, TVs, radios, or phones. In the rondavels, hammocks swing from stilts.

Dining/Entertainment: At the Pavilion, you can dine in the open or enjoy meals in the Sugar Mill Restaurant with its adjoining bar. Lunch at the Sugar Mill includes an Antilles fresh-fruit salad with coconut sherbet and sandwiches. On Thursday, all the guests at Little Dix are transported by car or Boston whaler to Spring Bay for a barbecue luncheon with a steel band. Entertainment is provided 6 nights a week.

Services: Unequaled service with a staff-to-guest ratio of one-to-one. One of the hotel's Boston whalers will take you to the beach of your choice with a picnic lunch.

Facilities: Free Sunfish, floats, and snorkeling gear; seven tennis courts.

EXPENSIVE

BIRAS CREEK ESTATE, North Sound, P.O. Box 54, Virgin Gorda, BVI. Tel. 809/494-3555, or toll free 800/223-1108. Fax 809/494-3557. 16 cottages, 32 suites (all with bath). **Transportation:** Hotel's private motor launch.
$ Rates (with AP): Winter, $425 double; from $625 suites. Summer, $350 double; from $500 suites. AE, MC, V.

This magnificent resort, located at the northern end of Virgin Gorda, is accessible only by boat. Perched on a hill, the fortress is surrounded by a 140-acre estate with its own marina, and it occupies a narrow neck of land, with the sea on three sides. To create their Caribbean hideaway, Norwegian shipping interests carved this resort out of the wilderness, but wisely protected the surrounding terrain. A greenhouse on the grounds provides a steady supply of foliage and flowers.

The guest accommodations (doubles and suites only) are along the shore. Rates include three meals a day, plus use of facilities and equipment. Cooled by ceiling fans, suites have a well-furnished bedroom, a sitting room, a private patio, plus a refrigerator.

Dining/Entertainment: Biras Creek's main open-air dining room is located in the hilltop stone "castle" and commands a 360-degree view. The restaurant is noted for its service and its cuisine: an imaginative menu features continental cooking and Caribbean specialties and offers fresh lobster every night. Biras Creek also boasts an extensive wine list. Cheerful by day and romantic by night, with candlelit tables and soft background music, the restaurant serves three meals daily. On Sunday, Biras Creek offers its popular curry luncheon buffet and, twice a week, guests are treated to the resort's outdoor beach barbecues. The dining room seats 120 people, with limited reservations accepted from nonhouseguests. A combo, with vocal performances, plays every Saturday night, from 9pm to midnight, on the stone terrace overlooking the water. On Thursday evening, a ballad singer entertains guests at the "castle."

Services: Free trips to nearby islands, taxi service in Virgin Gorda to hotel's motor launch.

Facilities: Swimming pool, snorkeling gear, Sunfish, two tennis courts, Boston whalers, dinghies.

BITTER END YACHT CLUB, John O'Point, North Sound, P.O. Box 46, Virgin Gorda, BVI. Tel. 809/494-2746, or toll free 800/872-2392 for reservations. Fax 809/494-4756. 92 units, 6 suites (all with bath). **Transportation:** From Beef Island airport, take NSX ferry to Bitter End Dock (½ hour).

$ Rates (with AP): Winter, $300–$395 single; $400–$495 double; from $950 suite. Summer, $225–$290 single; $325–$390 double; from $495 suite. AE, DC, MC, V. **Parking:** Free.

⭐ Guests at this rendezvous point for the yachting set have included treasure-hunter Mel Fisher and Jean-Michel Cousteau. Bitter End offers an informal yet elegant life, as guests settle into one of the "marina rooms," hillside chalets, or well-appointed beachfront and hillside villas overlooking the sound and yachts at anchor. Each room is suitable for two or more.

For something novel, you can stay aboard one of the *Freedom 30* yachts, yours to sail, with dockage including daily chamber service, meals in the yacht club dining room, and overnight provisions. Marina rooms are the same rates as live-aboard yachts. In each case, marina rooms and yacht rooms are the cheaper prices given above.

Dining/Entertainment: Dining is in the Clubhouse Steak and Seafood Grille or the English Carvery. The social hub of the place is the bar.

Services: Free sailing instruction, expeditions to neighboring cays.

Facilities (all included in rates): Lasers, Sunfish, Rhodes 19s, J-24s, Windsurfers, outboard skiffs, snorkeling equipment.

MODERATE

FISCHERS COVE BEACH HOTEL, The Valley, P.O. Box 60, Virgin Gorda, BVI. Tel. 809/495-5252. Fax 809/495-5820. 8 cottages. **Transportation:** Taxi.

$ Rates (with EP): Winter, $150 1-bedroom cottage; $250 2-bedroom cottage. Summer, $125 1-bedroom cottage; $195 2-bedroom cottage. MAP $40 per person extra. AE, MC, V. **Parking:** Free.

Ⓢ This group of cottages, nestled near the beach of St. Thomas Bay, has swimming at its doorstep. Built of native stone, each house is self-contained; the one- and two-bedroom units have a combination living and dining room with a kitchenette. If you want to do your own cooking, you can stock up on your provisions at a food store near the grounds. In addition to the cottages, a two-story unit has 12 pleasant but simple rooms that have private balconies with a view of Sir Francis Drake Channel.

Lunch, from noon to 2pm, costs $12 and up, and dinner, from 7 to 10:30pm, ranges from $22. Occasional entertainment is offered.

THE OLDE YARD INN, The Valley, P.O. Box 26, Virgin Gorda, BVI. Tel. 809/495-5544, or toll free 800/633-7411. Fax 809/495-5986. 14 rms (all with bath). **Transportation:** Taxi.

$ Rates (with EP): Winter, $125 single; $170 double; $195 triple; $220 quad. Summer, $75 single; $95 double; $115 triple; $135 quad. MAP $40 per person extra. AE, MC, V. **Parking:** Free.

This little Caribbean inn is a charmer. Owner Carol Kaufman runs the inn beautifully, with good food, good beds, and hospitality that ranks among the best in the British Virgins. The newly renovated rooms are located in a tropical garden facing the sea; each has its own patio. Scattered about are special accessories and local artwork. Four of the rooms are air-conditioned.

When you arrive, you'll be asked your interests. Perhaps you'll find a saddled horse waiting for a before-breakfast or a moonlight ride. Or you'll go for a sail on a yacht or a snorkeling adventure at one of 16 beaches, with a picnic lunch provided (perhaps lobster, pâté, champagne, or peanut butter sandwiches).

The French-accented meals served under a cedar roof are another reason for coming here. Steaks cut at the inn are from the finest fresh sirloin. If you're just visiting for the day, you can enjoy a lunch from noon to 2pm, costing from $10. Dinner, 6:30 to 9pm, begins at $16.75. Movies are available in the library, and there is live entertainment twice a week in the dining room during the winter season.

INEXPENSIVE

GUAVABERRY SPRING BAY VACATION HOMES, Spring Bay, P.O. Box 20, Virgin Gorda, BVI. Tel. 809/495-5227. Fax 809/495-5283. 16 units (all with bath).

$ Rates: Winter, $120 1-bedroom house for two; $185 2-bedroom house for four. Summer, $85 1-bedroom house for two; $130 2-bedroom house for four. Extra person $20. No credit cards. **Parking:** Free. **Closed:** 3 weeks in Sept.

These clusters of hexagonal white-roofed redwood houses built on stilts are available for daily or weekly rentals. Staying here is like living in a tree house, with screened and louvered walls to let in sea breezes. Each of the unique vacation homes has one or two bedrooms, small kitchenettes and dining areas, and a private elevated sun deck overlooking Sir Francis Drake Channel.

Within a few minutes of the cottage colony is the beach at Spring Bay, and it's possible to explore The Baths nearby. Your hosts can arrange for day charters for scuba diving or fishing, island Jeep tours, and horseback riding.

WHERE TO DINE

EXPENSIVE

CHEZ MICHELLE, The Valley. Tel. 55510.
  Cuisine: CONTINENTAL. **Reservations:** Recommended.
$ Prices: Appetizers $6–$7.50; main dishes $17–$27. MC, V.
  Open: Dinner daily 6:30–9:30pm. **Closed:** Sept.

Established on the ground floor of a clean and modern breeze-filled house by Michelle Noevere and her French-Canadian husband, Eric, this is considered the most competent and urbanized of the privately owned restaurants on the island. Menu specialties change frequently, but might on the day of your visit include lobster Rémy (flambéed with a sauce of cognac, cream, and tomatoes), conch à la meunière (with a sauce of shallots, white wine, garlic, and lemon), a pasta of the day, and steaks. Desserts are considered one of the high points of a meal here, with a separate menu of their own. You'll find Chez Michelle in Spanish Town just a short walk north of the yacht harbor.

MODERATE

TEACHER ILMA'S, The Valley. Tel. 55355.
Cuisine: WEST INDIAN. **Reservations:** Required. **Directions:** Follow the road to The Baths and turn right at the sign to Teacher Ilma's.
$ Prices: Full meals $16–$23. No credit cards.
Open: Lunch daily 1:30pm; dinner daily 7–8:30pm.

For some 45 years, Mrs. Ilma O'Neal taught preschoolers at the island's public school. She began her restaurant by cooking privately for visitors and island construction workers, and eventually became something of a legend. Today, retired from teaching and assisted by a handful of loyal helpers, she is one of the two culinary *grandes dames* of the island, beloved by many of her former pupils.

Call before 3pm of the day you plan a dinner here to order your menu. Meals are served on the screened-in veranda of Mrs. O'Neal's private home, near a pleasant bar and pool table. Begin with a sorrel-based rum drink laced with essence of island fruit, or perhaps with guavaberry punch. Main courses might include stewed or roasted chicken, lobster, johnnycakes, conch, pork, or grouper, followed by slices of guavaberry or coconut pie. Mrs. O'Neal emphasizes that her cuisine is not creole, but local in its origin and flavors.

INEXPENSIVE

BATH AND TURTLE PUB, Virgin Gorda Yacht Harbour, Spanish Town. Tel. 55239.
Cuisine: INTERNATIONAL. **Reservations:** Not required.
$ Prices: Snacks, sandwiches, salads, and platters $4.50–$15; tropical drinks $4.50; appetizers $4.50; main courses $10–$16. AE, DC, MC, V.
Open: Daily 7:30am–midnight.

This is the most popular bar and pub on Virgin Gorda, with an active local trade that is enhanced by its twice-daily happy hours (10:30 to 11:30am and 4:30 to 5:30pm). There's live music every Wednesday and Sunday (also Saturday in season) from 8pm to midnight (no cover charge).

At its handful of indoor and courtyard tables, you can order fried fish fingers, nachos, very spicy chili, pizza, Reubens or tuna melts, and an array of daily seafood specials listed on an oversize blackboard.

THE CRAB HOLE, The Valley. Tel. 55307.
Cuisine: WEST INDIAN. **Reservations:** Not required. **Directions:** Head south along the road to The Baths, and turn left at the sign to the Crab Hole.
$ Prices: Appetizers $4–$6; main courses $8–$15. No credit cards.
Open: Daily 9:30am–midnight.

This is a clean and decent West Indian restaurant contained within the private home of Kenroy and Janet Millington. Built in 1986, it occupies the ground level of a concrete house surrounded by fields and other houses.

Order your food from the blackboard posted above the bar. The menu changes daily, but might include stewed whelk with a creole sauce made from local spices and tomatoes, stewed chicken, fried fish, stewed oxtail, or hamburgers. Beer costs $2 a bottle.

MAD DOG, The Baths, The Country. Tel. 55830.
Cuisine: PIÑA COLADAS/SANDWICHES. **Reservations:** Not required.

$ Prices: Sandwiches $4; piña coladas $3.50. No credit cards.
  Open: Daily 10am–7pm.
Established in 1989, this is the most skillful and charming reconstruction of a West Indian cottage on Virgin Gorda. A wide veranda and the brightly painted 19th-century wooden timbers and clapboards create a cozy and convivial drink and sandwich bar where the piña coladas are absolutely divine. The owner and supervisor of this laid-back corner of heaven is London-born Colin McCullough, a self-described mad dog who sailed the BVI for almost 30 years before establishing his domain here.

THELMA'S HIDEOUT, The Valley. Tel. 55646.
  Cuisine: WEST INDIAN. **Reservations:** Required for dinner.
  $ Prices: Lunches $8; fixed-price dinner $18–$20. No credit cards.
  Open: Breakfast daily 7–10am; lunch daily 11:30am–2:30pm; dinner daily (only upon notification before 3pm) 6:30–9pm. Bar daily 11am–midnight.
Within a concrete house whose angles are softened with ascending tiers of verandas, one of the most outspoken *grandes dames* of Virgin Gorda, Mrs. Thelma King (who worked in Manhattan for many years before returning to her native BVI) runs a convivial gathering place for the island's West Indian community. Food choices include grilled steaks, fish filets, and West Indian stews containing pork, mutton, or chicken. Limeade or mauby are available, but many clients stick to rum or beer. Several evenings a week, live music is presented to crowds of listeners.

EVENING ENTERTAINMENT

ANDY'S CHATEAU DE PIRATE, Spanish Town, Tel. 55252.
  Solidly built of poured concrete in 1985, this is a large, sprawling, sparsely furnished local hangout with a simple stage, a very long bar, and huge oceanfronting windows which almost never close. There's a simple menu of hamburgers and sandwiches, and an endless supply of beer and rum-based drinks.
  The place is famous as a showcase for the island's musical groups, who perform at least four times a week (usually Tuesday and Thursday to Saturday) from 8:30pm to midnight, when lots of people congregate to listen and kibitz.
  Admission: Free most nights, otherwise $2–$15, depending on the entertainment. **Prices:** Drinks $2–$3.
  Open: Daily 11am–midnight. **Directions:** Lies ½ mile south of yacht harbor.

7. MOSQUITO ISLAND

The sandy, 125-acre Mosquito (also spelled Moskito) Island just north of Virgin Gorda wasn't named for those pesky insects we all know and hate. It took its name from the tribe who inhabited the small landmass before the arrival of the Spanish conquistadors in the 15th century. Archeological relics of these peaceful people and their agricultural pursuits have been found here.

GETTING THERE

You must take a plane to Virgin Gorda, then a taxi to Leverick Bay Dock. A boat will meet you and take you on the 5-minute ride from the dock to the resort. The island lies north of Virgin Gorda.

WHERE TO STAY

DRAKE'S ANCHORAGE RESORT INN, P.O. **Box 2510, North Sound, Virgin Gorda, BVI. Tel. 809/494-2254,** or toll free 800/624-6651; 617/661-4745 in Massachusetts. 8 rms, 2 suites, 2 villas (all with bath).

$ Rates (with AP): Winter, $265 single; $360-$370 double; $410-$420 suite; $520 villa. Summer, $205 single; $265-$275 double; $295-$305 suite; $420 villa. AE, MC, V. **Closed:** Mid-Aug to mid-Oct.

Today privately owned Mosquito Island is uninhabited except for this resort, which many patrons consider their favorite retreat in the British Virgins. The hotel offers comfortable rooms and two well-furnished villas that all have seaview verandas. The attractive, tropical restaurant faces the water and offers a superb cuisine featuring local and continental dishes, including lobster and a fresh fish of the day.

The resort provides free use of Windsurfers, snorkeling equipment, and bicycles. For additional fees, you can go scuba diving, deep-sea fishing, day sailing, or to The Baths at Virgin Gorda. The snorkeling and scuba here are considered so good that members of the Cousteau Society once came here to explore. There are four beaches on the island, each with different wave and water conditions.

8. GUANA ISLAND

This 850-acre island, a nature sanctuary, is one of the most private hideaways in the Caribbean. Don't come here seeking resort action; come only if you want a retreat from the world. It lies right off the coast of Tortola. The small island contains seven virgin beaches and nature trails, and abounds with unusual species of plant and animal life. The island is great for hiking. Its highest point is Sugarloaf Mountain at 806 feet, from which a panoramic view is possible. Arawak relics have been found on the island. It is said that the name of the island came from a jutting rock that resembled the head of an iguana.

To get there, take the Guana Island Club boat, which meets visitors at Beef Island airport (10 minutes).

WHERE TO STAY

GUANA ISLAND CLUB, P.O. **Box 32, Road Town, Tortola, BVI. Tel. 809/494-2354,** or toll free 800/544-8262. Fax 914/967-8048. For reservations write or call Guana Island Club, 10 Timber Trail, Rye, NY 10580 (tel. 914/967-6050, or toll free 800/54-GUANA). 15 rms (all with bath). **Transportation:** Private launch from Tortola.

$ Rates (with AP): Nov-Dec 15, $395 double. Dec 16-Mar, $530 double. Apr-Aug, $395 double. No credit cards. **Closed:** Sept-Oct.

Guana Island, the sixth or seventh largest of the British Virgin Islands, was bought in 1974 by Henry and Gloria Jarecki, two dedicated conservationists who also run this resort.

After your arrival on the island, a Land Rover will transport you up one of the most scenic hills in the region, in the northeast of Guana. You arrive at a cluster of white-walled cottages that were built as a private club in the 1930s on the foundations of a Quaker homestead. The stone-trimmed bungalows (with only two telephones) never hold more than 30 guests, and since the dwellings are staggered along a flower-dotted hillside, the privacy is almost absolute. The airy accommodations all have ceiling fans, private terraces, and attractive bathrooms; the decor emphasizes rattan and wicker. The panoramic sweep from the terraces is spectacular, particularly at sunset.

When guests want company, they seek out the convivial atmosphere at the rattan-furnished clubhouse. Dinners by candlelight are served on the veranda, with menus that include homegrown vegetables and continental and Stateside specialties. While dinner is a casually elegant sit-down affair, lunch is served buffet style every day. The self-serve bars charge guests according to the honor system.

Sports lovers and/or beachcombers will find seven beaches, some of which require a boat to reach. There are two tennis courts (one clay and one all-weather), plus fishing and snorkeling. Nature trails abound on the island.

INDEX

GENERAL INFORMATION

SIGHTS & ATTRACTIONS

U.S. VIRGIN ISLANDS

* = indicates Author's favorite.

BRITISH VIRGIN ISLANDS

ACCOMMODATIONS

U.S. VIRGIN ISLANDS

Key to abbreviations: S = Super-value choice; * = Author's favorite; B = Budget; C = Condo; Cg = Campground; E =Expensive; L = Luxury resort; M = Moderate; S = Self-sufficient units; VE =Very expensive

BRITISH VIRGIN ISLANDS

RESTAURANTS

U.S. VIRGIN ISLANDS

ST. THOMAS
AMERICAN
Blackbeard's Castle, Charlotte Amalie (*E*), 78
Eunice's, Red Hook (*LF$*), 85-6
Fiddle Leaf, Charlotte Amalie (*E*), 78-9
Greenhouse, Charlotte Amalie (*M*), 80
Iggie's Restaurant, Frenchman's Cove (*M*), 86-7
Piccola Marina Café, Red Hook (*M*), 83
Seagrape, Sapphire Beach (*E*), 84, 86
Victor's Hide Out (*LF*), 86
AUSTRIAN
Alexander's, Frenchtown (*M*), 80-1
BARBECUE
For the Birds, Compass Point (*M*), 82
CARIBBEAN
Algave Terrace, dining with a view, 84-5
East Coast, Red Hook (*I*), 83-4
CONTINENTAL
Hotel 1829, Charlotte Amalie (*E*), 79
Mark St. Thomas, Charlotte Amalie (*E**), 79
Raffles, Compass Point (*M*), 82
Seagrape, Sapphire Beach (*E*), 84, 86
FRENCH
Cafe Normandie, Frenchtown (*M$**), 81
Entre Nous, Charlotte Amalie (*E*), 78
GERMAN
Windjammer Restaurant, Compass Point (*M*), 82-3
INTERNATIONAL
Banana Bay Club, Charlotte Amalie (*M*), 79-80
Royal Palm Court, Red Hook (*E*), 83, 86
ITALIAN
Alexander's, Frenchtown (*M*), 80-1
Entre Nous, Charlotte Amalie (*E*), 78
Romano's Restaurant, North Coast (*E**), 84
LIGHT FARE
Iggie's Restaurant, Frenchman's Cove (*M*), 86-7
MEXICAN
For the Birds, Compass Point (*M*), 82
SEAFOOD
For the Birds, Compass Point (*M*), 82
Blackbeard's Castle, Charlotte Amalie (*E*), 78

Raffles, Compass Point (*M*), 82
Sugar Reef Cafe, Frenchtown (*M*), 81-2
Windjammer Restaurant, Compass Point (*M*), 82-3
STEAK
Chart House Restaurant, Frenchtown (*M*), 81
WEST INDIAN
Eunice's, Red Hook (*LF$*), 85-6
Victor's Hide Out (*LF*), 86

ST. JOHN
ASIAN
Chow Bella (*E**), 123
CARIBBEAN
Le Chateau de Bordeaux (*E*), 122-3
Pusser's (*M*), 126
CONTINENTAL
Ellington's (*E*), 123
Shipwreck Landing (*I*), 127
The Still (*M*), 126
FRENCH
Le Chateau de Bordeaux (*E*), 122-3
INTERNATIONAL
Caneel Bay Beach Terrace Dining Room (*E*), 122
Mongoose Restaurant, Cafe and Bar (*M*), 124, 126
Pusser's (*M*), 126
The Sugar Mill (*E**), 124
ITALIAN
Cafe Roma (*M*), 124
Chow Bella (*E**), 123
Paradiso (*E**), 123-4
SEAFOOD
Caneel Bay Beach Terrace Dining Room (*E*), 122
The Fish Trap (*I*), 126
Shipwreck Landing (*I*), 127
WEST INDIAN
Vie's Snack Shop (*B$*), 127

ST. CROIX
AUSTRIAN
Antoine's, dining with a view, Christiansted (*M*), 157
CARIBBEAN
Cormorant Beach Club Restaurant,

BRITISH VIRGIN ISLANDS

Now Save Money on All Your Travels by Joining
FROMMER'S ™ TRAVEL BOOK CLUB
The World's Best Travel Guides at Membership Prices

FROMMER'S TRAVEL BOOK CLUB is your ticket to successful travel! Open up a world of travel information and simplify your travel planning when you join ranks with thousands of value-conscious travelers who are members of the FROMMER'S TRAVEL BOOK CLUB. Join today and you'll be entitled to all the privileges that come from belonging to the club that offers you travel guides for less to more than 100 destinations worldwide. Annual membership is only $25 (U.S.) or $35 (Canada and foreign).

The Advantages of Membership

1. Your choice of three FREE travel guides. You can select any **two** FROMMER'S COMPREHENSIVE GUIDES, FROMMER'S $-A-DAY GUIDES, *or* FROMMER'S FAMILY GUIDES—plus **one** FROMMER'S CITY GUIDE *or* FROMMER'S CITY $-A-DAY GUIDE.
2. Your own subscription to **TRIPS AND TRAVEL** quarterly newsletter.
3. You're entitled to a **30% discount** on your order of any additional books offered by FROMMER'S TRAVEL BOOK CLUB.
4. You're offered (at a small additional fee of $6.50) our **Domestic Trip-Routing Kits.**

Our quarterly newsletter **TRIPS AND TRAVEL** offers practical information on the best buys in travel, the "hottest" vacation spots, the latest travel trends, world-class events and much, much more.

Our **Domestic Trip-Routing Kits** are available for any North American destination. We'll send you a detailed map highlighting the best route to take to your destination—you can request direct or scenic routes.

Here's all you have to do to join:

Send in your membership fee of $25 ($35 Canada and foreign) with your name and address on the form below along with your selections as part of your membership package to **FROMMER'S TRAVEL BOOK CLUB, P.O. Box 473, Mt. Morris, IL 61054-0473.** Remember to select any **two** FROMMER'S COMPREHENSIVE GUIDES, FROMMER'S $-A-DAY GUIDES, *or* FROMMER'S FAMILY GUIDES—plus **one** FROMMER'S CITY GUIDE *or* FROMMER'S CITY $-A-DAY GUIDE.

If you would like to order additional books, please select the books you would like and send a check for the total amount (please add sales tax in the states noted below), plus $2 per book for shipping and handling ($3 per book for all foreign orders) to:

FROMMER'S TRAVEL BOOK CLUB
P.O. Box 473
Mt. Morris, IL 61054-0473
(815) 734-1104

[   ] **YES.** I want to take advantage of this opportunity to join FROMMER'S TRAVEL BOOK CLUB.
[   ] **My check is enclosed.** Dollar amount enclosed_____*

Name_____
Address_____
City_____ State_____ Zip_____

To ensure that all orders are processed efficiently, please apply sales tax in the following areas: CA, CT, FL, IL, NJ, NY, TN, WA and CANADA.

*With membership, shipping and handling will be paid by FROMMER'S TRAVEL BOOK CLUB for the three free books you select as part of your membership. Please add $2 per book for shipping and handling for any additional books purchased ($3 per book for foreign orders).

Allow 4–6 weeks for delivery. Prices of books, membership fee, and publication dates are subject to change without notice.

Please Send Me the Books Checked Below:

FROMMER'S COMPREHENSIVE GUIDES
(Guides listing facilities from budget to deluxe,
with emphasis on the medium-priced)

	Retail Price	Code		Retail Price	Code
☐ Acapulco/Ixtapa/Taxco 1993–94	$15.00	C120	☐ Jamaica/Barbados 1993–94	$15.00	C105
☐ Alaska 1994–95	$17.00	C130	☐ Japan 1992–93	$19.00	C020
☐ Arizona 1993–94	$18.00	C101	☐ Morocco 1992–93	$18.00	C021
☐ Australia 1992–93	$18.00	C002	☐ Nepal 1994–95	$18.00	C126
☐ Austria 1993–94	$19.00	C119	☐ New England 1993	$17.00	C114
☐ Belgium/Holland/ Luxembourg 1993–94	$18.00	C106	☐ New Mexico 1993–94	$15.00	C117
☐ Bahamas 1994–95	$17.00	C121	☐ New York State 1994–95	$19.00	C132
☐ Bermuda 1994–95	$15.00	C122	☐ Northwest 1991–92	$17.00	C026
☐ Brazil 1993–94	$20.00	C111	☐ Portugal 1992–93	$16.00	C027
☐ California 1993	$18.00	C112	☐ Puerto Rico 1993–94	$15.00	C103
☐ Canada 1992–93	$18.00	C009	☐ Puerto Vallarta/Manzanillo/ Guadalajara 1992–93	$14.00	C028
☐ Caribbean 1994	$18.00	C123	☐ Scandinavia 1993–94	$19.00	C118
☐ Carolinas/Georgia 1994–95	$17.00	C128	☐ Scotland 1992–93	$16.00	C040
☐ Colorado 1993–94	$16.00	C100	☐ Skiing Europe 1989–90	$15.00	C030
☐ Cruises 1993–94	$19.00	C107	☐ South Pacific 1992–93	$20.00	C031
☐ DE/MD/PA & NJ Shore 1992–93	$19.00	C012	☐ Spain 1993–94	$19.00	C115
☐ Egypt 1990–91	$17.00	C013	☐ Switzerland/Liechtenstein 1992–93	$19.00	C032
☐ England 1994	$18.00	C129	☐ Thailand 1992–93	$20.00	C033
☐ Florida 1994	$18.00	C124	☐ U.S.A. 1993–94	$19.00	C116
☐ France 1994–95	$20.00	C131	☐ Virgin Islands 1994–95	$13.00	C127
☐ Germany 1994	$19.00	C125	☐ Virginia 1992–93	$14.00	C037
☐ Italy 1994	$19.00	C130	☐ Yucatán 1993–94	$18.00	C110

FROMMER'S $-A-DAY GUIDES
(Guides to low-cost tourist accommodations and facilities)

	Retail Price	Code		Retail Price	Code
☐ Australia on $45 1993–94	$18.00	D102	☐ Mexico on $45 1994	$19.00	D116
☐ Costa Rica/Guatemala/ Belize on $35 1993–94	$17.00	D108	☐ New York on $70 1992–93	$16.00	D016
☐ Eastern Europe on $30 1993–94	$18.00	D110	☐ New Zealand on $45 1993–94	$18.00	D103
☐ England on $60 1994	$18.00	D112	☐ Scotland/Wales on $50 1992–93	$18.00	D019
☐ Europe on $50 1994	$19.00	D115	☐ South America on $40 1993–94	$19.00	D109
☐ Greece on $45 1993–94	$19.00	D100			
☐ Hawaii on $75 1994	$19.00	D113	☐ Turkey on $40 1992–93	$22.00	D023
☐ India on $40 1992–93	$20.00	D010	☐ Washington, D.C. on $40 1992–93	$17.00	D024
☐ Ireland on $40 1992–93	$17.00	D011			
☐ Israel on $45 1993–94	$18.00	D101			

FROMMER'S CITY $-A-DAY GUIDES
(Pocket-size guides with an emphasis on low-cost tourist accommodations and facilities)

	Retail Price	Code		Retail Price	Code
☐ Berlin on $40 1994–95	$12.00	D111	☐ Madrid on $50 1992–93	$13.00	D014
☐ Copenhagen on $50 1992–93	$12.00	D003	☐ Paris on $45 1994–95	$12.00	D117
☐ London on $45 1994–95	$12.00	D114	☐ Stockholm on $50 1992–93	$13.00	D022

FROMMER'S WALKING TOURS
(With routes and detailed maps, these companion guides point out
the places and pleasures that make a city unique)

	Retail Price	Code		Retail Price	Code
☐ Berlin	$12.00	W100	☐ Paris	$12.00	W103
☐ London	$12.00	W101	☐ San Francisco	$12.00	W104
☐ New York	$12.00	W102	☐ Washington, D.C.	$12.00	W105

FROMMER'S TOURING GUIDES
(Color-illustrated guides that include walking tours, cultural and historic
sites, and practical information)

	Retail Price	Code		Retail Price	Code
☐ Amsterdam	$11.00	T001	☐ New York	$11.00	T008
☐ Barcelona	$14.00	T015	☐ Rome	$11.00	T010
☐ Brazil	$11.00	T003	☐ Scotland	$10.00	T011
☐ Florence	$ 9.00	T005	☐ Sicily	$15.00	T017
☐ Hong Kong/Singapore/			☐ Tokyo	$15.00	T016
Macau	$11.00	T006	☐ Turkey	$11.00	T013
☐ Kenya	$14.00	T018	☐ Venice	$ 9.00	T014
☐ London	$13.00	T007			

FROMMER'S FAMILY GUIDES

	Retail Price	Code		Retail Price	Code
☐ California with Kids	$18.00	F100	☐ San Francisco with Kids	$17.00	F004
☐ Los Angeles with Kids	$17.00	F002	☐ Washington, D.C. with Kids	$17.00	F005
☐ New York City with Kids	$18.00	F003			

FROMMER'S CITY GUIDES
(Pocket-size guides to sightseeing and tourist accommodations and
facilities in all price ranges)

	Retail Price	Code		Retail Price	Code
☐ Amsterdam 1993–94	$13.00	S110	☐ Montreál/Québec		
☐ Athens 1993–94	$13.00	S114	City 1993–94	$13.00	S125
☐ Atlanta 1993–94	$13.00	S112	☐ New Orleans 1993–94	$13.00	S103
☐ Atlantic City/Cape			☐ New York 1993	$13.00	S120
May 1993–94	$13.00	S130	☐ Orlando 1994	$13.00	S135
☐ Bangkok 1992–93	$13.00	S005	☐ Paris 1993–94	$13.00	S109
☐ Barcelona/Majorca/			☐ Philadelphia 1993–94	$13.00	S113
Minorca/Ibiza 1993–94	$13.00	S115	☐ Rio 1991–92	$ 9.00	S029
☐ Berlin 1993–94	$13.00	S116	☐ Rome 1993–94	$13.00	S111
☐ Boston 1993–94	$13.00	S117	☐ Salt Lake City 1991–92	$ 9.00	S031
☐ Cancún/Cozumel 1991–			☐ San Diego 1993–94	$13.00	S107
92	$ 9.00	S010	☐ San Francisco 1994	$13.00	S133
☐ Chicago 1993–94	$13.00	S122	☐ Santa Fe/Taos/		
☐ Denver/Boulder/Colorado			Albuquerque 1993–94	$13.00	S108
Springs 1993–94	$13.00	S131	☐ Seattle/Portland 1992–93	$12.00	S035
☐ Dublin 1993–94	$13.00	S128	☐ St. Louis/Kansas		
☐ Hawaii 1992	$12.00	S014	City 1993–94	$13.00	S127
☐ Hong Kong 1992–93	$12.00	S015	☐ Sydney 1993–94	$13.00	S129
☐ Honolulu/Oahu 1994	$13.00	S134	☐ Tampa/St.		
☐ Las Vegas 1993–94	$13.00	S121	Petersburg 1993–94	$13.00	S105
☐ London 1994	$13.00	S132	☐ Tokyo 1992–93	$13.00	S039
☐ Los Angeles 1993–94	$13.00	S123	☐ Toronto 1993–94	$13.00	S126
☐ Madrid/Costa del			☐ Vancouver/Victoria 1990–		
Sol 1993–94	$13.00	S124	91	$ 8.00	S041
☐ Miami 1993–94	$13.00	S118	☐ Washington, D.C. 1993	$13.00	S102
☐ Minneapolis/St.					
Paul 1993–94	$13.00	S119			

Other Titles Available at Membership Prices

SPECIAL EDITIONS

	Retail Price	Code		Retail Price	Code
☐ Bed & Breakfast North America	$15.00	P002	☐ Marilyn Wood's Wonderful Weekends (within a 250-mile radius of NYC)	$12.00	P017
☐ Bed & Breakfast Southwest	$16.00	P100	☐ National Park Guide 1993	$15.00	P101
☐ Caribbean Hideaways	$16.00	P103	☐ Where to Stay U.S.A.	$15.00	P102

GAULT MILLAU'S "BEST OF" GUIDES
(The only guides that distinguish the truly superlative from the merely overrated)

	Retail Price	Code		Retail Price	Code
☐ Chicago	$16.00	G002	☐ New England	$16.00	G010
☐ Florida	$17.00	G003	☐ New Orleans	$17.00	G011
☐ France	$17.00	G004	☐ New York	$17.00	G012
☐ Germany	$18.00	G018	☐ Paris	$17.00	G013
☐ Hawaii	$17.00	G006	☐ San Francisco	$17.00	G014
☐ Hong Kong	$17.00	G007	☐ Thailand	$18.00	G019
☐ London	$17.00	G009	☐ Toronto	$17.00	G020
☐ Los Angeles	$17.00	G005	☐ Washington, D.C.	$17.00	G017

THE REAL GUIDES
(Opinionated, politically aware guides for youthful budget-minded travelers)

	Retail Price	Code		Retail Price	Code
☐ Able to Travel	$20.00	R112	☐ Kenya	$12.95	R015
☐ Amsterdam	$13.00	R100	☐ Mexico	$11.95	R128
☐ Barcelona	$13.00	R101	☐ Morocco	$14.00	R129
☐ Belgium/Holland/Luxembourg	$16.00	R031	☐ Nepal	$14.00	R018
☐ Berlin	$13.00	R123	☐ New York	$13.00	R019
☐ Brazil	$13.95	R003	☐ Paris	$13.00	R130
☐ California & the West Coast	$17.00	R121	☐ Peru	$12.95	R021
☐ Canada	$15.00	R103	☐ Poland	$13.95	R131
☐ Czechoslovakia	$15.00	R124	☐ Portugal	$16.00	R126
☐ Egypt	$19.00	R105	☐ Prague	$15.00	R113
☐ Europe	$18.00	R122	☐ San Francisco & the Bay Area	$11.95	R024
☐ Florida	$14.00	R006	☐ Scandinavia	$14.95	R025
☐ France	$18.00	R106	☐ Spain	$16.00	R026
☐ Germany	$18.00	R107	☐ Thailand	$17.00	R119
☐ Greece	$18.00	R108	☐ Tunisia	$17.00	R115
☐ Guatemala/Belize	$14.00	R127	☐ Turkey	$13.95	R027
☐ Hong Kong/Macau	$11.95	R011	☐ U.S.A.	$18.00	R117
☐ Hungary	$14.95	R118	☐ Venice	$11.95	R028
☐ Ireland	$17.00	R120	☐ Women Travel	$12.95	R029
☐ Italy	$18.00	R125	☐ Yugoslavia	$12.95	R030